Derek Tangye has become famous all over the world for his series of bestsellers about his flower farm in Cornwall. The series, which began with A GULL ON THE ROOF, describes a simple way of life which thousands of his readers would like to adopt themselves.

Derek and his wife left their glamorous existence in London when they discovered Minack, a deserted cottage close to the cliffs of Mount's Bay. Jeannie gave up her job as Press Relations Officer of the Savoy Hotel Group and Derek Tangye resigned from MI5. They then proceeded to carve from the wild land around the cottage the meadows which became their flower farm.

Jeannie, who also illustrated many of the stories, died in 1986.

The Minack Chronicles

DEREK TANGYE

Great Minack Stories

The Way to Minack
A Cornish Summer
Cottage on a Cliff

Sketches by Jean Tangye

WARNER BOOKS

A *Warner* Book

This edition published in 1990 by Sphere Books Ltd,
Reprinted 1991
Reprinted by Warner Books 1993, 1994, 1996
GREAT MINACK STORIES © Derek Tangye 1990

Previously published separately:

THE WAY TO MINACK – First published in
Great Britain by Michael Joseph Ltd 1968
Published by Sphere Books Ltd in 1975, reprinted in
1980, 1981, 1983, 1985, 1988, 1990
Copyright © Derek Tangye 1968

A CORNISH SUMMER – First published in
Great Britain by Michael Joseph Ltd 1970
First published in paperback by New English Library Ltd 1972
Published by Sphere Books Ltd, 1984, reprinted 1985,
1987, 1988, 1990
Copyright © Derek Tangye 1970

COTTAGE ON A CLIFF – First published in
Great Britain by Michael Joseph Ltd 1972
Published by Sphere Books Ltd 1974, reprinted 1975, 1977 (twice),
1978, 1979, 1980, 1981, 1983, 1984, 1986, 1987, 1989, 1991
Copyright © Derek Tangye 1972

Printed in England by Clays Ltd, St Ives plc

ISBN 0 7515 0874 8

Warner Books
A Division of
Little, Brown and Company (UK)
Brettenham House
Lancaster Place
London WC2E 7EN

THE WAY TO MINACK

To my brothers Colin and Nigel

CONTENTS

ONE

'What do you miss?'

George Brown asks questions like an inquisitor. Casual, conversational, lighthearted questions have an urgency to them which makes them appear important.

'What do you miss?'

We have a stable door at Minack instead of a normal front door. It opens into the sitting-room, and near to the point where the top half swings indoors, we have an armchair with a high back. The occupant of the chair sits there comfortably enough, nine times out of ten will sit there safe enough, but there are occasions when the chair has been pushed back a little too far so that the top half of the stable door juts out an inch or two above it; and on such an occasion the occupant, should he get up suddenly, might possibly crack his head against the corner of the door. I remember thinking, as George Brown pressed his question, that the chair was so placed that this could be just such an occasion.

'You must miss something. Everyone misses something. Some section of your life must be unfulfilled. What is it?'

He and Sophie Brown were having a holiday at Lamorna, and they spent much of their time with Jeannie and me. There is no telephone at Minack, no noise of distant traffic, no sign of material progress in the boulder strewn, wild land which gently, then steeply falls to the sea of Mounts Bay. Here is a place which is poised in time. Here the old rocks have observed through the centuries the vanity of man, the fitful moments of his power, ambitions lost and won, the fleeing days of living. The old chimney of the cottage prodding into the sky awaits another gale, another sunny

9

day, another mist swirling in from the south, no different from the others it has faced for five hundred years. There it stands, a welcome and a farewell, sharing a landscape with the untamed, sharing the continuity of time. The years pass and the same moss is growing on the rocks, the same music of the waves plays at the bottom of the cliffs.

'What do you miss?'

I marvel at those who neatly analyse themselves and the rest of us. The motion of living appears so simple after reading the views of the theory-boys on this or that. Summaries of their solutions possess no edge of doubt. A huge house of cards is made to look indestructible. There is no grey in any problem. Reason is king. And although I distrust such exponents of logic, there goes with my mood a certain admiration. I admire their confidence because facts, in my own experience, so often lie, mocking the conclusions based upon them. I am, therefore, unable to pigeon hole myself. I am a don't know. I wend a long way round to find a solution to any problem, and when in the end I come to a decision it is usually instinct that motivates it. An inner force which I do not understand pushes me into action, so that afterwards I have to try and make the facts fit the deed. This, I know, is untidy behaviour and it sometimes lets me down. I find myself saying things, for instance, which do not do me justice. I blurt out a sentence which self-discipline would have made me smother, and I declare something which the listener interprets as the truth.

'What do you miss?' asked George Brown.

'Conversation,' I replied; and knew, in my wish to appear decisive, I was again trivially failing myself.

Jeannie and I had come to Minack, years before, because we had learnt to question the kind of life we had been leading in London. It was, in many ways, an enviable life. We were part of an environment of gaiety

10

and glamour which many people yearn for; and we had been lucky enough to have achieved a measure of those ambitions at which we had youthfully aimed. They may not have been important ambitions, but the gaining of them quelled in us envy of others and removed personal frustrations. We were, therefore, no longer restless. A stage in our lives had been reached when we could have a pause; and we realised that if we were not to recognise the moment we would find pleasure becoming a routine and the edge of any achievement blunted. So at any rate it seemed to us at the time.

There were also our failures. Failure can be tolerable when it is a stepping stone to success, and when it is leading to the fulfilment of a dream. In such circumstances you can ride over failure because you persuade yourself that next time you will have the success you desire. But when success is no longer a beacon to lure you, failure however small it may be, is a pointless tedium. Thus it was with Jeannie and me. Superficially successful we were racing along with the years and gaining no roots in the process; and without roots, we believed, all outward success was failure.

'Conversation,' murmured George Brown, half to himself, fingering the cover on the arm of the chair, 'conversation . . .' And I realised he had guessed I had spoken without thinking.

I looked at him from my kidney-shaped desk where I was sitting. A face that did not possess the obvious emblem of power; a chin which receded, kind eyes, a mouth which did not remind one of an orator.

'Conversation,' I repeated, 'because in the country it is easy to become insular.'

'Which confirms what I felt when I read *A Gull On The Roof*.'

'What was that?'

11

'I wasn't convinced.'

'How do you mean?'

He had irked me. Here was a challenge I had not foreseen. He had read my book, I had already realised, with care; for when a day or two previously he had met a man whom I had briefly mentioned in the book, he had flattered him by saying within a second of meeting: 'I know all about you!' He said this in a tone of attack. It was in the same tone he answered my question.

'I do not believe,' he said, 'that you and Jeannie really wanted to give up your kind of life.'

It is the woman who makes the sacrifice. It is easy for a man to exchange comfort for the primitive, to brace himself to accept a new way of living, to switch environment; but for Jeannie it meant giving up a suite of offices at the Savoy, entertaining the famous in her role as public relations officer, and becoming instead a housewife in a cottage without running water or electricity. This was ambition in reverse. This was the kind of action which the conventional expect to see fail. Our acquaintances waited expectantly. How long will she last in Cornwall? And over the years Jeannie has been monotonously asked by kinder minded people: 'Wouldn't you like to go back to the life you used to lead in London?'

George Brown found a distraction in bantering me. He envied us too in a way. He and Sophie are utterly devoted; and yet, after this brief holiday, privacy ended for them. ('If anything goes wrong,' he said as the four of us sat together at Minack, the election looming, 'we would like a farm, wouldn't we, Sophie? Somewhere far away . . . so that we wouldn't have to compromise.')

He has no ambition in the conventional sense of the word, he does not scheme for his personal advantage. He is absolutely honest. His philosophy is to immerse himself in

12

the job he has been chosen to do to the exclusion of everything else . . . in the manner of an evangelist.

One day when he was at Minack a reporter called and asked for an interview. George Brown blazed: he was on holiday, why should he be bothered on holiday? And the reporter retreated disconsolately. A few minutes later George disappeared from the room, and soon I found him outside sitting on a rock with the reporter happily beside him. He was sorry he had upset the man. ('I have a bloody temper, I know that,' he said to me once, 'but when I have a row with someone I immediately forget it.' Then he added, smiling, 'The trouble is . . . they don't.')

Achievement has not made him, as happens to some politicians, condescending. He seems always aware that eminence does not sever you from what you always have been; and so lurking beneath the surface is humility. I believe this is the cause of his outbursts, a. reaction to self-doubt. He responds quickly to the moods of other people. ('A dull chairman at a meeting often puts me off.') He is loyal, and very kind. He is quick to forgive. He hates feuds. ('The years after Gaitskell died were the most miserable of my life.')

But I felt as I was watching him that I was on the edge of a volcano, and it was not my business to stir him on a matter of such minor importance.

'Like you,' I said quietly, 'we didn't want to compromise.'

He had at this time given up smoking, and he did not know what to do with his hands. One moment he clasped them together, the next he rested them on his knees, then he began toying with the fabric of the chair. Suddenly he said:

'You gambled!'

He said it vehemently as if I had been caught committing a felony. Then he added:

'You had no idea what sort of life you were coming to, no training for what you were going to do!'

We *had* gambled. We *had* no idea what sort of life we were coming to. We had *had* no training. In a rational world such conduct is, I suppose, very foolish.

'Why?' he went on, 'why did you do it?'

Conversation, if it is to come to life, must be challenging; and George Brown, I realised, considered argument as a necessary way of passing the time. He was provoking me, but without malice. He was, at that moment, genuinely wanting to know the sequence of events which led us into taking such a rash, unreasonable step; and he was trying to flint me into defending myself.

I, too, have found myself at dull parties making a sensational remark or asking a pertinent question just in order to stir the pool of dullness. My attitude seldom succeeds in its object because the conventionality that breeds dullness retreats from challenge. I make a remark to awake the commonplace, and the response to it is often so dampening that I too feel dull. I am, therefore, on guard when someone tries to awaken my own lassitude; and I was aware that this was what George Brown was trying to do. In such a situation I am anxious, over-anxious, to be as bright as my companion would like me to be; but if my mood, if my temperament at the moment is engulfed by mental cotton wool I am inclined to conduct myself like an inexperienced schoolboy. I flounder. I react with a foolishness so that hours, weeks, months, sometimes a year later, I remember the moment with shame. A self-inflicted wound which no one else has observed.

'It's a story, I suppose, about a search for values,' I began reasonably enough.

Then I added tartly, as if I were aiming to counter his harmless bellicosity by a version of my own:

14

'And why should you be interested?'

As soon as I had spoken I regretted my tone. It was unnecessarily provocative. Almost rude. I waited.

'Well,' he said, smiling at my momentary impatience, 'it's now clear you and I have something in common . . . but I would like to know what decided you to give up the kind of life you both led.'

TWO

George Brown had disturbed our peaceful pool; and since he proceeded to peer at us week after week from the television screen, from cartoons and newspaper photographs, we were not allowed to forget it. He had succeeded in putting doubt into our minds. Perhaps, for instance, we were wrong to remain remote from the community age.

But ideas are inclined to float in timeless rotation when you live in the country. Unperturbed for the most part by man-made time-tables, you indulge yourself when considering a problem by never coming to a decision. Another spring, another summer, and you will find yourself contemplating the problem of the winter before; and so it goes on unless an incident produces an ultimatum.

More than a year had passed since George Brown had been at Minack before I was faced with such an ultimatum. I received one day an invitation to an elegant literary party in London.

I had once before been invited to a literary party, and the occasion has haunted me ever since. It was a month before war broke out and I had just spent a year travelling the world, and I was writing a travel book. On the way to the lunch the chairman of the occasion asked me to make a speech, and he said that all he required were anecdotes of my journey which would make the listeners laugh. I sat nervously through the soup, roast lamb, pêche melba and coffee, until the chairman rose to his feet.

'John Gielgud,' he said to the expectant few hundred, 'was to speak today but is unable to do so. J. B. Priestley was to take his place but he suddenly had to go abroad. I was then

16

lucky enough to persuade John Steinbeck but three days ago he went down with flu . . . and so we have Derek Tangye.'

The faint applause which greeted this introduction still whispers in my memory. So too does the quiet murmur which followed my anecdotal speech.

It was the end of freesia time at Minack and Jeannie and I were in the small greenhouse which we used for bunching. Freesias in the winter, daffodils in the early spring, tomatoes in the summer . . . that was our routine. It was an inevitable habit that we lapsed into long silences as we bunched, thoughts roaming in our minds as we picked up the blooms automatically, fiddled the bunch into shape, tied it, and placed it amongst the others. A long silence, then one of us suddenly out of the blue would announce a result of our roaming thoughts.

'Truth is always changing,' I suddenly announced on this occasion.

'And what prompts such a sage remark?'

'One moment I'm determined to go to London, the next I'm equally determined to stay here.'

Geoffrey at that moment came into the greenhouse with a basket of freesias, a scented tapestry of colour, and he dumped the basket on the bench and began to remove each small bundle of blooms and to put them into the waiting jar of water. He had been with us early in our time at Minack and I had proposed the toast of the bride and bridegroom when he married Emily who also now helps us with the flowers. But at that time we put our faith in potatoes proving to be the *el dorado*, and we were wrong. Geoffrey had to go after a potato season of great disaster, and it was four years before he was back again. It is easier now. We no longer grow potatoes. We have heated greenhouses and several tons of daffodil bulbs. It is more fun now than when he first came to Minack.

'What's so silly,' I said, after Geoffrey had departed to continue his picking, 'is that I'm making a mountain out of a molehill. I realise that. It's almost as if I'm afraid of a few days in London.' I was half talking to myself and Jeannie was silent. 'It's not just getting into a train, having a good time, and coming back,' I went on, 'there are other factors involved.'

'Don't be too serious about it,' said Jeannie.

If you live with someone and there are no office hours to separate you, no other life to lead, one has to be on guard against the groove. There you are, fulfilling the halcyon dream, two people who have come together, the end achieved which you hoped for at the beginning, daylight hours shared, boss to each other; and yet unless you remain separate, each a subtle stranger to the other, dullness sets in. There must be no quenching of conflict. Each sometimes must be misunderstood. Propinquity must not be allowed victory because conventional happiness has been won.

'How insensitive of you to say that,' I said.

'I don't understand.'

'You're mocking me.'

'Of course I'm not.'

The doubts in my mind had made me stupidly irritable. A sudden flare and it was over. But I felt angry with myself for feeling angry.

'I'm sorry,' I said.

I felt, however, as soon as I had calmed down, that my burst of irritation had done me good. It was as if a window had been opened on a stuffy room. I began to see more clearly what was irking me.

'Darling,' I now said soothingly, 'what's worrying me is whether another phase of our life is over.'

'In what way?' Jeannie had ceased bunching for the moment and was holding the flowers untidily in her hand. She wore slim grey pants and a white polo necked jersey with

18

her dark hair touching her shoulders. As always she provided an incongruous touch of sophistication to the artisan world around her.

'Take this invitation,' I said, 'five years ago there wouldn't be any doubt about turning it down. I would have refused point blank to travel to London however glamorous the invitation might have been. Yet here I am today half wanting to accept it.'

'Five years ago you hadn't written any of the books which make hundreds of people find their way here.'

'This so-called success, then, is making me restless, making me wish to see my old self again.' Then I added as if it were a joke. 'I don't think that means any good.'

'You can't go on forever seeing life through a chink.'

'See, you also have changed.'

When we finished the bunching we gathered the discarded blooms, the crooked ones and the short ones, those with damaged petals and warped petals, and brought them into the cottage for our own pleasure; and the others stood in their jars waiting for the morrow when Jeannie would pack them in their long cardboard boxes, and no doubt would call me because she could never take the beauty for granted: 'Come and see this box. It's special!' Then the boxes would be strung together in couples, an invoice made out and attached, and then they would begin their journey to some London home by being rushed to Penzance station for the Covent Garden train. And after that we were commercially minded, and the flowers became like tins in a grocery store. They were earning a living for us, and so the hopeful wait would begin for the letter which, in a couple of days, would bring news of the price they had fetched.

It was nearly lunchtime and I poured out a glass of wine for each of us, and I sat sipping mine on the sofa while Jeannie was asking what I wanted for lunch. 'We've got two cheeses to choose from but not much bread. I haven't had time to make any.'

I made my choice, then heard her say: 'You didn't object that other time we were going to London.'

This was true. But I didn't feel apprehensive as I did now. And in any case we never went.

We had been all ready to go, seats booked on the train, a room at the Savoy, when the Lamorna postmaster arrived at the door of the cottage with a telegram. It read: 'Got donkey, Teague.'

A short while before we had been to a pub near Redruth called The Plume of Feathers whose landlord, Mr Teague, was also a horse dealer. Jeannie while she was there murmured that she had always wanted a donkey; and so Mr Teague, a persuasive salesman, made a note of her casual remark as if it were a firm order. Hence the telegram. Hence also the reason for the cancellation of our visit to London.

For Jeannie was not the kind of person to ignore such a telegram, or to remain unmoved by the plaintive eyes of the donkey gazing at us on our arrival in a field at the back of the pub; and within an hour Penny was ours and on the way to Minack in the well of the Land Rover, nose resting on my shoulder as I sat in the driving seat. It so happened, however, that Penny was in foal, and the foal was expected at any time. We could not leave her, or Jeannie insisted it would be cruel to do so; and thus we stayed, and in due course Fred was born. The donkey who cancelled a holiday.

Jeannie's preoccupation with birds and animals was the result of her natural kindness. She wanted to like people but she had found that people sometimes let you down, animals never; and so she felt secure when she gave them her trust. I, however, have never become emotionally involved with them in the same way as Jeannie. An unhappy animal story in a newspaper, and she is part of it; and I have learnt now to tear out such stories

20

before she has a chance to read them. Nor have I ever set out to acquire an animal in a deliberate way, like shopping for a piece of furniture. I am aware of my weakness. I selfishly want to avoid the responsibility that an animal inevitably entails; and so they have to come to me by chance.

For when, in fact, an animal does enter my life, I am sure to become its slave. I hold out for a while, struggling feebly to keep my independence, then I surrender. So it was with Monty whom I first saw playing bewitching kitten games in Jeannie's office at the Savoy; and so it was with Lama, the once wild little black cat who became his successor. So also with Boris, the Muscovy drake, who was unwisely offered as a dinner to Jane, the girl who was then working for us, by a young farmer who was courting her. So also with Penny and Fred; and, more remotely, with the two gulls Knocker and Squeaker who have for years held firm to their rights of the cottage roof. All of them arrived without an invitation from me. It was always Jeannie who first made them welcome.

This capacity for kindness was the secret of her success at the Savoy. She drew to the hotel and to the others in the group, Claridges and the Berkeley, an international set of socialites, show people, politicians and newspapermen who were constantly surprised, sometimes disconcerted, that they were meeting someone who had none of the harsher characteristics of a career girl.

'You wouldn't think she would say "boo" to a goose,' wrote one columnist.

'The prettiest publicity girl in the world,' wrote another.

Her offices on the first floor, past the foyer lift on the right, up the green carpeted stairs, along the corridor and nearly opposite the outwardly ancient looking lift that once was called 'the moving room', were the meeting place of the currently famous; and the walls were covered by photographs signed affectionately by household names. Once a secretary in that office she became, before she was, twenty-one, its centre. And when an official history of the Savoy was written a year or two ago, Jeannie's *Meet Me At The Savoy* was in a special section of the bibliography along with two others; one was by Compton Mackenzie, the other was Arnold Bennett's *Imperial Palace* which was based on Savoy personalities of Arnold Bennett's time. She wrote her book when first we came to Minack; and as she was a wayward writer who looked hopefully for distractions, I used to lock her in the chicken house which we had converted into a spare bedroom. 'There's another hour before she can come out,' I would explain to a bewildered caller; and Jeannie would continue her typing. The same rough treatment has recently been repeated; and the result is her novel *Hotel Regina*.

She had shown no wish to return to her glamorous way of life since she had been at Minack; nor, for that matter, had she used the threat of wishing to do so as she might have done during some period of stress. Yet content as she was in the soothing, peasant way of living we had chosen, it was to be expected that a time would come when sophistication lured her again; and so perhaps it was reasonable for me to suspect that she was pushing me to accept this literary invitation. A relief from cooking, a change from bunching flowers, a reacquaintance with her other ego; clothes, wit, flattery, trivial gaiety, style, pace, another world. I could not blame her.

There was also the atmosphere of the Savoy that she should wish to sense again; for behind the lavish façade there is a strange heart. It imposes on those who work there the old-fashioned qualities of pride and loyalty, and these weave such a compelling tradition that even the humblest kitchen hand who can boast, 'I was at the Savoy,' possesses a passport to a job in any hotel in the world.

There is also another form of this freemasonry, and I have been a victim of it many times. Jeannie and I will visit a strange restaurant and suddenly Jeannie discovers that the maitre d'hotel or a chef or a waiter spent part of his career at the Savoy. I know then that my meal will be indefinitely postponed as old, wrinkled faces light up, accents excitedly become even more broken, and legendary names of the hotel world are bandied to and fro. I sit there patiently fiddling with a fork, waiting for the emotional memories to finish, growing hungrier and hungrier; and yet I understand. Jeannie was not alone in her feelings when she wrote:

'The Savoy was my whole life. I became friends with its most important visitors and humblest staff, and I grew to love it with a love that was as strong as it was unreasonable; a love that disturbed my dreams as well as my days until I thought and spoke of nothing else.'

That was the background of Jeannie's life before she gave it up and came to Minack with its paraffin lamps; and she had never been back to stay, and nor had I.

'Admit it,' I said cheerfully after dinner, 'you're pushing me to accept this invitation.'

Jeannie was sitting on the sofa close to the new stove. For years she had cooked on a day and night burning stove but recently we had changed to an electric cooker. The Esse had been dismantled and now within the enlarged alcove, we had a stove we could use as an open fire during the day. Lama, a black, silky cushion, was on her lap, murmuring with purrs as Jeannie stroked her forehead.

'I'm not pushing. Just in favour.'

I had found a pipe, had filled it, and was about to light it. I am one of those who are poor at lighting pipes, and I use one match after another; and having lit it, it soon goes out and I start again. There have been times when Jeannie has gone to an ash tray, counted the matches therein, then jokingly said: 'Fifteen matches . . . all in five minutes!'

On this occasion the flame was abreast of the bowl when

she added: 'You're quite right . . . I *do* want to go to London. We've been away all these years and now we can go back having justified ourselves. We were thought of as crazy to leave. People waited for us to creep back, hoped for it, some of them. But we have stayed and fought, and sacrificed all sorts of pleasures, and been patronised when we've had no money, and have always kept faith in what we were doing . . .'

She paused, and I was no longer trying to light my pipe.

'Go on,' I said.

'I would like to have some gay reward for all our struggles. I remember seeing you in a telephone box on a hot August day in Penzance when a cheque had been returned, and you were begging someone to help you honour it. I watched you clenching your fists, and knew the agony as the help was refused. I will never forget.'

'It wasn't as bad as all that.'

The pipe was out, but I did not mind.

'I want to feel superficial again, absolutely useless. I want to lie in bed and have a telephone beside me and be able to ask for what I want when I like. I want to be idle. I would like to have the fun of being greeted by Vercelli in the Grill, or walking into Claridge's and being welcomed by Luigi as if I had never been away, or going to the Berkeley and seeing Pelosi. All the gay things I used to do.'

'I understand.'

She was on cue for a fling. I could see that now. For years every penny that had been available had been spent on the flower farm; a new tractor, endless repairs to existing machinery, three or four years and another new tractor, vast capital outlay on daffodil bulbs, another greenhouse, heaters, oil for the heaters, and all the other mundane things we had to acquire to keep our business moving. Necessary, of course, but it had been Jeannie who had to make most of the sacrifices so that we could afford them.

'Well?' she said, smiling up at me.

Lama jumped to the floor and meandered over to the bookcase. There she sat, face looking upwards, hinting that she would like her saucer filled. Jeannie was quick to respond.

'I'm more solemn than you,' I answered, laughing, 'I wouldn't go to London just to be pampered.'

'You get that here,' she said mockingly, 'who cooks for you and does your laundry and supervises all your comforts?'

'The oldest stick to be used by women against man,' I said, realising she had scored a bull's eye, 'I submit, I beg your pardon. You deserve all the flippant hours you can get.'

'Thank you. I'll remember.'

She had filled Lama's saucer and had moved into the tiny kitchen. The kitchen had been her own design, and she had had it made soon after her mother had died . . . her house-proud mother who always marvelled how Jeannie managed so gaily to have people to stay under the then primitive conditions.

But that was in the old days. The new kitchen was like a galley in a boat, indeed it was made by a boat builder from Newlyn, and cunningly designed within a section of the sitting room . . . only ten feet long with a three-foot-wide standing space, a refrigerator, a sink, the electric cooker, and small cupboards of natural wood up to the ceiling. She used to potter about there too much sometimes for my liking. I would begin a monologue, then be mildly vexed by her lack of attention. 'I'm listening,' she would call amidst the clatter of pots and pans and water filling the sink. I would doubt it, and cease my talk, and wait until she had finished. No reason to be impatient on this occasion. She was out of the kitchen within the minute.

'You see,' I said, 'I want to find out whether this phase of our life *could* be over. You said yourself one can't forever go on seeing life through a chink.'

'Don't take me too literally.'

'I'm not, but I have to admit you made a good point. I'm wondering whether we have become too parochial, too self-satisfied with the rhythm of our life.'

'Why feel guilty just because you're happy?'

'Do you remember Christopher Buckley all those years ago,' I said, ignoring her question, 'when he was chief foreign correspondent of the *Telegraph* standing at the window of your office just before he went out to Korea and was killed?'

'One grey, wet afternoon.'

'He stood there quoting the lines from Barrie: "Do not stand aloof, despising, disbelieving, but come in and help . . . insist on coming in and helping".'

It was during the period when Jeannie and I were making up our minds whether to come to Cornwall. A grey, wet afternoon and I was listening to the voice of a crusader.

'We were involved in those days,' I went on, 'we were not standing aloof as we are now. We had struggled our way into the centre of things, and were successful, and were full of promise as long as we kept our nerve.'

'We didn't, did we?'

'Why?'

'We weren't ruthless,' she said, 'and we were too lazy to be cunning, and were hopeless at intrigue.'

'Lacking the ingredients of success.'

'If you like.'

'I suppose we expected too much of other people, expected them to have the standards we believed we had ourselves.'

I saw Jeannie smiling.

'You're having doubts,' she said, 'because you've forgotten what our life was like.'

'So have you in a way.'

'Possibly.'

'Well then,' I said, 'it's time to remind ourselves.'

I suddenly saw the motive for going to London. My restless mood had to be put to the test; and I would be able to do this.

Most of the important decisions of my life had been taken in London, and each decision had ended a phase which I thought at the time was permanent. Of course the stress behind a decision is easily forgotten when you are far away from its environment; yet each decision has built another part of you, sharing the responsibility of whatever happens.

I knew, therefore, what I had to do. I would set out to remember the kind of life I used to lead. I would go to see the places in London where I lived, and seek to catch my mood at the time when the decisions were being made. First, 38 Cranley Gardens off the Old Brompton Road where I arrived as an innocent from Harrow to become an office boy in Unilever House; then Joubert Studios off the Kings Road where I spent an idle summer, then 20 Elm Park Lane, also in Chelsea; then I would remember 56 Portsmouth Street, Manchester; then Cholmondeley House where I was to carry Jeannie across the threshold after our marriage; then Thames Bank Cottage at Mortlake where ghosts, I feel sure, will always shout on Boat Race day. All these in their different fashion led the way to Minack.

They could help me now. I would see them reflected against the present. I might then realise that the values I once believed important had no place in the community age. Perhaps this was the cause of my restlessness. Perhaps Jeannie and I were living in a fool's paradise.

We would try to find out.

THREE

A westerly gale was blowing the night we left Minack; and the roar was as if the cottage were a boat, the roof and walls the rigging. Outside, as I carried the suitcases down the path to the car which was taking us to Penzance station, I was pushed so violently by the wind that I had to drop the suitcases and steady myself. Far away across the bay, the Lizard light winked. The darkness hid the outline of the land around me but there in the distance curving towards the Lizard were the lights of Prah sands, Porthleven and Mullion. No sign of what was in between, only the sound of the sea's rage.

It was Sunday evening in the third week of January, and during the day we had wandered around the cliff meadows collecting the odd daffodils which were in bloom, a few from a meadow close to the sea, a few from another which edged the zone, enough to take to London to give away. Geoffrey and his young wife Emily would be in charge, and they would have no difficulty in coping with any daffodils which might become ready for market; and we hoped, too, they would satisfy Lama; and Penny and Fred the donkeys, and Boris the muscovy drake. There were the two gulls also, Knocker and Squeaker, who year after year had strutted along the apex of the roof or sat on the chimney warming their feathers. They, too, would expect the same attention paid to them by ourselves to continue in our absence. 'I'll bake a special lot of bread for them,' Jeannie had said. Over the years they had turned up their beaks to shop bread.

It is supposed that this country is a nation of animal lovers but sometimes I wonder whether this reputation is deserved.

Any branch of the RSPCA will tell you of the dogs and cats that are brought to them to be destroyed because their owners are going away on holiday. Apparently, in the minds of these owners, a domestic animal is an expendable object, useful between holidays. I should add, perhaps, that these animals brought by their misguided owners to the RSPCA may be considered lucky. There are many others which are left to roam the streets; and I have a friend who looks after such as these, who looks after them until he can find another home, keeping them in kennels often at considerable personal expense. He, too, sometimes doubts this country's animal loving reputation. For at Christmas time he will be pestered with enquiries for kittens and puppies ... and by holiday time they will be coming back to him as unwanted cats and dogs. Their time as toys are over.

We ourselves, of course, have always been extreme in the other direction. Foolishly so. There have been many times when we might have gone away for a night or two, only to be stopped by the thought: 'What will happen to the animals?' It was a vague, sometimes irritating, devotion to them; and yet if you live in isolation, no houses, no neighbours to be seen or heard, no constant reminders of the convulsions of conventional civilisation, it is easy for animals to dominate you. You revolve in a small world that is comfortable and reassuring. You are wanted, and you respond; and you receive rewards at many unexpected moments. It is a pleasant kind of domination.

In the days before our departure we fussed according to the varying vividness of our imaginations. We had been so long anchored to our routine of living that we behaved as if we were about to set off round the world. Would it be wise, we considered earnestly, to let Boris continue his roaming in the neighbourhood of the cottage, or should he be kept locked up in the hut which was his normal sleeping quarters? Boris's range of activities was limited. When first he came, seven years before, we were warned to expect him to fly the district enquiring for a mate; and we were advised to anticipate such adventures by providing him with a mate of our own choice. We did not do so because, in the first place we soon found that Boris had no ambitions to fly; and in the second, we cared not for the idea of endless little ducklings growing up to be eaten. Hence Boris remained a happy bachelor and free to roam as he liked.

He had a congenial routine. He would waddle to his hut in the wood on his own in the evening, and before nightfall one of us would lock him up. He would be let out in the morning and woe betide us if we were late, for then he would hiss and wave his head like a cobra; and if I were the one at fault I felt forced to apologise. 'Sorry, Boris,' I would say, 'I overslept.' His roaming, at first glance, seemed harmless enough because he never went further than the small section of land which surrounded the greenhouse in front of the cottage . . . apart from his ponderous walk up the path to the cottage door where he waited for any titbits which Jeannie was prepared to give him.

The trouble was that the foxes could watch him. For years, in a curious misguided way, we had never feared the prospect of a raid on him. The foxes, we knew, wandered about the field on the other side of the shallow valley and indeed they had given us much pleasure from time to time . . . especially the summer they chose to raise their cubs from the earth they had dug in a corner of the field. But we never thought they would have an eye for Boris until a well-meaning gentleman came along and put the idea into our heads. 'Do you mean,' he asked incredulously, 'that you allow the drake to wander unguarded? It's amazing that a fox hasn't got it long ago.' It was at that moment that innocence turned into anxiety. Darkness, we appreciated, was an obvious danger and hence our care to lock up Boris at night. But in daylight we had always felt that Minack was magically safe. We believed, or more accurately Jeannie believed, that there was a truce between Minack and foxes and badgers in the neighbourhood; and provided we did not allow anyone to persecute them, the vulnerable members of the Minack community would be spared.

A fox, indeed, had shared a winter in the stables with the donkeys; and Jeannie pretended that it was the cub she had once looked after whose paw had been caught in a trap. Every night it got into the hay alongside the donkeys, then slid away around breakfast time. Sammy, we had called the cub; but the fox was a vixen and she became Samantha. Many a time that year I heard Jeannie going down the path which leads to the sea calling: 'Samantha!' . . . with a plateful of food. And as many times I saw Samantha appear from behind a hedge, waiting, watching . . . but not running away. She could trust Jeannie. No wonder we had believed Boris was safe.

The same threat applied to Lama. She, too, never wandered any distance and was always ready to come in soon after nightfall, but just about the time we were warned about Boris, we were told what had happened to a cat at Sennen Cove adjoining Lands End. In broad daylight a fox was seen to sneak into the car park outside the pub, and snatch the pub's cat which was sunning itself on a wall. Out dashed the pub's customers like a pack of hounds, chased the fox up the road where it soon dropped the cat, badly mauled and minus a tail. We had known of foxes catching cats before, but never had we known so graphic an incident. It alarmed us.

For Lama herself believed she was immune from danger. When she first came into our lives she was a wild cat . . . so wild that I remember her hysterically flinging herself against the mesh wire in the chicken run where I had surprised her, in order to escape from me. She had been born in a cave down among our cliff meadows close to the sea, and when she was old enough she began to roam in the neighbourhood of the cottage. She kept always at a distance and Jeannie despaired that we should ever become friends with her. Then one day, a stormy day, we heard a cry at the door. It was Lama. From then on, a change in her serenely took place, and she became an indulgent, home happy little black cat. A strange transformation. A cat which once sped away when anyone came within a few hundred yards of her, became placid and amiable and very loving.

It was this loving which caused us concern. It was as if she believed a magic protected her from danger. A car or a tractor, for instance, was no threat to her and she would contentedly sit in its path. I saw her once advance towards a fox cub which was peering at her from a short distance away, a sauntering, friendly advance. And more recently, indeed only a week or so before we heard the story of Sennen Cove, I witnessed an incident which startled me.

I had gone into the wood near the cottage where Boris had his hut when I saw a young fox weaving about in the grass a few yards away. It was neither a cub nor a fully grown fox. It was elongated like a teenager, and it gave the impression that it was unsure of itself. Head down in the grass for a moment, front legs spread out like a puppy wanting a game, then upright again with head on one side in puzzlement. I stood there absolutely still, and for the life of me I could not guess what was happening. Perhaps it is playing with another fox, I said to myself. But suddenly the fox turned round and darted off into the undergrowth, and for a second I saw a black dash on its tail. Lama, of course.

Lama, therefore, courted danger without knowing it, and this we had to accept. So also did Boris; and thus we had to weigh up the hazards against the inconvenience caused to them both if they were kept shut in. They would be furious, that was certain; and after all, we said to each other, we might impose the same standard of caution on ourselves. A legion of buses were waiting to run us over.

Hence, we decided, our caution in regard to them could become a neurosis, and it would be kinder to allow them during daylight hours to continue their wandering ways. In any case Geoffrey would never be far away. He would be, we felt sure, an admirable guardian.

Penny and Fred, the donkeys, posed a different problem. Nobody was likely to attack *them*. In their case boredom was the enemy. They liked to have us around during the course of the day, liked us to be there if they felt in the mood to be taken from one meadow to another; and if we were not present to obey their whims, they were provoked into taking action. Such action, of course, depended upon the opportunities that might be available. A hiker, for instance, who might pass their way, knapsack hoisted on his back, was likely to feel as he marched head down intent on his journey, a curious sensation around his shoulders. It would be Fred. Fred had developed a technique of creeping up behind an unsuspecting walker, then pushing his nose into the mysterious contents of the knapsack. If there were no knapsack, if the passer-by took no notice of him, Fred would play the 'you're a ghost' game; and this meant that the unfortunate stranger suddenly found a donkey barging at him as if his presence did not exist. Fred found this very funny.

Penny's boredom was exorcised in other ways. Apart from her tuneless, excruciating hee-haw – a sound which was intended to make us rush to her help from wherever we might be in an anguished desire to stop it – she had other tricks. Tricks which she had also taught Fred. She was skilled at gate opening, nudging a latch off a hook. And no one was more talented in removing a bar from across a gap. She was an artist in finding a weakness in any field's defences. She was, in fact, a donkey Houdini; and when the trick had been successfully performed she would lead her son on a spree among our neighbour's fields. Such behaviour, as I have said, only took place when they were bored; and it would have to be Geoffrey's job to see this did not happen. Perhaps it would be his most difficult job, though fortunately he could have some help. 'I'll bring Julie and Philip here,' he said, 'and that will keep them quiet.' Julie was six, Philip four.

'Penny is mine,' Julie had always said.

'Fred is *mine*,' Philip had always countered.

When, therefore, we entered the night train at Penzance we believed we had done everything possible to cater for the idiosyncrasies of those we had left behind. There was food for them galore. We had anticipated their whims as best we could. The security measures were reasonable; and Geoffrey had been primed to forego any normal useful work should any of the creatures display a need for special attention. None of them had any reason to notice that we had gone away. We would have a complete rest from responsibility. Two slaves on holiday. And I had to admit to a great sense of relief. I do not think the train had rumbled along the lines as far as St Erth, before I said to Jeannie in a neighbouring sleeper:

'I feel my London ego is already taking over.'

I heard her laugh.

'Mine is doing the same,' came the reply, 'and by to-morrow I'll feel the Savoy is my natural home again.'

FOUR

I lay awake and listened to the rattle of the train and the occasional toneless hoot of the diesel engine. Camborne, Redruth, Truro. My old home was near Newquay and the station we used was Truro. As a child I never went to Penzance, though Penzance was of enormous importance to my childish self. I used to pretend that Paddington, Penzance and the Cornish Riviera Express combined together in some strange way to represent the journey of life. Heaven knows how I came to make up such a fantasy but for a long while it remained for me a delightful, secret game. Penzance was the mysterious beacon, a never-never land. And there I would be on Truro station either waiting for the Cornish Riviera to come up the line from Shangri-la, or watching it leave the station to go there. I think I had the idea in my mind that life would be as simple as that journey; scheduled stops punctually reached, courteous behaviour, unchallengeable values, a certain aura of romance, and a far-away moment of orderly conclusion.

On the platform of Truro station are the ghosts of my father and mother; and many greetings, many farewells. We would drive from my home, Glendorgal, in an old Wolseley tourer with me in the back, my old sheep dog beside me, my father and mother in front; my father in a large tweed motoring coat and a cap, my mother beside him with her Maltese terrier on her lap, and the three of us trying to talk naturally in these last few minutes before I went back to school. Or they would be waiting for me when I returned for the holidays, and when I leant out of the train window I would see them standing together with sheep dog on lead ready to bark wildly as soon as he saw me; and Maltese terrier tucked in my mother's arms. Safe days.

I was lucky in my parents. They were completely unselfish as far as my two brothers and myself were concerned and they repeatedly, by sacrificing their own enjoyment, helped us along our way. I am afraid that of the three of us I was the most unsatisfactory because I provided no evidence to counter the verdict of my Harrow housemaster who declared to me one day after I had missed a catch in an inter-house cricket match: 'You're useless to society, old man.'

My brother Nigel, for instance, who has now created out of our old home a famous hotel, won the King's Dirk (equivalent to the Sandhurst Sword of Honour) as a naval cadet at Dartmouth. My brother Colin was head of his House and captained Haileybury at Rugby football. Both were older. Both provided an incentive for me to achieve something of equal youthful importance. I knew that this was hoped for by my father and mother.

But I achieved nothing. I failed at the most simple of examinations, and except for a morning glory moment at the age of fifteen when I was captain of the junior football and cricket teams of my House, I provided only enthusiasm to my schoolboy sporting activities.

I had, however, an excitement for living, and this found an outlet in a correspondence course for journalism which I studied after lights out at the bottom of my bed with the aid of a torch. This secret gesture of protest against the teaching methods of my expensive education gave me great satisfaction until the proprietor of the course guessed the truth; and thereupon wrote me a kind letter suggesting that the remainder of my course should be suspended until I had completed my scholastic duties. I agreed reluctantly.

I had now to find some other way to divert me from the tedious boredom of my lessons, but in this I was to be frustrated once again. I wanted to find a master who would be my Svengali, someone who would talk to me about literature and history and ways of the past and the civilised beat of living, someone, in fact, who would counter the crude methods which forced me to write out pages of Shakespeare or many verses of the Bible when I was late or committed some other light misdemeanour, thus spoiling my pleasure in them.

Harrow is a romantic school. There are walls and buildings and paths there which remain unchanged from the days of Raleigh and Byron, Sheridan and Peel, Palmerston and Churchill ... and there are haunting songs which tear the heart in the innocence of their themes. All this I felt, but who was to fill in the details? I plodded at my examinations and when I failed yet again I yearned the more to find someone who would reassure me that failure at eighteen is unimportant. I was asking too much. Then, as now, the pressure on schoolmasters allowed them only to spend time on those with promise, and thus I remained alone with my hopes. Terence Rattigan, the playwright, was in my House at the time; brilliant scholar and cricketer, charming, kind and a conqueror of examinations. I once followed him and a witty classical master up the Hill, though many yards behind, willing them both to pause and see me and involve me in their clever conversation. They didn't.

Thus I left Harrow without an accolade, and at a time when there were three million unemployed. It was then my father received the reward of being kind to a man some years before. My father's friend was in Unilever and by his influential help I was able to exchange my life on the Hill for that of an office boy at the London headquarters. I was immediately filled with commercial enthusiasm and ambition; and I opened envelopes and ran messages with the zeal of a future tycoon.

Jeannie, meanwhile, seven years younger and living twenty miles away at St Albans, was faring more happily. She was clever, and this puzzled her parents. Her father, an extrovert, did not understand a daughter who enjoyed Charlotte Bronte and Trollope and Jane Austen before she had even reached her teens. He had never read any of them. He was a gay man, overflowing with the desire that everyone should be happy; and, he believed simply, that if everyone was generous to each other this could be achieved. But this eldest daughter of his ... he was slightly embarrassed, though proud, by the ideas she had. 'She's a bit of a blue stocking,' he would explain apologetically. Jeannie, however, was also an athlete. When she was older she played lacrosse for Hertfordshire, and later she was chosen to play for the South Eastern Counties on the wing. News of this particular honour came through the post, and she rushed excitedly to tell her parents. 'Rubbish,' said her father, thinking of his blue stocking daughter, 'it's a mistake. They've chosen Barbara not you. Go and ring the captain and tell her.' There was no mistake.

Barbara was her younger sister and she was very good at tennis. One summer, fellow members of the local tennis club kept urging her to bring sister Jean along ... it was the summer that a young girl called Jean Nichol (spelt with an h) had been chosen to play for the Wightman Cup. At last Jean Nicol (without an h) agreed to go to the club, and was overwhelmed by the enthusiasm with which she was greeted; and she was astonished, when she reached the court, to find that an audience had gathered to watch her. Jeannie may have looked slim and pretty but her play was deplorable. She was a rabbit. She was the Nicol without an h.

This tale of mistaken identity followed Jeannie around; and although she never appeared on a tennis court again, she was constantly being asked about her Wimbledon and other championship experiences. Soon there was to be a climax. Jean Nichol and Jean Nicol became engaged the same week, were married within a few days of each other, and each had the Savoy Hotel as their headquarters. The Press wanted to photograph them together but Jean Nichol refused to meet my Jean ... though it did not stop a confusion over wedding presents.

Jeannie came into my life a long time before I met her or had heard of her. A series of strange coincidences.

When, for instance, I was at Harrow I used to stay with my aunt in a pretty Regency house called Rutlands, set in a large garden, at Bushey Heath. Jeannie's father happened to pass by this house about this time, and from the moment he saw it he had a passion to buy it. He never did, but often he would say: 'Let's go for a drive and see *my* house.' And off the family would go in the car to Bushey Heath; and stop close to Rutlands. I was probably there at the time.

There were other coincidences. My parents, when I was a child, used to let our home, Glendorgal, during high summer, and we would go abroad or rent a house during the same period. I never quite understood the financial advantages involved, I was too young to do so in any case, but I knew that my parents felt triumphant if they let Glendorgal for X guineas while living somewhere else for Y guineas.

One summer a Y guineas house was in Newquay itself, a squat Victorian house in a row almost opposite the entrance to the Newquay Golf Club; and overlooking the patch of green where for decades all-in wrestling had taken place. How could it be that Jeannie's parents should take the same house? They did one summer, and it was in Newquay harbour that Jeannie first learnt to swim.

A schoolgirl memory of Jeannie's is when she went to Holland and Germany along with other members of her school at Westgate. The Westgate school was run by a Miss

Weber and her brother had a language school in Bonn. My brother Colin was at this school though, needless to say, Jeannie did not know this when she visited it.

Her first job was as a secretary in the firm that ran the Dorothy Dix column for the *Daily Mirror*. Jeannie remembers saying to herself as she saw my photograph on advertisements decorating London buses: 'What has *he* done to deserve all this?' Her doubts were justified. I had done *nothing* to deserve it.

Barbara was also now working in London, and she and Jeannie used to travel back to St Albans in the same train in the evening. They would arrive at St Pancras at different times, and so there was a standard arrangement to meet on the platform opposite a certain advertising poster. It advertised Tangye hydraulic jacks.

My own contribution to this series of tentative steps which brought us together took place on a Japanese cargo boat bound for Hong Kong from Sydney just before the outbreak of the 1939 war. A passenger aboard, an engineer on his way to a job in Hong Kong's dockyards, fancied himself as an amateur palmist. For some days I scorned his boastful claims and refused to accept his offer to read my hand; but one evening, after I had had my fill of saké, I yielded to his insistence. I myself was on my way to China, Japan, then home by the Trans-Siberian Railway; and I had a vague hope that this man would be able to tell me whether my journey would be completed before the inevitable war broke out. I held out my hand. 'You're going to marry in 1943 and the girl will be smaller and darker than yourself,' he said, 'and her initials will be J. E.'

This information at the time gave me satisfaction. A girl with whom I considered myself in love had waved good-bye to me at Waterloo Station when I set off on my tour of the world; and she was smaller and darker than myself, and her

Christian name also began with J. The engineer had given me good news, I said to myself; and good news it remained until a few weeks later I had a letter to tell me that the girl concerned had married.

The prophecy remained submerged at the back of my mind, but I certainly did not pay any importance to it; it was only an item in my diary. Jeannie, meanwhile, had become a secretary in the Press Office of the Savoy, then had been promoted to Public Relations Officer when her boss was called up. It was there that I first met her. The bombs were monotonously falling on London, but I had had a book called *Time Was Mine* just published; and I was in the Savoy foyer one evening when someone pointed Jeannie out to me. 'A girl of influence,' I was told, 'you ought to know her.' Her sphere of influence lay partly in the Savoy bookstall; and when, after our introduction, she arranged that the book should be prominently displayed on the bookstall, I felt that manners allied to desire warranted me inviting her to dinner.

Carroll Gibbons, at this period, was playing in what is called the River Room. The windows, overlooking the Thames, were boarded up as a protection against bomb blast; and men and girls danced there at night in uniforms of many different European nations seemingly unaware, just as Carroll and the famous members of his band pretended to be unaware, that death danced with the music. I sat with Jeannie against the wall beside the entrance, and once when Carroll passed us he asked in his drawl what Jeannie would like him to play:

'The Lady is a Tramp, of course!'

We had before us roast duckling in red wine sauce, peas and potato croquettes. We had also a bottle of claret. Already we had performed the first fencing of conversation. Polite noises had been interchanged and we were relaxing.

41

My book, I was saying to myself, had brought me luck which was quite unexpected; one question about each other, and another; and then came a wild impulse to ask her what other names she had beside Jean.

'The ghastly name of Everald,' she replied innocently.

I looked at her across the duck.

'Do you mean your initials begin J. E. ?'

'Yes. Why so anxious?'

Why indeed. How could I possibly tell her that a prophecy had begun to be fulfilled? Here I sat attracted, at the stage of getting to know her, trying to impress her, diffident because she was a girl of experience, and yet firmly written in my diary were the letters J. E. . . . the girl I was going to marry. I gobbled my duck, made an excuse and went out to ring my best friend. 'I've just met the girl I'm going to marry,' I said, giving him the details. 'Forget it,' he replied grumpily, 'it's war time. Be happy this evening.'

I fell asleep when the diesel broke down outside Bodmin Road station. A wonderful silence had come to the compartment, and I heard an owl hooting, and I began to remember the trees in which it lived, the trees which towered over me as a schoolboy when I fished the river for trout with my father; the river which twined beside the railway line . . . I thought of the car being parked by the station, pulling on my clumsy waders, fixing my rod and line, opening the small aluminium box containing my flies, and wondering which to try first, and then marching beside my father to the river hoping that all the trout in the neighbourhood would soon be deceived by my cast. I remembered . . . and fell asleep.

And so deep was my sleep that I did not wake again until the sleeping car attendant woke me up with a tray of tea and biscuits three quarters of an hour before we entered Paddington.

I got up and pulled down the window shutters; and soon, after all the years, I began to see London again.

Cranes. I saw these first. Huge, Frankenstein cranes straddling the skyline like monster crabs. Then, as the train dashed through Ealing and Acton, I saw the early morning commuters posed on the platforms, stiffly in lines like matchsticks; and they were black as well as white. And I thought with mild surprise that during the years I used to live in London a coloured man was an oddity. The train was slowing, and now it was no different from when last I came to Paddington. I was passing the same debris of buildings, the same seedy tall houses, the same grime, and broken windows. All the years of talk and nothing had been done. Time was standing still for me. Coming into Paddington that morning was like arriving there in the years after the war. Only the steam engines were missing.

'To the Savoy!' I said to the taxi driver, after we had taken our turn in the sleepy-eyed queue. And to Jeannie I said: 'I feel nervous . . . like a farmer up for Smithfield Show!' And already unknowingly I had made my first mistake. I had been so impressed by propaganda concerning inflated London prices that I read the scrawl for our tea and biscuits as eight shillings. Only later did I learn it was three shillings. A countryman on the loose. My London ego required time to acclimatise itself.

There is something opulent about the leather smell of a taxi, and now we were speeding through Bayswater and on into Park Lane, I felt the excitement of our adventure. An early morning in London, no traffic, no one yet to crowd the pavements, Jeannie at my side, familiar sights to please, the Vickers building and the Hilton to shock. I was nervous but very happy. I was, for instance, about to wear the cloak of a millionaire. Money was about to lose its control of me. Along Constitution Hill and into the Mall, then round

Trafalgar Square and into the Strand. In a minute we would be turning into the Savoy courtyard. In a minute banknotes would take the place of pennies. I had my arm through Jeannie's and I pressed her hand.

'Oh,' she said as the taxi drew up, and the porter advanced to the door, 'oh, I have such a *delicious* sense of being on the spree.'

We went through the revolving glass doors into the foyer, the familiar pillars, the sofas and chairs to the left where people sit to watch the world go by, the stairs past the Grill leading up to the American Bar; and on the right the flower kiosk, the bookstall where Jeannie had arranged for *Time Was Mine* to be displayed, the counter of the Enquiry Office, and a little further along, that of Reception with suave young men in morning coats already on duty. Ahead were the stairs leading down to the Restaurant and to the corridor off which were the private banqueting rooms and the lift which took guests to that side of the building; and ahead, too, were the stairs and the passage which score upon score of times Jeannie had walked as she went to and from Room 205 which was her office. There, too, were the news tape machines which men pretend to look at while waiting hopefully for an expected companion, and the lift which Bert, the liftman, had never left while the bombs fell, and the alcove of telephone boxes where Abel had ruled in an orderly confusion of telephone calls.

'Miss Nicol!'

The welcome had started. A hall porter in his dove grey uniform came forward. Then another. And this was to continue during the first days, as staff came on to their different rosters. The clerks of the Enquiry Office, the waiters of Grill and Restaurant, those of the American Bar, other people who work behind the scenes ... another and another would come up to her.

44

A young man from Reception escorted us down the stairs which led to the Restaurant, then turned left along the corridor which led to the far lift. The usual thought went through my mind, looking at the key in the young man's hand; I hope we're not going to be put somewhere at the back. Both of us knew of the subtle way in which the importance of guests was judged. Characters which the outsider assessed as important might be considered by an international hotel as only worthy of a minor room. A secret antenna was always at work. A millionaire or a film star, an established one or a rising one, were surprised sometimes by the treatment they received.

We were on the fifth floor, and the young man turned to his right, and we went along the corridor, and when we reached the end, the key opened the door of a river suite. The Savoy had welcomed Jeannie's return by bestowing a subtle compliment.

The élite the world over try to use their influence to secure suites overlooking the river at the Savoy. They have, apart from their opulence and the immaculate service, superb views of London; and those on the fifth floor are, by tradition, the most sought after. 'We stood at the window of our suite on the fifth floor of the Savoy Hotel,' wrote Charles Chaplin in his autobiography on the occasion he came back to live in Europe with his wife Oona ... 'we stood silent, drinking in the most stirring view of a city in all this world.'

When we were left alone, we too stood at the window. It was huge, like a shop's window, and it was divided into three sections and one section was ajar, so that as we stood there we heard the waking hum of London. Away to our right were the Houses of Parliament with the face of Big Ben clearly to be seen; and across the curve of the river were Hungerford and Westminster bridges. Opposite, and incongruous because it seemed to emerge from a patchwork of haphazard buildings, was the Festival Hall; and to the right of it were the eyesockets of the Shell monolith. Sleek tugs and their barges were busy on the river as the tide was high, and we were reminded again how long it had been since we had lived in London; for the tugs we knew when we had our cottage at Mortlake were as T Model Fords to the cars of today. Below us Cleopatra's Needle peered above the bare plane trees of the Embankment Gardens, and I thought of its curious connection with my family . . . it was hoisted into place by hydraulic jacks invented by my grandfather and his brothers, and one jack lies in the foundations to this day. On the left was Waterloo Bridge, and black beetles were beginning to scurry across it to their shops and offices, and Jeannie remembered how she was once one of them on her way to Room 205. Further to the left, past the spick and span *Discovery*, I could see Blackfriars and the Unilever building into which I once scurried myself. And if it had been clear, if there had been no clinging early morning haze, we would have seen ahead of us the hills, the surprising hills of Wandsworth, Lambeth and Lewisham; and beyond them those of Surrey.

'A good beginning,' I said.

'Marvellous,' said Jeannie laughing. And she picked up a telephone and ordered breakfast.

The elegant sitting-room had orange covers on the sofa and easy chairs, a glass cupboard with old china plates, a writing table, a television set enclosed in a walnut cabinet, two china table lamps, a standard lamp with orange shade, a thick green carpet, curtains of greenish grey; and the bedroom was ten times the size of our Minack bedroom, and there were cupboards galore, and layers of drawers, and the view again over the river; and there was a lobby adjoining the large bathroom with cupboards for my own clothes. At Minack we were confined, and our clothes were crowded into odd corners; and so, unexpectedly, it was space which also gave us pleasure in that first hour at the Savoy.

There was a knock at the door and Louis, the floor waiter, pushed a trolley into the sitting-room and breakfast awaited us. After he left I failed, as I had done many times in the past, to manage the Savoy coffee pot; and I spilt the coffee on the elegant pink tablecloth as I poured it into the cup.

And then I picked up my cup and walked to the window and I heard Jeannie say behind me:

'The last time I saw someone silhouetted against that window it was Danny Kaye.'

Danny Kaye in his hey-day always stayed at the Savoy. Nothing is forgotten. You come back to a hotel room and the last time greets you.

'He was pretending to cut my hair,' she went on, 'and the photographer thought it funny, and he caught the moment, and the picture was published when *Meet Me At The Savoy* was serialised.'

'Yes, he did look funny.'

There was another knock on the sitting room door, and a page boy and two girls from the florists appeared. They were laden with flowers, and the two girls came in to arrange them.

'Jeannie,' I said, looking at the cards, 'five different people have sent you flowers!' I was glad she was receiving the welcome she deserved.

She went later into the bedroom to unpack, and I remained in the sitting room, staring down on the river and the Embankment. I was thinking how pleasant it was to be back in London, free from any sense of involvement. So many of my memories were born of tension and frenzied activity, but now I was an outsider. I was still dependent on others, but I was also remote from them. I could observe the scene instead of being immersed in it. And yet, I said to

47

myself, such soothing thoughts might prove deceptive. Only in brief moments does one think one can ever change. The pace of London could still catch me again. The pace I longed to enjoy when I first came to London, and lived at 38 Cranley Gardens.

I would go there tomorrow, I decided. I would take the Tube to South Kensington, walk up the Old Brompton Road, and turn left at Cranley Gardens. I would see myself again as when I first stared at No. 38; a nineteen-year-old, sheltering behind the safety of *The Times*, along with my parents, my relations, and the rest of the middle class of that era; anything unpleasant, *Times* valuation, being kept out of sight.

I would remember again the first phase . . .

The Places

FIVE

There was an oak door at 38 Cranley Gardens. I used to face it late at night when I had forgotten my key, staring at its threatening solidity, wondering whether I could dare ring the bell and, after a jittery interval, have the courage to face my landlady in her dressing gown.

'If you forget your key *once* more, Mr Tangye . . .'

In daytime I used to hurry through the doorway, down the steps between the two massive stone pillars supporting the Victorian portico, and run at speed towards South Kensington station along the Old Brompton Road, past Cranley Place and Sumner Place, past Onslow Square Gardens, past the massive flower arrangements in the window of Wills and Seager, past people going to work more sedately. I dodged the traffic and into the station. I had to catch the 8.26 Inner Circle for Blackfriars if I were to sign on at Unilever House in the black column . . . instead of the menacing red one, reserved for those who were more than five minutes late.

I wore a bowler hat, a black city suit, and carried a rolled-up umbrella. I used to buy a third class ticket, then travel first class; and I would sit, eyeing not the reading matter, but the possible coming of the Inspector. So for twenty minutes I believed myself important, my vanity assuaged . . . until the train arrived at Blackfriars, and I rushed up the stairs and along to the back door of Unilever House.

'Mornin' Tangye,' some voice would say to me from behind, 'mornin' Tangye.'

I sat in a large hall of metal desks, and I was the junior

clerk in a section of five. I opened envelopes and ran errands, and copied invoices into a ledger; and was obsequious to the manager, a tall, gaunt man with a black drooping moustache like that of Bairnsfeather's Ol' Bill. I was nineteen years old and my salary was thirty-seven shillings and sixpence a week.

I was keen at that time, and studied business books, and was smilingly alert when the thin-lipped colleague who was the least favourite of my superiors, ordered me to fetch him a packet of cigarettes. I believed a show of willingness was the passport to success. I believed that if I set out to be liked, appreciation of my gifts and therefore promotion would naturally follow. I smiled at everyone, kept my temper when taunted, fawned for praise. I had yet to begin to learn about the mysterious forces that rule a career. I was simple.

The months went by and my promotion did not materialise. My keenness lost its edge, my smile its readiness, and I was now ready for diversions. The scope for these was limited, but one which gave me considerable pleasure was The Walk. I could not take it as often as I would have liked to. My absence would have been noticed.

The Walk was, in fact, a tour of the Unilever building. I briskly marched up the stairs, along corridors, up more stairs, along more corridors; and I did this with an air of such purpose that anyone observing me would have thought I was performing a mission, and not carrying out an escape from boredom. Up floor after floor, then down again, and back to my desk, and my colleagues with their faces close to their ledgers.

The fourth floor was my favourite. This was the floor of the directors, and it smelt of opulence. All the other floors had an anaemic smell which gave the impression of dull efficiency. The fourth floor smelt of spice ... as if the directors with their world-wide influence had ordered one of their companies to produce for that floor an exotic furnishing appropriate to its importance. I never discovered what it was but I can smell it now.

Anyone who worked on this floor, any typist or secretary, possessed prestige ... the élite worked for the directors of course; and when, on my walk, I passed these girls coming out of their sanctums, shorthand notebooks in their hands, lofty, distant expressions on their faces, I was annoyed to find they made me feel insignificant. Could not these girls guess that the young man they saw walking so briskly had been to a deb dance last night with Lady This and Lady That?

I then found that my heart beat a little faster when, going down from the fifth or up from the third, I approached the fourth floor. I felt as if I were about to play a game of roulette, for I had to coincide my walk along the corridor with the appearance of a pretty girl from one of the sanctums; a pretty girl, tiny with Slav eyes, whom I had first seen walking out to lunch with a clerk from margarine sales. Sometimes there was no sign of her; often, miraculously often, she would appear from the door just as I was passing. I would stare at her, my heart would flutter ... and I would continue briskly on my way.

This hesitation on my side to talk to her, apart from any natural lack of courage, was typical of my attitude at this time. I had been brought up to believe that social conformity was the yardstick which ruled the life of a gentleman; and I was that kind of gentleman. When, for instance, my Harrow housemaster bade me goodbye when I left school, he sent me out into the world with this advice: 'Don't be rude to servants in other people's houses.' He pronounced this as if he were giving me the golden key of wisdom ... and I was impressed. His superficiality was reassuring. It seemed to promise that I had only to be patronising towards those with accents rougher than my own for me to have a happy and secure existence. I, and all those like me, belonged to a race apart; and we did not mix with the others.

Hence my corridor courtship, though lasting for many weeks, only left me with unrequited desire. I never met the girl. I never learnt her name. Yet here I am after all these years remembering her, and for a very good reason. My unrequited desire for her, my missed opportunity, dented the confidence in my middle-class standards which hitherto I had taken for granted.

There was another diversion, long talks with Howard Clewes in the basement cloakroom about the books we were going to write.

'A pekinese belonging to a rich woman will be my hero. He will write in the first person about her flamboyant life.'

'Why not write a book from the viewpoint of a shoe lace?'

'I'm going to make an Earl the chief of London gangsters.'

Howard Clewes was a trainee and I therefore considered him a superior person, far superior to a clerk like myself. He was dapper, a high forehead, a neat moustache, a pale face, and a regular feature of his impeccable clothes was a fancy waistcoat, like the type I used to wear at Lords for the Eton and Harrow match. I listened to his ideas with admiration, and I goggled when the following week he would inform me he had, in the meantime, already turned one of his ideas into a novel. I never knew whether he was as industrious and prolific as he claimed. The first novel I read of his was *The Long Mirror*, and that was over twenty years later.

I myself preferred talking to writing; or just dreaming. I found it simpler to pour my undisciplined thoughts into a diary, a scrawling, gushing document which, like most diaries that are written without the future in mind, contained neither truth or lies ... only the flash of the fleeting mood with its consequent omissions.

'I'm so lazy,' says one scrawl, 'and if I don't pull myself together pretty soon I'll achieve nothing.'

I was now twenty.

I had enrolled again in a course of journalism, similar to the one I studied by torchlight under my bedclothes in my study at Harrow. I did so in the hope that the results would provide me with the prestige I so coveted; for, unlike Howard Clewes who wanted to write because he believed he had a tale to tell, I only wanted to write to see my name in print. I had been a nonentity at school, and this irked. I was still a nonentity, and I was determined to correct the situation. I cherished the belief, guilelessly and without a trace of cynicism, that clever, successful people chose friends on the basis of their publicised achievements; and so if I were to gain an entry into this circle, if I were to be part of this sophisticated Nirvana, I had to achieve some sort of notoriety.

My writing ambitions, therefore, though motivated by my instinct were governed by my head. I needed a halo, the same evergreen halo of one kind or another that the young always seek to boost their importance. In my fluffy world of debutante parties I wanted to say I was a writer, not just a clerk. Any kind of writing. Anywhere in print. Anything to create a mirage of achievement. And so when my little articles continued to be returned to me unpublished, the weak moment was certain to arrive when I would pretend. The shadow of myself as a writer would be born.

The occasion when this first happened was at a bizarre party given by Tallulah Bankhead. I had been taken there by a wealthy South American diplomat who himself had begun the evening in an unusual way. He had entertained myself and the other guest, Adrian Daintrey, the artist, to an elegant

55

dinner at his house in Eaton Square; and instead of offering us a cigar when the dinner was over, he suggested a pipe of opium. The three of us retired to an over-furnished room upstairs, the paraphernalia of opium smoking was produced, and in due course there I was puffing away like any old Chinaman.

After a while I said: 'I don't feel any effects.'

'Nor do I,' said Adrian.

'Ah,' said the diplomat, 'you come here often. Get the habit . . . life will become beautiful.'

It was beautiful enough for him that evening to take us uninvited to the hotel where Tallulah Bankhead was staying: and as I entered the suite and saw the numerous faces who previously I had only seen as photographs in *The Bystander*, I said to myself: 'This is it. At last I am a part of high life.' I was indeed. Never before had I seen any hostess of mine dance in such a provocative way before her guests. Nor in my wildest dreams did I ever expect to help carry a cabaret singer of world renown home to her bed. And in between times I had told my lie.

Tallulah Bankhead was a fabulous, lovely eccentric with a husky American voice, possessing little talent except a huge capacity for living. She was of the kind that each decade produces to provide headlines for the newspapers. Everything that Tallulah did or said was news. In an age when there was no television, her face was as well known as the heroine of a TV serial. Her activities astonished and pleased the humdrum. And now I was in her company. And sometime during that evening or early morning, I was sitting at the piano in a corner of the room playing my party pieces of Night and Day, then Stormy Weather, when she flopped her arms around my shoulders.

'Darling,' she asked throatily, 'darling, what do you *do*?'

Out of the corner of my eye I saw across the room a well

known playwright, a comedian in a Cochran revue, two Peers, the leading lady of London's longest running play, the leading man of another, and an industrialist who, I remember reading, possessed the world's largest yacht. I could not possibly admit I was a clerk.

'I write,' I said confidently, playing a fat chord.

'Darling, *how* exciting . . . what do you write? Plays? Have you a play running in London?'

I did not know then that some people ask questions without expecting an answer. I took her seriously, and was out of my depth.

'Oh, no,' I said airily, 'I write for magazines.' Then added in a panic: 'Small magazines . . . like *Answers* and *Titbits*' . . . I writhed at the thought she might ask for more details and I saw myself being shown up as a fraud before everyone present. I had, however, said enough. She had already lost interest and was 'darling-ing' somebody else.

Throughout that summer I was usually bleary eyed when I stared at my ledger in the morning. I was a bright young thing, a deb's delight, and my old Harrovian tie was a passport of respectability among the mothers. I had discovered, meanwhile, that a necessary feature of this form of entertainment was to develop the art of being a snob. Hence when I received the embossed invitation to a dance, along with an invitation from a well meaning hostess to one of the dinner parties beforehand, I would accept the former but dally with the latter. A deb's delight automatically accepted a dance invitation . . . but a dinner party, one of the formal dinner parties that preceded the dance, he was wary about. He did not want to commit himself to a commoner when a day or two later he could have accepted an invitation from a Duchess.

There was, of course, no virtue in such futile society games. No object either, except for the wealthy social climbers. Nor was there the excuse of escapism, because there was nothing these people had to escape from. Three million unemployed was only a figure to them. There was no threat of war to make them apprehensive. No mood of impermanence to make the young jittery. No cause to yell for. A comfortable smugness pervaded the scene. Ramsay Macdonald had deserted the Labour Party and was heading the Coalition. The King was solidly in the Palace, the Archbishop at Lambeth, and the Empire a vague wonder in the far distance. The smugness seemed likely to last for ever.

The season was nearing its end, and I was in a daze of tiredness. I used pointlessly to stay at a dance until three and four in the morning, have four hours' sleep then dash to the office, and often hurry back to Cranley Gardens in the evening to have an hour's sleep before starting the merry-go-round again. All very well to have experienced this kind of life, I said to myself, but what did it mean? Dull girls, dull conversation, and an impatience with myself.

It was about this time that I met the most beautiful girl I had ever seen. She was a ballet dancer and instead of being content with desire I found myself coping with infatuation. This had happened in light fashion to me before. There was one girl, for instance, a fair, pretty little thing who was the first girl I ever took out to a restaurant on my own; but the romance died the same evening. I took her to the Mayfair where Ambrose had his famous band, and the headwaiter observing my obvious inexperience in such a sophisticated world, dumped us at a table for two next door to the drums. The din was awful. The girl and I bawled at each other until two in the morning, and that was enough. I never saw her again.

Pearl was a ballerina of the Ballet Rambert company, but when I first saw her she had a part in a revue at the Comedy Theatre. It was a cosy, undistinguished revue, but there was a number in it called Mediterranean Madness which brought the house down; and in this number Pearl appeared from out of a dark blue backdrop, wearing precious little, and dancing to a sad little song sung by a young man from the side of the stage. I was overwhelmed with emotion. Dark hair to her shoulders, slim body sinuously dancing, a face like an exquisite Oriental, she seemed to me to be a young slave on display. I had to meet her. At any cost I had to overcome the obstacles in my way, and these of course were many. Pearl was the toast of the town, pursued by eligible young men and society hostesses ... and I was a twenty-year-old clerk knowing not a soul who could either fix an introduction or ask me to a party where she would be. Days passed without a solution, and in the evenings I would sit in the theatre gallery and watch her; then wait outside the stage door and see her disappear with some handsome companion. It was agony.

However, after one such evening when I was walking back to Cranley Gardens, I had a bright idea; and the next day I put it into effect. I reckoned that her admirers competed with each other in the amount of expensive flowers they gave to her, huge bouquets, dozens of roses; and so if someone sent her only a few, the very parsimony of the gesture might make her sit up and wonder. I therefore despatched six red roses to the Comedy Theatre along with a note of admiration and I added, this being the real purpose of my gesture, an unconventional request. Would she meet me at six o'clock the following Thursday at the Berkeley for a pre-theatre supper?

I arrived fifteen minutes early and my heart was thumping so loudly that I felt embarrassed. Surely all these people sitting around on the sofas must hear it? I looked at their faces and envied their nonchalance. Thump, thump, thump ... ten minutes, five minutes. Would she come? Or had she thrown my note away and made a joke of it among her gay friends? I fingered the red carnation in my button hole. I had explained in my note that I would wear one so that she would be able to recognise me. Panic ... supposing some other young man was also wearing a red carnation? I looked wildly round ... then suddenly, there she was. A slender dark figure wearing a black velvet dress, and more beautiful than even I had expected.

I suppose it was inevitable that the meeting would not be a success. We had a table in the alcove at the back of the restaurant, and as soon as she sat down she said: 'I think I am mad to have come here.' This unfortunate beginning only increased my nervousness, and my mumbling conversation did not make sense even to my ears. Nor did she make any effort to help, and I looked at my watch and saw half an hour had gone and there was still another half an hour before she had to leave for the theatre; and I wished I had never sent the roses and that I had kept my illusion. There she sat, polite, cool, exquisite, and I was thankful when Ferraro, the old maitre d'hotel, came up to the table and began talking to me. At least his gesture gave me *some* position. I knew him well, and knew also he sometimes said more than he should. There I was keeping him beside us as if he were a lifebelt when I casually mentioned that I was wondering whether to dash down to my home in Cornwall for the weekend.

'Ah,' he said, looking coyly at Pearl, 'I expect it all depends whether you say yes or no tonight.'

I never expected to see her again. I went to bed miserable, woke up miserable, and consoled myself that I had added something useful to my juvenile experience. I felt lonely. I even looked at my ledger with affection, as an object that was familiar. I went on my walk round the Unilever building and hoped to see my girl of the fourth floor emerge from her sanctum ... the sight of her would have given me comfort. And then two days later when I got back from the office, a letter was waiting for me. Pearl had thanked me. Then, of course, my agony started all over again.

It is the sweetness of youth that weeks are months, and months are years; and the real years are far, far away on the horizon. I knew Pearl for a year and a half, and it seemed a lifetime. And when we no longer had anything to offer each other, and friendship had become dull, there was a comical sequel.

My brother Nigel was three years older than I; and this meant, as far as I was concerned, that he wore the mantle of a sage although, in fact, he was only twenty four years old. He had a vast amount of talent, a musician, an artist, brilliant and witty, and after beginning his career as a naval officer, he resigned and went into aviation. He became in due course an instructor at the old Stag Lane aerodrome near London, and one of the finest aerobatic pilots in the country. He was wonderfully good looking, and one day when Alexander Korda had called him in to advise on the flight sequences of *The Shape of Things to Come*, H. G. Wells saw him in the studio.

'There he is!' the squeaky voice cried out, 'there's the man I want to ride naked on a horse at the beginning of the film!'

Possessing such qualities, and glamour, as he did, I was always a little apprehensive as to the impression he might make on the girls I myself fancied. I had a fright one night, for instance, after taking Pearl home to the flat where she then lived in Hanover Square, when I observed a Morris two-seater with canvas hood slowly circling the square. It struck me immediately as familiar, and I hid in the shadow of St George's Church to watch it pass by. The driver was Nigel.

We were such good companions, however, that when I

61

came out of the shadow into the road and held out my arm like a policeman we both laughed; and he gave me a lift home. Even so I knew that here was another rival; and when several months later I left London for Manchester, it was inevitable that Nigel should take Pearl around. I did not mind. Nor did I mind when that Christmas he brought her as a guest to our home in Cornwall. So often I had wanted her there but she had never been able to arrange it; and now she was in that lovely place as a stranger. 'Ashes,' I scrawled in my diary, 'are sad things.'

But in the meantime I had lost some of my edgy ways, and I no longer felt very young. Pearl led me into a world of people, books and conversation which I had never known before. My values began to change and I was no longer ruled by embossed invitations. Certainties became doubts, and I was the happier for it. At least I was moving. As for Pearl, her sole ambition was to become a great ballerina. She never did, although few who saw her dance will ever forget her. She married a film director, and died in Hollywood when still in her twenties.

One evening I will always remember. I had collected her after the theatre and we were in the balcony of the Cafe Royal. Gay people around us and below us.

'Look,' I said, handing her a copy of a newspaper, 'read that!' It was a copy of the old *News Chronicle*. I waited a minute, then saw her smile.

'The beginning,' she said.

The beginning: five hundred words I had written about archery. My name in print at last.

SIX

I left my two comfortable top floor rooms at 38 Cranley Gardens on my twenty-second birthday, and went to live at Joubert Studios in Jubilee Place off the Kings Road, Chelsea.

My single room faced an alleyway and saw no sun, a lugubrious place; but to me it seemed like a palace because it was another step towards my emancipation. My aim in life at this time was to rid myself of the strait-jacket standards my environment had brought me up to believe indestructible, and to find a way to be free of the restlessness inside me. I had no clue where this restlessness might lead me but, if I bottled it up, I knew I would never find happiness; and so leaving Cranley Gardens meant leaving conformism, and moving to Chelsea meant moving to intangible freedom.

'All I want out of life,' I wrote in my diary that first evening at Joubert Studios, 'is to be able to say at the end of it that I have lived vividly.'

Such a vague ambition suited the situation in which I now found myself. I had been faced with a decision to make. After making a nuisance of myself for months in Unilever, I had been offered a job away from a ledger. Here's your chance, I was told, here's your chance after all your grumbles about still being a clerk in accounts. And the plum I was offered was the position of a salesman of soap in Warrington.

Once I would have been excited by the prospect but the waiting had killed my enthusiasm; and in any case I was wiser. No longer did I see myself as someone dedicated to the pursuit of money, nor did I see any virtue in surrendering one's life to the whims of a great Company. 'A career,' I had read somewhere, 'is like a voyage through a long and winding pitch black tunnel . . . and when you come out of it, of it, your life is over.' A depressing description indeed, but it made me aware, even more sharply than before, that I must follow a career which I could enjoy.

Unfortunately I had no qualifications; and I was now twenty two. I was persistently reminded of these drawbacks each time I obtained an interview with someone of influence.

'I note, Mr Tangye, that you haven't passed any examinations . . . not even the School Certificate.'

'You see, Mr Tangye, without having a University background you are a little old for us to start training you.'

No one inside or outside Unilever had any real use for me. I was given a three week trial in the advertising company of Lever Brothers, writing copy, but this also ended in failure. I applied to other advertising agencies and answered advertisements in *The Times*, advertisements of the type which seek a young man with initiative. I wrote to provincial newspapers, enclosing a copy of my *News Chronicle* article on archery as evidence of talent, and received no replies. I cultivated the friends of friends of men in power, hoping a miraculous meeting might suddenly be arranged with some tycoon who would immediately give me my chance. On one occasion I thought my persistence had at last succeeded. I had manoeuvred an introduction to Geoffrey Dawson, editor of *The Times*, and I found myself sitting in his office in Printing House Square, sunk deep in an armchair.

Geoffrey Dawson, bearing in mind my background, seemed to me to be a god. He had not as yet achieved his footnote in history, that of being one of the arch appeasers of Hitler. His role at the time was simply that of guardian of the Establishment, an omnipotent censor of values good and bad. I was not, of course, concerned with his moral attitudes, I was only concerned with his attitude towards me;

and I sat in the armchair trying to look intelligent while he stood with his back to the fireplace and delivered a monologue.

I have learnt now that famous men periodically like to grant interviews to young people so as to remind themselves how clever they have been. Young people gaping earnestly, believing the interview is for their own good, represent shadows not themselves; and the interview has failed as far as they are concerned even before it has begun. So it was with my visit to Geoffrey Dawson. He had no intention of helping me. I was there only to listen, and to receive avuncular advice. One piece of advice, however, flickered my interest and for a moment I knew I was inside the mind of this editor of *The Times*: for Geoffrey Dawson, bottom to the fireplace, hands in trouser pockets, hard eyes behind a bland smile, suddenly displayed his hate for the Press Lords.

'Remember,' he said, winding up his monologue and speaking with some passion, '. . . remember this advice I give you. You may wish to become a journalist but I warn you, never *never* work for Lord Beaverbrook or Lord Rothermere. Such men would destroy you.'

I was to work for both their newspaper groups.

Meanwhile I had this decision to make. Should I become a soap salesman? It posed me with the perennial problem of youth, the problem as to the extent I should believe in myself; or whether my instinct was mixed up with wishful thinking, a case of bravado, or whether I was wanting to act the rebel just to pretend I had promise. One needs luck at such moments, someone to meet who pushes you; and it happened to me on this occasion in a ridiculous way.

A shop window in Ludgate Circus at this time advertised that it was the home of a phrenologist. There were models of bald heads facing the passers-by with weird hieroglyphics thereon; and placards of promises that the customer who allowed the bumps on his head to be examined would have the trends of his character and talents accurately described.

I had been passing this window for the three and a half years I had been at Unilever, on my way to lunch at the Mecca half way up Ludgate Hill; and I had dismissed the extravagant claims as the work of a crank. But now, because I felt vulnerable and puzzled, I was prepared to put them to the test. I had nothing to lose by seeking a bizarre opinion.

And so one lunchtime I found myself sitting in a chair while an old man gently pressed the bumps on my head. It was like a massage, and a quiet haziness was coming over me when suddenly the old man said urgently:

'You must not barter! You must not barter!'

Such a cry of warning at such a moment had, of course, a profound effect on me. He had said exactly what I wanted him to say. And when a few moments later he further declared that my bumps provided evidence that my future lay in advertising, interior decorating or journalism, I was certain an oracle had spoken. No bartering! Journalism! At the cost of a guinea, sitting in an old leather chair with the noise of Ludgate Circus in my ears, I had received the advice I had been searching for. There and then I decided to act before common sense intervened. I returned after lunch to Unilever House, formally refused the job in Warrington; and gave in my notice.

Gestures are wonderfully intoxicating. They provide the confidence which usually somebody else has to pay for. As I stumped out of Unilever House that evening, out of the cavernous doorway into New Bridge Street, I knew I was faced with a predicament. Once my notice had been worked out I wouldn't have a penny. No money in the bank, no income. And so there would be no alternative but to appear to blackmail my father and mother into helping me. That night I sent off a letter of explanation to my home in Cornwall; and began the nervous wait for a reply.

My parents were conventional in so far as they believed that there were certain standards, if maintained, which ensured a contented life. My father, for instance, had a sense of duty towards both his family and the community; and he would deny himself some pleasure time and time again in order to fulfil that duty. He was poor by middle class standards of the day; and one of my most vivid memories is the sight of him in his cramped study at Glendorgal, poring over papers and account books, trying to make one and one make three. He was always travelling to London and Birmingham, and such travelling he loathed. He had, however, a duty to perform in trying to help save our old family engineering firm; and this he succeeded in doing though it was years afterwards, after he died, that it paid its way again. He had no income from this source, nor was he paid as chairman of the Cornwall Quarter Sessions; and so one of the reasons he travelled was to earn money as a part time London traffic commissioner, a responsible job which he gained not only because of his reputation but his past, long ago, experience as a barrister.

He was very fond of music, particularly opera. He had joined up at the outbreak of the First World War, giving up his career as a successful barrister; and at the end of that war he decided, wrongly probably, not to return to his Chambers in the Temple but to continue to serve as an Intelligence Officer in BAOR of that time. Thus my young years were spent in Cologne, in a huge house on the embankment opposite the Bismarck statue. It is not the house I remember, however, but my visits to the Opera House. My father took me and my brothers there four and five times a week and, young though I was, I became so emotionally involved in opera music that if I heard an isolated bar being played I was able to recognise from which opera it came. Later, when my brother Colin and I were both working in London, we used to hasten in the early morning to Covent Garden before going on to our offices, put our names on a hired stool in the gallery queue, and see The Ring through together sitting on those hot, hard seats close to the roof. Then sometimes when I was staying at Glendorgal, my father would suddenly rush out of his study where he had an old fashioned wireless set with earphones, exclaiming: 'Come quick! I've got the Milan Opera House!' And, putting on the earphones, I would excitedly hear amid the crackling atmospherics, a faint Scarpia wooing Tosca.

My mother, I feel sure, would have carried a suitcase five miles if she thought it would help one of us. She and my father were devoted to each other, and I never knew them have a quarrel. Yet it was for her sons that she lived, and sometimes she had original ideas how to help us. She once read that someone with the same family name as her own had become a millionaire sheep farmer in Australia. She wrote to the *gentleman* inviting him to visit Glendorgal on his next trip to Britain. In due course he arrived; and his long lost cousin together with her sons were waiting on the Glendorgal doorstep to greet him. We were, of course, on our best behaviour. My mother had primed us that this was essential if her hopes were to materialise. Alas, something went wrong. The millionaire died a knight, but my mother waited in vain for the solicitor's letter she had planned for.

They were both worried when they heard I had left Unilever. Colin was safely in Lloyds, Nigel too was safe because he had proved his brilliance, and so only myself was a problem. The family which had grown up so happily and easily together, with such conventional smoothness, were faced with the odd man out. And yet when I received the reply to my letter telling them what I had done, my father and mother kept their concern to themselves. 'It's your life,' they said, 'and we will do what we can to help.'

I now became ensconced in my room in Joubert Studios with three pounds a week and time on my hands. My room cost me twenty seven shillings and sixpence without breakfast, so I had one pound twelve shillings and sixpence as weekly pocket money. This money was an allowance from my father and mother but it clearly had to be increased, and so I turned my attention to doing so. I had no intention of looking for a regular job because I had the intuition that only by remaining my own master would I gain the end I was aiming for. I had no calculated plan, just a vague belief that the opportunity would suddenly face me; and I had to remain free in order to seize it.

Thus I became a part time salesman first of electric light bulbs, then of ladies' stockings; and I had a splendid trade in both until I had saturated my friends who were householders with electric light bulbs, and my girl friends had lost their sense of humour. The flat racing season had now begun and I noticed one day a particularly tempting advertisement in the *Sporting Life*. A Mr Siebert of Sackville Street offered a foolproof system, the backing of the most newspaper tipped horses; and although this might be considered obvious enough, Mr Siebert had an ace up his sleeve. He had a complicated staking method of his own invention which defeated any sequence of losing horses; and every day by letter post the subscriber would receive the day's method of investment.

I was sufficiently cautious to pay a visit to Mr Siebert's address, and found him, an elderly grey haired man, on the second floor of number Thirty Six wearing a black suit, a high winged collar, and a cravat. He was sitting in an untidy room surrounded by newspapers. He looked bewildered but this greatly impressed me; for here, I said to myself, is an honest man burdened by the responsibilities of handing fortunes to others. He talked softly, reasonably, convincingly, in a broken accent, without boasting; and I left his presence determined to find the necessary capital to follow his system.

My mother and I had been in partnership before. A wayward, charming Etonian friend of mine had induced me, when I was at 38 Cranley Gardens, to put my faith in a greyhound racing system; and we used to visit together the different race tracks night after night. At one period when we were having a remarkable run of success, my mother was also staying at Cranley Gardens; and she became highly enthusiastic when she found me returning from a session at the White City with several pounds in my pocket. She offered to contribute to the venture so that I could increase my stakes and also, therefore, my winnings. I had, of course, no notion that she had decided to carry out a plan of her own.

Almost immediately, on that occasion, we entered upon a losing sequence so long that we were forced to give up the system; and yet the memory of this did not seem to deter her when I mentioned Mr Siebert. I had, however, guessed that she would be impressed that he had his office in Sackville Street; for in those days anyone who had an office off Piccadilly had a special prestige. It inferred that Mr Siebert was an expert; and I knew that experts of any kind, in my mother's opinion, possessed the magic of infallibility.

So my mother and I went into partnership again. Racing day after racing day, an envelope containing Mr Siebert's mathematical calculations arrived at Joubert Studios. Moreover it was not a question of putting the bets on in the morning, then waiting for the results in the afternoon. Mr Siebert's staking system depended on the results of each race; and so my afternoons were spent in hot telephone boxes ringing up my bookmaker and making the necessary adjustments. By the end of April I had begun to lose interest, by the end of May Mr Siebert's envelope had become a menace, by the end of June I could cope no more. We had neither lost nor won a penny, sheer tediousness had exhausted my desire to bet. But my mother's own deep laid plans had succeeded. She had cunningly controlled me while I indulged my fling. I was never to follow a betting system again.

By the end of June I had also become rattled by my mode of living. 'I'm fed up with myself,' I wrote crossly in my diary, 'I talk too much, and I spend hours worrying what people think of me. I'm living aimlessly. I must find a purpose.' I was like someone waiting his turn on the tennis court, performing any frivolous pastime until his name is called. I was, for instance, a deb's delight again but now, instead of being bleary eyed in the office, I stayed in bed at my leisure. This might have been fun had not my conscience continued to prick me. This was a Bertie Wooster kind of life without the money. I lay in bed with my hangover, mentally chastising myself for my misbehaviours of the night before; and I felt miserable and helpless and vapid.

I had, however, a practical consolation for being so annoyed with myself. My weekly funds were quickly spent, and although I was assured of an elegant dinner in the evening I had also to eat during the day. One early morning I was standing at the buffet of a coming-out dance when I observed one of my deb's delight colleagues stuffing sandwiches in the pockets of his tail coat. There was, of course, a pocket in each tail and he was filling both of them, wrapping the sandwiches first in handkerchiefs. He was in the same financial plight as myself, and he explained to me that he always relied on the dance of the night before to fill his larder for the following day.

I mentioned the moral aspect of purloining the sandwiches, but he correctly maintained they would be thrown away once the party was over. His chief concern, therefore, lay in the timing of acquiring the sandwiches, and it was to be mine too; for though we might be morally at ease, we certainly did not want the embarrassment of a hostess catching us redhanded. Thus I learnt it was necessary to wait, before taking action, for the moment when the band had stopped and its members were packing their instruments away . . . so that there was no chance of having to dance with the sandwiches flopping against the backs of my legs.

All went well for several weeks until I became over-confident. One night, instead of waiting for the band to pack up, I surreptitiously wrapped up some sandwiches while the band was still playing, intending to go home immediately they were safe in my tail pockets. I had stuffed one lot away, was pushing the other in my second tail pocket, when my hostess of the evening came gaily up to me and asked how I was enjoying myself. Manners required me to ask her to dance, and I foolishly led her to the floor. At this moment the band struck up Vienna, City of my Dreams, and instead of a shuffling foxtrot, I was forced to career around in a waltz. My partner and I had circled the floor but once when someone called out to me: 'You've dropped something!' And there on the floor, dancers all around them, were my sandwiches.

These untidy frolics had a value because they provided remorse, and out of remorse came introspection. Sometimes I would take a Green Line bus out into the country and walk the day long, asking myself questions I was quite unable to answer. I did not seem to belong to any groove, no banner spurred me. I thought of my friends who were contentedly following a career, and others who lived for the day without a moment's worry of their future. I belonged to neither group. Only an instinct motivated me, and it was leading me nowhere.

It was this sense of being in a no man's land that led me to read books in the way I did. The enjoyment of a story was of

72

secondary importance. My solemn purpose was to cull advice from authors of worldly experience, or to discover reflections of my own moods which hitherto I had been unable to put into words. Hence I pored through the works of such writers as Turgenev, Dostoievsky, George Moore, Keyserling, Somerset Maugham, Proust and many others with a pencil in hand to mark a significant paragraph; and then later I would conscientiously copy it out into a note-book. In this way I became gradually aware that my moments of puzzlement and despair were not unique; and I even discovered it could be an advantage to be intro-spectively depressed. It developed one's understanding of other people.

The deb dances were over and the social games had moved to Cowes. There was nothing trivial to occupy my mind, and I spent my idle August days meandering along the Kings Road, or lying on the grass in Hyde Park, or sitting stifled in my room at Joubert Studios. Months of waiting and nothing had materialised. Nor was I any wiser than when I left Unilever as to what I was expecting. Just a Micawber instinct, and I knew I could not pursue it much longer.

Then one morning I received a pound note from my father and with it came a message: 'Keep your pecker up. It's going to be alright soon.' And so it was. That lunch time I called in at the Six Bells in the Kings Road. Some people I knew were there, and one of them introduced me to a pretty girl; and while I spent my pound note I learnt from her that she had a boy friend who was closely acquainted with Max Aitken, son of Lord Beaverbrook. By closing time she had promised to introduce me to her boy-friend. Within a fortnight I had been ushered into Max Aitken's office in the *Daily Express* building in Fleet Street. Within another fort-night I was in Manchester.

I had been given a month's trial as a *Daily Express* reporter.

SEVEN

I was away from London for eighteen months; and when I came back I wore a brown trilby hat jauntily aslant to my eyes, and I dangled a cigarette out of the corner of my mouth. I had begun my trial period in Manchester as an assistant to the night news reporter, roaming round Manchester until half past four in the morning, calling at hospitals and police stations, keeping in touch with fire brigades, seeking news of casualties and crime and fires. On my second night I was in Ancoats Hospital when an ambulance brought in a man who had been found dead in the street; nothing unusual about that, just one of several incidents during the year. The dour, kind, blunt Yorkshireman, the chief night news reporter, offered me the chance to write up the facts. My first story. A man found dead in the street . . . but could I write it? The permutations of such a story were innumerable, and I tried them all. Five lines were required, yet I found it impossible to discover the magic formula; until at last . . .

> Charles Kemp, aged eighty-five, of
> Garden Street, Ardwick, Manchester
> collapsed in the street late last
> night, and on being taken to Ancoats
> Hospital was found to be dead.

I was launched as a reporter.

I was soon aware, however, that my presence in the *Express* office was an embarrassment. My colleagues were friendly and helpful from the beginning, but I sensed the management considered me an inexperienced young Londoner who

74

had been foisted upon them against their will; and the sooner my month was up the better. I can be deceptive when I am on the defensive. Outwardly I am inclined to court trivial favours. I seek smiles from those with power over me, soothing myself that smiles are acts of approval. And yet there is another part of me which judges such fawning for what it is worth. I fawned on this occasion, expressing obsequious good mornings or good evenings when I came within voice distance of the powers that be; and yet all the while there was this other part of me, plotting hard. They could not turn me away if I produced enough stories which were published in the paper. I would make sure that I did so.

I had, however, a set-back within a week. Another young man was foisted on the management, a Cambridge graduate called Ronald Hyde; and when I learnt that his sponsor was the great Lord Beaverbrook himself, I felt despair. Neither of us was wanted, but if there were to be a choice it was obvious that Beaverbrook's protégé would be preferred; and so I looked across the room from where I sat at my typewriter and watched Hyde with disquiet. Then three days later there was no sign of Hyde in the office and I heard murmurings about a party the night before, and conclusions were drawn; and I was overjoyed. A black mark against my rival, for certain. If a man was prevented from arriving at the office by a hangover, surely he must be considered unreliable; and I felt a little more secure. But I had much to learn about the ways of newspaper offices, for a few days later Hyde had a story on the feature page with his name at the end of it. His name in print! Injustice! Why should he receive such an honour? I was in a panic, for suddenly it dawned on me that I would soon be out of a job, and I would be creeping back to London into a vacuum. For six weeks I lived with this terror, and then the magical moment arrived when we were both taken on. And soon we were to become close friends, and years later we shared a house in Richmond, and it was from this house that I married Jeannie. And Ronald himself became the most famous news editor of his time.

I learnt during my period in Manchester that tolerance is one of the main virtues. There was an extraordinary naturalness among the reporters, and if one of us were having a lean time, out of luck, stories going astray, the others would always try to help. There was not a single occasion, except the one created by myself, that anyone was jealous of another; and so my belief that careerists have to spend their lives trying to score points over each other was put in temporary suspense. I knew after a few weeks, for instance, that I could commit any foolishness without having to fear that someone might take advantage of it. There was a quiet friendliness among everyone, and I was happier than I had ever been in my life. I believed that I had found, in the newspaper profession, a kindly camaraderie which was unique.

I was also introduced into the gusto of living, and discovered to what extent I had lived in the shallows. I had been so sheltered that I had never been aware of sadness. My life had been a kind of minuet, an absorption in frivolous details; but now I began to become aware of humanity which hitherto had been only a word. There was a realisation that nobility of mind and action is usually secret, belonging to ordinary people who accept the good and the bad with fatalism. These obvious truths were to me at the time a revelation. It was as if I had spent my life in a cell, and I at last had been set free; and naturally I was bewildered by what I found.

I was enriched by these discoveries, but not enough to check my personal ambition. I observed, that's all. I was anxious to show sympathy, but only on terms that did not interfere with my work. News editors have no use for the fainthearted, and so ruthlessness was an essential if I were to keep my job. Yet I found I had also a ruthlessness of my own making. I loved the chase. I would rush out from the *Express* building in Ancoats Street on some story and I would have the same pent-up excitement of the huntsman after the fox. This was the mood of youth, the untarnished enthusiasm of inexperience, the reason why the young are chosen for tough jobs, the reason why the not so young are promoted, and the middle aged discarded.

Sometimes I had to do jobs which had no meaning except to satisfy the sadism of a newspaper's circulation, and then I had no alternative but to pretend to myself that I was being clever, an elaborate self-deception like someone who believes that otter hunting is useful. Acquiring photographs, for instance. There was little sense of achievement conning someone to give you a photograph, some personal photograph kept in a frame, so as to prove that I was better at conning than a rival.

'I am very very sorry,' I would say in a sepulchral voice, 'your little son David was run over by a bus this afternoon . . .'

'I know, I know . . .'

'Could I have a photograph of David? His little friends will be glad to see it in the paper.'

And because the mother was helpless, and off guard, she would hand me the photograph off the mantelpiece; and already I could see the gleam in the eye of my news editor when I handed it to him.

'You will have it returned tomorrow,' I would say, thanking her profusely, backing away from her tears to the door.

The art of a news reporter is to learn how to lull a victim, because all good reporters are confidence tricksters in embryo. The brash approach is only of value when the victim is highly excited, part of a drama upon which he has had no time to reflect; and then the reporter has only to ask the right questions for him to collect the facts of the story. The subtle story, which has to be dug out of the victim, relies on the same kind of intuition as that of a centre three quarter when he swerves through a mass of oppoents to score a try. There are rules to obey, but intuition brings the success. I was shown an example of this soon after I arrived in Manchester when I accompanied a senior colleague on a murder story. He interviewed several people during the day, and each time I grew restless and embarrassed by the idiotic questions he asked. They were so obvious, so inane, that I kept saying to myself that he must be the worst reporter in the office. At last I had to show my innocence.

'Why waste your time with such questions?'

He grinned at me.

'To make them think I'm as stupid as you think I am.'

I soon showed I had learnt my lesson. News came into the office that a missionary whose home was in Didsbury had been captured by bandits in central China and was being held to ransom; and I was sent off to Didsbury to interview the man's parents. When I arrived I found a posse of reporters already there, standing in a group outside the house. The door was shut, the curtains drawn, and I was told by my rivals that the parents were refusing to see anyone.

I guessed, however, that my rivals would soon drift away back to their offices, bored by the apparent uselessness of their wait; and so I went off for a walk. Then after an hour I came back, and strolled the few steps through the garden and knocked at the door. I was alone. No one was watching me as I waited for an answer. A man's voice asked who was there.

'I've come to offer my sympathy,' I called back through

the closed door, 'I read about it in the evening paper.'

The door was inched open. 'Did you know Rudolph?'

I saw now it was an old man, and behind him, peering, was an old woman. A meek couple.

'I did not know him but I admired what he was doing.'

I was sitting in their kitchen with a cup of tea in my hand before I told them I was a reporter; and by that time I was so involved in their distress that they did not remember they had told my rivals to go away. I was mouthing sympathy, and listening, and they were relieved.

'Let's pray for his safety,' I said, and then the old man fetched a Bible, and the three of us knelt, and prayers were said.

Next day I wrote in my diary: 'Praise all round for me today for my missionary scoop. But does it mean I'm losing my soul? To my horror, as I poured out my sympathy, I found I was only thinking of the headlines I might get . . . *all I wanted was the story.*'

I consoled myself that if one remained conscious of one's hardness, the damage need not be too serious; as if the knowledge that it was wrong to knock someone over the head with a hammer was enough for the jury to bring in a verdict of not guilty. And yet, if the truth be told, nine times out of ten no one was hurt when a story was told against the initial wishes of the victim. Fury at first, but flattery from the notoriety often came afterwards. It was when a newspaper exposed a personal secret that the damage was done, and the hurt came to the innocent. Nonetheless, conning breeds a conscience though it may take some time to mature, and I had a long way to go.

Often, however, there were antidotes to tough reporting and I would be involved in some incident that moved me deeply. I was sent off to interview a man who had a painting in a local exhibition in Salford, and the point of the story was that the man was a chronic invalid. I found him in a dingy Salford street, in a grim little house with a broken pane in the window of the front room. His wife was large and bossy, her hair straggling over her forehead, a dirty blouse, and she looked to me as if she had permanently lost patience with life. He was emaciated, jumpy, and as he breathed there was a sound like ancient bellows. He had been gassed in the First World War, and had been told he would never be able to lead a normal life again. They had been married a week before he had gone to the front.

I stood there asking him questions, and although he fidgeted and was nervous and looked like a scarecrow and his wife interrupted him, he gradually passed on to me an extraordinary sense of peace. I ceased to hear the traffic outside, lost my awareness of the poverty of the house, forgot the sharpness of my reporter role. He was pouring forth to me about the ideals he had when he was a young man, of how he had tried to keep true to them, and how, despite his inexperience of painting, he had endeavoured to put the lessons of his life on the canvas which was now hanging in the local exhibition. Its title had a melodramatic Victorian air about it, easy to smile at. He had called it Courage and Despair ... two men representing despair, a third who symbolised triumph over evil. A crude picture, perhaps, but it had its truth.

My home in Manchester was at 56 Portsmouth Street, off Ackers Street where the theatrical touring companies used to have their lodgings. I had stayed my first few days in a house in Ackers Street, arriving there on a wet Sunday night after calling from door to door looking for a room; and with my journalistic future beginning on the morrow. I had been seen off at Euston by my brother Colin, my mother and two or three others including Stephen Watts, then a famous film journalist. I had met Stephen Watts while I was at Unilever, and one day I asked him to dinner to seek his advice on my search for a journalistic career. He, however, misunderstood my invitation. He arrived, consumed the dinner uncomplainingly, and only months later did he tell me it was his second dinner of the evening. When I was appointed to Manchester, he took the trouble to tell me the rudiments of a reporter's life, and he came to Euston to wish me luck. And so there I was that evening, the rain pelting down on Manchester, a landlady who appeared immediately suspicious of me, remembering nostalgically the party which had seen me off, scared stiff of the future, and trying to console myself by playing a tune called My Dancing Lady on a portable record player.

Within a few days I was as suspicious of my landlady as she was of me, and I moved out and found a home with timid Miss Robinson in Portsmouth Street where I was to be happy all through my time in Manchester. It was a little street with little houses, and Miss Robinson was a little woman. She was also the ideal landlady, and I paid her £1 a week for a sitting room and bedroom including breakfast; and when I didn't have breakfast she took 6d off, and when I was away for the night she took 9d off. The place was scrupulously clean, and she darned my socks and mended my clothes, was always anxious to please, and never objected to the gaiety of my companions when they remained late at night in my sitting room.

My companions were usually from the shows which came to Manchester on their way to London; and I loved and laughed with a succession of chorus girls from Cochran and Charlot revues; and got into debt because of them. One unwise evening, after a Charlot first night, I invited a party to the Midland Hotel where the stars of the show were having their parties. 'Magnums!' cried the girls in Gaiety Girl fashion when I asked them what they would have to drink. 'Oysters!' they cried again when they looked at the menu. I remembered the party with distress while, for months afterwards, I paid off the bill in instalments. My salary was £3 a week.

There were others I first met in Manchester who, if I were to meet them again, I feel would be the same friends as in the beginning. Dickie Murdoch with off-beat humour but compelled by André Charlot to be a romantic, singing sentimental songs in a croaky voice, dancing like Jack Buchanan with shuffling steps; and speaking kindly of everyone. John Buckmaster, marvellously good looking, a golden boy, full of original talent, adored by the chorus, and so quiet. James Mason touring with a play of his own production, dry humour, ambitious, laconic and who, years later after Jeannie and I came together, was to taunt me for being an anti-cat man when Jeannie was urging me to have one. Norman Hackforth, voice of Twenty Questions, whom I envied because he won girls by his exquisite piano playing. Clifford Evans whom I still see. Giles Playfair, then working for Imperial Chemicals, who told me how he had been offered £50 if he could get every national newspaper to mention potatoes on one and the same day. He went off to Oxford and arranged that an article should appear in Cherwell saying that the Oxford boat race crew required more potatoes if they were to win. The article appeared and there were headlines in the newspapers: Potatoes to Pull. He won his £50.

This flirting with the fringes of show business suited both the flippant side of my nature and also my news editor; and I was soon being ordered to interview celebrities who, outwardly confident, were, I found, scared of the impending reaction of their north country audience. The pattern was usually the same; the suave arrival of the impresario and the chief performers, then interviews during which a studied effort was made to avoid condescension towards the reporters; then rumours that the scenery would not be ready in time for the show's opening, then emotional jollification at a party after the first night, then disappointment with the reviews, then rumours of backer withdrawals and new backer arrivals, feuds between stars, anxiety among the lesser fry, more rumours that there was no London theatre available; and then finally after a fortnight the caravanserai would depart; and the Mancunians would blasily wait for the next lot.

Under these conditions I met for the first time many of those whom I was to know for the rest of their lives. Noel Coward, when I first interviewed him, had just completed playing a part in a movie called *The Scoundrel*. He had never been in one before and I asked him his reactions.

'It's terribly, terribly monotonous,' he replied in his clipped fashion, 'acting all day in front of a tired electrician . . . and a lamp.'

C. B. Cochran and André Charlot were the showmen of the day, and they could charm anyone into liking them. They both had exquisite taste and a panache for the subtle things of life . . . Cochran with his spectacular revues, Charlot with his intimate ones; and they both had an inability to keep any money in the bank for themselves. The first time I met Cochran, the legendary Mistinguet was about to arrive in his suite at the Midland Hotel. 'Look out,' he said, 'she may be over seventy but she'll think she's your age when she sees you.'

I was to know André Charlot best, or Guv as everyone called him, when years later I was in Hollywood. He had lost so much money on his shows in England that he thought he might begin a new career in California; and that the movie people would wish to draw on his experience which had discovered such stars as Gertrude Lawrence, Bea Lillie,

Ronald Colman, Jessie Matthews and a host of others. They didn't; and when I was there he was living a parsimonious life in a small flat on the outskirts of Hollywood and refusing ever to leave it. 'After all,' he said in his charming French accent, 'a producer might call, and if I were out . . . well . . . he would forget to call me again.'

Many show people came and went and I would present myself to interview them. I remember John Gielgud saying: 'I'll never rest until I play the Prince Consort on the stage.' He has never done so. And I remember Constant Lambert, the lyrical composer of the Rio Grande, the conductor of the first English ballet company which ever made a profit, one of the most fascinating young musicians of the time who died before this remark of his came true. I made a note of it in my diary: 'There's a young girl in our company whom we are keeping back until she is ready. She is only sixteen and her name is Margot Fonteyn. She is going to be the greatest ballerina of all time.'

I became alive in Manchester; and I loved the wet dreary streets and the rattle of trams, the good fellowship in rumbustious pubs and the gaiety of my colleagues; and the excitement of being part of a far wider world than I had ever known before. I began to learn to judge people for what they were worth and not for what they appeared to be; and my role of reporter, however harsh and trivial the missions could sometimes be, had begun to teach me that all men are not born equal; and, like racehorses, they cannot all win.

I was always happy in Manchester, and I realised that I would never again enjoy the same undergraduate spirit of freedom. Yet I could not smother the urge to go forward. Manchester had awakened my senses, but London was where I belonged.

EIGHT

'Go round the world before you're thirty,' was the parting advice of my Manchester editor as he bade me good-bye and wished me luck. 'The opportunity will come . . . seize it.' The kind of advice people give when their own hopes have been disappointed, and I noted it in my diary, and wondered what the opportunity would be like when it came; and whether it would come in time because Hitler was shrieking at Nuremberg, and the civil war in Spain had begun, and fathers like my own had begun to worry about their sons.

I was now a reporter on the *Sunday Referee*. The paper had a reputation in its time but it was slowly tottering towards its end. The offices were in Tudor Street off Fleet Street, and they resembled a rabbit warren. The reporters' room was a hole which had no windows, where electric light had to blaze all day; and there was no library of reference books or files of newspaper cuttings like those available in Manchester, and the furniture was in need of repair. I was being paid three guineas a week retaining fee, and extra for each story published, the size of payment being related to the importance of the story.

I quickly found that the atmosphere was different from what I had known in Manchester where we trusted each other, and were pleased at each other's successes, and saw no reason why we should fear one another. There was instead an invisible irritant at work around me as I sat at my desk. My colleagues were pleasant enough but they seemed strained and reserved, and I did not feel comfortable. There was, of course, rivalry for the space obtained for each story but normally this would not have affected me. I was therefore annoyed with myself for feeling pleased when I had done better than a rival; and I was annoyed again when I thought my rivals were pleased by a failure of my own. I was, in fact, as I realised later, having my first experience of the jungle; the subtle eroding of the wish to trust, the gradual awareness of the need to be on guard in casual conversation, the avoidance of too much enthusiasm, the veneer of charm and gaiety and goodwill which momentarily deceives, the tension created by the sudden changing moods of the hierarchy, the surprising promotions or dismissals. All this was new to me, and so I remember with backhanded gratitude the time I spent in Tudor Street; for it gave me a warning.

I did not in the beginning pay much heed to my disquiet, because I had the joy of living in London again; and London then was unselfconscious. There was no need to strive for effect, no need to rely on gimmick publicity. London was the centre of the greatest force for peace the world had ever known, and she knew it, and she was lazily insolent in taking it for granted that everyone knew it too. Small things made me happy; a fourpenny ride on the open deck of a number 14 bus through Fulham and the West End and further; five bob spent on an evening out in a pub, yet money enough for a hangover next day; listening to the fussy hoots of the tugs on the river or watching the Changing of the Guard because it was a routine and not a tourist attraction; sandwiches with a girl in the early morning at the coffee stall in Sloane Square; leaving front doors open without thought of theft; a safe stroll in the park on a warm summer's night; Queen Mary in her toque; a silent sky. Yet the pace of living at the time seemed fast enough. There were nervous breakdowns, and drug addicts, and people who tried to get away from it all, and morals didn't stop a girl from going to bed with a man if she wanted to. The base doesn't change very much.

I stayed at first with my father and mother who had rented a furnished house for a few weeks in Elm Park Gardens in Chelsea, a high storey house of endless stairs; and I used to hurry back to them from my unsettled kind of day, and climb the stairs to my room, and say to myself that although I loved my parents their normality did not fit in with my unreliability, and I wished I was on my own. I did not have to tell my mother this in words and, without saying anything to me, she began to look for a flat for me. And one evening, after I had arrived home late for dinner, irritable because I had left friends enjoying themselves, she broke the news that she had found for me the ideal flat.

It was not a flat. It was a mews cottage . . . and it *was* ideal. It was off Elm Park Road and between The Vale and Beaufort Gardens both leading to the Kings Road, and the address was 20 Elm Park Garden Mews, and you came to it after passing under a brick archway which seemed to have no reason for being there. It was a little street which ran towards the Fulham Road, and at the beginning of my living there it was a working street with chauffeurs coming and going in limousines; and these were always being washed and polished and tinkered with while children played noisily around watching their fathers in overalls, and watching them again in peaked caps and dark uniforms as they drove from the mews on the way to their dignified assignments. Then as people like myself moved in, and others who remodelled the cottages in fancy ways, the mood of the mews changed and the chauffeurs who remained became the odd men out; and there came a day when the authorities no longer considered it a mews and they changed the name to Elm Park Lane.

The front door of the mews cottage opened on a tiny stairway and this led straight up into the sitting-room which had a wooden balustrade, like that of a minstrel's gallery, overlooking the stairway. There was a bedroom, a kitchen, and a bathroom like a boxroom because it had no windows. Beneath the sitting room was a garage, and on the left of the front door was a ground floor spare room which was to be used by my brother Nigel when he came to London on visits from where he lived in Hertfordshire. The place was unfurnished and dilapidated but my mother, while I worked, supervised the decorating and went bargain hunting for furniture. I still have some of the furniture; the sofa is at Minack, and the kitchen cupboard which came from Peter Jones is in the barn behind a pile of fertiliser bags; and its contents are now nuts and bolts, and half used tins of paint. So the day came when I moved into the first home of my own, and I realised it was another of the original pleasures, and I felt I could conquer the world.

A limited world, however. I was only wishing to enjoy myself, and this meant spreading my contacts, and building up my ego, and living for the day. I rejoiced, therefore, when I was sent to interview famous people, or found myself on a murder story having a drink with the suspected murderer, or sitting in the hotel room of a young aristocrat who was believed to be the brains behind a jewel robbery, or commiserating with the parents of an eloping daughter. It exhilarated me to watch from the outside how other people behaved when assuaging vanity or avoiding danger.

One day my editor, R. J. Minney who was to become successful in wider fields than journalism, sent me to interview the legendary William Randolph Hearst who had arrived at Claridges with his friend, the famous Marion Davies. They were on their way to St Donat's Castle in Wales which Hearst had bought on a whim and had stuffed with some of the treasures it was his habit to collect. I was naturally a little apprehensive over interviewing the most powerful newspaper owner the United States has ever known, but I also thought it might be useful . . . one day I hoped to be going to America and if I pleased Mr Hearst many doors might be opened.

I found him sitting in a chair too small for him, heavy jowled and pouch-eyed, wearing a tweedy grey suit the jacket of which hung floppily around a waistcoat which was crumpled in folds. He reminded me of Toad when Toad was about to boast, except there was a wariness in Mr Hearst's eyes that Toad never had. I posed questions to him about his anti-British newspapers and the reason for this, and why it was he still liked to have a home in Britain. He replied, as owners of newspaper chains are inclined to reply, that he exercised no control over his editors; and that he harboured no ill feelings towards the British and so it was only a coincidence that his newspapers were so inclined to attack us. I asked him also about his art collecting . . . and at this moment I realised that within a couple of feet of my face was a winning Marion Davies offering me peanuts from a plate. Inexperienced though I was, I sensed conflict. I turned from Mr Hearst in his chair, and asked questions of Miss Davies instead. All the old questions.

'Which part did you like playing most?'

'Who is your favourite director?'

'Is there any part which you want specially to play?'

Old Mr Hearst sat solidly in his chair while Marion Davies played her charm on me; and when I left, she followed me into the Claridges corridor and said:

'The old man,' and a thumb went over her shoulder towards the suite, 'has been getting all the publicity this trip. *Could* you do a story about me?' And the limpid blue eyes had tears in them.

There was a curious sequel. I returned to the office and wrote one story about Miss Davies, the other about Mr Hearst. The first was a casualty of the sub-editors and did not appear in the Sunday issue. The second was given some prominence. I thought no more of it until my editor on the following Tuesday handed me a telegram addressed to him from St Donat's. It read: 'Deny ever having seen your reporter. Signed William Randolph Hearst.' No letter followed, no explanation; and my editor was as baffled as I was.

I sometimes had an unfortunate tendency to miss out the most important questions when interviewing someone, and I would realise my forgetfulness as soon as I had left. Usually I would return, ask the questions and all would be well; but there were occasions when the subject had been thankful to see the back of me the first time, and so I was barred from seeing him again.

I had arrived for instance on a Saturday morning in Belfast by the overnight boat with the aim of interviewing von Ribbentrop, then German Foreign Minister, who was staying the weekend with Lord Londonderry. It was a time when the latter was considered to be excessively pro-German and I had been instructed that an interview with him would be a good second best to an interview with Ribbentrop. I had a firm belief, however, as I set out in a taxi to the Londonderry mansion that neither would be willing to see me; and I was right.

I stopped the taxi at a kiosk near the estate and rang up, explaining that I had come over from London specially, etc. etc. . . . and after an interval while the message was relayed to Lord Londonderry, I was abruptly told I was wasting my time. Thereupon I told the taxi to drive to the front door where I was told to my face that I was not wanted. I was thoroughly dispirited because I knew my newspaper would not look kindly at the expenses of my journey if the result was total failure. I *had* to see one of them. My taxi driver now came to my help, for he informed me that he knew of a hole in the wall of the estate which was close to the kitchen garden; and the kitchen garden was not far from the back-door of the mansion. It was his suggestion that I should enter through the back door unannounced, then find my way inside to Lord Londonderry's quarters. It was risky but I had to try something, and so the taxi driver drove me to the hole in the wall, and within a minute I was alone in the kitchen garden.

I walked up a path with herbs growing as a border, past an old-fashioned greenhouse, then right along another path which led straight to the backdoor. I didn't see a soul. I now walked boldly inside, turned left because I sensed that this was the direction to the living-room, and then had a fright. A man was coming towards me. He came straight along the passage, went past me without a word, and disappeared.

I was now highly excited by my adventure. I walked on a few yards, came to an open door, went through it into a hall, and there I found myself being stared at by several Londonderrys who were hanging on the walls. And at the same moment I saw the real, live Londonderry through another doorway, and with Ribbentrop beside him. They were staring out through the french windows into the garden.

I coughed.

'Excuse me, sir . . .'

Had Lord Londonderry displayed surprise, annoyance or just plain anger, I feel sure my mind would have reacted with speed. Instead, while Ribbentrop turned a lazy smile on me, Lord Londonderry with utmost charm ignored my break-in and asked me what I wanted. I once again explained, and thereupon he gave me an innocuous statement which he told me I could quote; and I was so thankful that there was *something* I could report back to my editor that my nerve, which had carried me so far, promptly collapsed. It was only half an hour later as the taxi was speeding me back to Belfast that I realised I had been a fool. I had achieved the hardest part of my task by succeeding in seeing them. So why hadn't I asked any questions?

Schiaparelli was the Balmain of the late thirties. I had ghosted an article for her on the general subject of her life; and when it was suggested to her that she wrote a series of articles enlightening English women how they should dress, disclosing the fashionable secrets of a Parisienne and all those beguiling charms expected of the French, she agreed to do so on the condition that once again I was her 'ghost'. I was flattered, and I also thought what a useful education it would be for me. And when she further proposed that I should go to Paris every month to gather the material for each set of articles, I had expectations that I would be launched into a world of exquisite models and elegantly conducted affairs.

Schiaparelli had recently opened a branch of her House in London and the articles, therefore, were a means to advertise the branch without cost to herself; but she was not going to allow me to mix business with pleasure. Thus the first visit to see her, my first ever visit to Paris, set the tone for the others. I sat in her office overlooking the Place Vendôme, notebook in hand, watching her aquiline features and listening to her voice as it tattooed her views on the ways a woman can captivate a man. 'Accessories, these are important.' (She had recently opened a boutique of accessories.) 'Scarves . . . a gay scarf transforms a plain woman.' And so on. I still, however, had hopes that when the interview was over she would propose introducing me to the Paris of the gay Parisienne so that I would be able to taste the flavours of what I was writing about. Alas no. She introduced me instead to an elderly American publicity woman. We had dinner alone.

My pursuit of pleasure was aided by my being at times a

cabaret columnist, a radio columnist, a theatrical columnist, and a disc columnist. None of my columns had any influence because no one took the *Sunday Referee* very seriously, but they provided opportunities which would otherwise have been denied me. Discs, for instance, came to 20, Elm Park Lane from the recording companies in large packages; the cabaret column meant I was showered with invitations from night clubs and restaurants; the radio and theatrical columns enabled me to arrange a meeting with any girl I might admire from afar.

I had, for instance, loved a sloe-eyed film star called Sylvia Sydney; and there had been an occasion after seeing her in Elmer Rice's *Street Scene* at the Empire Theatre in Leicester Square when I had walked home praying for a miracle that the next girl I met would be her. In due course she did in fact come to London and when I saw that she was staying at Claridge's I realised the long awaited miracle could now come true. I rang up and asked to interview her.

She was as nervous as I was, this girl whom I had watched conquer Clark Gable, Burgess Meredith and other highly paid lovers. And this gave me momentary confidence, and I asked her to come out to dinner with me, and when she said yes, I guessed I would be wise if I took her somewhere away from the conventional restaurants if I were to make an impression on her; and so there we were at Quo Vadis with Leoni hovering around us, a lighted table lamp between us, and I with a feeling of unreality that I should be so close to this girl I had worshipped from my cinema seat. I had no car of my own, and I had borrowed one from a friend, a Baby Austin which was even smaller than a Mini; and after dinner I told her I would take her to the most beautiful view in London. This was the floodlit Battersea Power Station, the first floodlit building in London, and we stood on the Embankment on the opposite side of the river and watched in silence the white plumes of smoke disappearing into the night; and, long afterwards, she told an American journalist in an interview that it was her most memorable sight in London. Perhaps it was. As for me the tension of the evening had been too great. I was out of my depth. I had only admiration to offer and she had plenty of that; and I never dared ask to see her again.

This initiative I displayed, superficial though its intention may have been, did on occasions bring me a special reward. There was a girl called Jan, for instance. She was playing a part at the Criterion Theatre when I first saw her, and Twentieth Century Fox had just offered her a contract in Hollywood, and so I made this the excuse to interview her. She had recently come from Melbourne with her mother, and she was slim and dark with blue eyes, and highly intelligent; and there was a calmness about her which balanced my own frivolous exuberance. Sometimes people come together and remain content with each other for a while because their personal circumstances by luck coincide. Soon their friends take it for granted that they are always together, and neither is invited anywhere without the other. It is a soothing time; and yet both inwardly know they are living in a kind of suspense account. They do not belong to each other. They suit each other for the time being, that's all. They are waiting. Thus it was with Jan and me.

Jan was only in Hollywood for a few months, and one evening after her return I was telling her that Godfrey Winn was leaving the *Daily Mirror* and the column which he had made so famous. And I added: 'How I pity the man who succeeds him!' Godfrey Winn, of course, had won his fame by his courage, by being blatantly sincere, and by setting out to help his readers in a way that no columnist had tried to do before. His success and popularity was such that anyone who succeeded him could only be a pale carbon copy; and so hence my expression of pity.

The very next morning I had a telephone call from an executive of the *Daily Mirror* asking me to meet him in El Vino's, the Fleet Street wine bar. I had left the *Sunday Referee* and was now working on the *Sunday Express* where John Gordon was editor. I was also writing occasional magazine articles and one of these, a lighthearted piece on my likes and dislikes, had caught the attention of the *Mirror*. I had no clue of this when I arrived at El Vino's and found the executive in an alcove with a bottle of champagne on the table in front of him. I had no clue that half an hour later I would be leaving El Vino's as Godfrey Winn's successor.

The transformation in my life was immediate and startling; and I joined the procession of unknowns who become overnight stars because it is good business for somebody else. Within a month I had bought myself an elegant Buick, received numerous flattering invitations from people I had never met, and gazed at a hoarding in Trafalgar Square which hailed 'the brilliant young writer Derek Tangye' who was currently denouncing hypocrisy in his articles in the *Daily Mirror*. There were also posters on buses with earnest photographs of myself staring down at the traffic. My father, fascinated by these, would stand for hours with a camera, waiting for buses which halted long enough for him to photograph the extraordinary claims concerning his son: 'Derek Tangye exposes this,' 'Derek Tangye condemns that.' Nothing so peculiar had ever happened to a member of the family before. As for myself I realised I had become a celebrity without justification, but this did not prevent me enjoying the situation. The first taste of success, however tenuous, is always sweet.

But quite soon I received a warning to keep my ebullience under control; a witty comment from Cyril Connolly who lived five minutes away from 20 Elm Park Lane in a flat at the corner of The Vale and Kings Road.

I had met him first when I went with my father and mother for a holiday at Dulverton in Devonshire. We stayed at a hotel called the Caernarvon Arms and the object of the holiday was the trout fishing; and this my father and I did for most of each day. Indeed most of the solid looking guests were trout fishermen and the subject of conversation was inevitably limited to the trout which got away or the trout which was caught. In this setting the presence of Cyril Connolly was incongruous, more especially because he and his wife Jean were accompanied wherever they went by a marmoset. The other guests clearly did not approve of such unusual behaviour, and my father and mother called it absurd exhibitionism. I, on the other hand, was fascinated by this gesture against convention. It had an aura of intellectual bohemianism which caught my imagination. Not that I knew then who Cyril Connolly might be. He had still to write *The Rock Pool*. I had still to read and reread *The Unquiet Grave* which lies on my desk as I write.

I did not meet him again for some years, but when he came to live in the Kings Road there began a period when I saw him often. He was kind, and delightful, and witty. And I burst into his flat one day and told him about some graphic incident connected with my column. He sat tubbily in a chair listening to me, mischief in his eyes warning me of what might be coming, saying not a word until the appropriate pause occurred when he could deflate me. Then:

'Derek,' he said, mockingly solemn, 'you're selling your soul for a penny a day.'

Outwardly, I am sure, I appeared to be doing just that. I was rushing around too much, going to too many parties and theatre first nights, accepting too easily the praise of people who wanted to make use of my column; and generally behaving as if success had gone to my head. My behaviour, however, was in fact a nervous reaction. As the days went by I began to realise the extraordinary responsibility my column entailed. It was not a satirical column or a column which could win easy applause by knocking some public figure off his perch. It was a column which reached people who were too ordinary to be cynical and too close to the sadness of life to be insincere. Such people needed a focus in life; and Godfrey Winn had discovered this and the *Daily Mirror* had exploited it.

There was, therefore, another role for me to play; and it made me feel inadequate and humble. As a reporter I had had plenty of experience of nosing my way into the private affairs of people suffering from misfortune, but I had remained an outsider. I was now, however, embroiled. I had the usual numerous letters asking for advice, and I would try to answer them without my words sounding too remote; and people would visit me and tell me stories which were true but which were difficult to believe.

Then there was the Fund which Godfrey Winn had launched one day in his column, and which I now continued to operate. Its object was to help any reader in need, and when the Fund ran low I had only to write that more money was wanted, and the money would come rolling in. It was a salutary experience to discover how generous people could be, and equally salutary to discover the various ways in which I could dispense the money.

Lucid assessment of facts did not come into my calculation when I decided whether or not someone deserved help or not. I had to rely on instinct whether each case was genuine. I probably made many mistakes but, if there were such mistakes, they were compensated by the numerous times the Fund saved someone in a crisis. Such times were diverse in their nature. A city typist told me a long story how she had stolen the petty cash, and now full of conscience wanted to replace it before she was found out; a mother who was dying from a lingering illness wanted to take her children to look at the sea for the first time in their lives; a father with a son in the condemned cell in Leeds Prison needed the money for his fare so that he could see his son before the execution. I faced dramas like these every day.

Meanwhile, outside this private world, the Spanish Civil War became bloodier, Chamberlain wooed Mussolini, Anthony Eden resigned in protest, Hitler seized Austria; and the very few tried to wake up the public into realising that World War II was on its way. But the old preferred to remember their nightmares, and the young to live their dreams, and nobody took any notice. It was cosier to be fatalistic. It was easier to let history be in command. We were prepared to read about war, become emotional about it, so long as we did not have to think about it.

For a while my column seemed to go well enough; and then I began to sense there were forces at work which aimed at dislodging me. Nothing unusual about this if you are in a job which other people would like, for it is part of the price you have to pay for holding it. I carried on as if nothing was happening and I would clatter through the day, then return to 20 Elm Park Lane and flop into bed exhausted . . . only to wake up at dawn with a nasty feeling that in any case I was not fitted to be a true success at the job. I was therefore agreeably surprised when one morning a senior member of the hierarchy called me into his office, told me he was pleased with my work, and that he proposed to lengthen my contract. Moreover he outlined a plan to me whereby I was to visit a European capital every weekend, beginning with a trip to Paris the following Friday. On the Friday I came into the office with my suitcase, my seat booked on the afternoon plane, when the man called me in again and told me of another idea. He politely informed me that the policy of the *Mirror* had been changed overnight, and my column wasn't wanted any more.

Jan was playing the young girl in Robert Sherwood's *Idiot's Delight* at the Globe Theatre. In those days producers were not usually interested in presenting plays which stirred the conscience, but the fabulous Henry Sherek, most imaginative of conventional producers, gambled his money because he believed the public ought to see it. He wanted the public to think about war. He wanted the public to wake up. I loved the play myself and I used to go often to see it and listen to the sad, rasping voice of Raymond Massey who played Jan's father. It haunts me still.

I rang up Jan immediately after I had been fired from my column, and arranged to collect her after the theatre. I felt pleasantly calm about the situation. I suppose it was a relief that my forebodings had at last materialised, and I no longer had to pretend that all was well. Yet I was sensible enough to realise that I was in a fix. The over publicised kind of column I had been writing had no place in any other newspaper. Indeed the huge amount of publicity I had received was now a drawback. No other newspaper would want me. And I had a sudden chilly thought that I would have to creep back to being an anonymous reporter.

It was sometime during the afternoon that I had my brilliant idea. It had to be acted upon immediately. The secret of its whole success depended upon my securing the agreement of those who had fired me.

That night Jan and I went to the Berkeley, and we sat in a corner watching the dancers from a distance, and listening to Al Collins playing his violin. A waiter had filled our glasses with champagne.

'Well,' she asked, 'what happened?'

I gave her the details, then went on to explain the idea I had had.

'And they agreed,' I said, raising my glass, 'they're going to publish a column saying I'm resigning because I'm going round the world.'

'When will it appear?'

'I've written it . . . tomorrow.'

I had remembered the advice my Manchester editor had given me.

NINE

Algonquin,
West 44th Street,
New York.
June 29th, 1938.

Dear all of you,

How you'd laugh and laugh if you were with me. All my life I've heard of the beauty of the New York skyline; of the heat of New York's summer months; of the fuss they'll make of anyone on the celebrity fringe.

Well yesterday morning I was up at seven to watch us coming in . . . we were due to dock at ten. And I thought of all the carefully organised publicity dope which was to launch me into the money-earning newspaper world, and I wanted to be wide awake and ready when the reporters arrived to see me.

But I was to have a series of surprises. To begin with the skyline was hidden by a drizzling mist as cold as any in England. Well, I said to myself, that doesn't matter because I'll be able to pay all my attention to the press.

They came aboard the *Aquitania* with the immigration officials and began rushing round asking questions of one person and another. There I was waiting expectantly and when nothing happened I went down to my cabin thinking they might be there. Then back on deck. They were interviewing all and sundry, but did they approach me? No indeed. Not the faintest notice was taken of me! Oh dear it was funny . . . and then when I got to the Algonquin I hadn't been there an hour when the telephone rang and a man from some press agency asked if I would allow him to take my photograph. Ah, I thought, they have found me at last. Only later did I learn it was a trick . . . all visitors are asked and vanity makes them agree. Then they sell the visitors the photographs!

I had lunch with the *Daily Mirror* man here. He told me I hadn't a cat in hell's chance of making any money on New York papers. So all the publicity handouts have produced a puff ball!

D.

The Royalton,
44 West 44th Street,
New York.
July 10th.

Dear brothers,

I've moved from the Algonquin to this hotel across the street where I have a lovely room with bath at the top of the building and a skyline of Broadway skyscrapers for 15 dollars a week.

I went to Sing Sing yesterday. It overlooks the Hudson and has the atmosphere of a. public school, prisoners black and white wandering around at will in grey flannel trousers and white shirts. The warder who took me round pointed out to me the most distinguished prisoners, and then I was literally forced to sit in the electric chair in the murderer's wing which I thought pretty poor taste. The warder just laughed.

D.

The Royalton,
44 West 44th Street,
New York.
August 1st.

Darlings,

Apparently two letters have gone astray and I gather from daddy's letter today that one of them was from dear Colin concerning the disastrous state of my finances at home. I thought the sale of the Buick would pay my debts. I have at the moment £44 which isn't bad and that will last for another six weeks but it means I can spend nothing except on food and gives me no chance to go places getting material for articles. For instance when I went to Sing Sing the fare was 2 dollars and to tip the warder was another 4 dollars. And it will be a long time before I'm paid for the article. However, all will be well, and I'm sorry to cause all this trouble.

D.

The Royalton,
44 West 44th Street,
New York.
August 9th.

Darlings,

Colin's letter still has not arrived, and I still haven't the slightest idea about my finances except the gloomy remarks of yours like 'you can't walk on air' and 'what are you going to do?'

If it is as bad as you say there must be a mistake somewhere. Anyhow my reply to the news is to get as far away from England as possible, because I will do everything in my power to stop coming home before April next year. So I leave by Greyhound bus for San Francisco on Friday. The journey across America takes four nights and five days, but the price including food is only £10!

D.

Hotel Roosevelt,
Wabash Avenue,
Chicago.
August 14th.

My dears,

I started from New York on August 12th, 8.35 p.m. N.Y. time and got here last night after a hell of a battering in the bus with never a stop long enough for a wash or a shave. I start off again at lunch time for Salt Lake City where I'll stay a night or two and recover and do a story on the Mormons, then I go on to Reno. Part of the advantage of this bus trip is that I can stop over when I like, then take another bus.

D.

Sacramento.
August 22nd.

Dear all of you,

Next stop San Francisco! Meanwhile I'm sending you some notes I've made on the trip:

The woman whose head I brushed with my arm on the first night as I put on my coat. She was asleep in the seat beside me, and bellicosely as she awoke, she snapped: 'Did you hit me?' . . . 5.30 in the morning, a cafe in the Alleghany mountains sipping coffee with a gramophone blaring . . . the cloud of flies that filled the bus after Cleveland and the ferocious little man with flat ears and the eyes of Mussolini who spent his time wildly killing them, and who when we got to Chicago said: 'Watcha think of sharing a room? Cheaper you know' . . . 'So long folks,' said the drivers when they changed over every five hours . . . and the woman who kept her hat on all night . . . summer lightning above the plains of Iowa, grey, brown, black horses against the skyline standing head to head, flapping their tails because of the flies . . . non-stop quacking of the woman in the back of the bus. Just before Cheyenne she changed her place to one behind mine. I found she also smelt, so I got out and stayed the night . . . and it was the first time I'd seen cowboys in their full regalia. Everybody was drunk and I could get nothing out of anyone except slurred words . . . the little horror of a cowboy in the bar who was so proud of his belt. 'Yellow rat!' he cried, waving it in the air, 'you have to go far south to get that!' . . . there is a sign as you go into Reno: 'You can't do anything wrong here, we make it legal!' . . . I reached San Francisco with exactly ten cents left which wasn't enough to tip the porter who took my luggage up at the Pickwick Hotel . . . I feel rather depressed.

D.

956 Sacramento Street,
San Francisco.
September 9th.

Darlings,

The war news looks appalling and by the time you get this it may have begun. Even if it hasn't it is merely a question of time, a few months, a year. I am overcome by a sense of futility. If war does break I know I will come back. It would not be, as you know, from any raging desire to put on uniform but a quaint sense of loyalty to England. And yet am I right? Should one recognise one's country or get away from civilisation and live as an individual? Oh blast Hitler, hell to the man, as if there weren't worries enough when there's peace.

D.

Darlings,

Since my last letter Hitler has spoken and sounds as if he's climbing down. It's damnable how he keeps the world on a see-saw. However, to brighter things:

'I've been having a wonderful time with Gertie Lawrence. She's playing here in *Susan And God*, and every night I go to one of her parties. Lack of funds of course has meant that I haven't been able to do entertaining in return, but the other evening I had a brilliant idea. I was in her dressing-room with some other people, and I breezily told them how I had lost all my money gambling at Reno. I spoke so convincingly that they believed me and thought it very funny. Now Gertie tells everyone and hoots of laughter follow, and I don't have to spend a dime.

One night we had a hilarious evening in Chinatown which the Chief of Police arranged for Gertie. She is the most enchanting person, scatterbrained and gay, but never missing a thing. We went all over the place escorted by detectives, had a wonderful dinner at a Chinese restaurant and when we were walking home early in the morning we found bang in the middle of Grant Avenue a couple of English sailors . . . their ship H.M.S. *York* was in San Francisco on a courtesy visit. Up went Gertie gaily to one of them, because she – like me – felt homesick at the sight of them, and said: 'I am Gertie Lawrence!' The two men swayed, they were very drunk, then one of them murmured in reply: 'Well, sshow ush where we can get shome women.'

The play is moving on to Los Angeles and I will be seeing her when I get to Hollywood.

D.

Darlings,

This letter could be such a gay affair. There's so much laughter I could tell you about. But I have just come from the corner of this street and Hollywood Boulevard where I've been standing outside a shop listening, while for an hour and a half the mad Mullah of Germany tore the world to pieces punctuated by the organised hysteria of his followers. By the time you get this letter the bombs may have already come but at least, instead of the sudden horde of death that H. G. Wells foretold would come in the night, the horde will be expected. Last week I thought Chamberlain had surrendered totally, and even now I can find no saving grace for the manner he has handled it. The Americans jeer at us and all sorts of rude remarks have been made to me. But it is easy for them. They're safe. I do pray you are all safe in Cornwall.

D.

Blackburn Apartments,
1805 N. Wilcox Avenue,
Hollywood.
October 2nd.

Dear all of you,

Quite unbelievable. Like you and everyone else I just didn't see how it could be avoided. Such a miracle happening once may mean it can happen again, but now the first excitement is over I have a foreboding. Yet at least a lot of people who would have been killed have another year to live. War will come, that's certain, and I hope to goodness the country will rearm like mad . . . and meanwhile *how* I'm going to enjoy myself.

D.

Blackburn Apartments,
1805 N. Wilcox Avenue,
Hollywood.
October 14th.

Darlings,

I'm having a glorious time and the £50 you sent me has made me feel like a millionaire. You've been wonderfully generous and I for my part haven't been wasting a cent. Do you know that since August 12th my average expenses a week have averaged only £7?

Of course I haven't done badly though it means no entertaining whatsoever. I've got a lovely apartment here which really costs £10 a week but the landlady is letting me have it for £3 as there are not many people about. The other apartments seem to be filled with ambitious mothers escorting hopeful daughters. The whole place is geared to celluloid and the mirage of its riches. Of course it is all very synthetic but it's prettier than I expected; I never for instance expected the Santa Monica mountains to be so close. and I've never known such mass beauty. You walk along Hollywood and Sunset Boulevards and pass one exquisite thing after another. Golden hair and dark hair, slim figures and tapering legs, and always youth.

I'm seeing a lot of Miles Mander and Guv Charlot. Miles has just played the visitor in Wuthering Heights with Merle Oberon and Laurence Olivier, they say he's marvellous. He's so charming and gay, and vague, and kind. We went out to see his friend, an old silent star Jameson Thomas whom you may remember, and who is dying of TB in a tiny clinic in the Sierra Madre. A tiny room too. And when Miles told him I'd come from England, this gaunt, very good looking Englishman kept murmuring from his bed: 'I'm dying to see England again.'

Guv Charlot is absolutely broke, but is so amusing about it. He laughs and laughs about my Reno gambling story, and I must say it is working just as well here as in San Francisco. He himself who has launched so many stars including of course Gertie, cannot now have a meal even at the Brown Derby. He just sits in his apartment, waiting for letters, and wonderfully dignified. We've been poring over maps together plotting my journey to Tahiti.

I saw Gertie several times while she was at the Biltimore in Los Angeles. Once after the show I was alone with her in the dressing room, and she was hoping Douglas Fairbanks would call. Minute after minute went by, and I became aware that I was an interloper, and yet also my presence helped to hide the fact the man hadn't called and wasn't going to call. I thought she was very sad. And then a lucky thing happened. Johnny Green suddenly arrived, the composer and pianist, whom Gertie had known since her Charlot days, and the three of us went off to a hotel where there was no one in the restaurant except a couple of morons, a piano and ourselves.

As soon as we had finished our supper, Johnny went over to the piano and started to play. Then the morons moved out and we were left alone, and I asked Gertie to sing Some Day I'll Find You and she answered that she always sang it out of tune and Nöel always laughingly complained. Then she sang it to the empty room. And of course I never knew that it was Johnny Green who composed Body and Soul. He brought it to Gertie with three other songs when he was very broke, and she bought a share in all the songs, then she sang Body and Soul on the BBC and also took it to Ambrose ... well you know the result. So there I was that evening alone for an audience except for a waiter, listening to Gertie sing and Johnny Green play song after song until it was time to go home. Johnny Green is writing a musical for her, and she's thrilled because the show opens with her on a bicycle, pedalling furiously, with her bottom to the audience!

D.

Blackburn Apartments,
1805 N. Wilcox Avenue,
Hollywood.
November 2nd.

Dear Colin,

I couldn't believe it when I heard your voice just now. What a wonderful gesture to ring me, and now I feel I missed out everything I was going to say in excitement. Only three minutes when we're accustomed to talk for an hour when I'm home! Anyhow, you know my plans and that though I'll be on a shoe-string I think I'll be able to carry them out. I'll board the *Nyhorn* at San Pedro the day after tomorrow and we're due in at Panama on the 15th. Then I go over to Cristobal to wait for the French boat for Tahiti and I'll go steerage which only costs about £10. I'll wander around the South Seas for a while then go on to New Zealand and Australia, and after that the Far East and home by the Trans-Siberian Express. Doesn't it sound marvellous? It was Miles Mander's idea that I should go on the Trans-Siberian ... he says that if there's a war anyone who has just come from Japan across

Russia will be specially wanted. I've an extraordinary intuition that he's right.

D.

Hotel Washington,
Cristobal.
November 21st.

Dear all of you,

I sent a sheaf of notes off yesterday to you about my *Nyhorn* voyage. It was a fabulous saga. Now I'll be boarding the *Ville d'Amiens* for Papeete tomorrow, and I'll be thankful to get out of this place. The hotel is very ritzy but the town and that includes Colon is the filthiest, smelliest, hottest place I've ever been to. The only bright time I've had was when Tyrone Power flew in for a night. He had told me in Hollywood he would probably be there about the same time, and he called me as soon as he arrived, and we had a terrific evening touring the nightclubs. He is the nicest young American I have ever met, humorous, gay and sincere, and none of that flashy phoniness so many of them have. We finished up with a couple of girls, a bottle of whisky and a gramophone in his room at the hotel, but we hadn't been there twenty minutes when a manager told us the girls were not allowed. So the great lover had to take them home.

D.

Ville d'Amiens.
December 4th.

Darlings,

Have just heard that there is a ship leaving Tahiti for Vancouver tomorrow and I'm going to rush something out to catch it. We get in at dawn tomorrow. We've had glorious weather since passing the equator. But thank heavens the journey is over as there is no privacy in the steerage and all the time I have an appalling gnawing feeling of hunger. We eat on tin plates which have always a greasy smell and so have the glasses while the water doesn't taste like water. The food is just what is left over from the second-class plates and I haven't touched meat since I got aboard because it is always

109

high. The mattresses are of straw but that hasn't mattered. Sometimes I've slept on deck until the men washing the decks in the early morning have woken me up with the hose . . . but tomorrow it's all over and I pray it won't be raining, it's the rainy season, because I want my Tahiti dream to come true.

D.

P.S. – Have just arrived and am waiting to land. The arrival was beyond my wildest dreams. The sun rose as we arrived, and I wanted to shout and cry and pray for the beauty of it. The water was so still that it seemed solid, and the most wonderful scent brushed the air, hibiscus, the *tiare tahiti*, and all the luxuriant jungle of the island. I felt incoherent with happiness. As we slowly sailed towards Papeete I could see the weird outline of Moorea, then I saw a canoe with a white sail and a man naked but for his red pareu, and soon we reached the opening in the reef, and we turned to sail through it. Here at last was the land of Gauguin, Rupert Brooke, Maugham, Keable, here within my sight were the things they loved, and the tranquillity and happiness men dream about as they obey the conventions of civilisation. I feel I've found another dimension to my life.

D.

Papeari, Tahiti.
December 31st.

My dear brothers,

I am at the lonely end of Tahiti, the Presqu' Isle, in a bungalow built on stilts into the lagoon so that I hear the water lapping beneath me through the bamboo stilts, and through the bamboo which make up the walls I watch the moon and the stars. But it's not perfect because in a bungalow near me is an American who has a radio and who instead of being happy with the noises of the night, insists on listening to dance bands. Why do they always have to have their pleasures man made?

Otherwise I'm quite alone except for Mauu and his dozens of children. He is one of the characters of the South Seas. He is very fat, always with a red pareu round his middle, and with breasts sagging like those of an old woman. He knew Rupert Brooke, and he told me that he used to call him jokingly 'pareu of Tahiti' because Rupert Brooke could never tie his pareu properly, and it was always falling down! Mauu told me of an old priest who knew the Mamua of the poems, and I went and saw him, and he showed me where Brooke lived at one time, but there was nothing to be seen except jungle growth. He said that Mamua deserved the poems. She was very lovely.

A rat has just run across the floor. I've got used to such things and I don't turn a hair. At the moment I'm sitting on my bed in my yellow and red pareu, and I am thinking that all the world is mad except those of us who live in the South Seas. Your letters, all the letters I'm getting, are chatty and informative but it's amusing to sense the underlying worry and dread that pervade those countries who are the leaders of civilisation. Compare those civilised thoughts with those which exist here. Everyone wants to make love and be happy in undisciplined freedom, and yet mind their own business, and never have an argument . . . on the road if a driver is stupid or a bicyclist is foolish nobody shouts neurotic epithets. Everyone wakes up in the morning seemingly wanting to be happy. Our Western philosophy has become too complicated, losing its way from truth because it is thought clever to do so. Anyhow your letters have made me realise I must stay in the South Seas as long as possible. I'm just off to Taravao two miles from here on my bicycle for a New Year's Eve party. I'm the only European who will be there, and yet I'll not feel an interloper because there is no colour consciousness.

January 1st, 1939.

Happy New Year! I went to Taravao last night and on my way there I was caught in a terrific storm and got very wet. Then when I arrived I had a couple of Aaorai beers and went to a cinema which was in a barn and there were three young men who accompanied the film on their guitars though when the scenes got very exciting they stopped playing. The film was a wildly simple one made at the time, I should imagine, when we were schoolboys in Cologne. It was silent of course and the captions were in English but these were translated into Tahitian by a shrieking man at the back who had a continuous battle against the noise of the rain on the roof and the yells of the audience who loved it all. Afterwards I joined the party of Madame Kett, Tahitian herself with a half Spanish husband, and drank champagne provided by a Chinese. And everybody kissed each other, and then I trundled home the two and a half miles to Papeari. This morning the festivities have continued as Mauu had a native feast for his family and friends and we've been eating raw fish and curried shrimps and shell fish dressed in coconut juice, and wild chicken, and been drinking rum and red wine. I speak only French and Tahitian, and I even think in the language, and again I was the only European. Everyone is so happy without any sense of guilt for feeling so.

D.

Hotel Tahiti,
Papeete.
January 6th.

Darlings,

I am delightfully, deliciously happy. I woke up this morning around seven and went on to my verandah and within fifty yards was the blue of the lagoon and sailing boats that come from distant islands tied up to the wharf. I have finally made up my mind to stay as long as I can. I'll try and catch a boat for New Zealand on February 16th. Meanwhile I'm going on a glorious adventure voyage to Raiatea, Tahaa and Bora Bora, where the film of Tabu was made and White Shadows of the South Seas; and where they say it is all untouched by the vulgarity and beastliness the white man takes everywhere with him. I go first to Tahaa by a two-masted schooner, and she'll be loaded with cattle and smells and queer traders and Chinamen and Tahitians, and though desperately uncomfortable I will always remember the two days with pleasure. Oh the blue that is just beneath me and the blissful stillness. Just near is a schooner from the Austral Islands and another from the Tuamotus. Did I ever tell you of the old English colonel who won

112

an M.C. at Paschendaele and who is now living incongruously at a beautiful spot in Moorea? He gave me a lecture as to why he was there and he ended by saying: 'There will always be rivalry and bitterness and distrust between nations. They have the tortured minds of Bedlam. There is no rest, no peace. I tell you, sir, when I was part of that world I was the same. I myself was confusion. But here, from this place where we are now, I see that world as if it were a glass bowl and inside are the fishes swimming round and round, without end and without meaning.' All this probably sounds rubbish to you.

D.

Toopua.
February 14th.

Darlings,

I have written you a number of letters but there has been no means to take them away from Bora Bora, and so they will go with this one, and you will read about my different moods one after another. But I'll never be the same again after being on this island of Toopua. Only one family living here and it takes an hour to walk round, and it is twenty minutes across the lagoon from Bora Bora. There is a hill in the middle and I walked up it this morning and looked across the lagoon to the coral reef guarding the islands from the sea, and to my right was the mountain of Bora Bora and at its base the village of Vaitape edged by the greens and blues of the water, and almost hidden in the coconut trees except for the red brick spire of the church. I could hear a guitar and a man's voice singing.

My hut has a floor of white sand and the sand continues (there is no door) until the water laps it a few yards away and when I lie on my bed I can see the outlines of the coral rocks under the water and the multicoloured fish swimming amongst them, so clear is it. How seldom a dream comes true untarnished, but it has happened to me. And I am so cut off from the world that I really don't mind I now can't catch the boat for New Zealand. Hopelessly irresponsible I know! But the wind has been wrong for the schooner which was coming here, and I may have to wait days. I'm just not thinking what I'll have to do. And yet I am aware in my heart that I don't want to stay for ever among such happiness and that when you are young you must have a purpose to drive you. I just want to cram as many first hand experiences in my life as possible, then sit back and contemplate as to what I've done, thankful that reality has taught me and not second-hand stories. One day perhaps I will find an environment as peaceful and happy as my island of Toopua, and for the rest of my life I will be searching for it.

D.

ss *Stella Polaris*.
February 18th.

Dear all of you,

The doubts and fears and the old restlessness of mind are back. Here I am in the *Stella Polaris* along with a cargo of American millionaires and young heiresses. They sailed into Bora Bora on a world cruise yesterday morning, and I had to make up my mind immediately whether to sail in her or stay here indefinitely. We're now on our way to Pago Pago where Maugham wrote *Rain*, then Samoa, then Suva where I get off and take a boat to New Zealand. So the programme is on again, and I'm absolutely determined to come home via the Trans-Siberian if war has not already broken out. It is the only thing I can do to compensate me leaving my island of Toopua.

Meanwhile half the passengers disapprove of my presence, the other half are curious. I wear only a pareu and am bare-footed. I have one small suitcase because the rest I left behind in Papeete and I've wired the consul to send it on; and I'm quite sure the Captain is also doubtful about me. I've had to explain to him that I can't pay the fare till I arrive at Suva.

As for myself, I find that all my peace of mind has gone.

D.

TEN

I completed the journey as I had planned. A brief sojourn in Auckland with my uncle; a happy time in Sydney and Melbourne, stops at Brisbane and Thursday Island, through the Torres Strait and the Arafura Sea in a Japanese ship to Manila and Hong Kong. A week of Shanghai night life, then Tokyo and a wait for my Soviet visa before setting off for Korea and Manchuria on board the Trans-Siberian Express at Harbin. Ten days on the train silently sharing my compartment with two soldiers, an old woman and a little girl who every night periodically woke up crying in a small agonised voice: 'Mama! Mama!' Moscow, Warsaw, Berlin, and a sight of Hitler shouting. Cologne, and a visit to the Bismarck statue around which I used to play as a child, a day in Paris, then emotionally seeing the white cliffs of Dover. In early June my journey was over.

I went down to Cornwall with my mother and father, then once again I was living in 20 Elm Park Lane. I was in a vacuum. Articles I had written while away had not been published, articles I now proposed were turned down before I wrote the first paragraph. Hitler dominated insular Britain, and yawns greeted my suggestions of stories in other parts of the world. There was no interest in Australia or New Zealand, no interest, in fact, in any part of the British Empire as it was then called. Its loyalty was taken for granted, and no one asked me when I got back how these people, thousands of miles away, would react. There was an unthinking self confidence they would come and help us if need be; and they did.

Yet I found only the few accepted war as inevitable. Hitler, of course, provided the main source of conversation but only in the sense that his behaviour was like that of an annoying wasp; and the newspapers gave the impression that they headlined his pronouncements because they were a free gift to the circulation departments during the summer season. Nobody wanted to think, and perhaps they were right; news of the Nazi-Soviet Pact was to come soon enough. I went down to the Isle of Wight for the week-end to stay at the house that the mothers of my friends Bill and Lindsay Baxter and Ward Thompson had rented. Val Hussey was there, and James Mason languidly helping us all relax. During that week-end we revelled in the irresponsible gaiety of optimism; and within two years only James and I were alive, except for the mothers.

I had no wish to find a job because if I did I would not be able to write the book about my travels, and it was this book which held my future, or so I thought. But if I had no job I could not afford to live in London. Hitler would not attack until the harvest was gathered in ... was a current, comforting belief; and so I reckoned I had two months, and I asked 'Beakers' Penrose in Cornwall if he knew of a cottage where I could be alone for that time. He always helped his friends, and soon he found me Rose Cottage.

Rose Cottage was in a wood above Coombe near Truro, and I visited it not long ago with Jeannie. The roof had caved in and brambles thickly covered the path leading to the door; and although the two rooms on the ground floor were clear in their shape to me, I had difficulty in outlining them to Jeannie. They had lost their shape except in my memory. Here Roy, successor to my first old English sheep dog Lance, shared my days and nights, as I toiled at my book. Off we went together on walks during that heavenly summer, and he lay at my feet as I tapped at my typewriter. At the beginning of August I had at last struggled to complete two chapters and I sent them to a friend for approbation. His reply made me tear them up.

A passer-by told me that Ribbentrop had signed the Nazi-Soviet Pact with Molotov; and I remembered the American journalist in Moscow who had said to me, in regard to Britain's own wooing of Stalin, that the Russians thought us utterly insincere because the negotiations were in the hands of William Strang, a Foreign Office official, instead of a Minister. And so I heard the news, and patted Roy on his shaggy head, and said soon he would have to go back to my mother and father.

There is a telephone box above the creek at Coombe, and that evening I rang my brother Nigel. He said that he himself, a Reserve Flying Officer in the RAF, was probably being appointed to Training Command; and that Colin, because of his knowledge of German, had been asked to join the German section of Intelligence. I left the stuffy telephone box knowing that the moment of truth had arrived for me, and that I had to make up my mind what to do. I no longer could try to be myself. I had to conform.

I enlisted in the Duke of Cornwall's Light Infantry a couple of days afterwards and my Company was despatched to Pendennis Castle at Falmouth where our task was to guard the docks. We had no training and we had no weapons except for one rifle which was assigned to a coloured boy to prove there was no colour prejudice in the Army. I alertly patrolled the dock with a stick, and soon realised to my surprise that the opportunity existed for me to continue writing my book. My father had given me a £25 car, and when I discovered that no one objected to me parking it in the dockyard, it became my office; and in between patrolling the quays, during my rest periods, I used to sit in the front seat typing my experiences of the year before.

I had written five chapters when news of my scamper through Asia reached the War Office, and I was summoned to London. The brigadier who interviewed me seemed immensely impressed that I had volunteered, and he stared at my crumpled battledress murmuring: 'Damned fine show, damned fine show.' There was, of course, at this time no urgency in the fight against Hitler; and there was even a general air of contentment that the war, without bringing danger, had introduced a spark of purpose into dull lives. We all could feel important without too much concern. Thus I was scarcely surprised when the brigadier informed me that I was the man the country needed to look after the Order of Battle of the Chinese armies, nor when I was quickly made an officer, nor when a week later I was promoted Captain; for such an undeserved meteoric rise from the ranks was not unusual at the time. I had a few days leave in Cornwall, then drove up to London with my mother, and as we passed through Andover I saw an evening paper placard: '*Royal Oak* sunk in Scapa Flow.' I groaned, but my mother beside me said cheerfully: 'You'll have to get used to news like that, dear. We had to last time before we won.'

I sat in my room in the War Office, and found I was not only in charge of the Chinese Order of Battle. I had under my command the British interpretation of the activities of the Netherland East Indies Army, the Thai Army, and that of Indo-China. I had a card index for each army, the names of the officers and sketches of their careers, and I had maps with little flags denoting divisions which I moved about after finding informative paragraphs in *The Times*; for most of the information upon which I based my assessment, eventually if need be the Government's assessment, came from published paragraphs in *The Times*.

My Far East interests did not prevent me from observing what went on elsewhere. Indeed had I known what fascinating secrets I was to harbour during the next few years, and had I been a General, I would have kept a diary of them. I had, however, a sense of responsibility which made me worry that I might lose such a diary or someone unfriendly to the cause might pinch it. But sometimes I was so enraged by what I saw and heard that I allowed myself to scribble mysterious notes which years later I found difficulty in deciphering, so obscure had I made their meaning.

I was the War Office night duty officer when the Germans invaded Norway, the link between the outside military world and the Chiefs of Staff. I was resting on my iron bedstead when the telephone rang and a reporter from the *Daily Express* asked: 'Does the War Office know the Germans are in Norway?' I replied: 'No, thanks for the tip.'

Thereupon I contacted a senior officer in bed at home.

'Hitler's invaded Norway, sir.'

A pause.

'What a bloody fool the man is. Act quickly and we've got him.'

I found such obstinate, unreasonable confidence, time and again; and as an amateur I was bewildered. These military men of power were entrenched by pre-conceived ideas, and if anyone dared doubt them the reply was a stony stare or a bad tempered shout of: 'Nonsense!'

I remember the harassed senior officer garnering information for the statement to be made by Neville Chamberlain to the House of Commons about Norway. He glared at a meek junior officer who had told him Narvik had been captured. 'Dammit,' he said, 'you've got the letter wrong. It can't be Narvik, it must be Larvik.' Narvik was in the north, Larvik in the south; and of course Narvik had been taken by surprise.

And as our ill-equipped troops were about to land in Norway, urgent requests were made as to the conditions they might find. For instance: 'Is the railway line, Stoeren to Lillehamer, narrow or broad gauge?' Answer from the Norwegian Intelligence Section: 'Don't know.'

I kept wondering what these Intelligence Sections had been doing in peacetime and realised that their members, bereft of imagination, found life more rewarding spending their time writing and reading meaningless minutes. But the Norwegian campaign nudged the Chiefs of Staff to look into the matter and General Ismay on their behalf circulated a gentlemanly directive. 'I think,' he wrote, 'we were badly let down over the Norway affair and I think country sections should start immediately to collect proper data . . .'

I happened to be night duty officer again when the invasion proper began, and this time I heard the news over a crackling line from the Military Attaché in Brussels. Once again I forthwith contacted a senior officer. 'The balloon is up, sir,' I said. Came the reply: 'Good . . . now we can get moving.'

I continued, during the days which followed, to play with my divisions of the Chinese Order of Battle. All of us kept stiff upper lips, continued to write unnecessary minutes, and made silly little jokes to hide our increasing anxiety. We pounced on the top secret telegrams which were passing round the sections, and when the Dunkirk evacuation began we hastened in the morning to see the night duty officer who gave us the latest tally of the troops who had got away. I wrote a memorandum to a certain VIP proposing every man and woman should be mobilised into a defence force, and that an intelligence network (local agents, radio communications, etc.) should be formed immediately in those areas likely to be invaded. 'I always like new ideas,' was the reply, 'and for that reason your letter of May 20th was welcome. I do not say that what you suggest is practical, but it will receive consideration when plans are evolved.' It was obvious that there was not a minute to be wasted, and I talked to Michael Foot who at that time was writing superb leaders for the *Evening Standard*. He wrote a clarion call for civilian mobilisation and said he would talk to Beaverbrook. But it was a while later before Anthony Eden announced the formation of the LDV, later the Home Guard.

France fell, and we were advised to carry revolvers; but there were no revolvers. Then my brother Colin who worked in a room along the corridor from me remembered the two Mausers my father had in a show case at Glendorgal; and my father sent them to us along with some ancient looking bullets. One Saturday the two of us had a good lunch and went out to Richmond Park. We were wary of the safety of the Mausers which had been collected from dead Germans in the First World War by my father. So we loaded one of them, tied it to a tree with it pointing to another tree, attached a long piece of string to the trigger, then burst out laughing . . . and pulled. A shot cracked. The Mauser did not explode.

I had finished my travel book by the time the uselessness of my job had been realised and I had been sent on a Course to Swanage. I showed the manuscript to Alec Waugh who was on the Course too, and he liked it mainly because he had been in Tahiti too; and while the Battle of Britain was fought over our heads, and after each day of being taught World War One methods of warfare, we reminisced. 'When the war is over,' he said optimistically, 'you and I will go to Tahiti together.'

I had no faith in myself as an army officer serving in unit, and the Course was leading me that way. I did not seem to grasp the details which were essential if I were to be efficient. I was as dumb as when I used to fail at my examinations at Harrow. I also rejected blind obedience. I just could not see the point of risking my life carrying out some plan which I knew was idiotic. Hence, when towards the end of the Course I was summoned to London, to Wormwood Scrubbs, temporary headquarters of MI5, interviewed by a chain-smoking lady in a ground floor cell and told ten minutes later I had been appointed to MI5, I felt thankful I was to remain an individual. I was to be a member of MI5 in war and in peace for the next ten years.

I was sent first to Newcastle where I worked as an assistant to a delightful man who exasperated me. He was an old hand in MI5 and as a novice I was clearly in no position to query his views. I found, however, that whenever I suggested a possible line of investigation, his logical arguments against pursuing such an investigation speedily deflated me. We were poles apart in our thinking. My experience as a newspaper man had taught me that hunches could lead to a big story, and I believed the same kind of hunches might lead to catching spies. Hunches first, then painstaking investigation. But my boss did not believe in such things, and in this he was like many people I have known in my life. I have been vexed so often by those who go only by the book. Those with grooved minds who obstinately refuse to be flexible.

I had been a month in Newcastle with little to do when I was ordered back to London and instructed to form a special unit where my journalistic experiences could be of value. I was given a cell in Wormwood Scrubbs, a pretty secretary, and freedom to move around the various departments asking what questions I liked to ask ... for part of my new job was to produce a weekly news-sheet containing the activities of each department. I soon realised that in some quarters I was viewed with suspicion. Wasn't the fellow on the *Daily Express*? Even the *Mirror*? I was surrounded by a plethora of solicitors, barristers, dons, all of whom had arrived to augment the tiny permanent peacetime group of MI5, and I realised I was the odd man out. I had, however, the usual ace up my sleeve ... I could not be quite as bad a risk as I appeared to be because my father had been an Intelligence Officer AND I had been at Harrow. Public schoolboys, in those days, could not be traitors. I was tolerated therefore. I was a member of the caste. The truth is that when I joined MI5, it was being geared to combat the Germans; and the Germans as an Intelligence force had the rating of a Fourth Division football team. MI5, except in one, small, ignored corner of the organisation, was bewildered when faced by the naughty deceit of the Russians. Burgess, Maclean and Philby were already in orbit ... but they could act with gay confidence. They knew their caste.

I had not been long in Wormwood Scrubbs before it was decided to evacuate MI5 to the country. The bombs were falling on London and one of them could have destroyed the MI5 records; and so a place was chosen for us to move to, and the place was Blenheim Palace where the Duke of Marlborough and his family surrendered huge rooms to trestle tables.

I realised now that the time had come for me to leave 20 Elm Park Lane, and that when I did so I would in effect be saying goodbye to my youth. There I lived the gay days when there were oceans of time in which to make mistakes and to recover from them; and to be in despair at one moment but be filled with hope the next because there were so many years ahead. I lived there the time which one never expects to end, the ebullience of being young and successful, of passing fancies, of dominating views, of believing all youth is Peter Pan. I gave in my notice to the landlord, then although this notice had a period in which to expire, I decided to take away from the threat of bombs those possessions of mine which I valued most. There was a small kneehole desk of rosewood; my personal papers; a watercolour by Adrian Daintrey; and above all a small oil painting of a plantation

123

and a lagoon by a strange man called Gouwe with whom I had stayed on the island of Raiatea near Tahiti. These were my treasures.

I piled them into my car and drove them to Blenheim Palace, and I carried them into the room which had been chosen for me as my office. It was on the first floor of the south wing, above the archway which all of us used to reach the quadrangle. There they were, safe from the bombs, daily reminding me of normal times.

I was billeted a couple of miles away and in the morning I drove to Blenheim Palace. And one day as I neared the Palace, I saw a plume of smoke curling from the rooftops; and as I drove nearer still, I saw it was coming from a room above the archway. A crowd was standing there, a fire engine was hosing, when I pulled up. And there was also my pretty secretary.

'*Our* room,' she said, looking upwards.

Smoke was now billowing from the window.

A cleaner had inadvertently dropped a match in the wastepaper basket, and set the room ablaze.

ELEVEN

In the New Year I had begun to spend two nights a week at the Savoy, and my book *Time Was Mine* was published, and I met Jeannie; after the second occasion of having dinner with her, a bomb hit the hotel killing two guests, while I was asleep in the shelter knowing nothing about it. The Savoy was the headquarters of the American journalists, indeed of all top journalists, and it was useful for me to be with them. They all hovered round Jeannie who was barely out of her teens, and who was just beginning her reign as the most famous public relations officer the Savoy has ever had. She introduced them to the people they wanted to meet, booked their rooms, flirted with them, and was all the while in a gentle fashion seeing they were happy in London; and in so doing she was able often to influence their reports on Britain.

I was treated as a casual admirer but the people she wanted to know were also the people I wanted to know; and if we were not together we were frequently in the same party. We would be in Tich's Bar for instance. Tich was a bouncy little waiter of much character, and his Bar was not really a Bar but a collection of small tables and chairs on a landing, one floor up from the Embankment entrance. Here, into the early hours of the morning while the guns boomed outside, would come the men who moulded world opinion, the war correspondents and the political commentators; and they would sit, glasses repeatedly re-filled by Tich, arguing over the conduct of the war, recounting rumours, theoretically reshuffling the Cabinet, attacking the censor, discussing individual politicians and generals, revealing the trends of

125

Britain and of America and elsewhere. Jeannie was often with them and although she was very feminine I noticed they treated her as one of their own; and I remember her at a corner table with Quentin Reynolds, helping him prepare one of his famous broadcasts.

Within a day or two of *Time Was Mine* being published, the whole stock was destroyed when a bomb landed on the warehouse in which the copies were housed; and a week or two later the printing works was hit. No books and no type, and the publishers refused to reprint; and so it was a quick end to the high hopes I once had of my round the world story. Yet a few copies circulated and I had some rewards . . . the legendary Hannen Swaffer who had always seemed a god to me wrote a page about it, then I met him, and he said in his slow cockney voice, a stub of a cigarette in the corner of his mouth, ash over his lapels, wispy untidy white hair, a high collar and a black cravat: 'I don't read books . . . I've read yours . . . damned good.' High praise indeed from Swaff; and he was always to be my friend, and Jeannie's to whom he inscribed a photograph he gave her when we left for Cornwall: 'To Jean, in disgust with her for running away.' And there were humorous rewards too. A colleague in M15 said to me pompously on the steps of Blenheim Palace: 'You'll regret this book, Tangye, when you're older.' And shortly after Jeannie and I were married, one old lady who was our neighbour said to another old lady: 'I *do* hope Mrs Tangye hasn't read Mr Tangye's book.' And there was the vicar of St Columb near Newquay who denounced me from the pulpit for my frankness, much to the amusement of his parishioner, my father; for I had dedicated the book to my father and mother.

By May I was beginning to see Jeannie more regularly. I had been shifted back to London and because my work was of a special nature I was given a private flat to use as my office where I could be on my own, away from the formalities of headquarters. There was, however, the question of where to live, and this was solved one day when I met an American lady who had temporarily married into the Peerage. She had a furnished house to let on the river a few hundred yards below Richmond Bridge; and as soon as I saw it I fell in love with it . . . and at Cholmondeley House, nearly two years away, Jeannie and I held our wedding reception.

Of course it was much too large for me on my own, but two American journalists were with me on the day I first saw it, and we agreed to share it together. There was a beautiful room on the first floor with bay windows overlooking the river, and I was to stand there hour after hour observing the dirty old barges with jaunty names like *Pam* and *Willie*, or staring at the passers-by on the towpath during warm evenings and sunny week-ends, uniforms of all defeated nations, and those of the Commonwealth; and the girls. There was an island opposite, a deserted island of undergrowth and trees; that first spring swans had a nest there, and I came to the house in time to watch the cygnets have their first swim. Richmond at this period seemed to be a village and I believed I lived in the most beautiful part of it; but as I said Cholmondeley House was too large for me on my own. The dining room was as big as the room on the first floor and there were five bedrooms and two gardens; a tiny one between the house and the towpath, a larger one at the back alongside the garage which you walked through from Friars Lane to reach the front door. Bachelors couldn't run the house on their own and because the organisation was left to me, I chose the housekeeper to look after us. I did not know that one of my partners was never to appear again, the other was seldom to pay. But I had other friends who stayed from time to time as paying guests, and so I managed to

127

continue to live apparently beyond my means; and to pursue the job which enabled me to serve the men of power.

As the months went by it became a habit for people to come out to Cholmondeley House on Sundays, and from lunchtime to late in the evening there would be talk; and it became a kind of extension of Tich's Bar without the drink. Any subject might be discussed, any political argument debated. It was an uncomfortable period of doubts and suspicions, of views too vehemently expressed as a result; and the views might lunge in one direction one Sunday, the opposite direction the next. Cholmondeley House was a turbulent barometer.

Was Lloyd George, for instance, preparing himself to be the British Petain? The picture of the man suited the conjectures; his magic, a contemporary of Petain in age and war experience, the memory of his years of glory leading him to yearn for power again whatever the conditions might be. He fed the rumours around his name by giving occasional injudicious interviews to American editors on fleeting tours of Britain. One or two of these editors, ostensibly on a mission of top level reporting, were also emissaries of the Administration. America was still not in the war, and the scouts were searching for frailties in our determination.

I do not think the British took the stories about him seriously because we were all so conceited that we could not believe it possible a British Petain would be needed. The Americans were different. They watched from afar and many doubted our stamina; and so when Lloyd George unburdened his fears in 'off the record' interviews, there were some who believed him. I remember one American who arrived during 1941 with a letter of introduction to Churchill from President Roosevelt who went post haste to see Lloyd George at Churt; and when afterwards I saw him he said: 'The old man was terribly depressed. He believes he

128

is the only man who can negotiate a peace in any way favourable to Britain. He is convinced you cannot win the war on your own.' I do not suppose this particular American realised that Lloyd George was only getting rid of a mood when he talked in this way. His indiscretions were not calculated ones; and on great occasions it is the calculated indiscretion which you have to watch for in the political arena. Lloyd George was old, and tired, and sad.

But by June we were no longer alone. The Germans had attacked the Soviet Union, and suddenly Stalin was being cheered instead of being booed when he appeared on the newsreels. In December the Japanese bombed Pearl Harbor, and the Germans declared war on America. 'At last after two years we're in,' said Quentin Reynolds wryly, 'and we've managed it without declaring war on anyone.' And as for ourselves there now began the period of Churchill baiting.

One of my jobs was to keep in regular contact with the Secretary of the War Cabinet, the present Lord Bridges; and though this did not mean I was in possession of high level secrets, I probably knew more from my various sources about government activities than most of the critics to whom I listened; and I may have been right when I thought that Churchill's basic problem was the 'dead wood' he inherited when he took office.

This 'dead wood', those people in key positions of varying degree and placed in so many arms of government, both military and civil, were momentarily galvanised into life when Britain was on her own, but soon slipped back into their mediocre ways when the acute danger was over. These were the same people who muddled the country into war unprepared, the type who were responsible for the Norway fiasco, the same who helped the British Empire to die from boredom. There were tiers of such people and Churchill, absorbed by great decisions, could not get rid of them in a matter of months or a year or two because there were so many of them. They sat snugly in their homes and offices, hindering Britain's future by their lack of imagination. Churchill was aware of this, and it made him depressed and irritable. He was, like most men of brilliance, absurdly affected by the lowering influence of the third rate.

Hence the biting tongue of Aneurin Bevan, Churchill's most publicised critic, was a blessing in disguise. He may have angered Churchill but he was the only person to provide him with a rhetorical opposition in the House of Commons; and thus he also stimulated Churchill. The trouble with Nye Bevan, a man of such charm and wit and explosive oratory, was that he often allowed his emotions to influence his judgement; he made Churchill into a permanent Aunt Sally, Churchill could never do right.

Yet the venom of Nye Bevan was directed at the people who sheltered behind Churchill rather than Churchill himself. He was concerned with the class war as well as the fighting war; and when he lashed Churchill, he was in fact lashing the old order which he considered Churchill represented. But Nye Bevan's weakness lay in his interpretation of the facts upon which he based his talk and speeches. Too often his arguments seemed to fit his wishful thinking; and a speech, hailed as brilliant by his devoted band of admirers, would thus fail to hit the target because the content was too obviously tainted by prejudice.

Jeannie and I dined with him one night soon after the battle of El Alamein in a small restaurant off Leicester Square. A victory at last but Nye would not admit it, and he was wailing as usual about Churchill's conduct of the war. 'What does this victory mean?' he asked. 'If instead we'd sent our forces to Europe and left a holding force at El Alamein, the war would be over now. The opportunity was missed, and we've lost the war, we've lost the war . . .' Then he continued: 'We must find a Prime Minister who will choose Ministers who will purge their departments of all incompetents. Up to now it is the *people* of Britain who have carried Britain through, not the leaders or the ruling class.' And then, as often happened with him, his mood suddenly changed. He began laughing.

'The other night,' he said in his lilting Welsh voice, 'I had dinner with a Colonel in the War Office. The man said the House of Commons should be closed so that the leaders could get on with the war undisturbed. Fancy now, fancy saying a thing like that.' He had turned to Jeannie and was wagging a finger at her. 'So what could I say in the circumstances? "You're a middle class Fascist!" I shouted across the dinner table. The chap was very annoyed.' Nye paused again, the joke was ready. 'And what was he annoyed about? He didn't at all mind being called a Fascist . . . but I ought to have called him upper class!'

He never allowed his political convictions to interfere with his enjoyment of good living. Larry Rue, the pro-British correspondent of the *Chicago Tribune*, used to tease him about this. One day the three of us were having lunch together in the Savoy Grill when Nye complained about the food. He did not think it up to the usual standard. 'Ah,' said Larry mockingly, 'now you know how the poor live.'

Some people at one stage even wanted Sir John Anderson to take over from Churchill, but fortunately the idea petered out. It was during the period between the fall of Singapore and the victory of El Alamein, surely the worst period in Churchill's life, and men around Churchill were becoming exasperated by his refusal to listen to anyone. 'I sometimes think,' said one Minister acidly to me, 'that when Churchill wishes to carry out an important operation he considers the speech he can make about it first . . . then decides how the operation is to be carried out.' Unfair, but the comment represented the mood.

Towards the end of that year of El Alamein I spent a fascinating afternoon with Harold Macmillan. (My reason for interviewing him concerned a book I was writing about the British Empire, of this more later.) It was just before he was appointed Resident Minister in North Africa, and he was at that time Under Secretary for the Colonies. I saw him at the Colonial Office, and for a couple of hours I was alone with him except for occasional darting appearances of John Wyndham his aide, now Lord Egremont. Macmillan was then comparatively unknown, and I knew no one who tipped him as a future Prime Minister, nor was he a politician whose views were much discussed. He was just an efficient Under Secretary, a little frustrated by his job, yet soon to be on his way to take a place in history. There he sat at his desk, a rakish air about him, a sonorous musical voice dropping elegant witticisms, loads of charm, and inquisitive. He was also suffering.

'Wyndham!' he called, after I had been there a short while, and a door opened and Wyndham hurried through it, tall and thin, eager, attentive, like the head boy of a school seeking to please his headmaster. 'Wyndham, I am in great pain ... bring me a bottle of whisky.' The pain was the legacy from his severe wounds in the First World War. Wyndham fetched the bottle.

'First help Mr Tangye liberally to a glass.'

I sat sipping my whisky feeling that perhaps my presence was useful to him because he was in pain and he did not feel in the mood to concentrate his mind on serious matters. And he flattered me by listening to what I had to say, cross questioning me, then giving me his own views and telling me anecdotes.

'I'll never co-operate in an anti-Churchill movement,' he

said, and he made great emphasis on this, 'but he will have to be careful that he doesn't Asquith himself. He is surrounded by a crowd of inefficients. If something goes wrong again people will be crying for another government, and Beaverbrook will be sent for. Beaver will lay down his own terms . . . leaving Churchill as a figurehead, and becoming the power behind the scenes, getting rid of committees and so on.'

Wyndham was again at my elbow. 'Thank you,' I said.

'Aristocrats after the war,' Harold Macmillan was saying, 'may complain that they have lost their money and so on . . . but they've ruled England for a long time. They can go on doing so, go on having their shooting and fishing, but they'll have to change their titles to Commissars.'

American troops were now arriving in Britain in great numbers and although fraternisation up to that time had been surprisingly good, many influential Americans continued to bark their jibes about the British Empire. I told Harold Macmillan about the *Time Magazine* Bureau chief who said the British were robbers, and how I had a slanging match with him, yelling: 'Puerto Rico! Philippines! Hawaii!'

'They know nothing about the British Empire,' said Macmillan, half American, 'and it is an illusion that we make money out of the colonies whatever they say. Indeed the African colonies and the West Indies are a liability but of course we have to remember our own people who have made their homes in those places. They work very hard, you know, for very little.'

At this point he was smiling to himself, and so I guessed I was about to listen to a favourite point of view.

'The Yanks,' he said, and a quiet chuckle had already begun, 'always talk of the Boston tea party as the real reason for the American revolution. I never cease reminding my American friends that this is not so. The real reason, I remind them, was an edict of the Duke of Newcastle in 1776 that read something like this: "In the name of George the Third I order all lands to be returned to the Red Indians!" And of course as soon as the American colonials heard this, the revolt was on!'

The black-out hid Whitehall when I came away from his office; and his parting words to me were that he was there from 9.30 in the morning to 8.30 in the evening, and that I would always be made welcome. 'Come whenever you like,' he said, 'and tell me the news.' I never did see him again.

While I had been at Cholmondeley House I had edited a book called *Went The Day Well*. The title came to me during the time M15 was at Blenheim Palace, when I was billeted at a lovely old house in the village of Coombe where a hawk-eyed old lady made a great effort to pretend that my presence in her home was not a considerable nuisance. One day I was looking through her visitors' book and found these two anonymous lines against an entry of 1917:

> Went the day well? We died and never knew.
> But well or ill, England, we died for you.

I was very moved by these lines, and I thought that they exactly suited the theme of the book. I did, however, substitute 'freedom' for 'England' because the book was not only about Englishmen; and, after all, England and freedom were then synonymous. I explained the book in this way:

This is the story of men and women who bade goodbye to their days of peace to die for gains they will never share. They came from many different lands, spoke many different tongues, yet all of them gave their lives for the same beliefs.

They did not want to die. For dying meant leaving good friends, and happy homes, and clear blue skies, and the salt of the sea, and rounds of golf, and walks across the moors, and drinks at the club, and the wind at night, and the scent of log fires. For dying meant they would never know whether or not they had fought in vain.

Yet when the moment of cold decision ended the brightness of their lives their thoughts did not halt them; and they died so their beliefs might live.

Some may call them heroes, but they themselves would not wish to be considered such; because each, according to his fashion, did his duty . . . expecting neither reward nor recognition.

There is, then, no special standard of conduct in their way of life that has made them part of this story; only that their actions mirror what millions have already done and what millions are prepared to do.

They are of the cavalcade of freedom. Labourers and clerks, playboys and housewives, students and old men, typists and nurses; all these and many more who march the road of danger and sacrifice so that the lights of cities may blaze again and the lands be filled with song.

One Friday last November I spent an evening with a young Polish Air Force officer called 'Vladek' Grudzinski. In the passage of time I had not known him long; in the quality of mutual friendship I might have known him since the days he patrolled the skies above Warsaw. He was twenty-four, small like a jockey, with a round face and fair hair, and eyes that from being laughing and kind would at the mention of Nazi Germany suddenly look cold and cruel. He had fought almost continuously for two years and three months – in Poland, France and England. He had just been decorated with the Polish Cross after shooting down his seventh enemy plane in this country.

On that evening he was very happy. The English girl he loved had said she too loved him. For the first time, perhaps, since leaving Poland, he had someone to live for; because he had not heard of his family since the beginning of the war.

There was a cold moon lighting the house-tops of London when I said goodbye to him, and I remember well the shaft of silver light on his face as he leaned out of his car to wave goodnight. 'Till next week,' he laughed.

But there was no next week.

On Sunday morning he was out on a sweep over France with his squadron. Over Dunkirk he dived within fifty feet of an anti-aircraft battery, spraying it with bullets. As he pulled out of the dive a shell from the battery caught his plane amidships and blew it to pieces. Another gay life had gone.

Another gay life to join the procession of those who have died for the rest of us to go on living. Full of hope and courage and love of being alive. Unstinting in their willingness to sacrifice. Sure that the future will dawn bright. Firm in their faith that those who are left will not fail.

And so it was that on that evening when I heard the news of 'Vladek' Grudzinski I thought of the story of this book. A story not to be written by a single person, but by a company of people each of whom had known the savagery of personal loss. A story that would tell how men and women of this age lived full lives and met sudden deaths. How they gloried in doing their duty and how they paved the way for life to become normal again. How courage was their companion and tenacity their sword. How they were strong in defeat and sharp in attack.

Men and women who, through the centuries to come, will always be remembered.

This is the story . . .

I had asked a number of people, both known and unknown, to write of someone who had been killed during the first two years of the war, and whom they had cared for. Patricia Ward wrote of Billy Fiske, the American who volunteered for the RAF and who was killed in the Battle of Britain, the first American pilot to die in the war; there were tributes to the two MPs Ronald Cartland and Arnold Wilson, the latter a disillusioned appeaser who joined the RAF as soon as he realised he had been wrong, and was killed at the age of fifty-six serving as an air gunner; James Agate, the diarist and theatrical critic, wrote of the gay young Tony Baerlein, and introduced an Agate note on the day the book was published by telling me it had been published at the wrong time; the then Bishop of Southwark wrote of Prebendary Thompson who was killed by a bomb as he stood on the steps of St Peter's, Eaton Square, where he had been vicar for twenty-five years; Peter Quennell wrote of Christopher Hobhouse; Howard Spring wrote his little masterpiece about a conscientious objector, Arnold Baker, who was prepared to die as a merchant seaman but not as a member of the armed forces; there were stories about the MacRobert brothers whose mother bought a bomber as a memorial and presented it to the RAF, about a WVS member, about an auxiliary fireman named Jack Maynard and written by Hannen Swaffer ('Does it stand up to the others?' he had asked), about a housewife, and an ambulance driver, and a member of the Rescue Service; there were the stories of Sergeant Pilot Ward, the New Zealand VC, of other representatives of the Dominions and India; there were tributes to Ludovic Kennedy's father, Captain Coverley Kennedy, captain of the *Rawalpindi*, the armed merchant cruiser with six inch guns which attacked the *Deutschland* and was destroyed; each conquered country had a representative, and the Soviet Union, our then only fighting ally, had a tribute written by Leonide Bondarenko, the Tass Agency man, who was my friend and who often came to Richmond. All these stories had been written by people who, at some moment of a day, had heard the news that a friend had been killed, and felt despair. I ended the book with an epilogue:

. . . That is the story. If, having read it, we have a feeling of grimness it will not have been told in vain. For if out of the pages there stepped a ghost he might tell us there are some who forget, who forget the dead who died for them, who forget the blind who were blinded for them, who forget the maimed who were maimed for them.

He might ask us to close our eyes sometimes and vision the last moments of some who have gone – the airman who in a spiral dive struggles in vain to free himself from the cockpit; the bomber crew whose plane is ablaze; the seaman who lingers in the icy water; the soldier who chokes on blood in the desert; the patriot who stands against a wall in the dawn with a handkerchief around his eyes.

He might ask us to think sometimes about these men; about the anguish in their hearts and the twisting pain in their bodies; about the loved ones they left behind and about the children they will never see grow old.

He might ask us, then, to swear vengeance; vengeance not only against the enemy, but against the old world which preferred them to die young. He might ask us to show our vengeance, not in our bitterness, but in our defiance of the hell still to come; in our ruthless resolution to win the peace that will come too.

For out of the peace, out of the great new world those who are left will build, these men and women will find their memorial.

No one was paid for their contributions, and all royalties went to the Prisoner of War Section of the Red Cross; recently the book has been published again and this time the royalties are going to the Star and Garter Home of Richmond. During the war each story was broadcast to Occupied Europe and messages were received by the BBC asking for them to be repeated. My generation does not forget these men and women and what they did for us; but there are the others, who take the present for granted.

There was for me a sequel to *Went The Day Well*. A few days after it was published I was standing one Sunday afternoon with Jeannie at one of the windows of that lovely room of Cholmondeley House overlooking the river, when we saw below us on the towpath a legless member of the Star and Garter Home cruising slowly along in his wheel-chair; and on his machine was tied a Union Jack. We both felt the same. *There* was a man who had lost all the normal pleasures of living by serving the ideals of his country, and still had the faith he had done right. Of course, now in retrospect, I realise that we were being sentimental, but we both felt at the time enriched that there were people who believed that the British had something to be proud of. The man still had not wheeled his way out of sight when I excitedly turned to Jeannie.

'I've got it ... I'm going to write a book as to why that man still has faith!'

She looked at me, not knowing me except for the times we had been gaily together, a little suspicious of my sudden enthusiasm, ready to please but feeling she should be sensible.

'What sort of book?'

'I'll try and explain why he feels as he does.'

'You can't just write about enthusiasm.'

'There'll be more to it than that.'

I had already slowed down in my excitement; Jeannie, this passing friend beside me, or so she seemed at the time, had brought sense to me. The man in the wheelchair may have given me an idea, but Jeannie had halted me; and as a result during the following few days I looked at the idea pretty coldly, and the next time I saw Jeannie I thanked her for what she had said to me, and I told her she was quite right, and that instead of being emotional, I was going to write a factual account of the British Empire. So factual that my first chapter would be a series of questions: What is a Dominion? What is a Crown Colony? What is a Protectorate? What is a Mandated Territory? What are the powers of a Governor? What is the Executive Council? What is the Legislative Council? I would then write a chapter on every Colony and each Dominion, describing the history, the political and economic situation, and the prospect for the future; and at all times I would try to be objective and let the facts speak for themselves. Of course I had no idea what I had let myself in for; and nor had Jeannie any idea of the part she was going to play. It was going to take two years of my spare time to collect the material and write the book, interviewing scores of people and reading mountains of documents. I was a bachelor when I began it, and a married man of nearly two years when it was published. I had called it *One King*; and the two of us waited anxiously for reaction.

Meanwhile Jeannie began to visit Cholmondeley House regularly on Sundays from her home at St Albans, and I used to walk up Friars Lane to meet her. If I was late I would see her hurrying along under the trees which bordered the Green, and greeting her would tell her who had turned up for the day. Capa always came when he was in London, the legendary Capa who was the greatest war photographer of his generation, and who was killed stepping on a mine in Indo-China; dark and very gentle, with a cigarette drooping out of the corner of his mouth, making one think that he looked like an *apache*. 'Jeannie with the light brown hair,' his soft Hungarian accent would say, 'I love Jeannie with the light brown hair.' This always was his welcome to her. Claud Cockburn who wrote in the *Daily Worker* under the name of Frank Pitcairn, and wrote also a famous newsletter, would regularly display his exuberance; politics for him had the excitement of the countdown before a moonshot ... provided the countdown had hitches. Alec Waugh and Michael Arlen would drift in. Michael Arlen suffered severely from hangovers and usually wore dark glasses, and he was quite unlike the brittle characters he wrote about. He had an immense love, although born an Armenian, for Britain, and he had come back from America and offered to take any job in the Ministry of Information. They gave him a liaison job in their Midland division, and he was content to accept it, and did very well ... until a witch hunt began, and solid British citizens objected to an Armenian speaking for them. 'I had a dirty deal, I know,' he murmured to me one day, 'but who am I to make a fuss? There is a war on and I'm not going to bother the public about my small troubles.

There were Ned Russell, Bill White and Geoffrey Parsons of the *New York Herald Tribune*, and Cy Sultzberger of the *New York Times*; all of whom believed in the British way of life and never failed to make this clear in their despatches. Arthur Koestler came once or twice, bringing his sadness with him. Shelagh Graham giggled her way through a couple of visits during a trip from America; very feminine, watching all the time for stories with bite for her column, and described by Alec Waugh as a 'dream'. And years later to become famous for her book describing her life with Scott Fitzgerald. Robert St John, the bearded correspondent of the National Broadcasting Corporation, who wrote *From The Land Of Silent People*; and who, when my book *A Gull On The Roof* was published, remembered the times he had had with us at Cholmondeley House, and arranged with a Florentine bookbinder for a copy to be specially bound. And there were the exiles ... Joseph Luns now Foreign Minister of the Netherlands, Milan Gavrilovic the Yugoslav who gave me the wooden pipe bowl I have in front of me at this moment, Poles, Chinese, Norwegians. Jeannie never knew who might be there when she arrived at Cholmondeley House; and quietly took over the role of hostess.

Then at last she became the resident hostess.

'Will you marry me?' It was seven o'clock in the Coalhole, the pub in the Strand, and I had been waiting for her for an hour; and she had expected a row as she came up to the marble topped table where I was sitting.

'Yes,' she said quickly, glad to be let off.

TWELVE

We were married in the Lady's Chapel of Richmond Parish Church at quarter past twelve on February 20th. The Russians were destroying the German Army at Stalingrad, the Eighth Army had reached Tunisia; and the little blitz, the flying bombs and the rockets still lay ahead.

We had presented ourselves to the Vicar of Richmond three weeks beforehand, and after agreeing to marry us he asked me to pay his fee. I pulled out my cheque book and started to write. 'I don't accept cheques,' the Vicar said smartly. And as I had no cash, Jeannie had to look in her purse and produce the money; and she says I never paid her back. My mother came up from Cornwall to stay at Cholmondeley House a fortnight before the wedding, reluctantly because she was anxious not to interfere; and then, as soon as she arrived, she caught a bad cold but she wouldn't admit it because all she worried about was being a nuisance. She wasn't, and she helped us both in a thousand quiet ways; and, Jeannie, whom she loved, effortlessly made her realise she was needed.

My brother Colin was best man and as Jeannie came into the church, the organist playing Jerusalem, he murmured to me: 'Give her a winning smile!' She was wearing the veil of the Earl of Dudley's family which had been lent her by Patricia Ward who had written the tribute to Billy Fiske in *Went The Day Well*; and I remember thinking as she looked at me across the church how sweet was a quiff of her dark hair that appeared incongruously out of it. She didn't mean it to be there. She had dressed at the Savoy, surrounded by well-meaning relations who had fussed over her and who had a glorious time pulling the veil this way and that; and the quiff was a result.

There was the usual rumbustious reception, and savour was added to the occasion by the Thames threatening to flood the house. It had succeeded often enough before. I would watch it edging across the towpath, into the small garden, up to the French window where a board was supposed to keep it out . . . and then somebody would shout the alarm and I would realise I had been surprised in the rear. For the river would move along Friars Lane and enter the house via the garage, the large garden and the front door. The housekeeper naturally moaned despair, but I, watching from half way upstairs, would have the excitement of a schoolboy. 'Look! It's half way up the legs of the dining table!' or 'It's gone higher than last time!'

Jeannie and I left for our honeymoon as the tide had reached its height, and this time no damage was done, and the guests were safe; all we had to do was to walk nimbly along a small stone wall to the car, wheels awash, which was taking us to Victoria station. We spent our honeymoon at Brighton, and we were both in a daze after the parties which had led up to the wedding; and neither of us remembers very much except buying a Wedgwood jug from a shop in The Lanes which we still have, and spending lunch times at Pitt's Hotel where old man Pitt had lived since 1886; and where a luscious old gentleman named Bimbo, a retired clown, ceremoniously presented Jeannie with his buttonhole each day . . . an orchid, a camellia, and a red rose.

We returned to Cholmondeley House, and were soon informed that as the owner needed it again we had to leave. It was a disappointing beginning to our married life, but we soon had compensation in the excitement of looking for another house; and the house had to be on the river because both of us found peace watching the river. It was a necessary antidote to the life we led. Indeed it became an obsession to find such a house, and when, after weeks of searching, we found one called Mall Cottage in Chiswick Mall whose small garden had a parapet which fell sheer to the river, we were of course delighted. We arranged terms with the owner, and were ready to move in when we had a telegram. The owner had changed his mind. Naturally we were furious, and we did all those things that fury generates ... consulted solicitors, wrote harsh letters and so on. The owner was unmoved, and so in the end we had to accept defeat. There was, however, an aftermath ... a year later Mall Cottage had a direct hit, and the bomb went through the sitting-room.

So we were back to the beginning, and time was getting short; and it was then that one Saturday morning I stopped the car on Chiswick Bridge, where we got out, and stared down at the little cluster of houses which huddled along the river in the shadow of the huge Watney brewery building. There were only six, in fact, and a pub ... Riverside House with its roof blown off, Leyden House where, we were to learn, an indomitable lady crippled by arthritis was looked after by her husband, Thames Bank House where a very old couple also had faced the blitz on their own, Tudor Cottage where dogs barked, Asplin Cottage and Thames Bank Cottage. The little group looked scruffy, no hint of elegance like the houses lining the river at Strand-on-the-Green a couple of miles up river, or those at Chiswick Mall a couple of miles down river. Old cottages and old houses but they were dwarfed by the brewery and I felt that, except for Boat Race day, they represented a forgotten part of the river. Passers-by, I suspected, would look at the brewery not at them.

'I like it down there,' said Jeannie.

'Me too.'

And in five minutes we were in the pub meeting Gus and

144

Olivette Foster and asking why the cottage, next door to the pub except for a patch of waste land and an elm, was empty. 'The owners, Mr and Mrs Moore, are very particular,' said Mrs Foster primly, eyeing us.

We were to know Mr and Mrs Foster very well. It was easy to call Mr Foster, Gus, while it was impossible to call Mrs Foster, Olivette. They had been at The Ship for thirty years, from the period when maharajahs hired the pub on Boat Race days to the time we came to Mortlake and there was excitement if two customers called during the morning. Gus came from an old Music Hall family ('My father was manager for Lord George Sanger and booked Marie Lloyd for Margate'), and he had met Olivette when she was sixteen and champion diver of London. He had a rakish air, was owner at one time of twenty three trotting ponies one of which, Polly Pan, was the champion of England; and before the First World War he was a member of the National Sporting Club where he puffed cigars, and drank champagne, as he watched the now legendary boxers. Gus was a character, and when later Jeannie and he used to go racing, he always gave her an expensive bunch of flowers. We had many parties at The Ship. We had many occasions singing into the early hours around a battered old piano to the accompaniment of an unreliable Gus; and dear Mrs Foster, enjoying it all immensely herself, used to murmur again and again to herself: 'He's had enough . . . he's had enough.'

The Moores, owners of Thames Bank Cottage, accepted us after careful inspection. The care, as I was to learn, was due to the close knit grouping of the inhabitants of Thames Bank, Mortlake. They wanted the *right* people to live there and be one of themselves, and the *right* people had to belong to their way of thinking. In this, I am afraid, Jeannie and I were a disappointment. We were rather demure when we applied for Thames Bank Cottage. We played down that side of ourselves which steady people might have viewed with alarm; and as a result one glorious day we were told that Thames Bank Cottage was ours to rent at £90 unfurnished a year. I said to Jeannie that we had found the home which would be ours for always.

The cottage had a dunce's cap. The roof, instead of being a normal roof, rose from its four corners to a peak just like those paper hats in a Christmas cracker. The living-room was at the top of the house, oak beamed, and with windows looking across the river to the meadows on the other side, the winning post of the Boat Race almost opposite. On the left was Chiswick Bridge, on the right in the distance the silhouette of London. There was a bathroom on the same floor and in winter it was bitterly cold, and in those days there was no clever way of heating, and so every winter at some time or other the pipes were frozen. The stairs were of polished wood, and on the first floor were the large bedroom also facing the river and a spare bedroom at the back. On the ground floor was the dining-room where Monty of *A Cat In The Window* used to sit watching the passers-by and waiting for us at night to come back. There was the kitchen and off the kitchen was another little bedroom with its own bathroom; and the night before our last Boat Race party Gertrude Lawrence stayed there after her performance in *September Tide*. The small garden had high walls surrounding it, and at the far end was a pillbox of an air raid shelter where we used to crouch with Monty when the little blitz began, except on the night the cottage was full of people celebrating our first wedding anniversary, and the roof was blown off. Jeannie didn't like being in the shelter because she was frightened of the spiders, and she was concerned for the chickens we kept in the chicken house alongside. We grew vegetables in the garden, and planted a syringa bush which became large enough for Monty to shelter under on hot summer days and a cherry tree which he used as a scratching post.

We were lucky in the uneasy married life we led. We were together. We did not have to write letters which might not reach their destination, or wait for letters, or telegrams, or read about faraway news in which one of us might personally be involved. Our unease lay only in the pace of our life, and in the disquiet that we might not be doing enough. We were at the heart of affairs and we had power, and we could often succeed in doing something through our contacts when conventional methods of communication had failed. I always knew, for instance, that any matter raised by me and considered of paramount importance, could be on the Prime Minister's desk within a few hours. Such matters, however, were rare. And sometimes I doubted the worth of my luck, and wondered whether I should apply for a change.

I was still collecting material and writing *One King* . . . fifty thousand words, one hundred thousand words, one hundred and fifty thousand words. I thought the task would never end, and I had to find time at all hours for interviewing people. At night Jeannie would bring me cups of black coffee, and I felt despair at one moment and elation the next when another section of the Empire had been dealt with. I was a joke among my friends, and a nuisance; for when in the evening they were relaxing, I would drag Jeannie away and take her home where she would cook me dinner on the gas stove, and Monty would purr round my legs, and I would force myself to sit at my desk.

Occasionally we would have staying with us a man or a woman who had been on a secret mission to Europe, or someone who had defected to the British. These brave lonely people had an approach to life which shook me into realising that I had nothing in common with them except remote sympathy. I was in the same category as the

Americans who have never known bombs falling on their homeland. Pour out the words of commiseration, the words of admiration, the words of encouragement, but in doing so no hearts are touched except in the imagination.

There was a Pole, thin like a taut wire, who acted as a courier for the Polish underground, and who was perhaps the most important courier of them all. He had been three times out of German occupied Poland, three times back, and he had now brought with him a message from the head of the Jewish secret Socialist party in Warsaw ... a message about the slaughter of Polish Jews in the concentration camps which we in the West refused to believe really existed. In the upstairs room of Thames Bank Cottage, a log fire burning, curtains drawn for the blackout, Jeannie handing round the coffee cups, he described to me the assignment he had been given. He spoke calmly without heroics, and yet I had a strange sense that he knew that the hardest part of his assignment was in the present. He had to convince people like me that he was *speaking the truth*.

He had been ordered, so that the message he brought might be more convincing, to see for himself what happened in a concentration camp. And he told me how he had smuggled himself into a camp with false papers describing him as a German Camp Inspector. He saw an elderly man, naked, emaciated, sitting by himself. No one took any notice. He saw a dead baby on the floor. Nobody took any notice.

He described to me how there was a wooden passage leading to a railway. Thirty wagons were entrained there, each wagon had room for forty people. At a signal the Gestapo guards started shouting, and the Polish Jews in a panic rushed down the wooden passage and into the wagons. Instead of forty in each wagon, there were at least a hundred, and all the while the guards were shooting and punching and beating with sticks; and then drove more into

148

each wagon, forcing them to climb over the dying bodies of the others. 'The train shuddered with their cries,' said the Pole. Then the doors were banged shut, and the mass in each wagon continued to scream; and the guards laughed because they knew what soon was to happen. The floor of each wagon had been covered with lime, and fumes began to fill each one; and no person survived.

There is no answer to such a story which, at that period of time, was one among many competing for newspaper headlines. No answer at all except the inward knowledge that one had been hearing the ring of truth; and that politicians should hear about it and everybody else who had time to listen. But the Pole already had the answer to my thoughts.

'When I left,' he said, 'when I left Warsaw my chief who has lived in the West said to me: "They will not believe you, Witold. They will listen politely but they will not understand . . . you will be pleased because you have been invited to see an important person, and you will arrive at his office at half past eleven in the morning. You will give him all the evidence, you will be getting eloquent, you will be saying what we want done . . . then at quarter to one your listeners will look at their watches and one of them, to the delight of the others, will say it is lunchtime, and the interview will be over. They will not understand, Witold." '

The Polish link in London of the Socialist underground in Warsaw was called Sieglebaum. The Pole who was sitting in our upstairs room delivered to him the message which he had been ordered to give. 'You must tell the British and the Americans that they *must* make reprisals if any Jew in Poland is to survive. I beseech you!'

Shortly after receiving the message Sieglebaum committed suicide. 'I have failed,' he wrote in a letter he left, 'but perhaps by the way of my death, the world may be told what I was not able to tell in my life.'

He failed again. Only the few believed what was happening. The others waited for the evidence of their eyes.

Periodically, A. P. Herbert, on river patrol, would moor the *Water Gypsy* opposite us, and row ashore in peak cap and Petty Officer's uniform. Sometimes it was in the morning before we were up when we would hear the bleep bleep of the hooter announcing his arrival; sometimes it was late at night. I suppose the most satisfactory period of his life was when he, as a Petty Officer and a Member of Parliament, patrolled the Thames in his beloved *Water Gypsy*.

'Did you know,' he said as we had breakfast on a sunny September morning, sitting on the steps of the cottage during one of his early calls, 'that over there, under the towpath by the brewery, were buried hundreds of victims of the Plague?' And he went on about the cottage. 'It may have been the original inn because the legend is that it was kept by a waterman who married a Shakespeare player.' I was in due course to dig up from the garden many broken old clay pipes, sometimes part of a stem, sometimes a bowl, and when I sent them to an expert he confirmed they were Elizabethan. The evening visits were more lively. Alan's purpose in life being to have fun, he was as much at ease in a public bar as in the Savoy Grill or in our cottage. On one of these visits I suddenly heard amid our laughter and talk, the bleep of a Mayday signal coming from the river. The sender was one of the crew left aboard the *Water Gypsy*. The tide had ebbed, leaving the *Water Gypsy* high and dry on her side.

We went to St Albans to stay with Jeannie's mother and father after the roof was blasted, and Monty, an unwilling evacuee, went too. He was an uncomfortable companion because he took an instant dislike to Judy, the black Scottie, who was after all his animal host. Nor did Judy like Monty. She loathed Monty in fact, and she decided from the beginning to give him no peace. And so there was only one thing to do . . . they had to be kept apart. Thus Monty was shut in a room all day. He was kept a prisoner and his character began to change. Instead of the winning ways that won me away from being a cat hater, he became like a zombie. He was indifferent to my efforts to play with him. He lost his looks. I began to think to myself how right I had been to dislike cats, to consider them soul-less creatures, selfish and unco-operative; and I began to wish we had a dog. But when we returned to Mortlake, roof now intact, the charmless Monty disappeared. The change in him was extraordinary to behold. He was his old bewitching self. He was boss of the home again. And among the guns again.

The alert went at 11.40 p.m. on June 16th. Rain was falling in buckets and the guns began to bark, unsure of themselves, just like dogs themselves bark when there is a stranger about. I heard no bombs fall, and I assured Jeannie there was nothing to worry about although I already knew the flying bombs, the V1, were expected. At daylight the spasmodic gunfire continued, and it was unnerving because when manned bombers came over there was a glorious crescendo of gunfire; and in a weird way comfort was thus gained. At half past nine in the morning the all clear went, soon to be followed by another alert. The postman called at the usual time. The weather had cleared and he said cheerfully, 'Nice day, isn't it? Lots of mysterious goings on last night.' Thus did those react, who kept the life of Britain ticking.

I was driving along Millbank the same day at quarter past three and saw the people looking upwards. I stopped the car and heard the drone of a V1. I got out and made towards a shelter. Then I saw this particular V1 above Battersea Power Station, and its engine didn't cut out, and it continued northwards, so I went back to my car and went on with my journey. The following day I had lunched at the Savoy and I came out to the Embankment entrance where I had parked the car; and Chamberlain, the hall porter, said to me: 'Wait a moment, Captain, the alert's just gone, and the first five minutes are the worst.' I waited with him, and we heard four V1's buzz over in quick succession, then a few seconds' silence after their engines had cut off, then the crash; and we tried to guess where the people had been killed. For the people south of the Thames, within easier range, the flying bombs were hell. All night they were listening for an engine cutting out, then waiting for the seconds to pass before the explosion; and in the early morning too, and as they washed, and as they ate breakfast, and went on their way to the office, and when they were there, and when they had lunch, and in the afternoon, and as they went home, and as they cooked their supper, and as they waited to go to bed, and as they tried to sleep.

'I was in Harvey Nichols' this morning,' said Jeannie calmly as she was cooking my dinner, Monty looking at her hopefully, 'when the warning buzzers went and we all lay flat among rolls of carpet on the ground floor. We heard a V1 pass overhead, and then we all got up. A moment later we heard another coming, and we all fell on the floor again.'

I would ring up Jeannie from my office when I heard a crash in the Savoy direction and saw a plume of black smoke. 'All right?' 'Yes, it was in Kingsway.' Or she would ring me. And a slang developed among people. 'O.K., it's gone over' . . . 'O.K., I heard it drop' . . . 'This is a near one, get down' . . . 'Poor devils' . . . 'I should think it's Sloane Street.' And there were the clouds, the endless low clouds that summer which let the V1's fly unseen, and the questions which were asked: 'On which side is God?' Thus did people live and think and fear, and have a purpose.

In November *One King* was published. Three weeks beforehand Jeannie and I had gone to stay at a farm called

Treglossick on the Lizard peninsula for our annual leave. In the middle of the first week, my dear friend Jackie Broadbent, political correspondent of the *Daily Mail*, sent me a telegram: 'Manny Shinwell is going round the House praising *One King* to the skies.'

'Damn Jackie,' I said to Jeannie, after I had read the telegram in the sitting room which at night was lit by an oil lamp. 'Damn him, I wanted to be left in peace.'

Such is the perversity of life. My enthusiasm had been drained into the book, and there was none left in me to enjoy the results.

THIRTEEN

My life, after victory came, was not as straightforward as Jeannie's. I suddenly woke up to realise that I had passed the age of irresponsible dreams. And yet the dreams persisted, making me puzzled and restless and unsure. It was as if I were meeting myself again after five years wearing the same clothes ... there was the old self, however much I might have appeared to have changed in the meantime. I still wanted to play a lone role. I still knew that my mind would curdle if I were subject to an authority which I despised. These were the feelings I had always had; and they were supported by the knowledge that Jeannie felt as I did. We both believed that independence rather than conventional success was the greatest prize to possess.

But such an attitude has to measure up to reality. We were like countless others who, wanting to be free, had not the means which could provide such freedom. We could only muddle our way to the goal we were aiming at, hoping that fate would lead us there. We were not yet ready to do anything drastic. We were content to wait ... Jeannie, satisfied in the excitement of her job while I probed to find a compromise between the old self and the new. And I soon discovered how difficult this was going to be.

I pretended to myself, for instance, that a likely method to win our independence would be for me to write a novel. I foresaw that it would be sold for a movie, that I would become a script writer, and that Jeannie and I would then travel the world collecting material for further novels and further movies. The realisation of this delightful prospect depended, I felt, upon a period of total concentration. I had resolutely to refrain from becoming involved in any other activity. I would hide myself in Thames Bank Cottage for six months, and then emerge with a manuscript which displayed the knack and opportunism of a contemporary story teller. That was my superficial plan.

I had not, however, taken into account the after effects of my book on the Commonwealth. I was sought after. I was offered lecture tours. I was offered the job of Commonwealth correspondent on a prestige newspaper. There I sat in the top room of the cottage with the windows looking over the river, a blank piece of paper in front of me, turning down all these approaches, pleased with myself for my determination to do so, but aware that I was slowly weakening. After all, the novel was a ridiculous gamble. Would I not be wiser to cash in on the prestige that *One King* had given me?

A week or two later, and a blank piece of paper still in front of me, I was made another offer. The nature of it inevitably appealed to my vanity. Arthur Christiansen, the dapper, legendary editor of the *Daily Express*, rang me up.

'Meet me in the American Bar at the Savoy this evening,' he said.

'Why?'

'I want you to take over the William Hickey column.'

'Impossible.'

Chris hired and fired people with abandon. He had, I suppose, a kindly nature, certainly an engaging one, but loyalty to individuals was never allowed to interfere with his loyalty to the newspaper. This I knew, and I was on guard. And yet I was flattered.

The following day I was contacted by an emissary of Chris. Again I said no. I said no the next day and the next, and now I knew that Beaverbrook had decided he wanted me, and Chris, therefore, was determined to get me. The money was good, and the William Hickey column in those days was a plum job. Tom Driberg, the best columnist ever to work on British newspapers, had made its reputation; and there was no army of people contributing little paragraphs. The man who wrote the column was out on his own.

I still lived, however, in the shadow of MI5. I had surrendered my uniform and I had given up my flat, but there was still an arrangement whereby I was to operate on certain missions should the necessity arise. Of course the William Hickey column might provide me with a good cover, but clearly I was not going to take that into consideration in deciding whether or not I accepted the job. It was really a question of self indulgence. On the one hand I had learnt, during my years with MI5, the basic principle of reporting without prejudice about events and people; on the other hand I was tempted to experience again the thrill of the chase which always swept over me whenever I entered a newspaper office. I was sitting dolefully in the top room of the cottage, wondering what to do, not a word of my novel yet written, when Christiansen rang me again.

'Meet me at 6.30 at the Savoy.' It was an order, charmingly given.

'Yes,' I replied meekly.

I had been five minutes in the bar when he arrived in a hurry, wearing an unbuttoned teddy-bear coat, greeting others he knew before he turned to me. He considered me already his employee. The time for arguing was over.

'I want your column to be waspish,' he declared.

'Yes.' And I remembered the moment I had crept hopefully into the Manchester office of the *Daily Express* on a month's trial.

'I want you to write about people in such a way that their friends will be annoyed, and their enemies pleased.'

'Yes.'

'You'll be able to go where you like. Everybody will want to meet you. But remember . . . you must be waspish about them. Waspish!'

'Yes.'

'Harold Keeble will fix the contract. Three months' notice either side but . . .' in a spasm of extra bonhomie he called for another round of drinks, 'I believe you'll be with us for years!'

'Yes,' I murmured.

'I want your first column by 4.30 on Sunday afternoon.'

After he had gone I hastened to Jeannie's office, and found her having a party with half a dozen people so that I had to take her into the secretary's office, and tell her what had happened.

'It's ghastly,' I groaned, 'I've committed myself.'

'You must be the only newspaperman in the country who could feel like that.'

'It doesn't matter what I say. Accepting it is against all my instincts.'

'Never mind . . . meanwhile I can give you a story.'

I laughed.

'Let's go back to the others.'

My time as William Hickey lasted three days. I wrote my first column on a Sunday, my last on a Tuesday. Between-whiles I had not been waspish enough about my old friend Alec Waugh, nor waspish enough about the Governors of the Star and Garter Home, Richmond, which I had visited . . a visit which had deeply moved me. Indeed it was this particular visit that later made me rush to Jeannie to tell her the news.

'I couldn't stand it any more,' I said, 'I even said I would tear up the contract.'

'I'm on your side,' said Jeannie, as if I didn't know, 'but aren't you being impractical by not accepting the money which you can collect?'

157

'Of course I am . . . but it's a matter of principle.'

'Expensive.'

'I've never felt happier.'

So there I was again in the top room of Thames Bank Cottage with a blank piece of paper in front of me, and Monty sometimes sitting on my knees, purring gently. At last I could get on with my work without having outside pressure put on me; and one page was filled, then another and another. A soothing life, interrupted only when I accompanied Jeannie to parties at night; and this might have gone on for the six months I had promised myself, but Stanley Horniblow, the editor of the *Daily Mail*, asked to see me. Once again I fell into a trap.

A different kind of trap. A strip cartoon was required for the *Daily Mail* and I was invited to invent a suitable character to dominate it, then to write the story, and the dialogue of each day's series of drawings. I was offered a high salary, told I could work at home, and informed that my artist collaborator would be the urbane Julian Phipps. The pleasant prospect of working with him settled the question, and once again my good intentions were thwarted. The novel was put aside. Only for a short while, I thought. As soon as I mastered the technique of writing the strip I would have plenty of time to do both.

I had not, however, allowed for the personality of Judy. I have no idea why I chose this name but she was the girl who became the centre of my story, and provided the title for the strip. She was a sweet, sexy girl, and Julian Phipps interpreted her on the drawing board as being dark, thoughtful, and with a kind of sophisticated innocence. If this was the impression my story had given him, I have to admit he was partly wrong. The girl was sweet but she was also clinging. She wouldn't leave Jeannie and me.

She came between us. Jeannie and I went on holiday to a

farm in Cornwall, and Judy accompanied us. Every day, instead of relaxing, we would talk about Judy. We would go for long walks on the cliffs around Porthallow, and instead of talking about intelligent subjects, there would be Judy demanding that we should talk about her. How can she get out of such a situation? How can she condense her remarks into a single frame? Would she say that? Would she say this? The first story was about smuggling at a time when H.M. Customs in answer to my query declared in superior fashion: 'No one smuggles in this country.' The second was about the theft of the Gold Cup at Ascot. Julian drew beautifully and the strip looked good. Unfortunately a cleverer rival had suddenly appeared. Rip Kirby had arrived on the scene . . . and poor Judy was out. She had to wait to be seen until the *Evening News* recognised her charms. As for myself, frankly I was thankful to be rid of her.

The *Daily Mail* for a long time afterwards continued to pay my salary. Rip Kirby was a huge success, Judy was dormant, but the monthly cheque continued to arrive. Perhaps this unearned affluence was the cause of my feeling unsettled. I had the money, the time, but instead of concentrating on the novel which once represented so many of my hopes, I only played with it. I wrote articles for American magazines. I wrote a weekly column for the *Continental Daily Mail* and another one for a newspaper in Canada. I frittered my time, my career time, on passing opportunities when it would have been so much wiser of me to have remained true to my original superficial plan. And then an odd thing happened. I really went haywire. I decided to get rich quick . . . and the source of such riches would be a restaurant.

It was no ordinary restaurant. At the time we all had to have food coupons, and the cost of meals was limited to five shillings, and there was little entertaining at home, and there was a general dreariness about the food which was available.

Hence I conceived the brilliant idea, or I thought it was brilliant and this was enough to provide me with unrealistic enthusiasm, to open a restaurant where nobody ate. Instead, the customers entered the restaurant, came to the counter, read the menu, ordered their dishes which they could see were being prepared by a chef in the kitchen in the background, and then took them away in special containers. The site I chose for this strange venture was in Kingston . . . and I was quickly to find that the idea was long before its time.

I look back, in fact, on this period with dismay. I had had the amateur's notion that my personal appearance would not be required, and that my interest in the running of the concern would be a vague kind of overlordship. The chef would look after the kitchens, a manageress would look after the customers. I did not foresee that I would have to be behind the counter, and that Jeannie would have to be there on Saturday afternoons. Very foolish of me I know, but my initial enthusiasm had deceived me into such thoughtlessness. And so there I would be standing at the counter waiting for customers to come in. It was a distressing experience because there were never enough of them, and the weekly takings were always below the weekly expenses, and I had to borrow money to pay the wages, and I was often exasperated by the remarks of the public. 'Will a 2s. 6d. chicken salad be enough for four people?' 'I'll *try* one . . . I'll try anything once.' . . . 'I could make ten of these at home for the price of this.' (A Cornish pasty at 1s. 6d.) . . . 'The trouble is you're so expensive.' . . . 'What's it made of? Beef? Sure it's not horsemeat?' Perversely, as usual, one remembered such remarks, and not the compliments.

And yet there were compensations. The two chefs for instance . . . because I had found I had to have two. They both worked as if the business belonged to them, and when the two little men set off for the station at the end of the day,

I felt sad the battle was being lost. They had old-fashioned standards. Adao Almeida was a Portuguese who had been chef to Alice Delysia, the French actress, for many years. He always seemed to have a white patch of flour on his nose. 'When I return to live in my country . . .' he would say. He had only been to Portugal twice and he was never to go again. 'You live better with animals than with human beings . . . it's easier to find out which of them are honest . . .' And when business was bad, 'I cannot understand it, I cannot. All this good food and nobody.' And if a customer was difficult, 'She's wicked . . . wicked.'

The other chef was called Bunny Pessione, and I believe he was a great chef. He was too old for the hurly burly of a normal restaurant or hotel, and anyhow his artistic soul had been too hurt by the poor cuisine standards of postwar Britain. 'In the old days,' he said to me, 'the aristocracy were the aristocracy of culture. We chefs were artists who served them, and our hearts were there as we cooked the food.' His poetic choice of words became blunted when he continued his story. He spoke angrily, and what he said surprised me. 'Have you heard of Vatel, the great French chef for whom I worked at the Carlton? Vatel was preparing a banquet but when the fish failed to arrive in time he was so upset that he stabbed himself to death in a corner of the kitchens!' Bunny liked to dramatise. He was also kind and loyal and hard-working. When at last I had to tell him that I was selling the place, the old man's eyes filled with tears. 'Fancy us closing . . . after so much heart and soul has been put into it.'

And all the while MI5 remained my boss.

I was no longer an executive so I never went to head office or attended conferences or had a chance to look at the files. I cannot therefore write of this postwar period with inside knowledge. I was just an agent who was given tasks to do which for the most part seemed to be of little importance.

161

Despite this minor role I was still able to observe the mood of MI5; and the impression I had was that counter-espionage was in the doldrums. There was little to do. The ham fisted attempts of the Germans to plant agents in Britain had been successfully dealt with. Why should anyone believe it possible that the Russians could do better? At the end of the war there were only two or three people in the Russian section of MI5 . . . but already for a long time Fuchs, Pontecorvo, Maclean, Burgess, Philby and others had been performing their nefarious duties.

I met Philby on what was for me a dramatic occasion. An important member of an anti-Nazi group had escaped to Britain bringing with him a number of very useful documents. I was asked to have him to stay at Mortlake; it was during the latter part of the war, and I soon realised that the motive of his escape was primarily due to his fear of the Russians. The group he represented were convinced of Germany's inevitable defeat, but they were also terrified by the prospect of Russia occupying Germany. He had, therefore, been sent to Britain by the group to make their views known to the British.

The man himself was jittery; and Jeannie and I found the days he stayed with us very poignant. It was bitterly cold at the time and the cottage was like an icebox; and a pipe burst in the roof and water cascaded through the ceiling to the bathroom immediately below, and then froze into icicles. Hardly the time to entertain under any circumstances. But the man was twisted by doubts as to whether he was a traitor to his country or a patriot of a cause, and we listened to him for hour upon hour as he tried to persuade himself that he had acted correctly. Clearly he was disappointed by the reaction of the British he had seen. He had expected them to be as anti-Soviet as himself, but they had shown little sympathy. Their interest lay in the documents he had brought with him. In restrospect I realise only Philby was interested in his views.

Philby had recently been appointed chief of the Soviet section of MI6 known as Section V; and it was this section which had asked me to have the man to stay. At the end of his visit I had to report back to Section V, and it was then for the first time I met Philby. His office was in Ryder Street off St James's, in what is now a block of luxury flats. I entered his room and saw him sitting behind his desk; an untidy looking man behind an untidy desk. I was with him for ten minutes or so and came away with an uncanny impression that he had been sizing me up at the beginning, then decided to treat me as a foe. I am not being wise after the event. That evening I told Jeannie of the impression I had had, then I added: 'The extraordinary thing about this man Philby is that I feel I distrust him totally . . . and I've no reason to do so whatsoever.' Jeannie still remembers my vehemence.

I believe that one of the reasons for the MI5 failure after the war was due to over-sensitiveness. There was a strong undercurrent of prejudice against MI5 in many prominent circles, and it showed itself in a curious way. People would proclaim that they were being persecuted by MI5, and gained prestige by so proclaiming. 'My telephone is being tapped . . .', 'my letters are being opened,' 'I am being followed.' This persecution mania was probably fanned by Soviet agents as part of a nerve war against MI5; and it was a campaign which had a measure of success. My salient impression of MI5 had always been that it judged a person brought to their notice objectively . . . but this campaign influenced MI5 to be too objective. MI5 wanted at all cost to avoid the stigma of being called the British version of the Soviet secret police. MI5 was therefore scared into being too cautious.

Yet I had always found it difficult to get down to facts with

163

my MI5 colleagues. There was so much secrecy within secrecy. My colleagues were charming and amiable, conscientious and erudite, but sometimes when I was talking to one of them a glazed expression would come over his face; and I would try to make up my mind whether he was hiding information from me or whether he felt at a disadvantage because I had shown I knew more than he did. And on occasions I felt like a small boy unwillingly let into a prefects' pow wow . . . for a sudden change of subject would take place just when I was beginning to be interested.

I had dealings with Burgess but I never knew Maclean. Oddly enough, about this time in the late 'forties, there were officials who were grumbling about the Soviet Union's lack of appreciation of the Anglo-American determination to stop any aggression on her part. Open diplomacy had failed. The Soviet Union just would not believe that we were serious. 'If only the Russians had a spy in the Foreign Office,' said one of my friends lightheartedly, 'he could then tell them the truth.'

But I wish I had an explanation about the Philby affair which would quell my own puzzlement. The recruitment of university undergraduates by Soviet Intelligence was a known fact in some quarters. Soon after I joined MI5, one of the most experienced and imaginative among my colleagues said to me: 'The Russians are very patient. They will recruit a young man at a university with communist views, tell him to dissociate himself from the Party, watch him, and keep him on ice for years. Then one day they will come to him and say: "Now we want you to do this . . ." '

If such insight of Soviet methods existed within MI5 it is more difficult than ever to understand how Maclean, Burgess and Philby got through the net. And having done so how did they dispose of the information they acquired? The Portland spy ring needed the Krogers to transmit their secrets. Who was the courier, man or woman, of Philby and Co? He, or she, must still be in orbit.

I resigned from MI5 on the day Fuchs the scientist was arrested. Before I said goodbye I asked my chief whether it was a bad case. 'Shocking,' he replied, 'shocking.' There were certainly a few more shocks ahead.

And what about the novel for which I once had such high hopes? The week after we at last arrived at Minack, the manuscript was once again returned to me by a publisher.

I carried it down to the rocks, tore the pages in half, and dropped them in the sea.

FOURTEEN

When the war ended, Jeannie's job at the Savoy became even more absorbing for her; and more exhausting for that matter. We were out most evenings of the week, and we would come back late at night to Thames Bank Cottage to see Monty waiting for us in the dining-room window, his cross face lit up by the car's headlights, and we would feel sorry that we had left him for so long on his own. Then at week-ends we would sleep and recover, and be thankful we had such a peaceful home beside the river.

Jeannie loved her job. She was, however, a wise person. She had as much fun as anyone could wish for, but the pleasure from it was tempered slowly but surely by the realisation that the same kind of fun was being endlessly repeated; and that one day she would weary of it. Moreover in war time there was a purpose to her work, worthwhile achievements were to be gained by her efforts; but in peace time she was often made use of by those with trivial intentions. Some would try to lure her co-operation in a publicity stunt, others would earnestly ask her help, only to forget her once she had given it. She gradually became distrustful of people; and yet, and this was the charm of her, she was always ready to trust again.

I leave her now to tell you how she felt about her job in those years which were leading her to Minack:

I had been at the Savoy ten years when I decided it was time to leave. But as I gazed round my office after making my decision, with its pale pink walls, almost completely covered with signed photographs of celebrities, and its dark green curtains and carpet, I wondered about the next ten years. Could they ever be as challenging and gay and exciting as those that had passed? Would there ever be a sight so memorable as Churchill standing on a small chair which wobbled, in front of one thousand international hoteliers in the Restaurant and making the V sign while ecstatic bravos were shouted in many different languages? Would the entire Royal Family walk up the red carpet from the Embankment entrance to a wedding reception in the River Room? Would dozens of sufferers of infantile paralysis eagerly crowd the passage to Sister Kenny's suite? Would there ever be such a hilarious afternoon as the Mad Hatter's tea party, where the guests were Danny Kaye, Mae West, Olsen and Johnson, the Merry Macs and Harry Green? Would there ever be such a frantic search for the American Ambassador at one in the morning . . . and the Manager finding him (Lewis Douglas) at last in Room 205, my office, along with Derek, A. P. Herbert and Billy Butlin, earnestly discussing the Marshall Plan while I sat and listened?

I still have many of the photographs. There is a small one of Field Marshal Montgomery which was his favourite picture of himself, and he signed it on Luneberg Heath. Trumbell Warren, his Canadian A.D.C., came into the office one morning. 'How I curse Derek,' he said laughing, 'the Old Man has made all his Staff read *One King* then he cross-examines us about it every morning at breakfast!' And then Trum produced the photograph. 'I caught him in a good mood and he signed it specially for you. But it was a near thing . . .' Apparently a captured German flag was put outside Monty's door for him to use as a door-mat. He was very amused by the idea, and everyone shared his laughter . . . except Trum. Monty noticed his silence. 'Well?' he barked, 'and what do you think about it?' There was a moment's silence. 'I think it's in bad taste, sir,' replied Trum. Monty glared at him, then suddenly smiled. 'You're quite right. Have that flag removed at once.' A moment later he showed he had forgiven Trum for his frankness by signing the photograph. I had the photograph of A. P. Herbert alongside that of Monty in my office, suitable I thought because they were close friends, the teetotal Field Marshal and the merry, witty Alan. Alan stayed with him once at his headquarters and though Monty went to bed early, the Staff kept Alan up to four in the morning. Three hours later Alan groped his way to the table for breakfast, sat next to Monty, took one sip of his tea and said: 'Good God, sir! This is corked!'

I still have Karsh's famous photograph of Churchill. Karsh, a gentle little man, came into the office one morning and showed it to me. I naturally enthused about it, then quite unexpectedly he handed it to me. 'Thank you for your enthusiasm,' he said shyly, 'this is the second copy, take it with my compliments ... Churchill, of course, has the other.' I believe I was one of the first to be told how Karsh took it. 'He sat scowling with a huge cigar clenched in his teeth,' said Karsh, 'I begged him to remove it as it was spoiling the wonderful line of his jaw, but he refused and told me to hurry. So I got everything ready, and just as I was about to take the photograph I dashed forward and snatched it from his mouth. He didn't like me doing it, you know!'

There are many others. Two pictures of Danny Kaye. A quizzical, handsome Danny as Group Captain Mitty, and an endearingly scruffy Danny in his incredible golfing clothes. Tragic Carole Landis, the loveliest film star I ever knew. James and Pamela Mason at Olleberry Farm when they were married: solemn James with his dry wit; brilliant Pamela with a tongue which spared nobody. Ben Chifley, then Prime

Minister of Australia, sitting with his favourite film star Ingrid Bergman. Grace Moore who signed her photograph a few weeks before she was killed in an air crash. James Stewart, Ty Power – an old friend of Derek's, Bob Hope, Ronald Colman, John Steinbeck, Merle Oberon . . .

Radie Harris, the famous columnist of the *Hollywood Reporter*, Merle Oberon and Gertrude Lawrence were among my best friends during these years. All three were so gay and elegant, fun to be with, and kind. I have a picture of Merle stepping out of a taxi outside the Berkeley with the hotel porter beside her. The porter was in a newly designed uniform and I wanted to publicise this in some way; and so when one day Merle was coming to lunch with me, I asked if she would do me a favour by being photographed with him. I am afraid anyone who saw the photograph only looked at Merle.

Dear Gertie, so enchanting and vulnerable and contradictory and feminine and impulsively generous, gave us many photographs; and there is one of her in the wonderful part she played in *The Glass Menagerie*, the only major film part she played in Hollywood. 'And if you say you recognise me,' she wrote when she sent it, 'with me made up as the mother, I'll never speak to you again!'

Derek had first introduced me to her when she came over during the war. And when she went back to America she sent us food parcels, and to me she also sent the clothes she no longer wanted; and in those postwar years when rationing was still in force, she continued to send me her clothes. I was almost the same size as Gertie and the clothes seldom required any alteration; and because they were wonderful clothes I still could hand them on to somebody else when I no longer needed them myself. Shelagh of *A Drake At The Door* had one of the suits.

When she was in *September Tide*, the play by Daphne du

Maurier, she used to drop into the office or I would lunch with her every week. I remember the party she gave to the cast one night after the theatre in a room above a restaurant in Curzon Street, and Derek and I were the only two outsiders present. Derek asked her to sing but she refused because, she said, the cast wouldn't want it. It was a curiously unhappy evening because it seemed to us that the cast, except for Bryan Forbes who acted her son in the play, didn't realise what magic was present. She stayed with us at Thames Bank Cottage for our last Boat Race party, and we still have the badge of crossed oars and pale blue ribbon which she wore on her suit. She and her husband Richard Aldrich were our guests at our last New Year's Eve party at the Savoy. She raised her glass of champagne. 'Good luck to you two escapists from the rat race!'

Now that there is a movie about her, with Julie Andrews playing Gertie, I remember two incidents. One was when Derek and I had been at Minack for a year and things were going very badly with us. The postman one day brought Derek two letters from America. One from Gertie, the other from her lawyers. Gertie in the sweetest possible way, the lawyers with the offer of legal confirmation, asked him to write her story. 'I was given six names of English authors to choose from,' wrote Gertie, 'and I have no doubt in choosing you.' The lawyers proposed a trip for research purposes to New York, Hollywood, and of course London. Derek refused the offer. He never showed any doubt in refusing it. 'Jeannie and I,' he wrote back, 'have given up the kind of life such a book would entail. And anyway, Gee, aren't you much too young to have a biography written about you?' She was playing *The King And I*. A year later, she died.

The other incident concerned Julie Andrews. I went one day with David Milford Haven to have lunch with Ben Goetz of MGM at their studios in Elstree. And after lunch Ben

170

Goetz asked us to go to their studio cinema to watch a test which had just been made of a very young girl called Julie Andrews. I remember she was first interviewed in this test, then sang a song. When it was over Julie, dressed in jodhpurs and a high necked yellow sweater, ran up and down the aisle of the tiny cinema in high excitement; and while she was doing so Ben Goetz turned to us and asked our opinion of her. 'Not bad,' answered David grudgingly. And so that afternoon I saw a star born.

The Savoy directors allowed me much freedom, and there were no special hours for me to keep, but I was always in my office by ten in the morning although I might have been in the background of some function until past midnight. I loved my job and my overriding wish was to do it well. Sometimes I went through agony when a plan failed. During the Savoy strike which seemed to aim at disrupting the hotel arrangements during the Queen's wedding to the Duke of Edinburgh, a newspaper published a leading article denouncing the Savoy management. The article was very unfair. Indeed it was so unfair that the staff who had remained on duty demanded that they should be allowed to write a reply. The editor of the offending newspaper was a close friend of mine, and a frequent visitor to the Savoy, but I felt it was no use asking him to publish the letter. Hence I proposed to John Gordon, then editor of the *Sunday Express* and who now, of course, writes the most forthright column in Fleet Street, that he might possibly publish it in the letter column of the *Sunday Express*. 'I'll do better than that,' he said, 'I'll put it on the front page.' Then he added firmly: 'I'm not doing this for you, mind. But I strongly deprecate unofficial strikes . . . especially at times like these.'

I waited anxiously for Sunday morning, and I felt sure that my job was at stake. I had failed in my press relations to

keep a newspaper on our side, and if John Gordon failed me
. . . well . . .

On Saturday night I was in the Grill having dinner, and I
saw not far away from me the Savoy directors also having
dinner. I kept my eyes away from them and I longed for the
morrow and the fulfilment of my hope that I would be able
to rush happily to Claridge's, a copy of the *Sunday Express*
in my hand, asking to see the managing director who lived
there. Suddenly I saw John Gordon threading his way
through the tables, and I saw he had a sheet of paper in his
hand. In fact he had two. 'Here you are, Jean,' he said with a
kindly smile after a waiter had led him to my table. 'I've
brought you the dummy proofs of my leading article and the
letter. Now you can enjoy your meal and have a good night's
sleep.' John Gordon favours no one, but he possesses a
wonderful sympathy for truth. And his gesture took me away
from one of the most miserable experiences of my life.

The fact is that behind any glamorous job there is always
an undercurrent of strain. You have to be on top of the best,
incessantly playing a kind of Centre Court tennis. The
rewards are worthwhile if you are tough and have no other
interests; but if your ambition is to enjoy life, you must have
the luck to recognise the moment when it is time to go.

I had that luck.

The Return

FIFTEEN

We had a happy time in London. There was no doubt about that. Holiday London was a wonderful place. Yet we could not separate ourselves from the past. The past came bouncing into the present as we met again the same pressures which had led us to leave all those years ago.

There were the same languid bus queues, the same barging when the bus arrived; the same surge of people streaming across the Strand out of Charing Cross station in the morning, then nine hours later streaming back. There was the same unbearable stuffy heat in the big stores with the sales staff despairingly counting the hours; the same blocks of grey, expressionless faces on tube platforms waiting for trains which were already full. All these were as we remembered them. But now there was also the screeching noise in the sky to add to that on the ground, and the sinister stalking of traffic wardens, and danger at night. 'I was attacked in the Embankment Gardens the other night,' one old member of the Savoy staff told us, 'and I had to go to hospital with a cut eye.' And another, a chambermaid whom Jeannie had known since she first saw her clearing up the glass after an air raid, told how she was getting into a bus after evening duty, and three youths jostled her off it so that she fell into the roadway. 'And they did it for fun,' she said. The pleasure of London used to be that one could wander at will. How had it happened that lawlessness had become conventional? London had gone back to the days of the footpad.

But Jeannie and I were holidaymakers, and Jeannie had never woken up in London before, saying to herself that she

175

could do exactly what she wanted to do. Even now it was not as simple as that. If you have been away a long time there are many people to see. And so we rushed from one appointment to another, from the Strand to Chelsea, from Chelsea to Hampstead, from Hampstead to Bloomsbury, and back again to the Strand.

And when we were not rushing about, people drifted in and out of the river suite, and Louis the floor waiter brought in the drinks, and we would take our guests to the window saying: 'Isn't it a glorious view?' The same words we used when visitors to Minack looked across the bay to the curve of the Lizard.

Old friends came who were following the same pattern of living as when we had last seen them; and new acquaintances whose attitude suggested they couldn't unwind. Thus some of these new acquaintances, prominent in professions dependent on the exploitation of transient ideas, seemed to show an uncomfortable tenseness. The stakes they played were higher than those we had known because they had little security. There was no escape route waiting for them, as it had been waiting for Jeannie and me. The cost of primitive living was now too expensive. Yet successful and full of promise at thirty, they were expendable at forty. There had been no war to halt the growing up of youth, and so creative business had a relay of brains to choose from. 'All my present bright boys,' said an American head of the British branch of his firm, glass of whisky in hand, as he stared down at the river, 'can go within a year. And I can engage replacements who will be *fresher*.'

Downstairs Joe Gilmore, the laconic head barman of the American Bar welcomed us. Jeannie once had a greyhound called Gold Bounty which raced at the White City, and after one spectacular win Joe amusingly invented a cocktail named Gold Bounty. Indeed everyone at the Savoy used to follow Bounty, and Jeannie enjoyed reflected glory when she arrived in the morning at the hotel after one of his victories.

'What happened to Gold Bounty?' Joe now asked; and we told him.

Bounty was not good enough to go to stud so we were asked whether we would like to have him in Cornwall. He arrived at Penzance in the guard's van of the Cornish Riviera Express, and such was his excitement that I could hardly hold on to his lead as we walked out of the station to the Land Rover. We arrived back at Minack . . . and forthwith chaos ensued. He thought Monty was a hare, and within a couple of days we realised we could never train him to think otherwise; and so we found a farmer who kept greyhounds for coursing, and we left Gold Bounty with him. Three months later the farmer arrived at the cottage door. Gold Bounty was dead. He had died of a heart attack.

'I can still remember,' said Joe, 'the roar of the crowd as he came round the last bend: "Bounty! Come on, Bounty!"'

We were standing at the bar and I asked him if he knew the whereabouts of a friend of ours called Dave Golding. One of the pleasures of the Savoy is that you can usually trace friends by asking at the bar or at the enquiry office. Years may have passed since you have seen them. No matter. You will be told this one has married again and is living in Rio de Janeiro, or another died a year ago in Vienna, or another was in the hotel only the other week. Dave Golding, Jeannie and I had first known when he shepherded the famous Goldwyn girls to London after the war for one of the Royal Command performances, and he had been Sam Goldwyn's personal publicity man. Dave Golding, said Joe, was in London again and acting for Charlie Chaplin; and so to trace him further I went to the enquiry office and asked Fred Snow if he knew his home address. He didn't, but within half an hour he somehow produced it; and I rang Dave up. He came round to the Savoy not long after, where we had a gay reunion. Other old friends happened to come into the bar, and Joe said later: 'Just like old times.' Then Dave said he would send a studio car round in the morning to collect Jeannie and me, and we would drive, the three of us, to Pinewood to watch Charlie Chaplin at work.

So around ten o'clock next morning, Jeannie and I sat in the back of the studio car as it cruised along the Strand, across Trafalgar Square and along Pall Mall, up St James's Street, then round the Ritz into Piccadilly, on our way to pick up Dave Golding at his office towards the Hyde Park Corner end. I had only slept four or five hours, and I felt a little unreal. The car had travelled to the point when it was time to turn full circle into the other lane so as to draw up outside Dave Golding's office, when we had an accident. I was sitting in the left corner seat when a huge lorry behind us, carrying waste debris from a tube extension, skidded on the damp road surface while braking. It missed my seat by inches, slicing along my side of the car, making me feel like a Lilliputian. Then I sat fascinated, after I knew I was unhurt, as the lorry swung round and rose upwards on its back wheels. For a second it looked as if it were going to turn over on top of us. Then with a bang it righted itself and came solidly to a stop. It was within a yard or two, huge bonnet facing us, and leering.

When we reached Pinewood later we discovered that Charlie Chaplin had lost his patience. A scene between Marlon Brando and Sidney Chaplin had proved difficult to take; and Charlie Chaplin had issued an edict that everyone was to be banned from the set. Only those directly concerned with the scene were excepted. It seemed, therefore, that our day had been wasted. And so it would have been had not Marlon Brando come to our rescue. 'I'll fix it,' he said to us in his caravan, 'I'll introduce you to him, and say I've known you all my life.' And the introduction was made.

There seemed nothing particular about the scene in question, but Charlie Chaplin clearly paid much importance to it. He led us to a couple of studio chairs, and we sat there watching, alone except for the technicians; but it was Charlie we were watching, not the others. First he showed Sidney his son how to play his part, then he showed Brando how to play his. Each gesture, every tone of voice. It was a small masterpiece of acting, and when the scene was finally shot, a cabin scene on a liner, the two actual participants were only shadows of the performance we had previously watched. Anyhow Charlie Chaplin was satisfied, and Jeannie and I decided to creep away before rehearsals for another scene began.

We walked across the floor of the vast studio and had reached the door when Jeannie turned to have one more look at the little man. He was among a number of people but he saw her, and waved, then hurried towards us.

'Did you like it?' he asked eagerly, and he was so obviously pleased the frustration of the morning could be forgotten, 'didn't you think Brando gave a magnificent performance?'

He was addressing his remarks to Jeannie as if, strangely enough, he was seeking praise from her. And Jeannie with only a slight hesitation replied: 'Yes ... but we also saw a magnificent performance by Mr Chaplin.'

There is a sequel to this story. Some months later Jeannie received a letter at Minack from the Chaplin organisation. She was offered a handsome sum and all expenses to handle the publicity surrounding the premiere of *The Countess From Hong Kong*. She was tempted for a moment to accept, thinking that by working with Charlie Chaplin she would be watching greatness. Perhaps she was wrong to refuse. She doesn't think so. Our London visit had reminded her of the rat race pressures which would have been involved.

Sentimental returns are necessary indulgences. I had been already to Cranley Gardens and Joubert Studios and Elm Park Lane before I went with Jeannie to Richmond and Mortlake; and I found I had no envy of my youth. I did not wish to be young again. There were moments, of course, which I would have liked to re-live, but only because I wanted to correct a foolishness. And as I looked at the doors through which I used to pass, I also thought of time wasted. The pleasure and sadness of youth is that the speed of its passing is never thought about; and so you say that you will do this or that in a year, in five years, only to wake up one morning to realise that what you thought was infinitely prolonged has ended. My generation for the most part was in any case doomed; but those of us who were lucky enough to survive, endlessly remember those of our friends who died. This is not sentimental nonsense on my part. My generation imposed upon the world a gallantry of spirit, a belief in a cause, which may now perhaps be unfashionable. But I wonder. As I wandered round, looking at my old homes, remembering eager, young faces, I thought how lost we ourselves once felt; and how it needed a match of purpose to light our awareness, to release us from our inhibitions. So too today. The gallantry is dormant. The belief is waiting for the cause. It will come.

We went to the church at Richmond where we were married, before we went to Cholmondeley House. We had never been back to the church; and I made Jeannie laugh when I reminded her of my ex-housekeeper who refused to leave our side while we walked, I in my uniform, Jeannie in white bridal dress, from the church door along the stone path to the street where the car was waiting. 'Go away, Mrs Clark,' I kept murmuring urgently, 'go away.'

Cholmondeley House had a faded air about it. The paved garden across which I had carried Jeannie, and which backed on to Friars Lane, now looked lugubrious; but the front of the house, facing the river, charmed us again with its Regency curve. There was a wicker chair behind one window on the first floor; and on the ground floor, into which the river periodically flooded when we lived there, we could see through muslin curtains the blurred outline of a dining-room table. In front was the tiny garden, edging the tow-path, where witty friends used to loll on Sunday afternoons before austere suppers of liver sausage, potatoes fried by Jeannie, and lettuce; and where we stood with our families for our wedding picture. There was an untidy hedge behind the railings which nobody had bothered to trim.

I saw no change on the other side of the river. It had never been pretty to look at; the cabin cruisers moored offshore were as battered looking as those we had known, like second-hand cars waiting to be sold at the side of the road; and the bungalows squatted, a monument to a tasteless pre-war architect. Of course the swans still looked proud but they had lost the trees on the little island beneath which, that first time I had come to Cholmondeley House, I had watched a pair with their cygnets.

And there was the bridge. Surely no bridge is such an anachronism as Richmond Bridge; and as a result so beautiful to look at. It must be a nightmare to planners ... a narrow, graceful arch, built nearly two hundred years ago, queening the river with elegance; and choking traffic. Jeannie and I strolled along the towpath towards it, then along the cobbled road below the terrace, until we reached The White Cross. This was the pub where we used to gather with our guests who ordered their drinks in broken English, American accents, Canadian and Australian voices. Dolly Crispin used to reign there, a wonderful person, who made

181

one feel that she rightfully belonged to the age when land-lords were expected to be larger than life; and her old mother used to sit in a seat at a window facing the bridge, day after day, sipping gin, stroking a tiny dog on her lap, commenting on the passers by. A pleasant pub.

We left Richmond and soon we were staring at the outside of Thames Bank Cottage; and at The Ship next door, our other favourite pub, where Gus and Olivette Foster used to live. The Ship was now smartly painted a light grey but the cottage . . .

'What a ghastly colour!' said Jeannie.

Had we been looking at the cottage for the first time, we might not perhaps have thought it so awful; but through the years we had carried in our minds the colour the cottage used to be, a harmless creamy white, fitting the quiet mood of the old houses facing the river between the brewery and Chiswick bridge.

'It's terrible,' said Jeannie again.

The cottage had been painted the red of an over-ripe tomato.

'Anyhow,' I laughed, 'the rest looks the same.'

The elm still stood alongside the cottage up which Monty once climbed, then refused to come down. The same panes were there in the dining-room window through which he used to glare while he waited for us to come home; and where on Boat Race days the crowds used to watch him, making comments about the pale blue ribbon around his fox-coloured neck. As Jeannie and I stood together we could see his shadow.

I gazed detachedly at the porch and its flat roof. On Boat Race days guests climbed from our bedroom window to stand on it; and suddenly I remembered a March morning, an hysterical moment of excitement when Gertie Lawrence, David Milford Haven and Alec Waugh were standing there, shouting wildly, dense crowds roaring below them on the towpath ... and Cambridge winning by a quarter of a length. Boat Race parties! The tide timed their start at such strange hours, and guests would begin to arrive at ten in the morning, and in the oak-beamed room which stretched across the top floor of the cottage Joe Gilmore, being there for no other reason except that he wanted to help us, would dispense drinks from the bottles everybody brought. They were marathon parties. The Grand National, being often run on the same day, helped to revive the party while tickets for the sweepstake were drawn, and the race run. On the day that Cambridge won by a quarter of a length, Russian Hero won the race, and Frank Bowles held the winning ticket; Frank Bowles who became a Peer and Captain of the Queen's Bodyguard after giving up his seat at Nuneaton, so that Frank Cousins could endure his brief stay in Parliament. Jovial and witty Frank Bowles who was one of Aneurin Bevan's closest friends; and whom I first met in Hollywood.

We went up the alleyway at the side of the cottage to look at it from the back. I could not see into the garden because of the high wall, the same high wall which Monty used to patrol; and where he used to crouch, glaring down on the Rhode Island Reds we kept at the top end of the garden alongside the pill box air raid shelter. We did not use the shelter often. We used it sometimes during the flying bomb period and at the beginning of the rocket period ... the first rocket in London landed a quarter of a mile away. But we were not there that night when a bomb blew off the roof. We were in the cottage celebrating our first wedding anniversary with a number of friends. There was not in those days a fear of death on the roads, the fear came from the skies; and yet people irrationally used to risk their lives for comradeship. That night the party was happily in progress though the guns were noisy, when we heard the whistle of a stick of bombs falling towards us. We stood still like Madame Tussaud figures, holding our glasses; and we listened to Capa, the greatest war photographer of them all, counting each bomb of the stick as it fell, cigarette drooping from his mouth, standing by the half open door: 'One, two, three, four, here it comes . . .' Wham! And the place was a shambles.

Now here we were, years later, the tide low, a warm day for January, no traffic on the river, and I said to Jeannie: 'Shall I knock on the door and ask if we could see inside?'

'Oh, no,' she answered, and I knew I had been silly to ask such a question, 'I've seen enough. Let's go back.'

Sophie, George Brown's wife, lunched with us the day of the party which had brought us to London, and I am glad she did. Jeannie had bought a little black dress with a wide white collar from some boutique, and when she tried it on I said I didn't like it. So when Sophie arrived, Jeannie immediately asked for her aid; she put the dress on again and Sophie was full of praise, and I found myself liking the dress after all. Sophie has that kind, comfortable manner which makes you believe she is right.

The party was to begin at six o'clock and it was being held on the sixteenth floor of New Zealand House in the Haymarket. The object was to celebrate the selection by Hatchards of the top twenty Authors of the Year; and *A Donkey In The Meadow* had won me a place among them. But as the party drew near I had a queer sense of sadness, as if I were remembering all my other selves whose morale at the time would have been boosted, had they been able to foresee such an occasion.

At 5 p.m. A. P. Herbert arrived in our suite. He was one of the special guests and we had agreed that the three of us would go together. This kind, humble, marvellous original, had shared with us many happy moments. The continuous achievement of his life had been to protest with wit but without malice. He had this wonderful gift of debunking humbug, and he did this without any wish for personal showmanship. I suppose his philosophy was that everyone should have fun, but it should never be fun at somebody else's expense ... unless the somebody was a kill-joy. He never created, artificially, subjects and matters to attack. Wit, for him, was never a commercial commodity. He waited until injustice aroused him.

The three of us stood at the window of the sitting room looking down on the necklace of car lights passing along the embankment. On the other side of the river the windows of the Shell building popped one by one into darkness as the staff set out for home. On our right, beyond the trains of Hungerford Bridge, was the Lantern Light of the Big Ben Tower ... the lantern is always lit while the House of Commons is sitting. Below us on the river, the tide full, were the tugs and their barges, port lights and starboard lights, and as we watched them Alan Herbert started to sing a song from the musical play he wrote with Vivian Ellis soon after the war, called 'Big Ben'.

> London Town is built on London River
> And London River flows sixty miles to sea.

He finished a verse, and started to sing it again. It was a moving moment listening to him, and funny too. He didn't take his voice very seriously. And when he finished the verse for the second time, I said he ought to persuade someone to put on a festival of Herbert musical plays. *Derby Day, Tantivy Towers, Helen, Big Ben, Bless The Bride, Tough At The Top, The Water Gypsies*. It was a good list.

'Meanwhile,' I said, 'it's time to go.'

We went along the corridor to the lift, and soon we were in the hall waiting for the taxi which the porter was calling for us. Alan went over to the florist's kiosk which stands by the revolving doors. And when he came back, he held out to Jeannie two tiny pink orchids. They looked perfect on her dress.

'Your taxi is here, sir,' said the porter.

A quarter of an hour later I was gazing at the twenty books of the year; and in the middle was *A Donkey In The Meadow* with its picture of Fred as a foal on the jacket. And I suddenly longed for Minack.

'Jeannie,' I said, as the two of us looked at it, 'within forty-eight hours we'll be back.'

SIXTEEN

Spring had come to Minack while we were away.

'It has been very warm,' Geoffrey said when he met us off the train at Penzance, 'and the daffs have come in with a flood. The flower house is full of them.'

There was a pleasant reassurance in his words. I was sleepy and tired and a little dazed, and I was glad to be shocked into reality.

'Mostly Mags from the cliff,' Geoffrey went on, 'they've jumped. And I picked eight baskets of Golden Harvest from the wood yesterday.'

He continued to talk about the daffodils as we drove beside the sea towards Newlyn, then up steep Paul Hill, then along the winding road towards Minack.

'What about the donkeys and Lama and Boris?'

'Good as gold.'

'Didn't they miss us?' Jeannie asked hopefully.

'Didn't notice you'd gone,' he answered, smiling.

I laughed.

'You wait and see, Jeannie.'

The lane to the cottage now had primroses in the hedges, scattered drops of yellow, and when we turned the corner to approach Monty's Leap we saw the wild daffodils were in bloom in the banks on either side. It was a clear soft morning and the Trinity House vessel *Stella* was a mile or so off shore, and a fleet of Stevenson trawlers was sailing west to distant fishing grounds. It was a perfect morning to return to Minack.

Jeannie ran ahead of me up the path when we arrived. She wanted to be the first to see Lama because she had the doting cat lover's apprehension that Lama might be off-hand, even give us a can-do-without-you reception. An unnecessary fear as it happened. As soon as she opened the door, she knew it was unnecessary. For Lama was waiting, and when she saw Jeannie she showed her delight by performing the gesture which she reserved for moments of great pleasure. She folded up and turned upside down, paws in the air and yellow eyes watching; and by the time I entered the cottage such was her emotion that she seemed to be trembling with purrs.

A moment later I saw the donkeys. They were standing, head beside head, staring alertly down at the cottage from the corner of the field above the little garden ... their favourite position whenever they wanted to impose their will upon us. I picked up a couple of apples from the bowl on the table and went outside; and when she saw me Penny pushed her white nose into Fred's brown woolly neck, a habit of hers when she was excited. Then, as I came up to them, they began a gentle hee-haw, a whinnying murmur which got nowhere. 'Fred,' I said, giving him his apple, 'I saw a lot of people in London who thought your picture as a young donkey quite beautiful.' He looked at me sorrowfully for a moment. He was now bigger than his mother.

As I spoke the gulls arrived on the roof, and Knocker and Squeaker turned their beaks to the skies, and called for attention. They had not long to wait for Jeannie appeared and threw bread up on the roof. Then she collected two more apples, and while I set off for Boris's hut in the woods she stayed talking to the donkeys. I came to the hut and turned the rusty key. 'You all right, old Boris?' I said as I opened the door.

He was not in his usual place on the perch. He was on the floor crouched in a corner. He looked at me brightly enough and gave me his good morning hiss, then he got to his feet and waddled slowly towards me. There was nothing really I could fault about him except that he wasn't in his usual place on the perch. Nothing really. And yet I felt apprehensive. I described my feelings to Jeannie when I got back to the cottage.

'I expect you're only imagining it because you're tired.'

'Perhaps.'

And at that very moment I looked out of the window and saw him plodding up the path . . . plod, plod, plod on the grey chippings until he rounded the corner of the cottage and arrived at the door.

'Hello, Boris dear,' said Jeannie greeting him, 'what's all this I hear about you?' He seemed happy enough as he pushed his beak into the biscuit Jeannie had crumbled for him.

We changed and had a quick breakfast, and then went down to the flower house. Rows of galvanised pails stood on the benches, each pail jammed with daffodils in bud. In the old days we would have had to force them into full bloom before they were ready to send away but now the public is wiser. There is value for money when buds are bought.

'Heavens, Geoffrey,' I said, 'there are a lot here.'

'Sixty dozen I reckon.' He was already bunching. 'Not much time to waste,' he added firmly, 'if we're to catch the flower train.'

We bunched them in time and by two o clock they were all on their way to Covent Garden. Emily had come in to help us, and as we bunched Jeannie and I told her of some of the things we had done in London. London to Emily was as distant as the moon, and more dangerous . . . she had never been further away from St Buryan than Plymouth. 'And did he ever get lost?' she asked Jeannie, looking at me.

I did get lost in a way. Incidents tend to enlarge them-

189

selves in retrospect; and sometimes they become more important, sometimes funnier. The air conditioning failed on the floor where the party was held. I did not realise this at the time. I stood there making casual conversation, drinking vermouth, becoming hotter and hotter, mopping my brow with a handkerchief, feeling a fool, and explaining to myself that I was paying the price of being a countryman. I had seen it happen before. The open air type asphyxiated by city standards of temperature. I soon felt as if I were in the hottest room of a Turkish bath without prospect of escape. My conversation floundered. I was off balance. I was like someone who, on being interviewed for a job, had to sit in a low armchair while the interviewer towered at a desk above him. I was lost.

Then over a loud speaker system came a jaunty male voice: 'Sorry ladies and gentlemen, the air conditioning has been out of order. It has now been repaired.' Too late for me.

We went to bed early after that first day of bunching; and I awoke in the morning to the sound of unsolicited purrs from Lama at the bottom of the bed, purrs that had no reason except to express the sheer joy of living. I put out a hand and touched her, then lay thinking with pleasant anticipation of the day ahead. No train to catch. No hurried lunch in a smoky atmosphere. No appointments. No aimless rush from one point to another. All day Jeannie and I would be bunching the daffodils. Geoffrey would arrive from time to time with full baskets, and Emily would gossip, and sometimes our attention would be diverted. The sight of the *Scillonian* sailing by or a gaily painted French fishing boat bound for Newlyn, perhaps a fox hunting mice in the field opposite, or a hawk hovering which Jeannie would frighten away by clapping her hands. All manner of small diversions.

190

'What are you thinking about?' asked Jeannie beside me.

'I thought you were still asleep.'

'Just dozing.'

'I was thinking what a wonderful day lay ahead of us.'

'Were you? I've been lying here dozily thinking we were mad.'

'That sounds a bit harsh.'

'Just remember why we talked ourselves into going to London. We wanted to find out what values prevailed, whether we were right in still opting out, whether our phase, as you called it, at Minack was over.'

'Don't forget you also wanted to have a very frivolous time.'

'I loved all that part of it.'

'But you're saying we were mad ever to doubt our life here at Minack?'

'Yes.'

'We didn't really doubt it you know … we were just suffering from that mid-twentieth century malady of feeling guilty when you're happy.'

'There was something deeper as well. You had reached a moment in your life when you needed to go back in time in order to reassure yourself.'

'One only remembers part of the past. Truth is always changing, especially when it is related to the past.'

'But it has been useful, hasn't it?'

'Well,' I said, 'I've refreshed myself with memories of the mistakes I've made, and find I go on making them.'

'Such as?'

'The list is too long.'

She laughed.

'But, darling Jeannie,' I went on, and as I spoke I was trying to edge round Lama and get out of bed without disturbing her, 'I've also learnt something else. The art of living lies in balancing, early on in life, one's ability with one's hopes, then keeping the hopes under control.'

'You're beginning to be too bright for me . . . it isn't seven yet.'

Lama was still purring, and I was now out of bed. 'Stay there,' I said to Jeannie, 'I'll make the tea.'

She smiled.

'Did you hear that, Lama?'

A CORNISH SUMMER

To Amanda Vyvyan

ONE

When did it happen? Three, five, ten summers ago?
Incidents merge into each other leaving timeless intervals.
I do not remember the summer when the drought dried up
Monty's Leap, or the summer when I killed an adder outside
our door, or the summer when a hoopoe paraded on the
grass in front of the cottage, or the summer when I caught a
conger eel in my lobster pot, and scared Jeannie when I
brought it to her in the kitchen. Important incidents at the
time, they have faded into one summer; so too have the
pleasant hours I have watched Lama, the little black cat,
and Boris, the muscovy drake sitting incongruously side by
side, the one purring, the other ready to raise his head
feathers and hiss harmlessly the second he was disturbed; so

5

too have the stares of Penny and Fred the donkeys, looking down at us from the field above our porch, demanding our attention.

When did it happen? I do not know which summer it was when we watched the fox cubs playing in the field on the other side of the shallow valley, fearing that some stranger would see them too, and disturb them. All soft scented days when woodpigeons clapped their wings in courtship, when a raven grunted overhead, when green woodpeckers called to each other in the wood, belong to one summer; all still nights when voices of fishermen, a mile or more out to sea, sounded so loud that they were like ghosts talking in the front garden. There are no dates in my memory. No dates until this summer.

Our land stretches from a wood in one direction to the cliff and the rocks and the sea in the other. A community of gulls use our rocks as their home, and only when the easterlies blow from the Lizard do they go somewhere else. The southerlies, the northerlies, the westerlies, see them gathered side by side, young gulls and old, aimlessly watching the sea, dozing, like lazy holiday-makers.

When Jeannie and I first came to Minack this community of gulls spent their time on a great, sloping rock of blue elvin half a mile away to the south, roosting there at night as they do now at Minack.

High above this rock are the meadows we used to rent, years ago, for the growing of early potatoes. It was a period when we believed that an eldorado lay in the production of new potatoes. We grew them already on our own land, but we were greedy, and we imagined ourselves becoming the largest growers of new potatoes in West Cornwall, and so we rented these meadows. We loved them in the beginning, then grew to fear them; the ground was stony and in dry springs the potato plants refused to grow; and in wet springs when the plants were lush, a gale would come and scythe them, blackening the leaves so that only the useless stalks were left. We slaved in these meadows yet, because of this hard labour, a remnant of affection remains in our memories of the time we spent there. I walked around them the other day, and I found an old boot still lying in one of

6

the hedges . . . a boot which had to be cut from my foot
after my rotovator had overturned and one of the tines had
pierced my foot. The ancient construction of galvanised
iron known as the pink hut, partly hidden by laurel, is still
there . . . the pink hut where we used to sprout our potato
seed, and where we once helped to nurse a badger back to
health after it had been caught in a gin trap. And still I can
see in my mind those who aided us in our work. St Just
miners who came between shifts to pick up the potatoes,
Geoffrey Semmens, fast shoveller from St Buryan who had
to leave after one disastrous potato harvest but who for long
has been back with us; and Jane, and Shelagh. I can see a
picture of Jane on a blazing May afternoon, barefooted, fair
hair falling over her shoulders, pausing from her task of
scratching in the ground for potatoes, and picking up a long
handled shovel, then waving it angrily at an aircraft overhead because, it was rumoured, it had a device which
detected uranium . . . Jane who came to us when she was just
fifteen, lived in a cottage edging the cliff nearby, and who
hated progress. And I can see Shelagh, a year older than
Jane, wistful, tragic little waif who would suddenly break
the silence as we filled the potato baskets: 'Do you know
there are only one hundred and ninety-nine shopping days
to Christmas?' We would laugh.

Down below us as we laboured were the gulls. Summer
days of blue seas, and fishing boats hurrying to Newlyn. A
buzzard hovering. Swallows skimming the meadows as
they flew in from the south. A fox's silhouette on the mound
of what was the old quarry. There was a primitive and
beautiful wildness about these meadows. What would Jane
have done had she then known that a lighthouse was to be
built adjacent to the great rock of blue elvin, and pylons
carrying electricity lines were to cross the meadows, a
hundred years too late for those who might have needed it?
She would at any rate have understood why the gulls took a
dislike to the white building, and to the electronic note of
the fog signal; and moved to Minack rocks.

We like them there, except we are made to feel as trespassers when we wish to be on the rocks ourselves. We reach
the wicker gate at the top of our cliff and look down at our

7

pocket meadows, then to the granite rocks (we are on the dividing line between granite and blue elvin) . . . and the gulls. Reason, of course, says it does not matter if we walk down the little winding path, past one meadow and another, past the palm tree I planted when my mother died, past the bottom meadow of all, until we reach the point when the gulls have observed us and are stirring, flapping wings in annoyance, a cry from one then from another, until a general commotion disturbs the rocks and the sea, and the gulls fly away squawking with irritation that humans have invaded their privacy. Reason says it is absurd to feel self-conscious because we have interrupted their rumination. We intend no harm. We are not foxes . . . for foxes sometimes slip from the bracken, bramble covered hideouts on the cliff, to slink away at nights to the rocks, the rush of the waves silencing any noise of their approach. The foxes snatch, and take their trophy away, so it is not on the rocks I find the left over feathers, but in some corner of our land.

One day I saw a vixen set out to raid the gulls in mid afternoon, a warm, May afternoon; and I supposed she behaved so recklessly because she was craving food for her cubs. I watched her, through the gaps of an ancient stone wall, advance towards the somnolent gulls, using the path we follow ourselves. She had no cover as soon as she reached the top of the rocks and, although she slid like a huge snake towards them, she didn't fool the gulls for a moment. Up they went into the sky, crying out their fury, and I watched them hovering above her until a half dozen peeled away from the rest and began diving at her while she crouched in bewilderment. After a while they grew tired of this baiting and some of the gulls settled on the sea while others flew off down the coast.

I expected the vixen to give up her adventure and return to the undergrowth, but she was undaunted by the disappearance of her intended victims. A pause, and she was off again and reaching the rocks she began to scour them like a scavenger, pushing her nose into this crevice and that, then finding nothing to satisfy her, she hopped from one rock to another until she arrived at the seaweed covered rocks which are only seen when the tide is low. I had moved

8

from my hiding place to secure a better view, and if she looked up she would have seen me. I watched her leap across a pool, then another pool, then run along the edge of the deep one where we bathe on hot summer days. She halted there for a moment and stared at the still water as if she had been startled by her own reflection ... then on again until she reached a terrace of rocks that rose upwards, fifty feet or so, to the undergrowth. She was up and gone and out of sight within a minute. Nothing to show for her trouble when she returned to her cubs at the earth.

Did this happen three, five, ten summers ago? I do not remember.

Perhaps this summer I will remember ...

TWO

I had seen the first swallows of the year the day the daffodil harvest was over. I was standing late in the afternoon a few yards away from the cottage on what is called the bridge. The spot has no resemblance to a bridge, and it only received its name because, when standing or sitting there, you have a panoramic view before you . . . as if you were on the bridge of a ship. On summer days we spend much idle time on the bridge. We have levelled part of an old stone wall with dark blue slate at table height, and we sit on a bench in front of it. The wall is a wide one, and there is enough room for a narrow strip of earth above the dark blue slate; and this is encased in stone so that we have a flower bed as

10

well on the wall. We grow mignonette there every summer, and on still days and evenings the air is full of its sweet scent.

Behind us, as we gaze at the view, is a field where cows from our neighbour's farm, look inquisitively down at us. On the right is what looks like an old building without a roof, and it is where for many years we stored the coal. It is small in area, and growing out of the base of the stone walls are blackthorn, and in the summer the small green leaves cover the area like an umbrella. We have cleaned it up, and made flower beds where the coal used to lie in a heap, and have lily of the valley in one bed, cyclamen in another, Christmas roses in a third; and every year we sow night scented stock in all three of them. We have painted white wrought iron chairs and a table in the middle, and when it is hot in the summer we sit there in the shade; or when a breeze is blowing which makes the bridge too cool, we sit there because it is sheltered.

On the left is an ancient stone pig trough cornering the wall where we have the blue slate and the bed of mignonette. It is square, and massive and we heaved it there after finding it hidden in the undergrowth. Pigs drank from it in olden days and now we keep it filled with water for the birds; and the gulls who spend their days on the roof use it. Alongside is an escallonia bush which we planted over eight years ago, and after taking a long time to settle, is now growing at a pace. This evergreen with its shiny little leaves which scent, and pink flowers which bloom twice a year, is the home of small birds at night, and Jeannie has given it the fanciful name of Escallonia Towers. Then comes the path of grey chippings which leads downhill past the cottage, window-less this side except for the window of our tiny bedroom, to the space where a caller parks his car. Here is the old barn, clay binding the stones of the wall, where the donkeys shelter in winter and where Lama used to hide in the rafters when she was wild; and opposite is the white seat with the verbena beside it where Jeannie's mother was quietly reading the paper when Fred, then a three-week-old donkey startled her by bashing his head into it. And it was on this white seat that Lama sat for the photograph that Shelagh

11

secretly took to give us a surprise present for Lama's first Christmas.

Away past the barn runs the lane which did not exist when we first came to Minack, through the little stream which is called at this point Monty's Leap after Monty of *A Cat in the Window*, then winding up the hill to the farm buildings of our neighbours at the top, then on to the Penzance road over a mile away. We cannot see the farm buildings from the bridge. We cannot see any building except a farm in the very distance on the other side of Lamorna valley. So when we stand on the bridge we gaze at wild land, except for a field or two; and at the expanse of Mount's Bay, and the sweep of the Lizard.

Between the fields behind us where the cows graze, and the field where the donkeys spend hours of their time staring down at the little garden and the porch, trying to will us to pay them attention, lies a stony stretch of land at the top of which is our well. This well, we were advised by a dowser, would gush water at fifteen feet. This depth was reached by the miners we engaged to dig it; and the soil remained dry as a desert. There was the splendid hole, so splendid that farmers would come from miles around on Sunday afternoons to have a look at it; and all our money was going down it. Twenty feet, twenty-five feet, at last at thirty feet a great shout went up from the bottom of the well: 'Water! Water!' It was still not enough and we had to drill a special hole four feet long before there was any quantity to pump to a storage tank. There is not enough even now in a dry summer. But when the main supply was brought to the farms of our neighbours, we ourselves refused to have it. The well may be inconvenient, but the freshness of the water is incomparable.

On the way up to the well, there is a small wooden gate into the donkey field. From there they can watch us on the bridge, and if they are bored they will paw at the gate, rattling it, so that we have to look. I was looking at them when I saw the swallow skimming the field behind them. And when I shouted out: 'Swallow!' to Jeannie the donkeys thought I was shouting at them, and they began to hee-haw. Fred's hee-haw is a fine trumpeting, but poor Penny

12

groans up and down the scale as if she had never known how to hee-haw properly. There they were then, singing away in their own fashion, as Jeannie came out of the cottage to join me.

The first swallow is one of the original pleasures. Nature triumphing over man is always a pleasant act of reassurance that we have still a long, long way to go before computers rule the universe. Humans may be drilled into uniformity, but no one is going to control a bird who flies thousands of miles to Africa in the autumn, and back again in the spring to the same cave of a house, the same barn. So when I see the first swallow I rejoice because freedom still is with us.

Swallows had never nested at Minack. I supposed that the reason may have been that we were so close to the sea, or because we were almost their first landfall, or they needed to see more of the country before they decided to stop; or it may have been that the buildings just were not suitable. There had been times in other years when, for a day or two, we thought the luck had changed; and we would see a pair flying in and out of the narrow doorway of the barn, and up and around the cottage, and Jeannie would hope her wish would come true. But the swallows always failed her. They were not satisfied with the arrangements at Minack. And on they would fly.

When the swallows arrive, and the whitethroats, and the chiff chaffs and the warblers, and other migratory birds, the holiday season has begun. Robins, wrens, blue tits and coal tits, hedge sparrows and dunnocks and all the other birds who never move a mile or two from their base, find the foreigners pecking about beside them. Favourite perches at night are occupied; and nesting sites. And a branch which a robin thought was his own is now the branch whence a flycatcher from Morocco dashes on his short-lived expeditions. This is the beginning of a period of justifiable upset among the local inhabitants. Cornwall is under occupation in woods, gardens, shore and towns. But the donkeys, within the restriction of their own standards, are at peace. Holidaymakers will be coming to flatter them. Cameras will be pointing at them. Rides will be asked for by shy children. The summer is their time.

We watched the first swallow soar and swoop over the wood for a minute or two, then on it flew towards Lamorna valley. Others would be following but the first, it is always the first, that one remembers. It meant the prospect of summer, and the coming of unexpected adventures, and the gentle illusion that we were as young as we always had been. We stood silently on the bridge. This was one of its pleasures that we could sit or stand there, gazing our lives away. There were so many small incidents taking place that were of great importance to ourselves, but would not appear important to those who have to drive themselves to pursue conventional values. Why waste time observing a fox, the same fox you saw yesterday and the day before, nosing about looking for mice? Why be surprised again at the way the rabbits sit on their hind legs like a dog doing a begging trick, watching the fox at a distance? Why not bolt for a hole? Why does the fox if he is looking for food pass them by, except for token attacks? What was that wild cry? A water rail? There is a green woodpecker rapping at the trunk of an elm in the wood. Which one? And are the blue tits nesting in the box we nailed to the tree by the camellia? The willow tree is greening. I'm glad the flowers of the cherry tree have not been spoilt by a gale this year. The Scillonian is late, isn't she? She's coming round the point now. The Stephensons' fishing fleet went out this morning so the weather will be staying fine. What glorious colours the French paint their crabbers . . . look at the brilliant green of that one. I saw her last week in Newlyn harbour. Someone is coming down the lane. No, false alarm. Get the glasses, quick, there's something moving in the corner of Bill's field . . . oh, it's only his dachshund. Bill was one of the farmers at the top of the hill.

When we stood on the bridge we did not see the path because of the escallonia. We could see Boris or Lama begin to walk up the path, then they disappeared behind the escallonia, and we heard them instead. Lama was a little cat but the noise of her paws on the grey chippings as she came towards us was loud enough for Jeannie to joke sometimes: 'An elephant is coming.' And the elephant would appear beside us, collapsing on the grey chippings, turning on her back, inviting us to bend down and stroke a greeting. Boris never came to the bridge. We would listen to his plod, plod, plod on the chippings, then he would turn right instead of left and would waddle his way to the door of the porch where he would wait for one of us to attend to him.

We used to ask people who we thought might be knowledgeable if they had any idea how long muscovy drakes lived; and some would answer they didn't know because the only muscovy drakes they had possessed went sooner than later into the pot; and others gave us the answer we wanted to hear, that muscovy drakes were long living birds. 'I remember one, when I was a boy,' said a bird fancier whose views were particularly welcome, 'which flew over our farmhouse when he was sixteen.'

Jane had brought Boris to us eight years before, and we didn't know how old he was then. She appeared one morning with Boris in her arms, having carried him across the fields from the cottage in which she lived overlooking the cliffs a half mile away. A young farmer had given him to her in a mistaken gesture of courtship. He had arrived at her door with a sack, and explained he had brought her a good dinner. Thereupon Jane opened the sack, saw the muscovy drake inside, and burst into tears. She kept Boris for a couple of days in her bedroom until her mother decided it was not a suitable place; and so she brought him to Minack. I remember I did not want him. I did not want the responsibility of looking after such a bird. I was devoting all my attention at the time to maintaining the existence of the flower farm, and I did not want my interest diverted by the problems which might come with a muscovy drake. Might he not fly round the district, resulting in hours of wasted time searching for him? And would he be content to remain a bachelor? I raised these points and nobody listened. Jane, Shelagh and Jeannie just went on with their work, quite aware that I would soon surrender, just as I had surrendered a few months before when Lama had first come on the scene.

He was christened Boris after Boris Pasternak. There was a boy that summer staying nearby on holiday called Julius, and he would come over every day and spend it with us and Jane and Shelagh. Sometimes he would arrive before breakfast as we were cutting the lettuces for the Penzance market; and he would arrive full of the pleasure he had had from his walk along the cliff and across the fields where he was staying. He was sensitive and erudite for his age, and he was an admirer of both Dr Zhivago and Boris Pasternak's poetry. He it was who decided that Boris should be called Boris; and he it was who dug the hole where we placed an old galvanised bath. I remember filling it with water, then hopefully waiting for Boris to take his first swim, waiting discreetly at a distance along with Julius; and then the shout of Julius: 'He's in it!' Boris, as happens with such birds and animals, was not just loved by us for himself. He was a link with a past which we often like to remember. A year after that first bathe in the galvanised bath Julius was killed in a motor accident; and a year later Shelagh died.

Boris had become slower in his movements, and that was the reason why we had begun to worry a little about him. He no longer perched on the wooden bar, a couple of feet from the floor, in the chicken house at night. The effort of reaching it seemed too much for him, and so he squatted in a corner instead; and during the day he squatted more than he used to do in the various places of his territory he occupied. There was a lichen covered rock he passed to and from the chicken house which was a favourite place of his; and we could see this rock from the bridge. We had now built a small cement based pool for him in front of the shed where Geoffrey sits at lunchtimes; and after his bathe, after flapping his wings in the pool so that the water was in turmoil, he would plod to the rock and dry himself. He would flap his white wings again, and there was a sound in the air as if a carpet was being beaten; and then for a while he would stand on the rock with his wings a little apart from his body so that the breeze could dry his feathers. When he believed himself dry, he would waggle his beautiful green black tail feathers, tuck his head and yellow beak inside a wing, and go to sleep. And if he wasn't on the rock he might be by the old stone wall which faces the sun and which was also a favourite dozing place of Lama's And the two of them would be there, side by side. There were other

16

places he would like to go, and they were all close to the cottage. So we were startled when, one afternoon that April, we found he was in none of them.

'Perhaps he has gone to bed early,' I said. And I went down to the chicken house and found it empty. At that moment I began to feel afraid.

When Boris first came to us, indeed for years afterwards, we were blind to the possibility of foxes attacking him. We, of course, locked him up at night, but during the day, despite the fact we would often watch a fox roaming the field on the other side of the shallow valley, we never considered he was in danger. Then a neighbour said he was astonished at our foolishness. 'Do you mean you let him wander about when you are out?' he asked in amazement. And from then on we were always on guard.

But on this particular April day we had left him on his own. We had taken the car to Sennen and walked along the beach, and when we returned, Geoffrey had already gone home. Lama was waiting for us by the door and we let her in, and Jeannie filled her plate with a spoonful of fish. The donkeys were peering down at us from the field, and so I took a couple of chocolate biscuits to them, and stayed a minute or two beside them as they munched. Then I went down below the cottage and found Boris missing.

We both panicked. We rushed hither and thither calling for him at the top of our voices, hysterical behaviour which was to be funny in retrospect. After ten minutes we were no longer looking for a live Boris, and were searching instead for a trace of his feathers. I ran through the wood with my eyes on the ground, then back across the donkey field, past the cottage and down the lane. I felt enraged with myself for being so careless, and sickened at the thought that Boris should end his days as a meal for cubs.

And then suddenly I saw him.

I had dashed into the field where we have our mobile greenhouses, still scanning the ground for feathers, when I became aware of a white blob at the far end. I went racing across the field shouting: 'Boris! Boris! What the hell have you been up to?' He had never strayed so far in his life, and when I reached him he was quite unperturbed, and he

17

looked at me as if he was asking what all the fuss was about. Perhaps he was thinking he had played a funny joke on us. Perhaps it was his way of telling us that it was foolish to worry about his well-being. He would still, at the age of sixteen, fly over Minack.

Nor was Lama a wanderer. Indeed I have never seen her except on Minack land though once, when she was a wild kitten, she was seen by a neighbour in the old quarry which bordered the land we once rented. This was less than a year after Monty had died, the cat who had come with us from London; and on the day he died I had sworn that I would never have another cat unless a black cat whose home was unknown came to our door in a storm. I said this to Jeannie because I had been an anti-cat man before Monty had come into my life; and though he himself had won my heart, I did not believe that any other cat would win me again. But I had always been superstitious about black cats. And so some spirit within me moved me to make this stipulation which I naturally never expected to be fulfilled.

Lama, after roaming our meadows for a month beforehand, did in fact come miaowing to the door in a storm. And there was nobody in the area who had lost her. And she *was* quite black except for a wisp of white on her shirt front.

So where had she come from? Jeannie's firm opinion is that she was born in a little cave down the cliff. The clues are these.

For a time before Lama was first seen in our meadows, we had observed a small grey Persian cat passing occasionally within sight of the cottage. There was no question of it ever wishing to be friendly, and it ran away if we ever came too near. And after Lama at last chose to come in from the wild, and become a normal, home-loving cat, we continued to see the grey Persian at intervals in the distance.

We did not for a moment associate her with Lama, and we would never have done so had we not had the strange experience of finding another black kitten, the replica of Lama, six years after Lama had come to us.

This second black kitten was discovered by Jeannie curled up asleep in a little cave down the cliff. For a few

18

days afterwards, Geoffrey and I and another man who was helping us to plant bulbs would catch a glimpse of it in the undergrowth, darting about like a wild rabbit. We had already noticed that the grey Persian was regularly in our neighbourhood, and now we observed it repeatedly coming up and down the cliff when it thought we were not watching.

Then one evening as dusk was falling we found the grey Persian crouched on the branch of an elm near the cottage ... and a couple of feet away on the same branch was Lama. We had never, of course, seen them together before, and we could not help but notice that they were the same shape and size. And what was so puzzling was the way they were treating each other. They appeared to be so deep in conversation that they were unaware that we were watching them. Guess as you please what subject they were communing about. All I can tell you is that the next morning I found the black kitten curled up on a sack in the barn.

During its stay we used to watch it through a window on the lane side of the barn. Shy as ever, it spent most of its time hidden from sight amongst the paraphernalia of fertiliser bags and various implements; and only when Jeannie had placed a saucer of bread and milk on the cobbled stone floor were we able to see it. Then it would creep from its hide-out, crouch by the saucer and nervously lap. There was no doubt about its similarity to Lama. Indeed it was the exact double of Lama when she was a wild black kitten.

It was now that Jeannie christened the grey Persian Daisy. Jeannie was convinced that the grey Persian was the mother of the black kitten as well as the mother of Lama, and so she merited a name. Why Daisy I don't know. I think Jeannie thought the name gave an idea of what the grey Persian, and her brood, looked like. But once the kitten had disappeared we did not see Daisy again for several months.

Such an absence had happened before. It still does. So many weeks go by without us seeing her that we come to the conclusion she must be dead ... and then she reappears. One of us may suddenly find her down the cliff, or Geoffrey will call to us that he has just seen her in the donkey field, or we will be on the bridge and catch sight of her slowly following the route she has always followed when she passes through Minack. She comes through the greenhouse field, over the hedge and into the lane, down the lane towards the cottage and across Monty's Leap by a wooden plank, then she turns left over the bank into the stable field where the Cromwell daffodils have been left undisturbed for thirty years and more, across this field to a foot wide track which badgers have padded for centuries, then on to the top of the cemetery field where she either takes the path to the cliff, or goes right towards what we call the onion meadow, past the meadow where I first saw Lama, staring at me, assessing me, from beds of calendula. Her return journey does not always follow the same route. She chooses instead, to be surprised by Jeannie passing the washing line. The line is beside the well above the cottage. Wherever she is, she will never permit us to come too close.

You have a good view of the stable field from the bridge. I was standing there one afternoon when I saw Daisy again after an interval of two or three months. She was following the route I have described, exactly the same route that she was following before Lama came into our lives. But instead of being excited at seeing her again after such an interval, I was annoyed that she was there at all. She was distracting me. My purpose of standing on the bridge was to watch a pair of swallows whose behaviour promised that at last Jeannie and I would have the pleasure of saying that swallows nested at Minack. They had been flying in and out of the barn for the previous few days and now, at the very moment I should have been exclaiming to Jeannie that I had seen Daisy again, I had observed the swallows swoop down to Monty's Leap, settle for a few seconds beside the stream, then dip their beaks in the shallow mud bordering it . . . and a moment later fly back to the barn, diving at speed through the narrow doorway. A minute passed, and out they came again, down to the stream, beaks into the mud, then in a flash into the barn.

No wonder I wasn't interested in Daisy.

For the first time since we came here, swallows had chosen to spend the summer at Minack.

THREE

There was another cottage in our lives before Minack. We found it one summer day when we were taking the Poljigga road towards Land's End, the road which runs out of Penzance by the promenade, across Newlyn Bridge, then up steep Paul Hill, winding its way a couple of miles distant from the coast, past the curiously named village of Sheffield and up Boleigh Hill past Lamorna turn on the left, and on past Boskenna then Treverven Farm and Sparnon, down and up the beautiful valley of Penberth, past Treen, then Poljigga and a mile or two later joining the A30 for the last stretch to Land's End.

We were on holiday; Jeannie from her job as Press

Officer of the Savoy, Claridges and Berkeley; and myself from my job as a member of MI5.

We had no purpose in mind except to roam the countryside, pausing now and again, discovering a part of Cornwall that neither of us knew. In a way I am wrong to say that I did not know it. When I was a small boy spending holidays at my home of Glendorgal near Newquay, I always felt a mystical attraction for these far west lands of Cornwall; and presumably this attraction was developed by fleeting expeditions, picnics with aunts and uncles crammed in some ancient car, great voyages across the wastes of Camborne and Redruth, to St Ives and Zennor and Land's End. I do not remember any details, just a vague sense of adventure, though there is one such adventure I remember clearly.

My father's old friend was the Chief Constable of Cornwall at the time when my brothers and I were children; and every year he gave us a treat which lifted us into a sphere of great importance. He was a precise man, a bachelor, and he fought at Omdurman with Churchill; and as a child I never tired of his telling the story of that battle over and over again. He was a fascinating story teller, quiet voice, quiet humour; and as Chief Constable he was looked upon as a father figure by his men. He knew each member of his force individually, took a personal interest in their families. From the moment I first remember him, he suffered from imaginary ill health; he died peacefully when he was eighty-six.

His official car was a Sunbeam, an open tourer, and he would arrive in it, driven by a chauffeur in police uniform punctually at eleven o'clock on the chosen morning. Our host would sit in the front, and my two brothers and myself in the back with our feet making room for the inviting looking hamper on the floor. The hamper, of course, gave us a pleasant sense of anticipation, so too did the moment when the luxurious vehicle glided away up Glendorgal drive, my mother and father waving us goodbye, and set off for Land's End. But the real excitement, stimulated by our childish vanity, was the knowledge that our host had organised a surprise which was not in fact a surprise. The Chief Constable, we secretly knew, had arranged that every

22

village constable on the route, every inspector, sergeant and constable that could be spared in the towns of Redruth, Camborne and Hayle and Penzance, were waiting for us at strategic points; and as the Sunbeam hove into sight they jumped smartly to attention and saluted as we passed. We took their salutes as if they were our due.

I loved my home of Glendorgal. There was an occasion when I was at Harrow that I startled my fellow Harrovians by preferring to go there instead of attending the then great social occasion of the Eton and Harrow match at Lord's. The night train to Cornwall, just two days there then the night train back? Quite mad. Missing two days of strutting round Lord's in the finery of morning coat and elegant trousers and double-breasted grey waistcoat, cornflower in buttonhole? Extraordinary.

But Glendorgal was the most beautiful place in the world for me. This low, granite house with fat granite chimneys, now made famous as a hotel by my brother Nigel, lay snug beside its own private cove with views of rugged loveliness up the coast to Trevose Head in the far distance. The grounds were of wild Cornish moorland dropping cliffs into the sea, and here I used to hunt rabbits and to play with Bruce, a white, long-coated mongrel, and Lance my old English sheepdog, and Roy his successor. Here, too, aged six, I once started to dig to Australia because I had been told that the continent lay at the other side of the earth. My father had a fierce passion for Glendorgal. I have seen him by the hour standing by the sundial which is still there, gazing at the sea and the island opposite, and wandering around the grounds puffing his pipe; and when he went away on some business he would return in two days when others might have been away for three; and when we three boys began to bring girls to stay at Glendorgal we used to warn them that if they were to be liked by my father they must tell him how beautiful they thought it was. If they didn't feel as he did, we would have been aware that they had not been accepted. Such a situation never arose. It seemed impossible for anyone to be cool about the rugged loveliness of Glendorgal.

Jeannie never stayed there. When she came into my life,

my father had been forced financially to rent Glendorgal, and he and my mother were living in a cottage called Cavern Cottage on the other side of the bay from where my father used to look endlessly at our old home through a telescope. 'Every inch, every pebble, every blade of grass,' I heard him once say to himself as he stared through his telescope, 'I know intimately . . . and a damned stranger has to live there.' He was then a Deputy Lieutenant of Cornwall, Chairman of the Quarter Sessions, and Commandant of the Special Constabulary. It was war time, and he was also organising on behalf of Stuart Menzies, late head of MI6, a network of agents, wireless experts and couriers in Cornwall, who were to go into operation should the Germans invade and occupy the southwest. My father was, in fact, an unpaid public servant.

He had already sold the island opposite Glendorgal; and his way of doing so made certain that this island belonged to those who loved taste, rather than convenience, for all time to come. Newquay council had begun to negotiate for the island, connected to the mainland by a fifty-foot footbridge, before the time of compulsory purchase, before the National Trust had become the vogue. My father needed money, not for any extravagances on his part, but because he wanted to maintain Glendorgal, and my mother, and perhaps give some future to his sons. The council offered a good price, for they foresaw that this area of the Newquay environment had a huge holiday future, and my father was about to accept. Then suddenly, as he sat at his big Victorian desk which my brother Nigel still uses, he realised what would happen. He knew that Cornish councils tended to build public lavatories on beautiful sites; small ugly buildings, breeze block and cemented, which gave councillors a great sense of pride. He suddenly imagined such a building perched on the island where mounds of ancient burial grounds had hitherto reigned supreme. He thereupon demanded that in any conditions of sale no public lavatory should be built on the island; and the council agreed and took a thousand pounds off the price, and the skyline was preserved for ever. If you ever go to this island, you will find a granite seat with my father's name on it, and which my mother put there in his memory. It faces Glendorgal.

Jeannie, therefore, was never part of my home when we lived there, but she had a bond with my father, and when we became engaged my father gave us dinner the same evening at a restaurant called the Good Intent in the Kings Road in Chelsea. We sat at a corner table and he drank our toast and wished us well; and within a year he had died. But at this dinner he was telling Jeannie that there was only one other home in Cornwall which he considered compared to Glendorgal; and this was Boskenna. The Boskenna which was on the Poljigga road to Land's End. There we were a few years later driving past it.

I had no intention of stopping, indeed, I was not even sure that it was the place concerned. Cornwall is full of huge estates with myseterious drives to great houses you cannot see from the road; and there was no sign to show that this was Boskenna. Two huge stone pillars acted as sentries to the drive, and there were the usual woods, and the usual question mark as to where lay the house. We went on, the woods sprawling the landscape towards the sea, following the road which dipped into a valley then up again past a farmhouse with a thatched roof.

Jeannie said suddenly: 'I'm quite sure your father is telling us to stop. I mean it ... that *was* Boskenna we passed, and we *must* turn back.'

I respect Jeannie's intuition. Indeed we both find it wiser for us to follow our intuition than it is for us to follow reason. Reason, with all its pros and cons, its good sense and caution, makes us woolly minded and negative. Intuition, on the other hand, has led us again and again to behave irrationally, providing us with the chance to achieve the impossible. Jeannie's intuition at that moment, for instance, changed the course of our lives.

I turned back; and intuition guided us again. We might normally have made a call at Boskenna, if it was Boskenna. My father had been a friend of the owner, and my mother used to recount that at dinner parties he would flirt with her. His name was Colonel Paynter, a relic of this country's feudal past, a landowner who had a paternal interest in

25

those who worked for him, believing that their welfare was his duty, and not that of the Government. His attitude seemed praiseworthy at the time, and so it was within its narrow sphere. He benevolently ruled the district, giving a sense of permanent security to all his subjects. His word was law, his favours came from heaven. The first time we met him, he took us to a meadow where men and women were lifting new potatoes. It was a hot June afternoon; and the Colonel, small and bent, leaning on a walking stick and incongruously wearing a bowler hat, his pockets bulging with apples, shuffled round to each person, handing out an apple as if it was a golden coin. It was received as such.

But that day I turned back we did not call at Boskenna. I stopped the car instead by a gate in the valley below the farmhouse with the thatched roof. The gate is still there, on the coast side of the road, and it is painted white now. The path we then followed was only a foot wide, and it ran through the woods beside the stream until it passed two cottages, then it dipped towards the stream which was crossed by stepping stones on up the other side until it faded away from the woods into a small field which edged the sea. I remember we hastened along this path as if we had an urgent mission to perform, an appointment to keep; and as we reached the small field, marvelling at the gentle swell of the sea which was sparkling a bay guarded by boulders, not by cliffs, we suddenly saw St en Dellon.

It was an old cottage in so isolated a position, in a setting seemingly so perfect, that it is understandable that we both jumped to the conclusion that it was our dream cottage. How could we know at that moment that it was an illusion, that we were in fact seeing Minack?

For until we saw St en Dellon we had never considered the prospect of having a cottage in Cornwall. We had never thought of leaving London and uprooting ourselves from the life we were leading. But the sight of St en Dellon on that summer's day brought another dimension into our lives, and we knew we could never be the same again.

We had no chance of acquiring St en Dellon from the beginning, but this did not stop us from imagining that we could do so. And we took courage from the attitude of the old couple who lived there. They told us that they did not like the cottage because it was so lonely, and that they would prefer to live in the village. This sounded most promising. We visited them a second time and the old man, thick white hair and a face like Popeye the Sailor, told us that the sooner he could leave the better. We listened attentively, made sympathetic noises, and believed every word he said. There was a small boy, some relation, living at the cottage too, dark and sturdy like the true Cornishman, and he used to stare at us silently as we talked. On our third visit I thought I caught sight of him disappearing up a path as we approached the cottage. We had another pleasant conversation with the old couple, and as by this time we had met the Colonel (he owned St en Dellon), I explained that I was trying to persuade him to offer them one of the estate cottages in the village. They nodded politely but their manner on this occasion gave me the uncomfortable feeling that all the time they had been humouring us . . . the old Cornish way of agreeing with all that an up country visitor has to say and only telling him what he wishes to hear. There was still no sign of the boy when we said good-bye, and set off back to the car. There it was as I left it by the gate . . . except for the tyres. They were flat. The valves of all four had been loosened.

We were undaunted. Nor were we put off by the lack of decisiveness on the part of the Colonel. He appeared to be helping us yet there was no positive sign that he was actually doing so. He was intrigued, however, by Jeannie and the setting in which she lived and worked; and this we thought might be in our favour. This was the world in which he used to move many, many years before; and he used to question her about people long since dead. He asked for the gossip about them. He seemed not to realise that he had been left behind. And after our holiday and we were back in London, he would still write and ask for news. Like the old couple at St en Dellon, he was humouring us along. Like them, he had no intention of furthering our ambitions. Might we not be as lightweight as others from a city who came to Cornwall gushing their wish to be away from it all?

He had seen them many times before. All froth and excitement as they upset some standing situation. Then grumbles and disenchantment, and away . . . leaving another failure for the local people to remember.

The following May we returned to continue our campaign, and we stayed at Lamorna, three miles down the coast. We did not know that we were close to Minack. We did not know as we set out that first morning of our holiday to walk along the cliffs to St en Dellon that we were indeed about to see the cottage of our dreams.

We had reached a high point of the cliffs, and had sat down on a rock, the sea surging far below us, the sweep of the Lizard peninsula to our left, the rugged coast running away towards Porthcurno and Gwennap Head on our right, the land behind us a jungle of yellow gorse and young green bracken and savage brambles; and while we sat there, the soft sea air on our faces, we saw a buzzard gliding high in the sky above us. It began to drift inland, and as we watched its motionless wings, marvelling at the way they effortlessly made use of the eddies in the atmosphere, we suddenly saw below it in the distance, a small grey cottage on the edge of a wood. It was as grey as the boulders heaped haphazardly in the land around it, as grey as the ancient stone hedges which guarded long forgotten meadows. This was Minack. We knew at the instant of seeing it that it was to become our home.

We now no longer courted the Colonel. A prominent farmer in the district took his place, and months of more frustrating negotiations then followed. It was more than a year later that we saw the Colonel for the last time. We were outside the Lamorna telephone box and we had at last been told that we could rent the cottage of Minack and the land around it. He peered through the window of his old car, bowler hat perched on his head, and looked quizzically at Jeannie for a moment. Then he enquired:

'And is the casket worthy of the jewel?'

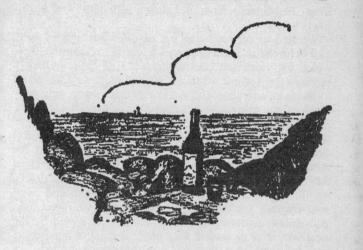

FOUR

Minack had no water or electricity when we first came to live here. The land was a wilderness, there was no lane for cars, the living room had earth for its floor. Neighbours were sure we would be back in London within six months. Jeannie, they said, could not possibly stick it. She might tolerate the summer but the winter never. Yet she was not to mind cooking meals on a primus stove, or lighting paraffin lamps with a wick soaked in methylated spirits. Primitive living, as others find, is the perfect antidote to over sophistication. There was space in the sky, and time was ours, and the air we breathed came to us from far away across the sea, and we listened to birds singing which we

29

hadn't noticed before, and we were able to watch them without having to hurry forward to heaven knows where. There were no conventions to obey, and all we wanted was to live the same kind of life as the crofters who once lived at Minack. Such a halcyon situation was hardly likely to last.

We had to earn a living out of the wilderness of land, and before this could happen we had to reclaim meadows which for years had been neglected. And then we had to begin to pay for our mistakes. We had only our enthusiasm to teach us and time and again this enthusiasm went very much astray. Nor could these mistakes be quickly corrected. A crop had to fail several times, due to the permutation of causes for its failure, before we could finally decide to discard it. Thus we grew massive amounts of potatoes for several seasons in succession before we were convinced they were uneconomical. This happened also with violets, wallflowers, calendulas, forget-me-nots, stocks and even with freesias; for there came a time when we invested in greenhouses and we were sure that freesias would be the ideal winter crop, and it was, until so many other people had the same idea that the market became glutted. We have reached the stage now when we only grow tomatoes and daffodils; and the daffodils in the spring of this year I am writing about gave us the best harvest we had ever known since we came to Minack.

So on the sunny April morning after we had loaded the last of the daffodils into the flower train at Penzance station, we celebrated by taking the winding path down the cliff to the rocks and the sea below. We had brought in a basket beef sandwiches of home-made bread, a couple of wine glasses, a corkscrew, and a bottle of *Côtes du Rhône*. It was one of those pleasant moments when one could look back on past efforts with calm detachment. The daffodil harvest is the foundation upon which we can plan the year; and now we could foresee a summer without financial concern.

Daffodil seasons are seldom orderly. The aim of a daffodil grower is to spread the harvest over several weeks, and so he stocks his flower farm with bulb varieties that follow each other in sequence.

In our case we begin with the deep yellow trumpet called Magnificence which professionals call Mags, and follow on with another golden yellow called Golden Harvest. Then comes a miniature King Alfred with the ugly name of Oblivaris but exquisite to look at and wonderfully long-lasting once picked; then a lovely large yellow trumpet called Joseph McLeod; then a variety with two names, California or Pentewan, a bright yellow cupped narcissi with a sweet scent and which thrives on our land; then a few Rembrandt, and a charming daffodil with the atrocious name of Sulphur which we now call Lamorna because it fetches a better price by so doing; and then the whites . . . Early Bride, Brunswick, Barrett Browning (a beautiful creamy-white perianth with a brilliant red cup), White Lion and Actaea. Actaea is a prolific cropper with a large pure white perianth, a brilliant scarlet eye and an exquisite scent; and when the last box of these has been sent away to Covent Garden, our harvest is over.

This may appear to be a simple sequence of events, a kind of factory conveyor belt which needs only the efficiency of man to turn out the goods required. Factories, however, can slow down output when the shelves are full, or increase it when they are emptying, whereas daffodil growers are at the mercy of the weather. Too warm a spring and all the varieties come rushing in together; too cold a one and they are held back, thus producing a glut as soon as the weather changes.

Such an untidy situation has attracted the attention of the planners who sit in their Whitehall offices, anxious to help the men of the soil; and I once attended a conference where a gentleman from Whitehall explained what should be done about the matter. Among his audience were some of the largest growers of daffodils in both Cornwall and the Isles of Scilly, and they were at the time being confronted (it was one of the warm springs) with acres of daffodils without the time and labour to pick them. The neatly dressed fellow talked to us as if God had no hand in the affair. 'You should have planned your varieties more carefully,' said he. 'You should hold the blooms back so that they do not flood the market . . . you should co-operate.' And so on. There we were puffing at our pipes, gaping at the fellow, while the sun was blazing and the nights were as warm as those of mid summer.

Yet there were some growers, in the Lincolnshire bulb area for instance, who listened to such advice, and they began holding back their surplus blooms in the refrigeration plants (pre-cooled bulbs produce, of course, earlier blooms). Then when they thought the market was more favourable, they took them out of the refrigerators and despatched them. Unfortunately they had not foreseen the effect of the refrigeration on the daffodils. The florists soon told them. 'Your daffodils melt,' came the cry, 'as soon as we unpack them.' One, therefore, prays for a spring when the weather is persistently cool, a steady even temperature which neither forces a variety or holds it back so that it clashes with another; and this is what happened this time.

It was one of those years, too, when every bulb seemed to produce a flower, and that is by no means a usual experience. Many a time I have walked the daffodil meadows a week or two before the season would normally begin and observed with dismay that few buds were showing, that the bulbs had only thrown up foliage. Some varieties are more temperamental than others, and one of these is the golden trumpet Magnificence. More often than not we have dolefully said to each other: 'The Mags are going to be light this year.' There they would be in lush rows of green foliage, and hardly a flower to be seen. I had bought them in the first place as the result of listening to the advice of an old man in the pub at Treen not far away. He told me, as he downed his pints, such heart warming stories of the money he had made from his Magnificence that Jeannie and I forthwith decided to follow suit. It was one of our failings, when we first came to Minack, that we listened too readily to those who set out to please us. We wanted to be assured that prosperity lay ahead of us, and so wise old men were good-natured enough to tell us what we wanted to believe.

Yet I have to admit that much of the failure to produce bulbs that flower regularly was due to our method of cultivation. We have to be old-fashioned in our methods because the contours of the land prevent us from being otherwise. The stretch of coast between Penzance and Gwennap Head used to provide those first early daffodils from the mainland which set the heart and the soul alight when you suddenly saw them for sale in mid January. Those were the true daffodils, and still are when you find them in the shops. They are grown in small pocket meadows, high hedges attempting to protect them from the salt of the gales, and the warm climate hastening their blooming. They demanded, however, much attention. Every stage of cultivation, for instance, was done by hand. When in the summer the daffodil foliage had died down, the bulbs every three years were hacked, though with great care, out of the ground and laid in rows to dry; and later they were picked up, put into bags and taken to the steam sterilisation plant for a three hour sterilising period . . . sterilisation of bulb fly and eel worm which are the scourge of daffodils. And when that was done, the bulbs were not returned to the same meadows. Early potatoes would in due course fill their meadows, while the bulbs filled the potato meadows. And all the work was done by hand.

But the price obtained for these very early daffodils – perhaps three or four shillings a bunch less commission and cost of freight – made the work worth while; and a daffodil grower was indeed foolish if he didn't look after his bulbs. Unfortunately for us cliff growers, stories of the prices we obtained tempted others to discover methods that enabled them to compete with us. The method of pre-cooled bulbs grown in greenhouses, resulted in the market being swamped by factory grown daffodils, weeks, even months before the true, naturally grown daffodil of the cliffs was ready to be picked. And inevitably the price dropped so that today we have to be satisfied when we receive a shilling a bunch.

This competition, and the regular increase in expenses, make it economically impossible to look after the cliff bulbs. The big growers, on the other hand, can use sophisticated machines in their large fields, machines which can lift two acres of bulbs a day; machines which sort out the sizes of bulbs, machines which can replant the bulbs at great speed;

all the paraphernalia, in fact, that comes with big business in any sphere. Such treatment guarantees that most of their bulbs will flower every year.

We, on the other hand, have to leave our cliff bulbs virtually untouched, just a very few being lifted in a year; and thus some of them have been lying in the ground undisturbed for ten years and more. Indeed, according to the experts, it is a miracle that the bulbs are still there at all. Disease, bulb fly and eel worm, should have decimated them. But many still thrive, the foliage in any case. And this year, the year of our success, they all flowered. No one could explain what had provoked them to do this.

The Mags, even the Mags were in profusion. The Oblivaris or Obs as we call them, which had lain in meadows long before we took them over, which had never before shown a bud, these too came bursting into flower. And there were blooms in all the hedges, and they came from bulbs which had been tossed there during the war when bulb ground had been required for potatoes, and the order had been made that the bulbs should be thrown away. There they were, Scilly Whites, Obs, Buxton and other old varieties which I did not recognise. Over twenty years later and they were still ready to bloom.

Apart from this bonanza of flowers, apart from the amiable weather, there were other reasons for the best season ever. Up to recently the market, and the public, wanted to buy daffodils only when they were in full bloom. We had to gear all our sendings to suit these requirements, providing ourselves with a vast amount of extra work, and doing harm to the daffodils in the process. We had to have a heat room, for instance, separate from the shed where we bunched because, with daffodils being picked in great numbers there could not possibly be enough room in the shed to allow them to come out naturally. Nor could they be left in the meadows because of the threat of wind damage. Hence the method had to be used by growers of forcing them into full bloom by putting them overnight in a room so heated by paraffin stoves that the water in the galvanised pails next morning was warm.

But all this belongs to the past; and we have largely to

thank the Dutch for the change. The Dutch are not interested in marketing daffodils in this country, but they are interested in exporting ever increasing quantities of bulbs. Thus the leaders of their bulb industry came to the conclusion that they themselves were being harmed by our traditional methods of marketing daffodils; and that sooner or later the public would turn against buying daffodils which in turn would affect the sale of their bulbs. Thereupon they decided to launch an advertising campaign in this country to persuade the public to buy daffodils in bud.

The success of the campaign has not only meant you can buy a bunch of daffodils which will last twice as long in your home. It has also produced splendid benefits to growers like ourselves. Our work is done more quickly. Picking, for instance, is easier. We don't have to worry so much about gales because the daffodil is now picked as soon as the head has dropped, the calex is broken and the yellow of the bud is showing. Nor is there the tedious task of filling the heat room with galvanised pails, then transferring them laboriously to the packing shed in the morning. Bunching is quicker as well. Since, in the old days, every bloom of a bunch had to be wide open, it often meant searching the pails for them, temporarily discarding the flowers which were not fully open. Packing, too, is easier, and more economical. We used to pack fifteen bunches in a box; now, because buds don't take up so much room, we can pack thirty bunches in the same size of box; and so money is saved on boxes and money is saved on freight.

But there still remains the problem of warm weather. At the beginning of the season, in January and February, picking in bud can be kept under control. In March, however, when it is warm and the bulk of the crop is maturing, control is impossible, and the meadows become a mass of open daffodils. At least they have not been forced in a heat room.

Therefore, remember this about early daffodils. The old-fashioned, Cornish grown, unforced early daffodil will never appear in the shops until the middle of January . . . except the heavenly scented narcissus Sol d'Or which comes from November onwards from the Isles of Scilly. Most of those others you see are artificially grown in vast hangars of greenhouses. Would Wordsworth have written a poem about such daffodils?

So there we were, Jeannie and I, the daffodil season behind us, on our way down the path to Minack rocks. The gulls rose in usual annoyance into the sky, wheeling and crying, leaving a cormorant silhouetted for a moment on the pointed rock where sometimes I fish for pollack; and then it too flapped its wings, and flew away low over the sea towards Lamorna Cove. We reached the flat rock where we had decided to picnic, and the sun warmed us as I brought out the bottle of wine from the basket, and Jeannie unwrapped the sandwiches.

'Do you realise,' she said, as I was opening the bottle, that this is the first summer since we came here that we have a chance of living in the present?'

I am one of those, as it happens, who find it difficult to live in the present. I am inclined to worry about some incident in the immediate past or to anticipate some gloomy situation which I imagine may materialise in the future.

'Sounds pleasant,' I said, my mind upon the two glasses balanced unevenly on a ledge of rock and the wine I was tipping into them.

It is not an easy age for peace of mind. The dull and unimaginative can achieve a version of it, as too those young enough who still believe that youth is everlasting, so too can those who are ruthlessly ambitious, so too the men and women who are so busy organising other people's lives that they forget to organise their own. All these have peace of mind of a kind. They do not suffer the pain of self questioning and remorse. They are certain that their standards are the right standards. They are normal.

But the rest of us, those of us who have to endure the doubts and personal complexities imposed by our imaginations, are labelled maladjusted and insecure, inferior beings in fact. It is curious how the phrase that he or she is 'insecure' has become a phrase that means a bad mark. As for myself I do not understand how any human being can feel

36

secure in the modern sense of the word unless he is unbearably conceited. Philosophy, after all, is based on the premise that those who are trying to find the truth about themselves, have a sense of insecurity. Aristotle, Tagore, de Keyserling, any philosopher throughout the ages indeed, would have had no place in history if present values existed in their time. Contemplation was the motive power of their faith, periods of loneliness developed the truth of their wisdom. I wonder in what category an appointments bureau would place them if they were living today. Is there any doubt that they would be considered maladjusted and insecure?

One therefore has to try and find out about oneself against the wishes of convention. Convention needs to pump knowledge into you, not wisdom. Convention, in order to preserve what it represents, must act in the manner of a dictatorship, forcing each person to follow patterns of behaviour which, however distasteful to him, however ugly, results in the end with the declaration: 'I've got used to it.' The most repeated, the most despairing phrase of this period of the twentieth century.

When I was a schoolboy, at other times of my life too, I have sometimes felt the need to be accepted in some conventional circle whose members seemed to accept each other for granted. But such acceptance can never take place. I have felt all my life that members of a group, however worthy their intentions, are running away from themselves. I believe one has to learn to face oneself alone, to try to come to terms with all the opposites inside oneself. Groups, it seems to me, exist to blur their members from the truth, becoming mutual admiration societies except when jealousy begins to irritate. Groups, in my mind, have always mirrored escapism, not the individual who travels alone.

When Jeannie said that this was the first summer since we came to Minack that we could live in the present, my instinct was to reject her belief. I could not see myself being separated from the personal conflict which is part of me. A wonderful daffodil season, a new book to be published in the autumn. the same book to be serialised during the summer . . . these are the sort of pleasures which should have made me feel secure. I should have quickly been able to react to Jeannie's gay suggestion by saying yes. But I didn't.

I was still involved in the struggle which had brought us to this stage in our lives. I was suspicious about my ability to relax.

FIVE

When disgruntled people in cities march to meetings on May
Day holding high their banners of protest, the white flowers
of the blackthorn lie in drifts in Mincak woods and along
the shallow valley which slopes towards the sea.

Chunky patches of golden gorse line the lane to the farm
at the top of the hill, blue periwinkle spatter the banks; late
primroses, wild violets, and early pink campion shelter
amidst the growing grass. Fields of our neighbours where
they have sown spring corn are covered by a film of green;
white blossom clusters on the pear tree which we planted
two years ago; and by the wooden plank which crosses
Monty's Leap, the sticky leaves of the trichocarpa exude
their exotic scent.

Persian Carpet wallflowers colour the beds around the cottage. Aubretia, white and mauve, fall over moss-covered stones. Dandelions are beginning to prove their invincibility again, piercing the joints of the stones in the path outside the cottage door. Foolish bumble bees buzz against the glass of the porch. A cuckoo, dipping its tail, calls on the rock at Carn Barges. A vixen in the lane in the afternoon warns us that cubs have made her fearless. A wren sings among the willows beside the stream. The first bluebells are in flower down the cliff. A blackbird in the elderberry close to the barn proclaims that she has a nest nearby. Rabbits chase each other in the field opposite. Last year's tadpoles crawl as frogs from hibernating hideouts. The sunset is noticeably further to the west. Woodpigeons hurry to and from the wood, larks sing above the field behind the bridge, small birds perform aerobatics in their excitement, gulls' cries have an enlarged vocabulary. This is May Day. These are the pleasures that have brought happiness to man over the centuries. No computer can halt their repetition, no politician, or shop steward, no passing mood or fashion.

I did not find the swallow nest in the barn for some days. At first I did not want to investigate, fearing my presence might upset this sudden acceptance of Minack as a home. I felt like someone who had sold a house to an enthusiastic buyer, but who was still awaiting the contract. Any little matter might upset the completion of the deal. I had to be careful. If the swallows thought the barn was regularly used, they might also think the place was dangerous. Hence my caution, and Jeannie's, and why we warned Geoffrey not to go into the barn at all during this crucial period when the swallows were settling in. I hoped the donkeys would be equally considerate.

We had acquired Penny one late Spring evening after calling at a pub called the Plume of Feathers at Scorrier, near Redruth. The landlord was also a horse dealer and from time to time sold donkeys; and he had, on the evening we called, this black donkey in a field at the back of the pub waiting for a buyer. She was an Irish donkey imported from Connemara a few months before, and she was not in good condition. But her soulful eyes looked at Jeannie, and Jeannie

40

was conquered, and I said I would buy her. She was also in foal. 'Two donkeys for the price of one,' said the landlord cheerfully as he collected my cheque. We put Penny in the back of the Land Rover and drove back to Minack; and a month later, on the twenty-eighth of May, Fred was born in a field overlooking the sea.

He was now a large donkey. Indeed when people came to see him there was sometimes a note of disappointment in their voices. 'He's bigger than his mother,' they would say doubtfully. And so he was. Penny, while Fred was growing up, was an also ran as far as visitors were concerned. Everybody wanted to take photographs of Fred and Penny just mooched about in the background. But then came the time when Fred lost the luxury of youth, and suddenly someone said; 'I prefer the black donkey.' This became a trend. Penny began receiving the attention which she hitherto had been denied.

Fred, nevertheless, was splendid to look at. He had a fine, intelligent head with a rough coat of chocolate colour in winter, and a shiny smooth chestnut coat in summer. He was, when the swallows arrived, in the changeover period from winter coat to summer coat; and though temporarily he had an untidy appearance, the mark of his cross was as prominent as ever. It was this cross which gave him an advantage over Penny. Penny's cross merged into her black coat. You could hardly see it. Fred's cross was quite clear, winter and summer; the dark line along his back joining the dark lines pointing down his shoulders.

One summer's day a little girl was brought by her mother, a stranger, to see him and Penny. I told the little girl the traditional story of the cross, how Jesus rode into Jerusalem on a donkey and how all donkeys were blessed with a cross ever after. Some while later I had a letter from the mother saying that the child had been seriously ill and had two operations in the Great Ormond Street Hospital for Children in London. It seemed that Fred and his cross had made a great impression on her, and she would murmur about him as she lay in her ward. The mother said that she was now recovering and wanted to give Fred a present . ... carrots came by another post, and inside the parcel there was also a drawing. A primitive picture by the little girl of Fred and his cross.

The donkeys normally ignored the barn in the summer and so it was perverse of them to decide to take notice of it when the swallows arrived. The barn was their winter home. Here they sheltered when the gales raged, here we would spread hay on the cobblestone floor when the grass had lost its bite, here they would stamp and snort as they waited for the weather to clear. But in summer, though they preferred to spend the night in the stable field with its entry to the barn, they never sheltered in the barn itself. A summer storm, and they would stand side by side with bottoms to the hedge, their heads drooping, miserable donkeys looking as if they were in a trance. Yet we had long ago given up the idea that we were doing them a favour when, Mackintoshes over our heads, we dashed out into the rain and led them disconsolately into the barn. Once inside, they soon came out. We were considered a nuisance when we interrupted their wet ruminations.

It was Fred who changed the routine. No sooner had the swallows begun to swoop in and out of the narrow barn door than Fred became curious as to what they were up to. He would disappear inside while Penny, too experienced to be interested in such matters, remained munching among the buttercups. After a minute or two Fred would reappear in the doorway, but instead of coming out into the field to join Penny he would stand stationary, blocking the entrance. It is possible that this was a deliberate act on his part to hinder the swallows, more likely it was a ploy to relieve the tedium of the day. He enjoyed diversions. His floppy ears almost reached the stone lintel of the doorway, and his frame filled the rest of the space. Would he annoy the swallows? Would they twitter angrily with frustration? He was quickly to find out. Each swallow dived at him from a height, and flew into the barn between his floppy ears like supersonic aircraft between two peaks in the Alps.

I was ignorant of the ways of swallows. I had never lived in a house where swallows nested. I knew, of course, that the nest was made of mud, but I had never considered how the nest was lined until one day I was standing on the bridge and saw a swallow playing in the air with a feather. One of Boris's feathers. Boris's annual moult came at a convenient time for the birds in the area. He used to squat near his pond on a bed of London Pride, preening himself, scattering his under feathers about with abandon; and I now watched the swallow collect one, then aonther, then another. It was a gay procedure. Up in the sky above the greenhouse, the swallow would let go of the feather, and the feather would float in the air while the swallow performed acrobatics around it before seizing it again, then letting it go after a yard or two and soaring into the sky, then returning, and at last in serious mood dive with it into the barn. I was now as curious as Fred. I had to find out the mysterious spot to which these furnishings were being taken.

I went into the barn one early morning, and promptly a swallow flew away in fright. I did not notice from which corner it was startled but I imagined it came from somewhere near the rafters. The nest must surely be attached to one of the beams. But it was an ancient barn, the plaster had crumbled away from the slates in the roof, the battens straddling these slates were in many cases broken, and it seemed a miracle that the roof had not been blown away many gales ago. And when I looked up to find the swallow's nest, I realised suddenly there was no safe place for it to be. Not directly above me in any case.

There was, however, to the right of where I was standing a kind of first floor not more than twelve feet square. It was a haphazard affair reached by ladder, a floor of wooden planks which rested on the wall at the far end, and an oak beam which had come from a long ago wreck at my end; and in between there were three lesser sized cross beams, and two upright ones which Penny and Fred liked to gnaw when they were looking for something to do in the winter. In decades gone by these wooden planks were used for 'shooting' potato seeds, potatoes spread out on the planks in October and planted in February when they had sprouted; and while we have been at Minack, they have been the scene of two minor adventures. Before we came to live here, we brought Monty, our ginger cat, down from London for the weekend; and when we were due to return he was nowhere to be found . . . desperate hours later we discovered him hidden in a cobwebbed corner where the planks rested on the wall. Then Lama hid up there when she was wild, and it was upon one of the planks I placed the first saucer of milk I ever offered her; and which she consumed as soon as I had disappeared. For years, however, we had not made use of the space except to dump things which we believed we might need in the future but never did. I now realised that above all the bric-à-brac must be the nest. The rafters, the batterns, and the plaster were certainly more secure at that end of the barn. And I decided that as I knew the swallows were absent, this was the time to go up and have a look.

The planks were only a foot or two above my head, three rungs up the ladder and I was standing on them. In one corner there were a dozen and more old fashioned wooden flower boxes . . . old fashioned because freight costs had outpriced this once normal way of sending flowers safely to market. Alongside them were rolled up bundles of netting which we once used over the freesias to help the stems to stand upright; and which I remembered buying from an old fisherman who made fishing nets in Porthleven. There were a couple of discarded deck chairs, their once bright orange material punctured with moth eaten holes. I saw an old window frame without its glass; a worn, well-travelled suitcase with faded labels and which would never be used again, a fishing rod, and a tin of weedkiller which should not have been left there and this I would take back with me and throw away. But I saw no swallow's nest.

I came down the ladder and went back to the cottage and saw Jeannie. I told her I could find nothing, and she said I must be blind because the swallows were nesting in the barn without question. I waited until Geoffrey arrived, then he and I went into the barn and had another look; and as we went in a swallow flew out again. Geoffrey, one feels, can deal with most situations that can occur in the countryside. He belongs to one of the oldest families in our parish of St Buryan. His father is a craftsman carpenter and these two, father and son and a little help from outside, built in their spare time two adjacent houses in the valley below Moorcroft between Minack and St Buryan. It was a painstaking effort, and took over four years to complete; and when at last the work was over Geoffrey and his family lived in one half and the other half was occupied by a couple and their child from Wales. Geoffrey's was a splendid house with a great window in the sitting-room looking across the fields and hills to the Ding Dong country on the other side of Penzance. So peaceful was the setting that one could never consider tragedy would be connected with it.

The two of us clambered about the planks and, as I expected, found nothing. I realised that the more frustrated I had become, the noisier I had been; and the anxious, considerate thoughts I had had about the swallows not being disturbed were now being disrupted by my own behaviour . . . I was, in fact, playing the routine role of someone who is unselfish when he is not involved but selfish when he is. We returned to the cobblestone floor and almost immediately Geoffrey said: 'I've found it!' We had been floundering about on the planks looking at the rafters when all the while the nest was just *under* the planks. It was on a ledge of one of the cross beams, and it was not a customary cup-shaped swallow's nest. The packed mud ran along the beam so that the nest was a shallow dip; and the site was open enough and low enough for it to be knocked to pieces by one swipe of an inquisitive donkey's nose. As we stood looking at it one of the swallows flew into the barn, and hovered, twittering, then flew out again in unhappy excitement.

'That,' I said to Geoffrey, 'settles it for the donkeys. They can't come in here this summer. We'll have to keep the bottom half of the door shut.' I heard snorts behind me. Penny and Fred were looking in at us from the doorway, two donkey faces which looked apprehensive. 'Donkeys,' I said, addressing them, 'the barn from now on is out of bounds.' And so it was until the swallows in the autumn flew away to the south.

I was greedy for bird's eggs when I was a boy. I was at a preparatory school called Copthorne not far from East Grinstead; and on my twelfth birthday I was given a small, darkly varnished box so designed inside that there were compartments for eggs of various sizes. I cherished that box, and I used to carry it along with me on my bird nesting expeditions in the woods around Copthorne, encouraged by a master we called Cobble Wobbles because he was always shaking his head; and who believed that the theft of birds' eggs offered a practical lesson in natural history. I had no qualms that I might be doing wrong because I had been brought up to obey authority without ever challenging it; and Cobble Wobbles was God as far as I was concerned. The more successful I was as a human magpie, jackdaw or carrion crow, the more pleased he was with me; and when the egg collecting season was over I turned to butterfly collecting. Cobble Wobbles would lead the Form on hot summer days, nets in our hands, in exciting chases through the woods after the beautiful, fleeting objects; and there was a sense of triumph when we returned to the school with a record catch of once shimmering loveliness.

I do not remember when my mood changed, when I decided I wanted the life around me to live rather than to die for the sake of providing me with a macabre pleasure. It was a gradual process, not even completed when I first came to Minack; for in the beginning I shot rabbits without thinking of those I failed to kill and which disappeared wounded, into the undergrowth. But if you live in isolated country there comes a time when you have to decide whether your life is to be that of a hunter or a member of an untamed community; and I chose to look upon myself as being one of the latter.

As a child, however, I would have taken one of the swallow eggs; and I would have punctured a hole at each end and cleared it of its yolk. I would have placed it in its chosen hole in the wooden box and would have boasted about what I had done. I would have taken eggs from other nests at Minack, and there would have been one less blackbird to sing, one less thrush, one less green woodpecker to fly dipping its way through the wood. This summer, safe from my childish ghost, the birds had only their own kind to fear. Not even Lama would bother them. Like Monty she had no interest in catching birds.

We used the bridge as a lookout for discovering where

birds were nesting, and we would stand there observing the comings and goings, as if we were observing the activities of a street. There were the thrushes, snug in the evergreen foliage of the camellia just below the shelter. In the shelter itself where we keep the tractor and the garden tools, where the forty-gallon tank of paraffin is stored which we use to keep us warm while we bunch during the daffodil season, a pair of blackbirds had chosen to build their nest on the blade of a scythe; a scythe which had remained unused during the winter but which was urgently required as soon as the blackbirds arrived; we of course did not use it. A wren had chosen a small hole in the wall a couple of feet from the barn door. The chaffinches which stuffed themselves throughout the year on the bird table, had built their tiny nest in the gorse bush beside the lane opposite the door of the old stable which I use as an office. A pair of robins had created a cup of dried grass between two stones in the wall close to the white gate through which we take the donkeys into the field above the cottage. The magpies, as usual, were in the blackthorn copse towards Carn Barges, and, as usual, I resented their presence though admiring their splendid plumage. An ornithologist told me once that one need never be ashamed of shooting a magpie or a carrion crow; and one was justified in taking their eggs, the exception to prove the rule, because of the appetite they had for small birds. Yet each year would go by and I would do nothing, an example of confused thinking; for on the one hand I wanted to safeguard the lives of birds, yet on the other hand I was avoiding taking action against those who killed them. But where would the list end? Hawks, jackdaws, buzzards would also have to be on the list if I were to take the task seriously; and I would become like a lady I know who believes that a vital duty of her life is to destroy wasp nests . . . friends and acquaintances from miles around notify her as soon as a wasp nest is discovered, and the lady jumps into her car, however inconvenient the hour, and hastens with her poison to the offending nest. It was easier for me, I decided, to let nature look after itself; at any rate until I had visual evidence to enrage me.

Around the meadow where stands the small greenhouse

is a circle of elm trees, and each year a pair of green wood-peckers nests in one of them, a pair of tawny owls in another. The owls, of course, are very secretive; and I never know for certain they are there, though passing the tree every day, until the time has come for the young to fly . . . and then one early morning I become aware I am being watched, the watcher being one of the parents in the willows opposite the tree where the young, one or two, have been brought up in a hollow. Each year it is the same hollow. Once a baby owl fell out in some mysterious way and we found it alive, a white feathered object the size of a child's fist, at the base of the tree with a dead mouse beside it. The parents, presumably, unable to get it back to the nest, were making a futile effort to look after it where it lay. We picked it up, climbed up the tree, and placed it in the hollow alongside another; and a few weeks later we saw deep in the wood two young owls sitting on a branch, side by side like Tweedle Dum and Tweedle Dee. But this summer there was only one young owl. I first saw him perched on the top of Boris's hut when I was on the way to open the door in the morning, still so young that curiosity overcame the sense of possible danger; and because I did not want to disillusion his trust I decided to leave Boris inside for a moment, and went on past the hut further into the wood. Out of the corner of my eye I saw him continue to stare at me, turning his head in human fashion to follow me as I passed. Yet in a week or two I realised, he would be frightened by the sight of me, and he would be gliding away silently between the branches of the trees, miraculously silent; and I contemplated, as I passed him, that the trust he now had in me was a reflection of all the innocents, the original trust. Talent and brains are distributed unevenly, and so is good fortune. Trust is the only quality the new-born momentarily share.

The circle of elms are pockmarked with holes that have been tapped out of the trees by past generations of green woodpeckers, and one of the holes is chosen each year for redecoration. The chosen hole this year was fifteen feet from the ground between the small greenhouse and Boris's hut, and the rim of its entrance was freshly pecked as if it were a newly painted front door. I feel sure the woodpeckers would like to keep their nesting habits as secretive as the owls but their characteristics make it impossible. They are, for instance, so exotic to look at. The crimson crown and green plumage are striking enough to attract attention under any circumstances, the more so when the trees are bare of leaves; and as the leaves are always late in our part of Cornwall, there is no cover for them to hide in when the nesting period begins. They are noisy too. They draw attention to themselves time and again by calling out their rapidly repeated note whenever they believe danger is about; and the note sounds on these occasions like a nervous laugh. So everyone knows when the woodpeckers arrive to nest at Minack, including the two carrion crows who have their headquarters at the other end of the wood.

There was another nest this year in this circle of elms. Three elms from that of the woodpeckers, high up on a fork of the tree, was a mistlethrush's nest. I had watched two courting while we were bunching the late daffodils, and I hoped they would stay in the neighbourhood because the mistlethrush, or storm cock as it is called, has a special significance for us. It is a bird of the gales. I have seen it on days when I have had to bend double to fight my way into the wind, when our gulls have been too scared to parade on the roof . . . I have seen it defying the weather, perched on the elder down by the stream, singing its song into the storm. A bird which, in such circumstances, brings re-assurance. So I was glad that it had chosen to nest with us; and we felt it a compliment in an undefinable way.

Mistlethrush, woodpecker, swallow . . . these were the nests which interested us most. Only the swallows were to be safe.

SIX

The jackdaws hunt in packs during May and June, and sometimes they come swarming over Minack cackling with greedy cries. Their home is less than half a mile away in a cliff which falls sheer to the sea, a mass of crevices providing hideouts over the centuries. The cottage where Jane lived is close by; and the small meadow where she used to go on moonlit nights to dig the soil with the Cornish longhandled shovel and plant her bulbs which still flower there in the spring, lies to the side of the cliff half way down, a pocket of unexpected land only reached by those who know the secret route. Commandos were once trained to climb this cliff, approaching it by boat from Newlyn, and clambering ashore on the rocks, then up to the top with uncanny speed. In early summer they faced the angry jackdaws as they climbed between the nests, and I met a commando who, after he had been dived at and pecked at, said vehemently: 'I'd rather be shot at by humans.'

We, therefore, fear the jackdaws when they come to Minack because they sweep into the trees and bushes, hopping nimbly but inquisitively from branch to branch, cackling ceaselessly, inevitably threatening all the fledgling and egg-filled nests in the neighbourhood. Yet we know it is partly our fault that they come. All through the year we have a jackdaw or two on watch near the cottage, ready to seize any scraps we throw to the gulls on the roof, that the gulls do not like or are too slow to take. We accept the presence of these jackdaws, even regret that they remain so wary of us, because we are bemused by their beady eyes as they wait alertly the chance to dart at a delicacy. But at nesting time these jackdaws proceed to act as scouts on behalf of their colleagues, sending them a message as soon as we have put food on the roof or grain on the ground for the small birds. Thus, just as a gull is deliberating whether or not to slide on its bottom from the apex of the roof to the bacon rind lodged near the gutter, a bevy of jackdaws suddenly appears overhead.

The first gull on the roof was called Hubert; and he had been visiting us for a long time when one day he arrived with a leg dangling, and blood on his feathers. He had been shot by a boy with an airgun on the rocks where he roosted; and there was nothing we could do to save him. Then there was Gregory, a gull with one leg, the other no doubt lost in a gin trap which is now illegal; and he used to wait on the other side of the shallow valley, a white spot in the field, until dusk was falling and he felt safe to fly to the roof without the likelihood of being attacked by another gull . . . we never saw him again after a gale which raged for two days. And there was Knocker. Knocker was a very intelligent gull who rapped his beak on the roof with such purpose whenever he required attention that strangers in the cottage were apt to say: 'There's someone knocking at the door.' Knocker too has now disappeared.

Knocker used to come to the roof in the company of a gull we named Squeaker because she was always making a hiccuping, squeaking noise like a young gull just out of the nest. Squeaker still comes to the roof, and she still squeaks. She flies up from Lamorna Cove direction; and she has a new companion, Peter, who is so nervous when he is on the roof that any wideawake jackdaw pounces first on the food we have given him. Philip is our favourite gull because he has a detached attitude towards life, a gull who likes to contemplate a great deal on his own, and when we see him musing away up on the chimney we have the impression that he is often sagely thinking about us below him as we go about our business. He is fussy about his food and will have nothing to do with shop bread. He is very fond of bacon and in the summer when we are having breakfast outside on the bridge and the breakfast consists of bacon and eggs, Philip is certain to be within a few feet of us, beak watering, waiting for the inevitable choice portion to be given to him.

Both Knocker and Philip were victims of the *Torrey Canyon* oil, and Philip was the worse sufferer of the two. Knocker was filmed with oil, Philip when I first saw him had his underparts saturated. The sight of them both naturally enraged me but the sight of Philip also surprised me. He was the first *Torrey Canyon* victim I had seen but I knew at the time that the main oil slick still had not reached my part of the Cornish coast. Hence Philip must have collected his oil some distance off Land's End and what was he doing so far away? We treated him in the only way we could. We bought him five pounds in weight of bacon during the course of the following week. He stuffed himself on it; and it gave him strength to perform his own cleaning and the fat, it seemed, countered the effects of any oil he might swallow in doing so. Within three weeks he looked his old self, and so also did Knocker and they were both wise enough to stop wandering afar while the *Torrey Canyon* affair lasted. There was never any oil on the rocks along our stretch of Mount's Bay, and so they were safe if they stayed in the neighbourhood. Our own particular hell was

52

watching the guillemots. We could see them floundering off-shore, struggling needlessly to reach the supposed safety of our rocks . . . needlessly because they had become so soaked with oil long before coming within sight of our own rocks that there was no chance of them living.

Nor was there any chance of the young mistlethrushes living. The nest was as obvious as a television mast attached to a lonely house. There were no leaves on the elm to camouflage the nest when the eggs were laid or when they were hatched. The nest sat on the fork of a tree for all in the sky to see; and although the leaves were fat on the branches a week before the birds were ready to fly, they had blossomed too late. The jackdaws, and the two carrion crows at the other end of the wood, had already marked down the nest; and its occupants were doomed.

It was ironic, therefore, that we should help the jackdaws with their own nests. Or Penny did. The jackdaws apparently considered her black hair as an enviable adornment to their nests on the cliff and when they came to Minack in search of food, they also showed a desire to acquire part of Penny for their furnishings. I would look out of the bathroom which faces the big field, and observe two jackdaws with their grey heads resembling quaint grey hats, perched on the rump of Penny pecking at her coat until their beaks were so full that they appeared to be wearing moustaches. Penny never objected, behaving all the while as if she were flattered that her black coat was in such demand. We, on the other hand, faced with the bare patch at the end of the nest-making season, had to make excuses on her behalf and, for that matter on our own behalf. The bare patch looked as if she had mange, and we would notice visitors staring at it with disapproval. 'It's the jackdaws,' we would explain apologetically, 'she allows them to take the hairs, you see. She doesn't mind at all.'

Fred minded. The jackdaws showed no interest whatsoever in his upholstery. His winter coat which he was only too anxious to be rid of, had a fine texture which one would have imagined was ideally suited for any nest. But it was the wrong colour, and so the jackdaws passed him by. This annoyed him. Fred indeed, always minds when Penny re-

53

ceives more attention than he does; though it is not jealousy that causes him to feel so. It is just that he wants to join in the fun. Penny hurt her foot one day and the vet came out to inspect it; and as he was inspecting it along came Fred. He was tossing his head about in a way which denotes that he has found something to laugh at. Snorts reflect his laughter, and up he came to the vet snorting his head off. 'Go away Fred,' said the vet, and I, who was holding Penny, gave Fred a push. Thereupon Fred collapsed on the grass within a few feet of us, rolled on his back displaying his large tummy, and keeping his eye on us as if he was saying: 'Look at me, aren't I worth your attention?' He behaves like a clown when he is wanting notice. Life in his opinion is very funny.

Penny, meanwhile, is a lady who enjoys poor health when she has a chance to enjoy it. Her foot, so the vet explained to us, had a slight sprain and no more. Yet it was far too much trouble to walk even a few steps towards us when we brought her carrots and chocolate biscuits. Indeed her interpretation of the role of an invalid was so exaggerated that she would lie comfortably in the furthest corner of the field expecting us to walk to her, kneel beside her, and push our offerings into her mouth. This desultory behaviour would naturally have alarmed us had we not had the reassurance of the vet that there was nothing to worry about; and also the added evidence of our own eyes when we saw her, a few minutes after we had disappeared from her sight, gadding about the field like a two-year-old. Ill-health for Penny was an entertainment.

The jackdaws and the carrion crows ravaged the mistle-thrush nest in the third week of May, a week before Fred's birthday. I have a feeling that one of the carrion crows started the attack, and that the jackdaws joined in. I had woken up to the sound of the cows being called in for milking by my friend Jack, one of the farmers at the top of the lane, and I saw through the bedroom window that it was a lovely early morning, and I was cross with myself for not waking sooner. I lay there for a moment looking out through the window, and listened to a thrush singing ebulliently, and then with irritation to the harsh caw-caw-caw of the carrion crow. I would have continued lazily to lie there had it not been for Lama who came in from the sitting-room where she had been sleeping and proceeded to tell me to get up. I never know whether Lama is waking me up because she wants to go outside, or whether it is a selfish desire to have her breakfast, or whether she is performing a favour by drawing to our reluctant attention that a beautiful early morning awaits us. The hour depends on the daylight, and so in mid-summer I can expect to hear her beside me at five in the morning. She comes to the side of the bed and makes a tiny strangled cry as if she is being garotted; or she is content with a squeak that sounds like: 'Ee-Ee'. Both have a pene-trating effect.

I seldom, however, display any immediate reaction. I hear the noise in my half sleep, and try to make up my mind as to the significance of the sound. If I decide it is prompted by greed, I bring out my hand from under the bedclothes, make contact with her, and give her a push. I promptly regret my action though hoping that as a result she will now be silent. She isn't. The strangled cry is repeated. So also the 'ee-ee'. And they are repeated again and again and again until I clamber out of bed.

We have the wire-framed contraption across our open window at night that we had made for Monty. He used to be free to go out through the window at night until we found a fox waiting for him directly under the window sill; and then his freedom was curtailed, as Lama's freedom is curtailed. Thus I often suspect that Lama, when she wakes us up, is taking revenge for the discipline we impose upon her. She remembers the mouse she nearly caught the previous evening and she wants to return to the hole where she knows it is hiding. Or she just wants to go a-wandering because it is a lovely morning; and she is comforted by the thought that *she* at any rate will be able to catch up on her sleep during the day. Whatever her wishes may be it is our job to obey them. However reluctantly.

On this occasion, however, she was surprised by my pleasant welcome. I clambered out of bed murmuring flat-tering noises at her, then, much to her delight, I went to the fridge and brought out the saucer of John Dorey fish, part of which she had relished the previous evening. A few minutes later I was outside my dressing gown, shuffling down the path of grey chippings in my bedroom slippers, looking across the valley for the cubs I expected to see; and filling my lungs with the air coming off the sea, and grass growing scents, and those of wallflowers, and that of the verbena by the white seat.

It was a Saturday, and on Saturdays during the summer the *Scillonian* makes a double trip to the Scilly Isles; the first leaves Penzance at six in the morning and returns about mid-day, then sets out again at half past one. But it is the morning trip which always intrigues me. How is she so full? Who are these people who crowd her decks at such an early hour of the morning? I watched her sail by Minack, loving the white smartness of her hull, and the way she provides in a turbulent world evidence that a duty can be honoured; for whatever the storms and the strain of the crew, she will keep to her schedule so that the islanders can be sure their produce arrives on the mainland. I watched her disappearing out of sight behind the may tree, soon to bloom, that edges the path on the way down to the cemetery field and the cliff, when I was startled by the commotion among the elms on my left.

It was a terrible noise, similar in its tone of hysteria to that of a pack of hounds after a cornered fox, only it wasn't the noise of howls that filled the air but that of a ghastly cackling; and it was high up. Of course I didn't have to think twice to know what was happening, and I ran towards the tree clapping my hands and shouting. I could do no more. I couldn't climb the tree and if I had fetched a ladder it wouldn't have been any use. The nest was destroyed in a matter of seconds. There would be no young storm cocks to shout their songs into the gales next winter.

The incident was a warning as to what might happen to the woodpeckers. Nothing could hurt them at the moment because they were safe deep in the hole, but as the days went by they grew mature enough to become inquisitive, and they began poking their heads out of the hole. One in particular we noticed; and no doubt he had been the first of the brood to be hatched. His was the head which was frequently framed in the hole, and we could see others of the brood jostling for position behind him. His excitement was always greatest when one of the parents was in the neighbourhood about to bring to the nest the result of a foraging expedition, and then he would make a burbling note which was a miniature version of a woodpecker's laugh. He was still quite safe. A carrion crow or a jackdaw could not enter the hole. No doubt its whereabouts had been marked, no doubt that the signs that the woodpeckers were growing up had been observed. But no attacks on them could be made until they left the hole on their first wavering flight.

Fred, meanwhile, had received fifty-two cards on his birthday, and most of them came from the children of St Buryan. The village of St Buryan is three miles away from us, and it is a sturdy village which has an atmosphere that suggests it has an inbred awareness of its past. Historically it dates back to the sixth century when an Irish girl saint called Berian travelled this way and founded a shrine in the then encampment; and later in the tenth century King Athelstan, after defeating the Danes at Boleigh Hill, worshipped at the shrine before setting out with his army from the beaches of Sennen to drive the Danes from the Scilly Isles. He made a vow, when he was at the shrine that he would endow and build a church at St Buryan if the expedition was successful. He kept his vow, and the original church lasted until the fifteenth century; then the present one was built, a beautiful building with a fine tower which in the days of sail was a landmark for ships far out to sea. Yet it is not just the historical aspect which gives St Buryan its strength. This is a village which has belonged so much to the soil, the storms, the droughts, the daily struggle of living with nature over the centuries that the villagers whose families have lived here for generations are instinctively loyal to the basic values. They hold firm opinions, are kind and generous, but are never strident. Outsiders are now coming to live in the village, and whereas five years ago there were only solid granite cottages to live in, one now sees on the outskirts an increasing number of bungalows with outside walls faced with *ersatz* stone. Old men, sitting on the bench in front of the church, see someone go by and do not know their name; old men on the same bench a few years ago knew the intimate personal story of everyone they saw.

We buy our weekly groceries at St Buryan from the shop which is simply called the Shop. ('I'm going up shop' say the locals). It is run by a couple called Lily and Ted Chapple who offer that personal service to their customers that a computer might tell them was uneconomic. They know the special whims and fancies of all who come to them, young and old; and at Christmas time they follow a custom that the computer would certainly condemn. Each regular customer receives a present, and a handsome one at that. The Shop is indeed in tune with the character of St Buryan, though it now has to compete with a flush of supermarkets that national chains have introduced into Penzance after buying up old fashioned concerns. Tempting advertisements, promising twopence off this and fourpence off that, try to lure the ladies of St Buryan to transfer their allegiance from the Shop to Penzance. There is, however, the bus fare to be paid; and the personal attention to be lost.

Across the road from the Shop are the pub and the Post Office. We used to go regularly to the pub in the days of the landlord called Jim Grenfell; and ten years ago before the mains were brought to the village, I used to stand at the bar window watching the villagers queueing up with their pails to collect water from the village well opposite. The pub has now been redesigned, and the present landlord is known as one of the most welcoming in West Cornwall, but we seldom go there ourselves. There is no fun now in going to the village pub if you live outside the village. Instead of having a roistering time, there you are standing by the bar clinically deciding whether the law will allow you another half pint. Maybe it is a worthy law but it is a law that has resulted in the loss of a legion of friendships. And the teetotallers drive as fast as ever.

The Post Office is presided over by Leslie Payne, a kind man whose occasional vagueness endears him to the many who appreciate his gentle character. His courtesy is famous and if you are engaged in some post office business, you may find yourself being offered a sweet from a large tin. He takes infinite trouble with any inquiry and, if you are accustomed to some city post offices, you will regret that Leslie Payne is not your local postmaster. He also sells fruit and vegetables, sweets and a few groceries and also newspapers. We have our Sunday newspapers from him, but he does not have a high opinion of newspapers. 'Another load of rubbish,' he will say as he hands the bundle over to us. Or during the week he may hand us, instead of the paper of the day, an out-of-date issue saying we will not notice the difference. He also sells ice-cream and on Fred's birthday this summer he organised Fred's customary gift to every child in the school.

It was a beautiful morning, and we were up soon after the sun rose across the bay above the Lizard peninsula, and from our bedroom window we could see a clump of mackerel boats off-shore, their owners trying to make a catch for the morning market at Newlyn. The donkeys were in the field above the cottage, the field now yellow with buttercups, and we went out in dressing gowns to call them. 'Fred!' I shouted, 'Fred!' When he was born our vet nicknamed him His Nibs and he still calls him this. 'How is His Nibs?' he will ask when we see him in Penzance. His Nibs, on this occasion, came across the field at the gallop leaving Penny far behind him. Penny is always more lethargic, realising I suppose that there is all the time in the world for anything she decides to do. 'Happy birthday!' we both called, and I found myself thinking that no time had gone by since last year, and the year before, and the year before that. The same pattern. The same instant of pleasure. And for Fred the same eating delights awaiting him.

In due course, before they had to hurry off to school, Susan and Janet from the farm at the top of the lane arrived at the cottage. Both have known Fred since he was born, and every summer they remember, and bring him a special birthday card, and a bunch of carrots; and this summer they brought with them the school birthday cards as well.

They were really drawings, not cards, and one was a four foot long poster with the message: HAPPY BIRTHDAY FREDDY FROM ALL IN CLASS 3. Each member of this junior class had helped to draw against the backcloth of a green field a Breughel-style version of children at a donkey's

59

party; merry colours, movement, humour and tremendous gaiety. There were drawings with splashes of colours that an adult would have been frightened to use unless he did so with self-conscious intention; and the designs were equally free from inhibitions. A drawing with an ice-cream in one corner, carrots galore, a chocolate cake with candles on it, all in reds, greens, blues, browns, yellows and the message: ONLY THE BEST DONKEY IN THE WORLD COULD EXPECT THIS CARD. Another of a donkey in a field at night with dark clouds overhead except for a patch in the sky where the full moon is bright. Another of a donkey in a stable made of carrots. Another of a donkey in a field with carrots floating about in the sky. Another decorated with butterflies, cakes and hearts. Another of a donkey wearing bright yellow harness and carrying a purple pannier. Endless messages of HUGS AND KISSES, LOTS OF LOVE, I HOPE YOU HAVE A HAPPY BIRTHDAY WITH LOTS OF CARROTS. And some of the drawings showed Fred smoking a pipe. It is his parlour trick. And a few of the children had once seen him performing it. We treated these greetings with the solemnity they deserved, and after we had had our breakfast, we read them out to the donkeys and pushed the drawings against their white noses. This charade which we have performed each year has a special purpose, for it is a gesture to the children for the efforts they have made; and the donkeys, of course, are quite ready to tolerate our foolish behaviour. After a few drawings have been pushed against their noses, we give them an interval in which they sample their presents.

The lush period of summer had now begun. Young green bracken was thrusting through the thickening grass, through the mass of leaves of the fading bluebells, draping the sides of lanes and blanketing the moorland, hiding paths which were once easy to find. Coarse docks and thistles sprouted in the daffodil meadows among the dying foliage of the daffodils. Ought we not to be efficient daffodil growers and keep the meadows sprayed with herbicides instead of relying on the motor mower in due course to cut them down? But we prefer to let the wild flowers be free, the good ones and the bad ones, and in June this summer the insects were humming in the meadows, butterflies stretched out their wings on useless weeds, chattering whitethroats clung to the thistles pecking at the first seeds. Up the lane from the cottage the stream had already become a trickle across Monty's Leap, the may tree beyond the gate on the right was a dome of white scented petals; nettles and foxgloves, Queen Anne's lace, clouds of pink campion and inevitable cow parsley filled the verges and the ditches. And the leaves were now thick on the branches of the elm where the nest of the mistlethrushes used to be, and on the branches around the woodpeckers' hole out of which the eldest one, at any moment, would be ready to fly.

The window of the bathroom looks out on to the donkey field with the wood running along the right, the first part of which contains the elms. There is also, close by, a pole which carries our electric cable to another pole in the wood in one direction and to a spike plunged into the ancient end wall of the cottage in the other direction; and the end wall is where our spare room and bathroom connects to the main cottage. I have never been happy about this arrangement. We both hate the sight of the cable threading its way through the wood and across the field; and we both fear, though we are assured our fears are groundless, that the gales which swing the cable, will produce a swing one day so vicious that the spike will bring the end wall down in a pile of debris. Meanwhile the birds like the cable, especially the swallows as we were to learn, because it is a convenient place to perch; and the carrion crows like the poles because they can sit there high above the trees observing, like big brother, every activity.

I was shaving in the bathroom, looking at my face in an inadequately small mirror, when there was the same hysterical cackling sound that I had heard a few weeks before. It was obvious what was happening, and I glanced quickly out of the window before dashing to the backdoor. Sure enough, I saw through the window that two carrion crows and the jackdaws were fighting over something up there on the electricity pole; and by the time I got through the door and had run into the field, clapping my hands and shouting, the fight had become a din; and it only became silent after they saw me, after they had dropped with a thud the object they had been fighting over, after the jackdaws had hurried away, after the carrion crows, cawing, had left for the far part of the wood.

The object was our young woodpecker. They had watched and waited and caught him on his first flight.

DEREK TANGYE
ST. BURYAN, PENZANCE
Tomatoes Grown for Flavour

SEVEN

In summer we depend on tomatoes to earn us money. The
prices are good in May and June, they dip in July, they dip
steeply in August. In May and June we gaze at the green
fruit on the trusses, willing them to turn pink quickly.

We have five greenhouses (in professional language we
have one greenhouse and four mobile greenhouses), and
also the small one surrounded by elms which we use now
only as a packing shed. At first we used this small one,
thirty feet long and twelve feet wide, both as a packing shed
and for tomato growing; daffodil bunching and packing in
the spring, cold house tomatoes in the summer. The tomatoes proved to be a modest success. There was a holiday demand locally, and so there was no problem about disposing

of the crop; and most important from a cost point of view there was no carriage to pay as there was with flowers and potatoes.

This modest success gave us ideas about changing our pattern of growing. We had become disenchanted with potatoes as a summer crop. Year after year at some crucial time of the potato growing season there would either be a violent gale or an exceptional frost; and our crop would be laid waste. Apparently we were living at the time in a ten-year cycle of such weather. The year we stopped growing potatoes, the harvest was bountiful. It has been bountiful ever since.

It is easy to forget the anguish that surrounds past endeavours. That last summer of potato growing we had hoped to harvest twenty-eight tons of potatoes, and we harvested twelve tons instead. We were as near defeat as we have ever been at Minack. There have been many times when we did not possess the cash to pay for our groceries, or for petrol, or for a drink at the pub. The bills and our hopes would mount up as we waited for a potato or flower harvest to mature; and the harvest would seldom equal our bills and our hopes, and so little would be left to carry us forward. We were maddening to our families. They grew exasperated with our optimism. For weeks before a daffodil or a potato season we would regale them with our high expectations; and then they would notice a silence while the season was in progress; and then, monotonously, they would receive our report after the season was over, a report that the weather had been the worst that old men in the district could remember. The harvest, whichever it was, had failed.

Yet Jeannie never wavered in her confidence that one day all would be well. It was I who became jumpy. I remember one desperate occasion when I seized my gun, not with the dramatic intention of shooting myself, but in an unreasoned, hysterical gesture of protest against the fates. Unfortunately in my rage I raised the butt of the gun so savagely that it hit my mouth; and to this day I have a damaged tooth which my dentist threatens to remove each time I visit him.

One winter, it was our third at Minack, our finances were in a particularly bleak condition. Nobody was helping us on the land. I spent my days rotovating the steep slopes in preparation for the potatoes, or helping Jeannie to pick violets, or performing any of those other tasks which are associated with fourteen acres of land. The cottage was almost as primitive as when we had arrived. No running water, no electricity of course, and Jeannie did most of the cooking on a paraffin stove; but we were happy except for the usual financial worries. Nevertheless we were not prepared to meet the situation with which we were suddenly faced.

The previous year a New York couple whom we had known for some years paid us a week-end visit, sleeping at a nearby farm but spending the daytime in our company. The fact that we were living under such primitive conditions did not seem to matter. Curiously neither Jeannie nor I thought it at all unusual that we should be entertaining under such difficulties; and therefore we felt no need to make excuses for the simplicity of our life. For example, when Jeannie washed up after a meal, she boiled a kettle and emptied it into a bowl; and when the washing up was done she took the bowl outside, as there was no sink, and poured the dirty water away on to a patch of waste ground. It was a practical method in the circumstances, and no doubt it had been used by the various occupants of the cottage for the five hundred years of its existence. The week-end passed, and it seemed to be a very happy one.

A few months after the couple had returned to New York they wrote to tell us they had written a play inspired by their visit to Minack; a play about an American couple visiting an English couple who had given up a sophisticated life for primitive living in Cornwall. We were intrigued by the news, even flattered; the more so when we learnt that the play was to be performed in the West End with a distinguished actress and actor playing the parts inspired by Jeannie and myself. We informed friends in London who booked seats for the first night; and my cousin organised a box to which he invited my mother who, although not well, was determined to see a play which promised so much amusement. The programme described the setting of the play as 'a cottage near Land's End'. The New York couple believed they had written a play which we would appreciate. We had not, however, seen the script.

The day following the first night the Lamorna post-master arrived with a telegram, an hour or two later with another telegram, then a third. Their contents were highly disturbing. The first nighters had not seen anything funny in the play at all, the jokes had turned sour after crossing the Atlantic, and the unmistakable message of the telegrams was that action had to be taken by us to stop the play. Then that evening my cousin arrived. He had driven specially from London to deliver to us an Act by Act account; and he was in a high state of indignation.

What were we to do? We hadn't the money for the fare to London, let alone the money to indulge in legal conferences; and in any case there was work to do, and there was no one to look after Monty if we went away. Nor were we in the mood to become involved in a legal battle. We were gloomy about our financial prospects without this added worry. We appeared to be losing our personal struggle to survive in the kind of life we had chosen, and we didn't have the toughness to enter another fight. Nor did we have any sense of humour to balance our distress. The cause was too close to us; the reviewer in one of the Sunday papers said the play was about a Failed Market Gardener. The theme of the play, therefore, touched a raw nerve; and the ingredients of the play inevitably made our nerves still rawer. Our friends were quite right to expect us to take action, and after we heard a review on the BBC which described the hero and heroine in unflattering terms, our fighting spirit returned. We decided, however, to do the fighting from Minack. We would not disrupt our lives more than necessary; and so we welcomed the help of a London solicitor who happened to be in our area advising a neighbour on a property deal.

Meanwhile at seven o'clock each evening as the jaunty tune of the Archer serial faded away on the battery set, we sat before the fire, aware that three hundred miles away in London an audience was settling down in its seats to enjoy a mocking version of the kind of life we led. It was hateful. It was particularly hateful for Jeannie because there were various jokes in the play of a domestic nature; and the set of the play (a friend recognised the interior of the cottage from the photographs of the set outside the theatre) accentuated the primitive way with which she had to cope with guests. A feature was that we had no sink; and this was made a great joke in the play. In one Act the heroine, after doing the washing up in a basin, carried the basin to the side of the stage and through the front door, then emptied it into the garden (just as we used to do). As the lady performed the task, the audience roared with laughter. We sat by ourselves in the cottage hearing that laughter.

A writ for libel was served on our behalf in due course, and the play was withdrawn after five weeks. The legal wrangle over the libel suit, however, meandered on. The management denied responsibility, arguing they had accepted the play in good faith; and the fact the authors lived in New York further complicated matters. The costs began to mount. We hadn't a penny for an evening out, let alone for an armoury of lawyers; and we became more and more enraged that as a result of the hospitality we had dispensed on that week-end visit, we had now been placed in such an invidious position. Heaven knows what would have happened had not that knight of losing causes, A. P. Herbert, come to our aid. We had known him for many years, and had shared many an incongruous adventure; and he had stayed with us at Minack and been quite unruffled by the then inconveniences. When he heard of our predicament, he marched into the offices of the theatrical management concerned, declared that he was on our side; and he would be glad for the world to know it.

The case was settled within a week; and the judge who announced the settlement, listened to the apologies read out on behalf of the offenders, and proclaimed that Jeannie and I were to receive 'substantial damages.' They were not as substantial as this sounds, nor as substantial as they might have been if we had had the tenacity to take the case to court. But it was enough. The first thing we did was to arrange for the water from the well to be piped to the cottage, then buy an Esse stove . . . and have a sink.

We were fortunate enough to have a kindly bank manager when we decided to have greenhouses. Perhaps his patience had been exhausted by the stories of our woes, and therefore he was in the mood to be receptive to this new idea; for we dazzled him with facts and figures of our financial prospects were we able to possess greenhouses. At any rate he loaned us the deposits. The instalments we were ready to worry about later.

We had pointed out to him that wind, and the salt it carried, was the most persistent danger to our crops; and so if, in the equable Cornish climate, our crops were protected by glass we would have guaranteed, factory produced results. Thus we would be able to grow flowers or lettuces in the winter, and tomatoes in the summer; and we would be able to leave our hazardous potato career behind us. We began with a splendid greenhouse with cement foundations, a hundred feet long and twenty-two feet wide; then later two mobiles each seventy feet long and eighteen feet wide; then another two mobiles seventy feet long and twenty feet wide.

The sight of them was impressive. The fixed greenhouses in front of the cottage, the mobiles in the field beyond. This field had been rocky and uneven, and we had to bulldoze the rocks away and level the site for the mobiles. Unfortunately the field was not long enough for us to gain the full benefit of the mobiles. Ideally a mobile should have three or four sites. Each of our seventy foot mobiles had only two. If we had four, for instance, we might have grown early, middle and late varieties of daffodils, winching the mobile along the rails on its very small wheels to cover each site as one variety succeeded another; and still have been able to grow tomatoes on the fourth site. Hence for the same capital expenditure we would have had four crops.

As we only had the two sites, however, we were forced to decide upon the most profitable crop to dovetail with the tomatoes; and we tried at various times forget-me-nots, chrysanthemums, lettuces, Beauty of Nice stocks, wallflowers, iris, polyanthus and freesias. Freesias were the most satisfactory until over-production everywhere brought down the price and made them uneconomical; and there was in any case a snag about freesias. Their picking time began in January (we had heat by now in the greenhouses) and the picking reached its peak during March. Hence the tomato planting had to be delayed because the mobiles were covering the freesias; and the consequence of this was that we missed the high tomato prices of June. There came a time, therefore, when we decided to give up such winter flower growing. We would devote all our efforts to the tomatoes.

Today the mobiles have become static greenhouses. We no longer winch them from one site to another; and though outsiders sometimes gaze at the bare soil in the winter and declare that we are not showing economic good sense, that we are failing to earn the interest on our capital, it seems we are conducting the right policy. It is wiser to be idle; and the idleness is also a benefit to the tomatoes. For during the winter the soil is sterilised by a chemical powder roto-vated into the earth, and this has to be left undisturbed for several weeks with the green-houses kept closed so that the fumes do not escape. The advantage gained by this can mean an extra two pounds a plant; and this in terms of money, can equal the returns of a winter crop. This, and the fact that the tomatoes are planted in good time, justifies the barren sight of our greenhouses in winter.

There are other advantages too. We plant the tomatoes at the beginning of March when the daffodil rush is on, and so when the sterilisation has been done we can make pre-parations. Vast quantities of peat are rotovated into the soil, and also fertilisers that are based on the soil analysis carried out by the Ministry of Agriculture in the autumn. Then, in the waiting time of early January, the strings are tied to the overhead wires that stretch from end to end of each greenhouse above where the rows of tomato plants will be. Each plant has this five-ply string to support it, and the earth end of the string is tied to a short galvanised stake which is plunged into the ground alongside the plant. The plants come from a specialist grower near Truro who delivers them in relays in his van. Everything is ready when they arrive. We may be in a period when there is a deluge of daffodils. It doesn't matter. No switchover from a winter flower crop. The tomato plants will be cossetted from their beginning.

This summer we grew two and a half thousand plants, and we chose a type called Moneycross and another called Maascross because both these types tasted like true tomatoes. This age of uniformity has cast its spell on tomatoes like everything else; and this summer it was officially decreed that when tomatoes reached the shops each pack must contain tomatoes of the same size. Government appointed inspectors now cruise around the wholesale markets checking that growers have obeyed the orders to pack their produce according to the official grades; and they will downgrade any pack which does not come up to their standards. These standards are outlined in a booklet which growers are expected to keep handy as they rush to send their harvest to market. The top grade, we are told for instance, must fall 'within one of the following size ranges as measured by the maximum transverse diameter of the fruits'.

A. 77mm (3 in.) and above but less than 87mm (3 7/16 in.) and so on down to F.
F. 35 mm (1 3/8 in.) and above but less than 40 mm (1 9/16 in.).

The instructions continue: 'The size range packed must, be marked on the container, either in millimetres or inches showing the minimum and maximum for the range (the lower figure to be stated first) or by the appropriate code.'

There are a further three grades each diminishing the standard required. No mention is made of flavour. If the shape fits the grade, the tomato can taste of soap or of nothing at all; and so the housewife, oblivious of the pressures directed upon her buying habits, comes to believe that a neat, uniform plate of tomatoes on the table is an emblem of wise buying. It happens, however, that the tomato varieties most used for uniformity have no flavour; top grade they may be, and of exquisite shape, but they are tasteless.

Jeannie and I soon lost patience with the grading instructions; and we devised a means to circumvent them. We decided to have two grades of our own choice; and on the little piece of paper, stuck to the container, that officialdom demanded should show the grade code number, I put the figure '2' or the word 'small'. The latter described all the very small tomatoes we sent away, while the figure '2' described the rest. Now by marking our tomatoes as second grade we had an immediate advantage. We were saved from any pedantic complaints about the size and shape of our tomatoes which an inspector might make; the tomatoes had to be of very poor standard indeed to be considered third grade. On the other hand we were not doing our tomatoes justice. Hence we had invented a slogan. In bold red letters printed on a card with my name on it, which was stapled to the container alongside the little piece of grading paper, was the slogan:

TOMATOES GROWN FOR FLAVOUR.

It worked wonders. Supermarket minded shops continued to stock the uniform tomatoes; but the others, the small shopkeepers, the hotels and restaurants, made special requests for ours. They were in great demand, and the wholesaler was delighted. And the inspector said nothing. The price we received always topped his Grade 1.

We also took care to grade the tomatoes according to ripeness. I let Geoffrey do the picking because he was faster doing it than I had ever been. I even persuaded myself that my presence and my fumbling slowed his work, and that he felt happier on his own. I preferred to be with Jeannie and deal with the tomatoes when Geoffrey brought them to us in baskets. It was certainly a cleaner job. Tomato foliage acts like a dye; and so when you make your way between the rows, either when pinching out unwanted shoots or when picking the fruit, everything about you becomes green . . . green clothes, green hands, green face. At the end of a morning's picking, Geoffrey's eyebrows were green. He never complained. He would empty the baskets, having first weighed each one so as to keep a record of the output from each greenhouse, then he would proceed to grade them, taking special notice of their colour. I am sure this helped us to collect the best price. A buyer always knew he would never have ripe tomatoes mixed with near ripe ones.

By the middle of June, this summer, it seemed we would have a good season. We were receiving 2s. 6d. a pound, or 30s. a chip (we call a container a chip); and we were despatching to the wholesaler in Penzance one hundred and fifty chips a week. Had such an output continued it would have been splendid but it didn't happen that way. The peak period lasts about three weeks, then tails off, and so do the prices; and against the tomato income we have to balance the cost of the oil for the heaters, two thousand gallons or more; and the four hundred gallons of liquid fertiliser which is fed to the plants throughout the summer by the automatic irrigation; and the cost of the plants at £42 a thousand; and the price of chips at 9d. each; and the cost of peat, basic fertilisers and the sterilisation powder; and of course the price of Geoffrey's labour and our own. Tomatoes, therefore, are our bread and butter, and not a way to a fortune.

This summer the tomatoes had, in fact, been late in coming into market ripeness. We had invested in a new heating system which we thought would be foolproof in its efficiency. Each house had a heater of its own, burning on oil, and the heat was circulated by a powerful fan through perforated polythene ducting that was fixed along the inside of each house. The heaters were automatic. Each house had a thermostat which controlled the temperature required; and the theory was that once the heaters were installed the tomato plants would grow in an ideal artificial environment.

Unfortunately the heaters, though expertly installed, refused to fulfil their function. For one mysterious reason or another, the heaters took turns to break down during the crucial period of the sharp March and April nights. Machines have often broken down at Minack. Second-hand machines or machines delivered straight from the factory, have brought despair to mechanics and to ourselves. The faults are always unusual, always unique. Hence when the heating engineer expressed amazement that the heaters should behave so temperamentally, I myself displayed no surprise. I had long ago become familiar with the sentence which followed:

'Never in all my experience,' said the man vehemently, 'have I known this happen before. Never . . . and I've been in this game for thirty years.'

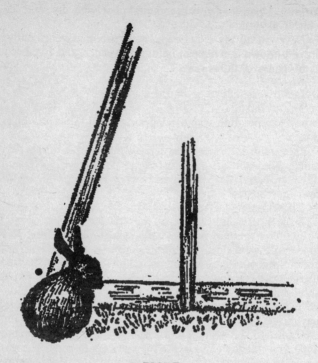

EIGHT

I soon became exasperated by the time involved in dealing
with the consequences of the breakdowns . . . letters, telephone calls, telegrams, hours just staring at the offending
heaters, more hours having sterile discussions with Geoffrey
about them, waiting for engineers to call, forcing myself to
make jocular remarks as they worked, all the while having
regrets that I had had the idea in the first place of modern-
ising the heating system. Then there were the nights. I would
wake up in the early hours, naggingly curious as to whether
the heaters were operating; and I would lie wondering, trying to make up my mind whether I had the energy to satisfy
my curiosity. At last I would clamber out of bed.

'I'm going to have a look at the heaters,' I murmured one

early morning to Jeannie.

Half an hour later I returned.

'How were they?'

'Number three was out.'

'What did you do?'

'Kicked it.'

'Did that help?'

'No . . . it's still out.'

My exasperation was driving me to childish demonstration.

The manufactureres, however, were helpful. They despatched an expert from their base at Watford who declared on arrival that similar heaters were operating amiably all over the country.

'The same model?'

'Exactly the same model,' he replied.

I felt, at this moment, that he was thinking that I had invented the misdeeds of the heaters. His firm had an impeccable reputation. If, therefore, the model had proved itself elsewhere there was no possible logical reason why it shouldn't be equally successful at Minack.

'Well,' I said boisterously, forcing a joke, 'the pixies must have got at them.'

A part of the heaters had to be re-designed in the end; and then the heaters began to operate normally. Eight weeks after their installation they were at last looking after our tomato plants automatically. Thereupon the thermostats broke down. They went mad. Sometimes they pushed the heat up to 90 degrees when it should have been 60 degrees; sometimes it went to 20 degrees. They too were changed by the manufacturers who now shared my opinion that we all would have been better off if we had never heard of each other.

On one of my excursions to look at the heaters I had become acquainted with a rabbit that appeared to suffer from an obsession to have its young in number three mobile.

Every night for a month if had been digging a hole under the rail upon which the mobile rested; and every morning I had blocked it up, only for the rabbit to dig another hole as soon as darkness fell. Once inside, the rabbit excavated a burrow with such speed that by morning the burrow was seven or eight feet long and three feet deep at the far end; and here also was the nest of dried grass and peat. This nightly activity could not be expected to help the growth of the tomato plants. True the rabbit avoided digging up the plants themselves, but the burrow played havoc with the roots; and there was always the threat that one morning I might find the young in the nest.

I was advised to set a snare. Snares have taken the place of the now illegal gin traps, and I regret to say that they are a necessity where rabbits have become too plentiful again after myxamatosis. Rabbits used to cry out in the fields around us when they were caught in a gin trap, then they waited until the morning before the trapper arrived to kill them. The snare catches the wretched rabbit; and provided the snare is set at the entrance of a rabbit hole no other animal is likely to be harmed. Unhappily the law allows the snare to be set at random in the fields. This can mean a prowling cat can be caught. I have never known this happen but the possibility exists; and so when snares are in the neighbourhood, Lama is never out of sight. I believe the most humane way of dealing with rabbits is by the use of nets and a ferret. The net straddles a warren and the ferret drives them into it where they are quickly killed by the hunter. Gas, pumped into the hole of an otherwise sealed warren, is often used. I once saw this about to happen at a spot where I knew badgers occupied the underground chambers, not rabbits. I raced across a field towards the men who were in charge, shouting at the top of my voice, and was half a minute too late. They were looking the other way. They sent a whiff of cyanide gas into a hole; and for weeks afterwards Jeannie and I were waiting to see badger tracks in the area again. We saw tracks *coming* to the sealed sett. It was six months before we saw the sett had been opened up again. It was meagre satisfaction that I had screamed at the men when I reached them. One badger more or less was not going to affect their sleep at night.

I would not set a snare for my rabbit at any price. I had, in any case, become involved in its struggle for a home.

Absurdly sentimental, I can hear the cynics say, and so I suppose I ought to feel ashamed; and yet I have never been able to understand why the description of a person being sentimental is derogatory, while the description of a person being cynical denotes a certain superiority. The sentimental are at least trying to be kind, the cynical on the other hand are trying to find a way of proving themselves by doubting the value of sincerity. As I have found that truth is always changing, I am also aware that I can, at one moment, be sentimental, and at another a cynic; but I have no doubt that, of the two roles, I prefer myself when I am sentimental.

I had destroyed the burrow many times, and the rabbit still persisted with its intention to have its young in the mobile. Surely, I argued, it would come to its senses when it realised my determination. There were normal burrows galore. Why not give up the futile battle against myself? The burrow filled in, the nest destroyed, the hole under the rail blocked up . . . all this night after night. Any sensible rabbit ought to have realised it couldn't win.

Then I met the rabbit face to face.

It was early morning and I was half asleep, and I had dragged myself from my bed to satisfy my neurotic curiosity about the heaters. Dawn was just breaking and the sky was already reflecting light although the sun had not yet risen. An owl hooted from the wood on my left, and out to sea I noticed the starboard light of a fishing boat bound for Newlyn. I walked barefooted across the grass wet with dew, and reached the mobile number three, and began to walk along the side of it keeping a look out for the spot where the rabbit had made its nightly entrance. I found it at the far end this time, adjacent to the sliding door; and I looked around for a stone with which to block it up, found one, and proceeded to bend down to put it into position.

As I did so I found myself at nose level with the rabbit. It had come round the corner of the mobile at a pace, and it had stopped at the sight of me with its forelegs in front, like a racehorse refusing at a fence. And its mouth was stuffed with dried grass.

It never came to the mobile again. The fright brought

77

sense to it. No doubt it found a nice burrow among those on the other side of the hedge to the field; and its young were probably among those who later on in the summer ate our carrots. My own last sight of her was as she raced away from me across the field, her mouth still stuffed with dried grass; and as she disappeared the sun was rising behind Porthleven across the bay, and the dawn chorus had begun to sing around me.

Others were interested in our tomatoes; blackbirds, for instance, relished them, and when I opened up the vents in the morning before Geoffrey arrived I could spot certain blackbirds who were impatiently waiting for me. There were, this summer, a couple of males with bright yellow beaks who kept watch for me in the willow trees; and there were a female or two who perched patiently on the mobiles. As soon as I had pulled down the lever and the vents rose skywards, I would observe these characters pause for a second, then disappear through the opening; and I would know they were hurrying to their breakfast. At all times of the day a blackbird would be in one greenhouse or another; and in the evening when I closed down the vents I had to be careful to see that I didn't catch a blackbird as it came out of the greenhouse through one of them; but we did at any rate find a way of minimising the damage they did.

We left the tomatoes they had pecked where they had found them, whether on a stem or on the ground, and the blackbirds went on pecking them before they started on a fresh one. This was considerate on their part. The tomatoes they demolished were not therefore so many in the long run; and anyhow Jeannie believed that a lost tomato was cheap payment for a blackbird's song.

Boris also liked tomatoes. In fact he liked them so much that he appeared to behave as if he were a connoisseur of tomatoes. He was fussy about each one he selected, and he was not so co-operative as the blackbirds. He preferred to waddle along a row biting a piece out of one tomato then another as, in another sphere, an experienced wine taster sips importantly a range of wines. Boris never finished, as the blackbirds did, a tomato he had once tasted; and so he was a menace when the first truss was ripening because the tomatoes were easily within his reach. Thus he had to be prevented from entering the greenhouse; and the greenhouse concerned was the one in front of the cottage, the others being too far away from his normal perambulations.

It might appear that it was easy for us to stop him, and indeed it was; all we had to do was to block the lower part of the open doors, the doors we kept open on warm summer days to help ventilation, with the two wire-framed trays that we had nearby for the purpose. Unfortunately we were always forgetting to use them. Time and again there would be a cry from one of us: 'Boris is eating the tomatoes . . . nobody has put the trays across the doors.' Then one of us would go in and tell him that he had to leave; and he would hiss and waggle his tail feathers, and slowly plod outside. Later in the season, when the trusses were out of his reach, we did not have to disturb him if he chose to spend the day in the greenhouse; and sometimes Lama would be there too. Lama curled up in a small black ball, Boris with his head tucked inside his wing. Both sound asleep.

Incidents like these filled our summer days, trivial moments of diversion, the minutiae of living. I would sit on the bridge, staring across the shallow valley, the sea to my right, listening to the sounds that belonged to these summer days . . . pigeons cooing in the wood, a lark singing, a cuckoo in the distance, the flap of waves on rocks, a girl's voice calling in the cows, the chugging engine of a fishing boat, the donkeys' snorting. Yet unimportant in themselves these passing pleasures posed the question, the everlasting question of the twentieth century . . . has anyone the right to slow down the tempo of his life in an attempt to come to terms with his inner self? Or should he surrender to the pressure of conventional living, accept the tribal customs, sacrifice truth in the pursuit of power, view life as if from an express train?

Most of us conform. We stifle the secret hopes we have for personal freedom but find we cannot kill them. They were with us before we were smoothed by habit; and though sometimes they seem to fade away as the years pass, we suddenly find ourselves faced with them again in the form of frustration. There they are, challenging our weak selves,

79

demanding why we have betrayed them.

Expediency, we reply, we had to earn a living. We became involved in a career, and we were chained to its progress. Or we may be practical by explaining that we never had the capital, never could hope to acrue the capital, that would have made it possible for us to break the pattern of our lives. Or we may admit that we lazily allowed time to slip by. Or we may say that the chance for change never came our way, or perhaps we didn't have the wit to recognise it when it was there.

Yet whatever the reason the middle-aged of today have an excuse if they believe they have failed themselves. They were caught unawares by the great god efficiency which is the deity of progress. They were passively passing their lives away, vaguely expecting their dreams to be fulfilled in some distant future, when suddenly they were forced to worship this new god; and this god, uncontrolled by any humanitarian definition as to what he should give in return for the upsets he causes, decrees the closing down of old established businesses, orders victims of takeovers to look for jobs elsewhere, force homes to be sold as a consequence, children to be removed from their schools, and the lives of people to be disrupted at any age when they might expect to be consolidating. The efficiency cult can become the human tragedy of the seventies. It is obsessed with the cutting of costs. Nothing else matters; and so quality suffers, and service, and the dignity of individuals.

The young, some of them, are alert to what faces them. They are moving into an age which has no precedent in British history. For there has been no war to decimate a generation as in 1914 and 1939; and so there will be a larger supply of young brains and energy competing for key jobs than ever before. There will be relays of such young brains; and the god efficiency will exploit them. Thus clever minds will be squeezed dry, physical stamina exhausted, in the service of combines and governments because fresh replacements will always be waiting in reserve; and brilliant men, so occupied by the immediate problems of the day that they have no time to keep up to date with contemporary research, will suddenly find themselves discarded for being old fashioned; full of promise at thirty, unwanted at forty.

There will be no place for the mediocre, or for the dreamers, or for those whose talents do not blossom in the examination room, or for those whose minds develop late. Fail a paper by five marks and they will be blackballed for ever in the career they want to follow . . . a dead-end by the age of twenty-one, smarting from a failure they believe to be unfair, a disappointment to their parents, frustrated with life before it has really begun. No wonder the seeds of revolt germinate. What has society to offer youth in such circumstances? The shallow compensations may await, but these provide no basic satisfaction to the inner self. An inflationary wage for unskilled work does not help to bring peace of mind if there is no pride or pleasure in doing it; or if it offers no future except to grow old as a unit in a computer, electronics giving orders for ever. So when youth rebels today, he is in fact rebelling against the prospect of his organised future; for he too is wanting personal freedom. The middle-aged may disapprove of his tactics, but the aim is shared. Both seek to own their souls.

Meanwhile the middle-aged faced the present. Those who have been successful, the ambitious and the power hungry, chase the prizes which beckon them, then find the prizes have turned to ashes when they have been won. Material ostentation, making people jump to obey their whims, living a jet existence around the world, creates a spiritual vacuum, or ill health, or a broken home. Speed has destroyed quiet moments of reflection by offering the successful too many alternatives, too many opportunities. A safety valve is missing. They have no time to contemplate, are scared to do so. Then suddenly the party is over, and they are lost.

The others, the undistinguished and the unimportant, always loyal to their families, leading their conventional lives out of a sense of duty, watch the prices go up, the fares go up, and then are forced to sacrifice another small pleasure which had helped to compensate for the queuing, the sardine travelling, and the noise which dulls the senses. They fear the change which is taking place around them, but are mute. This is progress for the common good so it is useless to protest. They gaze at the monster earth-moving machines clawing at the ground, and watch buildings familiar as old friends disappear into lorry loads of rubble. Nothing is secure. The fields where the Sunday walk is taken are scheduled to be the site of the new housing estate. The road in front of the house is to be widened, and it will demolish the front garden. Only the insensitive can be the winners. Only those who, in the name of efficiency, dictate the orders. And perhaps even they may sometimes wonder whether their own lives have become victims of their own actions.

Yet these forces of material progress will be moving even more quickly. There are no logical reasons to stop them. We have to accept the fact that, because of the population explosion, because of the trends existing today, the rights of the individual will become increasingly subservient to the demands of the community. So what can anyone do to shake himself free?

Conventions have always been the enemy of individualism, the herd always ridicules the odd man out. But today it is even more difficult to be the odd man out because regulations have been devised to control him. He cannot, as I did once, wake up one morning and decide to live in the country and live on virtually nothing.

The time was during the last few weeks of summer before war broke out. I had returned from a year of travelling round the world, and I was offered a derelict cottage near Truro where I began to write a book about my travels. I was alone, and free, and thankful I was able to live the life I wanted. Nobody was ready to interfere with me provided I obeyed the law; and the law, then, wasn't too complicated to obey. Nor did I have to be registered, except for my birth certificate, with any of the government departments of the day. No self-employed National Insurance stamps to find money for. I was totally free except for my personal doubts.

I have chased the mood of that time ever since; and another time, a few months before, when I lived on an island called Toopua two hundred miles away from Tahiti. Then, without communication with the outside world, finding myself so close to nature that I looked upon myself as a stranger, part of a community who were so natural in their behaviour and so untainted by western influence that they were effortlessly happy, I promised myself that after my return to England I would immediately make plans to live for a long while on the island. Needless to say I never did go back. Needless to say that the time came when Toopua was bull-dozed into an airstrip, providing western civilisation with another triumphant example of progress; and it then became, like the other islands of the South Seas, a tourist centre for the trivial. And instead of Toopua, I found Minack.

Money, of course, is the bogey, however fervent the desire, however mature the determination to be free. When Jeannie and I came to Minack our weekly expenses were £3 a week. But if anyone today wants to break away from his customary environment, he has to act with a banker's common sense. That's the bore. He can't act rashly, impulsively like Jeannie and I did. He has to calculate, and in the course of calculating, enthusiasm is inclined to dim; and so no change is made in the end.

It is, however, easier to feel free in the country; and cheaper. In a city there are too many diversions which give people the illusion of participating in real living, when in fact they are watching as outsiders. To feel free, in the sense that you become aware that you were born to belong to yourself and not to a Fuhrer, you have to possess certain traits of the hermit; and it is simpler to be a hermit in the country than in the city. You do not have to pretend. You do not have to spend money on non-essentials in order to keep up appearances. Clothes can be old. Vegetables are the cost of the seed. Blackberries stock you with jam for the year. You can brew your own wine, make your own bread, grow your own tobacco for that matter. And you will find yourself re-adjusting your ideas as to what constitutes wealth. Getting up in the morning without hurrying is worth a good deal. So too that you have no traffic jams to join. So too that you can stand and stare without appointments to keep. So too that there is no neighbour's radio to annoy you. So too that you can look up into a silent sky. All these are put on the credit side when you calculate the cost of changing your life.

For although we are living in the affluent age, a peasant's way of life is coming into its own again. Basic goods are becoming luxuries, and so those who can learn to be self-supporting will be the lucky ones. This return to simplicity is the only practical method that any one with limited funds can follow; and yet it is so easy to say this, so difficult to put into practice. I sometimes think of the succession of crofters who lived at Minack over the past five hundred years, and envy them. They did not have to compromise as Jeannie and I have to compromise. Sometimes I touch the old rocks around the cottage which they also touched, and the years run away in my mind, and I feel close to these people whose lives were governed by the seasons. Then they believed God was in charge, not governments. They had a natural faith. Simplicity was an uncomplicated virtue taken for granted. Wisdom was instinctive, not a product of theory. Nature crushed them, and exalted them; and they were a part of the world around them as the hares, and the corn, and the wild seas, and badgers on moonlit nights, and the cries of vixen, and haywains, and the swallows coming in the spring.

Jeannie and I are aware that we possess what constitutes the new kind of wealth. Seldom passes the day during which one of us does not exclaim to the other that the life we lead is the happiest that we could imagine, and small things will prompt us to exclaim this. The sight of a Red Admiral butterfly on the feathery white flowers of a privet, bees roaming the escallonia, the croak of a frog in a hole in one of the stone walls, a dunnock feeding its young, the first whiff of the mignonette scent on the bridge, the Mediterranean blue of the sea. And yet we have to compromise.

We have to perform sophisticated tasks in order to preserve the basic simplicity which we love, because there is an inevitable conflict between our work on the land and the results of my books about Minack. Neither would exist without the other, but the books have taken us away from the hard slog which used to be our daily routine. Perhaps this is just as well. Yet we sometimes look back with nostalgia to the days when nothing else filled our minds except the earthy task in hand.

Nestlings were now in the nest in the barn, and the parents were skimming the stable meadow, soaring into the sky, snatching the invisible flies, then swooping down and darting through the doorway of the barn. No lavish spectacle devised by man could offer greater pleasure. A summer's day, green bracken covering the moorland across the valley, foxgloves pointing pink arms to the sky, the white plates of the elderberry flowers, carpets of buttercups in the donkey field with the donkeys lying outstretched among them.

We had finished packing the tomatoes around midday, and Geoffrey had gone off in the car to Penzance to take them to the wholesaler close to the harbour. Jeannie, meanwhile, had disappeared into the cottage to be with Emily, Geoffrey's young wife, who was helping with the cleaning; and there was I on the bridge when I heard the sound of a car's wheels on the gravel way up the lane.

At first I thought it was an ordinary visitor. Then suddenly I realised it was travelling very fast; and when it reached the turning before Monty's Leap the driver started tooting his horn. The car had reached the Leap before I saw who it was; and it was my friend Jack from the farm at the top. I could not for the life of me understand why he was driving so fast. In a second I knew.

Geoffrey's house was on fire. The house he had spent years building himself in the valley on the way to St Buryan.

I hurried into the cottage to collect Emily.

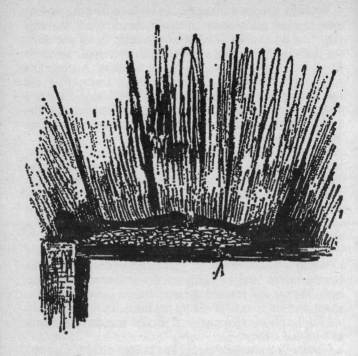

NINE

I saw the smoke billowing in the valley to my right as we
passed the Merry Maidens, that circle of stones which represent, according to legend, nineteen girls caught dancing
on a Sunday. I saw the smoke whenever the hedge was low
or there was the gap of a gateway; and I knew for certain that
this was a bad fire, because the smoke was black and thick
and in command.

'It will be all right,' I said to Jeannie and Emily beside me
in the Land Rover, 'I can't see any flames. The fire engines
must be there and damping it down.'

One tells lies on these occasions. I wonder sometimes
whether one tells them out of tact, or out of cowardice.

'Oh my home, my home,' I heard Emily crying.

We turned right at Boskenna Cross, and I put my foot down on the accelerator; and I wondered where Geoffrey might be. His habit was first to drive the Cortina with its load of tomato chips to Jennings Street where he was greeted by Fred Galley, the foreman of our wholesalers; and then park the car somewhere along the front where he ate his lunch from the pack Emily had provided. Both Jack and Bill, the farmers at the top of the hill from Minack were, I knew, trying to trace him by telephone. He had, however, another journey to do . . . he had to drive to Long Rock just outside Penzance to collect a fresh supply of tomato boxes. If he was caught at Jennings Street, he would be back within twenty minutes; if he was missed there because he had already departed for Long Rock he might be back within thirty minutes. If he had lunch between assignments he would not be back for an hour. At the moment we arrived at the fire, Geoffrey was munching his sandwiches on the front unaware that his home was being destroyed.

We joined the spectators, and spectators we could only be. There was nothing to do except watch; and when the watching became too emotional for Emily, friends took her to one of the council houses on the main road, and Jeannie went off to fetch her mother from her home two or three miles away. The fire had started in the adjoining house. The occupant had left for Penzance in his van around midday, and ten minutes later Geoffrey's mother, who lived a stone's throw away, saw smoke coming out of the porch. She ran up the hill to the road to give the alarm. There was a team of County Council workmen at work on the roadway, and while one rushed off to telephone the fire brigade, the others ran down the four hundred yards of track to Geoffrey's house. It was useless for them to try to put out the blaze, so they proceeded frantically to bring out as much of the furniture as possible; and when we arrived the grass field above the house was witness to their courage, for lying there at random was a bed, and an electric cooker, and a gramophone, and numerous other household belongings. But the bulk, including all the clothes, was still in the house; and though the firemen were doing their best, the flames, fanned by a south-westerly wind, were sweeping through the rooms;

and the glass of the great window which looked across the countryside to the Ding Dong country in the distance had already been broken into a thousand fragments by the heat. We all just stood and stared and muttered to each other our theories as to how it had begun; and I remember seeing Geoffrey's mother, a fine character who has always seemed to me to represent the best in country life, sitting on a rock, looking with resignation at the flames eating away the roof of this house which she had watched her son build with the aid of his father, a craftsman carpenter. The adjoining house was now a smoking shell; and all the fury of the flames were concentrated on Geoffrey's house. And there was still no sign of Geoffrey.

Fires hypnotise. People will stand staring at the flames snaking through rooms, watch timbers fall and walls collapse, gaze at the helmeted firemen training their jets of water through broken windows, like rabbits dazed by car headlights. This behaviour is not caused by a macabre pleasure. It is the awesome sight of an element let loose which seems alive in its viciousness. The first big fire I ever witnessed was in the Ancoats district of Manchester, and I had been sent to cover the story for the *Daily Express* by my news editor. It was night, and the building concerned was a ten-storey warehouse, and when I arrived it was already an inferno. I was fascinated into inaction. I stood staring up at the flames which were quite out of control. I saw a vast side of the building totter, then crash to the ground. I forgot why I was there. I was so hypnotised by the sight of it all that it never occurred to me that I had a job to do. Some two hours after my arrival I felt a tap on my shoulder. A senior colleague had arrived. 'I've been sent,' he remarked gently, 'to find out if you are alive.'

I did not, however, on this occasion stay gazing at the fire. I wanted to be on the main road when Geoffrey arrived, and I was up there talking to the officer in charge of the fire tender when I caught sight of the Cortina; and in a flash it had reached us and drawn up at the kerb. There is nothing one can do in such circumstances except to hold out a hand and convey sympathy by silence. He was calmer than I could have ever been.

'Everything has gone, hasn't it?' and he spoke as if he did not want an answer.

The generous village of St Buryan immediately came to their help. A home was offered to them and the two children, Philip and Julie, so that the family would not have to be separated; and clothes were showered on them, and toys. But as far as Geoffrey himself was concerned, I knew his calmness was only bottling up his emotions. Every inch of that house he knew intimately. Every nail, screw, floorboard, beam, slate, breeze block, and polished refinement he had planned with his father, and bought, and installed . . . and now they were a charred mess. Two years after the house had been completed it had become a shell for no fault of his own. An experience which might make anyone feel bitter.

I let him be on the Saturday, then went over on the Sunday morning. I walked down from the road, unpleasantly aware of the acrid smell coming from the desolation, and could see no one. Then I passed along the slope beyond the entrance to the house, and found two silent figures poking in the debris outside that great window which looked upon the distant Ding Dong country. Geoffrey and his father were picking up broken glass, and as I murmured my condolences I quickly realised that my tone may have been appreciated, they were not requiring any pity. They possessed the fatalistic outlook of the countryman, and this fire was part of the pattern of droughts, and storms, and ruined crops and lost harvests. The disaster had occurred, and it was no use to sit back and do nothing but moan about it. And so I found they were already planning the rebuilding of the house, and looking forward to the day when it would be a home again.

There was a fire at Minack many years ago, and there is a dark line along the granite lintel above the fireplace where a blazing beam left its mark. I have asked octogenarians in the neighbourhood whether they remember the occasion, and their replies are vague. Minack was a far away place which few people from St Buryan ever visited. The full name for the cottage is Dominack, but it has always been called Minack, pronounced Mynack, by those born and bred in the St Buryan and Lamorna area. In the neighbouring

89

parish of St Leven is the Minack Rock from which the famous cliff theatre takes its name. This Minack, however, is pronounced Minnack. Hence when I have talked to old people about the fire, they have replied: 'I think blind Trewern was down Minack that time.' Or: 'I don't remember. I've never been down Minack in my life.' But it seems that the fire took place just before the first world war or perhaps shortly after it started. The cottage was thatched in those days. Jeannie and I have often said that we would like to have it thatched again; and I once asked a thatcher how much this would cost. The price, I suppose, was not really excessive, but the thatcher, a formidable personality, laid down a condition that we could not accept. He insisted that the work would take three months, and during that period he would have to live in his caravan close to the cottage.

At the time of the fire there were upstairs rooms. The black line along the lintel is on the same level as the ledge which surrounds the living room, proving that this was the ceiling level; and if the ceiling existed today at that level I would always be stooping. Nor could there have been much space between the floor side of the ceiling and the roof. Thatch has to be very steep or the reeds become a bog after rain; and so the upstairs rooms, closed in by the thatch climbing to the massive, granite chimney must have been tiny. And where did the reeds come from which provided the thatch? There is an area of land sloping steeply down to the sea between the Minack boundary and the jagged point of Carn Barges in which reeds grow. They are not the type which thatchers use today, but there is little doubt that they were used in the past; and so the reeds I see when I walk to Carn Barges with the donkeys are the same stock which may have thatched Minack for centuries.

Geoffrey was back on Monday. By half past eight he had filled a couple of large baskets with tomatoes and he said to me that the morning's picking would amount to over five hundredweight. He always had an instinctive knowledge as to how much he would pick, and he was seldom wrong. It was the instinct of someone who was interested in his job, the result of enthusiasm he had shown for the plants all though their growing time. I went back into the cottage and told Jeannie. We liked to have an estimate of the quantity of tomatoes to be picked; we then could gauge how long the grading, weighing and packing would take. We decided on this occasion that if we were not interrupted we would finish by midday, and the tomatoes would reach the wholesalers before they closed for lunch. By eleven o'clock we were well up to schedule, and I was happily remarking upon this to Jeannie when I heard a car coming down the lane, then draw up outside the cottage. 'Hell,' I said, and went off to see who it was, passing Boris on the way, head tucked under his wing, squatting asleep on the London Pride which edged the rose garden. I reached the car, saw there was only one occupant, and immediately guessed he was a Government official. I observed that he had that purposeful but remote manner which always puts me on my guard. I greeted him suspiciously.

'Good morning,' I said.

'I'm from the Training Board,' he replied, 'you asked me to call.'

Indeed I had. A few weeks before, the newly constituted Agricultural, Horticultural and Forestry Training Board had summoned me for failing to pay the annual levy. The levy was £3 for each person employed; and as there was only Geoffrey to pay for, it might seem churlish that I had withheld the money. I was, however, one among thousands of growers and farmers who had failed to pay. We believed the Board was out of touch with reality, and so we made this gesture of protest against those in far away offices who devise ill-conceived regulations.

Horticulture is so different from the car, steel, and any other industry; and yet the theory boys had put it in the same category. The heavy industries are concentrated in large areas, the horticultural industry is splintered in small units all over the country; and while the heavy industries deal with mass production, the horticultural industry growing a multitude of different crops and facing all the vagaries of nature, has to deal with each problem individually.

Thus staff training is a commonsense affair; and everyone, boss or employee, has to continue his training throughout his working life. Every day you learn something from your practical work. Every day there is a new problem to face, a result of unusual weather, an unexpected pest, a mysterious plant disease. There is very little which is rational in horticulture. You cannot even organise the marketing because it depends on climatic conditions which are uncontrollable; and when expenses rise you cannot even put up your prices because you are governed by the wholesale market to which you send your produce. Horticulture does not need theoretical training schemes. It already has practical methods of helping itself. If a grower, for instance, needs specialist help he can visit one of the well-organised Government sponsored horticultural stations, or receive personal visits from helpful members of the National Advisory Service. For new recruits to the industry there are various Institutes and Colleges which teach the basic knowledge. You would say, therefore, that horticulture was well enough served by instructional opportunities. The theory boys think otherwise. Here are two extracts from their leaflets:

'It is advisable to teach an employee to teach instructional techniques to key workers who can then instruct others at their place of work.'

'Instructor training can provide the following benefits to the employer. Organised training on his own holding, tailored to meet the employee's need, an opportunity to follow without difficulty his employee's progress and capability. The instructing employee normally enjoys increased prestige and job satisfaction.' Sheer verbiage.

Nevertheless I decided to change my tactics after the summons had been served. I would challenge the Board's usefulness. I would pay the levy, then seek the Board's advice. I would behave as a reasonable employer, anxious to take advantage of Government paternalism, eager to look for ways of improving Geoffrey's horticultural techniques. I would discover at first hand how the Training Board operated; and hence my request that an official should call on me. What horticultural education would he suggest?

Jeannie said afterwards that when she saw me disappear

with the official into my office she waited for raised voices. She is, in a way, more impatient than I am, more quickly aroused by injustice, personal or social, real or imaginary; and she will sometimes want to go on the attack while I am advising caution. On the other hand I have a quick temper when caught off guard, and then I rush into an argument with fury. If, however, I have had time to contemplate upon what has vexed me, I attack with stealth. This, for me, is one of the advantages of not possessing a telephone. I can seldom be surprised. The irritations usually come by post; and I have to reply to them by post.

The irritation, on this occasion, had arrived, however, without warning; for although I had asked to see the official, he had in fact caught me by surprise. And so Jeannie was correct in thinking she might hear raised voices when he and I were alone in my office. My quick temper might dominate, and I was aware that I would let it do so if the man gave me half a chance.

He didn't. Instead of adopting the official tone of superiority I had expected, the man was disarming. I found myself feeling like a boxer who, all ready for a fight, sees his opponent throw in the towel before the first round begins. He agreed with the points I made about the Training Board instead of contesting them. He agreed that the Rosewarne Experimental Station at Camborne was one of the finest horticultural stations in the country; and that visits to see the practical work done there during the course of the year was the best possible educational value. He agreed that this area was served from Truro by highly efficient advisers from the Ministry of Agriculture National Advisory Service. He agreed that the Training Board could not offer any better training opportunities. So why should I pay a levy?

The official left without providing the answer; and I went back to Jeannie to help her finish the tomatoes.

'You seem deflated,' she said.

'I am.'

'Why? Didn't he annoy you?'

'He was far too nice.'

'What a shame,' she said laughing.

'But he left me with something to think about.'

'What exactly?'

'Well, it's an old story which only comes alive when it happens to yourself, I mean being a victim of the bureaucratic machine, and there are thousand upon thousand like me. Not just in this Training Board business, but in dozens of other different spheres. A decision is made in a wall carpeted room in Whitehall, and the man who has made it goes out and has a good lunch, walks around St James's Park, feeds the ducks, goes back to his office and already the consequences of the morning decision has been set in motion which leads in the end to the victims being angry when they first hear about it, then frightened, then resigned when they realise they cannot do anything about it.'

'Protest campaigns often succeed.'

'Only if the protesters have power to blackmail. The rest of us are ignored, we have to be obedient. We can bleat as much as we like but we will be forced to accept the decision however foolish it may be.'

'I just don't agree,' said Jeannie, she was weighing the last chip of tomatoes, 'time and time again ordinary people have made their views felt so strongly that decisions have been changed. Remember Alan Herbert saying to us long ago that people must always protest whenever their genuine feelings are aroused?'

'I do.'

A. P. Herbert, forerunner of those who wave banners in front of television cameras, attacked injustice and humbug with wit.

'It is a question of alerting people,' went on Jeannie, 'Alan said you must make people aware of an issue and the battle is half won.'

'He has always been an optimist.'

'You *are* cynical today,' said Jeannie, 'it seems to me to be time for lunch.'

I stapled the card on the last chip, and stacked the chip along with the others, all sixty of them.

'The man insisted that I will still have to go on paying the levy,' I said.

'If everyone continues to protest,' Jeannie answered

cheerfully, 'the law will be changed.' It has been; but not before I was summoned again for non-payment of a second levy.

The wind had shifted to the south, and although the weather was still warm and gentle I felt rain was not far away. I went into the cottage and poured each of us a glass of wine, then went ahead of Jeannie to the bridge. It was pleasant and sheltered enough there to sit down on the wooden bench, and stare, and eat the sandwiches which Jeannie brought to me a few minutes later.

'I saw Daisy this morning,' Jeannie said. Daisy, the little grey cat, mother of Lama.

'That's strange,' I answered, 'we seldom see her until the afternoon.'

We had often observed that she never appeared in the morning. She made her sedate way along her regular route any time from noon onwards, although over the years I remember several exceptions. There was a very cold winter, snow feet deep over our daffodil meadows in early March; and one morning I saw these paw prints on the way to the onion meadow, then caught sight of Daisy just ahead of me. Daisy was too much a part of nature ever to be unduly concerned by the contrariness of the weather. It was a part of her life, like the scent of the daffodils in the meadows in which she wandered, like the hot soil she stepped on after cliff potatoes had been dug in blazing summers, like the gales she hid from, behind lichen covered granite hedges. Strange that a cat one never touched should become so familiar.

'Heavens,' I said suddenly, 'the swallows are dive-bombing Boris!'

The bridge seems to breed inconsequential remarks. No discipline in the conversation is needed in order to have pleasure. One is watching a passing scene, and this warrants interruptions, or sudden changes of subject; a sudden flight of birds across the sky, a cuckoo calling urgently in the wood, Lama stalking a mouse in the grass by the apple tree, scores of such incidents are considered by ourselves as moments of importance. So now with Boris. Boris attacked by the swallows! The old boy was wagging his tail feathers in embarrassment. He had been up to the cottage for a meal of crumbled homemade bread scattered in front of the door by Jeannie; and he was beside the lavender bush on his way back to the grass around his pond when the attack took place.

Swish! One of the swallows missed his beak by inches. Swish! The other swallow skimmed his back. Poor Boris was bewildered.

'The young ones are soon to fly,' I said to Jeannie, then got up and went down the path to walk beside him. He plodded very slowly these days, and stiffly as if he had rheumatism. We had been more anxious than ever about him, although he gave no positive sign that he was ailing. He still had a good appetite. He still flapped happily in his pond. But there was an air about him that gave the impression of age, of a general slowing down of his ways.

'Come on old Boris,' I said, 'I'll be your escort.' He hissed fussily as he waddled on. He wanted me to know that he was perfectly capable of looking after himself.

He was, of course.

I was only showing my affection for him.

'Boris!' I suddenly shouted, 'they're dive-bombing *me*!'

A swallow had passed so close that I felt the rush of air on my face.

TEN

The flight of the young did not take place for a week. We would spy on them through the window on the lane side of the barn, pressing our faces against the glass because the dark inside made it difficult to see the nest on the ledge. Or I made a quick investigation by entering the barn itself, and looked at the nest at eye level. There were four in the brood. They would stare back at me, unafraid for a second, their heads rimming the nest, a line of fledgling white along their tiny beaks, incongruously reminding me of black and white minstrels. Their twittering would suddenly cease, their heads disappear, and I would then hurry away before a parent discovered me.

The parents, meanwhile, continued to dive-bomb the inhabitants of Minack. No one was spared their attention. Lama, Jeannie, Geoffrey, Fred and Penny, the gulls on the roof, jackdaws, woodpeckers, magpies, crows, all were to share the experience of Boris. Jackdaws, magpies and crows deserved any rough treatment they might receive; but not the rest of us. Indeed I began to wonder whether the object of the dive-bombing *was* to attack. No one was threatening the young, safe inside the barn, not even the jackdaws, magpies and crows. So were the antics perhaps a form of celebration? Were they a young swallow couple rejoicing in their achievement of producing the first brood of their lives? Were they, by their daredevil flights, trying to share the pleasure of their good fortune? If so, the response from the inhabitants of Minack must have proved disappointing.

Lama, for instance, did not find it amusing. She liked on a summer's morning to stroll towards Monty's Leap, taking her time, alert for any rustle in the grass, sniffing sweet scents, until she reached the stream where she leisurely partook of the water. The essence of this ritual was the way she could carry it out undisturbed. I would not have dared to interrupt her while the stroll was in progress; and I feel sure that if a stranger driving a car had seen her in the lane ahead of him, he would not just have stopped the car. He would have backed it out of sight. It was so perfectly obvious that she was communing with her soul, and had at all costs to be left alone.

The swallows, however, did not get the message. They observed the black plush creature below them, and thought what a delightful gesture it would be if they acknowledged her presence by slipping past her whiskers at speed. I happened to be watching Lama the first time the gesture was made; and she had momentarily paused by the elderberry tree beside which was a small syringa bush. Both were in flower and the scents clearly delighted her. She had her face up-turned to a white bloom on the syringa when a swallow dived from behind her, skimming both her nose and the white bloom, and forcing her to leap round automatically in cat-like defensive reaction. Her fury was increased by her failure to spot the enemy. Only myself was in sight, and I was certainly too far away to have been the offender. So she looked foolish; and was obviously very annoyed. Then, after a minute or two's pause, after a courageous and successful effort to subdue her annoyance, she set off again towards Monty's Leap.

She had reached the small, unused well at the side of the lane a few yards further on, when the swallow did it again. He whistled past her tail. She was at that moment totally absorbed by some activity inside the well, and I suspected she had heard a frog croaking within it. It is a shallow well, prettily placed beneath a great rock with a slab of stone overing the top of its entrance. It is a collector of land water and so it dries up in early summer, and then it becomes a comfortable hiding place for a frog or two. In spring it echoes with frog songs all day long; and when Jane and Shelagh were with us, when we used to bunch and pack our flowers in the old stables which is almost opposite, we used to play a game giving words to the croaking songs.

Lama never noticed this swoop on her tail. Her one-track mind was intent on the well, and she crouched beside it, head alert, and she seemed to me that she was about to leap inside it. Then, just as suddenly as the mystery sound had caught her attention, she lost interest; and the stroll was on again, a casual sauntering stroll denoting a cat who was at peace with the world.

The swallow, of course, was observing her. I could see him gambolling in the sky, high above the elms, then across the stable meadow and over the old hut where we used to shoot potato seed, then behind the cottage and up to the well. Then he turned, and like an aircraft lining up for a bomb attack, he swept over the bridge down the path which joined the lane, diving lower and lower, faster and faster, until with perfect timing he brushed the two little black ears of the lady who was so benignly enjoying her morning.

This time she did not ignore what had happened. She saw the swallow flash over the Leap a few yards ahead; and then belatedly displayed her displeasure. The swallow did not witness it. He was high up in the sky by then, and out of sight; and anyhow no harm would have come to him if he had. Lama's only weapon was a snarl, a turned-up lip, an ugly face. It might have scared a mouse, but not a swallow.

The jackdaws, magpies and crows were unperturbed by a swallow attack, for they were born to expect to be hated. The green woodpecker dipping its way up the valley to the wood was, however, surprised that any swallow should give him attention; and he laughed in apparent nervousness. It is an uncanny sound the woodpecker's laugh, for it is gay yet sad; and I have listened to it sometimes and wondered fancifully whether it represents the laughter of someone who died when they were young. Such a thought is too romantic; but the truth remains that a woodpecker's laugh makes me remember sometimes those I have known.

The gulls objected strongly to the swallows' behaviour. They considered the attitude of the swallows so impertinent that they would point their beaks to the sky as they stood on the flat top of the chimney or on the rim of the roof, and cry out their views on the subject. All through the year they were accustomed to treat the chimney and roof as their home during the day; and to expect their measured flight to the rocks and back to be undisturbed. Then these upstarts from South Africa who basked in the sun all those months when they themselves coped with the rain and the gales, suddenly started to bait them. It was intolerable. Yet they were powerless to stop the baiting. The swallows would skim over them as they cried, or dart at them as they glided towards the sea. It was easy to realise that the swallows infuriated them; but I have also to be fair to the swallows. The gulls are solemn creatures. I have never thought they had much sense of humour.

The donkeys, however, were very tolerant. They were banned from entering the barn, but they were not banned from the small paddock outside. The barn wall facing this small paddock caught the sun in the early morning, and its warmth often lured the donkeys to stand alongside it. This meant they were adjacent to the stable door through the top half of which flew the swallows as they went to and fro feeding the young. Not unnaturally the donkeys were intrigued by this activity; and, on awakening from a doze, they would decide to brighten their lives by having a look inside. Thus the swallows, having spent five minutes collecting insects up in the sky, would return to the barn door, beaks filled, to find two donkey bottoms facing them; while the open half of the door through which they had to fly was half blocked by two heads with large ears, peering into the semi-darkness.

There seemed to be an understanding between the donkeys and the swallows; and although the donkeys would stamp their feet when the swallows flicked past, the showed no other signs of surprise. These were donkeys in docile mood. They were curious to find out what was going on in the barn, but there was no tension in their curiosity. Fred's curiosity on other occasions can become so tense that he trembles with excitement, and then he will often blare out a bellow that sounds a little hysterical; and he will usually perform this bellow galloping across the field. He is too excited to keep still.

Various incidents can prompt this excitement. If I play hide and seek with him, if I have been so cunning as to elude him and he is at a loss to know which way to go and find me, he will often set off this bellow as he races in this direction and that; and I am then so moved by this demonstration that I emerge from my hiding place, and he will rush up to me, and there is a reunion.

Fishing boats and ships will also occasionally produce a bellow. Fred keeps a keen watch on any activity on the sea along the Minack coast. He appears to know the regular fishing boats, for although you may find him looking at them you do not receive the impression that he is particularly interested. A strange vessel, and his mood is quite different. Ears alert, nostrils quivering, you can see into his mind . . . what's that strange boat doing here? Or he may become fascinated by some craft which has anchored off shore, and although it is probably there for some quite simple reason, there are sometimes exceptions. He was fascinated, for instance, one summer evening, by a fishing boat whose skipper was repeatedly blowing a klaxon horn. This was a ready made situation for query and excitement, and Fred, who was with Penny in one of the cliff meadows at the time, responded as if he were a coastguard on duty. He was quicker to realise the skipper was in trouble than I was. He started to prance up and down the meadow, pausing every few seconds to stare out to sea; and indeed making me feel that if he had a telescope available he would have put it to use. It was a still evening, and the klaxon horn must have been heard over a wide area. So too Fred's bellow. He let out one of the loudest bellows in his repertory and it must have echoed over the water to give comfort to the distressed skipper; and it also appeared to have had an even more practical result. Within seconds I saw a distant fishing boat alter course. The combination of a klaxon horn and a donkey's bellow had alerted the crew; and soon afterwards they were towing the boat towards Newlyn.

The nautical aspect of Fred's character received a further boost more recently when the Q.E.2 passed within a mile of Minack. We knew she was coming; and we had been asked by Captain Warwick to put up some kind of signal. The wooden stake which propped up Jeannie's washing line was purloined, and a large orange tablecloth was nailed to it. The stake, now a flagpost, was then sandwiched between two boulders on the edge of a field close to the cottage; and there we waited.

We had chosen this field because the passengers aboard were being given a running commentary by the Chief Purser; and the placing of the flagpost in this field would enable the passengers to see the cottage at the same time as the orange tablecloth. We were, however, prevented from watching the approach of the Q.E.2 by the brow of a hill; and we depended upon Geoffrey to shout from a vantage point news of her coming.

Suddenly she was upon us. It was as if she had sailed out of the hill. The sight was stupendous, so unexpectedly beautiful that I found myself wanting to cheer; and this was exactly how Fred felt too. He was so excited that he literally quivered with emotion; and when the Q.E.2 sounded three deep blasts from her siren in greeting, I felt he might leap over the cliff into the sea and swim to her. Seaman Fred had come of age.

The interest of the donkeys as to what the swallows were up to in the barn never lasted very long. They would move away in to the stable field, and if it was a fine early morning and there was a rabbit or two about, they would create a diversion for themselves by giving chase to a rabbit. I have seen them chase a rabbit from one end of the stable field to the other, though they did so in harmless fashion. They were not chasing to catch the rabbit, and the rabbit knew this; so the chase was only an innocent game.

Jeannie once saw Fred chase a fox cub through the wood. We do not allow them in the wood because they have this foolish habit of gnawing bark whenever they are bored. Some people say that they gnaw the bark so as to sharpen their teeth. Whether or not this is true, the bark is still gnawed; and as a tree will die if the trunk is made bare of bark at any circular point, it is obvious that the wood had to be put out of bounds.

However at the time Jeannie watched Fred chase a cub, we had not awakened to the damage they were doing; and they were allowed to roam as they wished. It is a very small wood, a copse in fact, but they then had its freedom. In one corner Jeannie has a small cabin where she paints and draws; and where she wrote her novel *Hotel Regina*. She was there one afternoon when she saw a cub saunter past the cabin window oblivious of her presence, or the proximity of the donkeys for that matter. It appeared to be going into the inner wood when it changed its mind; and Jeannie watched it turn, then advance towards where the donkeys were standing out of sight, close to the hut where Boris lived.

Suddenly Jeannie heard a commotion, and the cub came scampering back past her window; and a few seconds later came Fred, nose to the ground like a foxhound. But instead of the tense face of the hunter, Jeannie says that Fred was obviously laughing; and that Penny, a yard or two behind, was laughing so much that she was flinging out her back legs as if she was kicking someone when, of course, there was no one to kick. The cub, a future of danger and serious chasing and narrow escapes lying ahead, hastened speedily away; and as Jeannie watched it disappear over the wall into the inner wood she wished it well, as anyone wishes a traveller well. The donkeys, now baulked by the wall, just stared across it to the uncharted world beyond. They were not frustrated. The chase had been a momentary game. They were not trying to prove anything. Life was fun for them.

It was not much for us, however, when we had to chase *them*. One would have thought there was no reason for them ever to wish to escape from their environment. Few donkeys had such space in which to wander, such variety of grass, such succulent different delicacies in the hedges. I had had a postcard from an R.A.F. man in Arabia this summer with a message for Fred. The postcard was a photograph of two donkeys laden with packs, and it came from Muscat in the Trucial States. 'These are *working* donkeys,' wrote the sender, 'Fred never had it like this! They have never seen grass.' I showed the postcard to Penny and Fred, rubbing the photograph against their soft noses. 'Now you realise how lucky you are!' I said . . . and they both promptly started to hoot.

Their escapades are only mischievous adventures; and I have learnt that Penny is usually the leader on these occasions. She is a sly one. She appears to be such a reliable matron type of donkey, she is always in the background when Fred is showing off, she seems always more slow in her movements; and yet I have several times realised that she urges Fred to commit the initial misdemeanour. Then if Fred succeeds in opening the gate or lifting the bar across a gap which I thought I had fixed securely, Penny will push past him and take the lead; and I have known her on a walk (on walks along the cliff we always take off their halters) behave so naughtily that she succeeds by some deception in slipping past us, then rush into a gallop with Fred fast behind her, and they are away in the distance before we realise what has happened. I have known them gallop up the lane in this thundering fashion. I saw them one afternoon munching the heliotrope around Monty's Leap, and I advanced slowly to capture them, murmuring friendly noises while doing so. I learnt later that their escape on this occasion was not their fault, a gate had been left open; but I would have been in any case furious when I saw them ignore my kindly approach, and set off up the lane. Within a few yards they put on the pace. There I was panting behind them, when I saw Penny's bottom disappear round the corner, Fred on her heels. This is the type of occasion when donkeys have you at their mercy. There is nothing you can do. They are up and away, and that's that. Fortunately Bill, who has one of the farms at the top of the lane, was walking down it; and he met them coming towards him at such speed that he said afterwards they would have continued to the main road a mile away and on to Penzance had he not been there to stop them.

Escape routes, however, are not always the result of a left-open gate, a bar cleverly removed from a gap, or a latch nudged by a nose. The donkeys, during the nights they spend in the open, become well acquainted with the badgers and foxes that live in the area; and when they watch them padding across a field, they also observe the path they take to get out of the field. At the bottom of the stable field there is a stone hedge which over the years has become overgrown with couch grass. On the stable field side it is about three feet high, on the big field side because the ground is lower it is a foot higher; and I have always taken it for granted that there was no chance of the donkeys jumping over it.

This summer, however, badgers had padded down the couch grass, and made a foot-wide path up the stable field side of the hedge, then over into the big field. I half noticed its existence, even caught sight of a badger one moonlit night, as he went his way over the hedge, then on towards the sett that lies hidden in the undergrowth half-way down our cliff; but I never thought this path might give ideas to the donkeys. Geoffrey once said of them after some particular escapade: 'I knew they were educated . . . but not that educated!' And I was soon to remember his remark.

It was a pleasant July evening, and my aunt was staying with us, and we had just finished dinner; and I happened to look out of a window which is close to my desk. Far away across the moorland I saw two familiar figures on Carn Barges.

'Jeannie!' I shouted, although she was only within a few feet of me, 'the donkeys! They're on their way to Lamorna!'

There was good cause for this panicky outburst. Never before had the donkeys received such a start. If I ran it would take me the best part of ten minutes to reach them, and when they saw me coming I was certain they would take evasive action. Ingenious donkeys who had escaped from the stable field by a badger path, who were now enjoying the full flush of freedom, who knew they were on the route to the Lamorna pub, were not going to surrender tamely. And anyhow, although they had paused on Carn Barges and from a distance seemed to be meekly grazing, would they stay there long enough for me to reach them?

'They're off!'

It was Jeannie who shouted this time. She was just ahead of me as I came out of the cottage; and she caught sight of Penny leading the way down the little path from the Carn, then disappearing inland along the rough path we always went with the donkeys. We called it the donkey walk. If it had not been for the donkeys the undergrowth on either side of the winding path would have joined together, and obitereeated it. But the donkeys have always liked this walk, and so I keep it open by taking a pair of secateurs along with me, snipping the tendrils of the brambles as I go. The path is like a steeplechase course. There is a point where the donkeys have to jump on to a low stone wall, then plunge into a deep gully which is always squelching with mud; and there is a stream to jump which in winter makes such a noise as it rushes downwards to the sea, that Fred at first refused to jump it. It would not stop him now, certainly not in summer when it is only a trickle.

'All I can do,' I said, 'is to take the car and meet them in Lamorna.'

'Jeannie laughed.

'You make it sound as if you are going to collect a friend who has been out for a walk.'

'I think the only thing for you to do,' I went on, 'is to walk along the path just in case they've stopped on the way.'

'All right.'

The lure of Lamorna for the donkeys lay in the potato crisps that Tommy Bailey, then landlord of the pub, provided for them; and in the carrots that Mrs Murley of the post office always offered them whenever her shop was open. They were also fussed over by numerous children, photographed by adults who rewarded them with more potato crisps, and were in fact treated as honoured guests. They loved the place. Moreover, as I will tell, they had been invited to open the annual Lamorna Gala. They felt at home in Lamorna.

But I did not find them in the village. They had lost their nerve. I had driven straight to Tommy's pub and asked those present if they had seen any donkeys, and nobody had. So I took the car up the lane which continues up the side of the valley until it fades out in moorland except for the path of the donkey walk. Halfway up I saw in the growing dusk three holidaymakers coming towards me.

'Have you,' I asked after I had stopped the car, 'by any chance seen two donkeys?'

The eccentricity of the British is their normality in unusual situations. The holidaymakers were politeness itself.

'Well,' said one in a manner that suggested I had asked whether she could tell margarine from butter, 'two donkeys did run past us earlier on.'

Ah! I said to myself, I know what has happened. They had lost their nerve on the last part of the journey to the village. Even when we were with them they had always been disconcerted. They thought a dustbin was an enemy, or the steps to a cottage, or a gutter beside the lane, or a parked car. Sometimes they would refuse to pass an object which puzzled them. They behaved, before they reached the potato crisp, like primitive tribesmen seeing the bright lights for the first time.

And so, I guessed, they had turned off on a lane to their left which ended in a cul-de-sac. I was correct. I drove the car up this lane and discovered the two of them, shamefaced, longing-to-be-home donkeys. I had no halters so I took Penny by her mane; and I frogmarched her up towards the moorland, and when I reached it Jeannie was there. We kept the donkeys ahead of us as we returned to Minack; and after they were there, after we had put them in the field above the cottage and made sure that the gate and all other possible escape routes were secure, I went back to Lamorna to collect the car.

Next morning, as had been my habit since the eggs were hatched, I peered through the barn windows to see how the young swallows were progressing. They were out of the nest.

Two were perched on top of a daffodil wind-break which was leaning against the wall opposite. The other two I could just see on the top of the galvanised bin in which we normally kept the donkey food pellets during the winter.

For three days they never flew from the barn. They used it as a nursery.

ELEVEN

When the swallows flew out of their nursery and began to play games in the sky, and perched on the slates of the stable waiting their turn for insects to be brought by their parents, the shine on the green of the bracken was fading, docks were seeding, the bulb meadows needed scything, the cuckoos were soon to leave, the brightness of butterflies had taken the place of June gaiety of birds. Early July time, and the mood of Cornwall was changing. Cars rushed along the narrow lanes, meeting at places too narrow to pass where drivers shouted at each other, each refusing to be the first to back. It is always the same in the first half of July. The visitors are in a hurry. They seem to have brought their grievances with them.

'Why the hell do you have this stone post here?' demanded a driver of a friend of mine. He had just smashed into it.

'It's my gatepost,' replied my friend plaintively. She produced a hammer to help beat out the damaged mudguard, found a glass of milk for the child in the car, carried a cup of tea to the mother.

'Ugh,' said the mother after sipping it, 'you've put sugar into it. I don't take sugar.'

'The gatepost should never have been there in this narrow lane,' went on the husband, bringing the hammer down with a bang, and breaking it. 'And why have a cheap hammer?'

At night the entrances to fields, the laybys, the grass verges, are the parking places of caravans disguised as cars. In the morning they disgorge their occupants who eat out of tins brought from home, then leave their litter for County Council workmen laboriously to collect. During the day other cars are parked; and men in braces, women in flowered dresses, enjoy their Cornish holiday by the roadside, brewing tea on Calor gas camp stoves, sitting on the metal-framed chairs that fold neatly in the boot of the car, reading newspapers.

Early July time . . . and one local inhabitant will say to another: 'A lot of people about but they aren't spending any money.'

A publican will interrupt.

'Three nice looking people came into the pub yesterday lunchtime, said they were thirsty but didn't ask for beer. They asked for three glasses of water, and although I didn't like this I didn't want to be awkward and so I obliged them. They carried the glasses outside and sat on the bench. Then I saw them through the window dropping those lemon powders or some other flavour into the glasses. They didn't even bother to bring the glasses back when they left.'

A café proprietor betters the story.

'A couple asked for a cup of tea. Then shared it.' And he added, 'Never mind, a better lot will start coming next week.'

The local inhabitants can be edgy in early July time, thinking of overdrafts to be cleared by the season's end;

and, unused to city manners, they are sometimes inclined to take offence when offence was not intended. Sometimes, of course, they are also accused of being greedy, but the friendliest people in the world towards strangers who want to be friendly too; but they are quick to react against those whose manners they consider abrupt or supercilious. But the pleasant stranger will always be made to feel welcome; and he will find certain aspects of the Cornish character, politeness and enthusiasm for instance, that will charm him.

Cornwall, however, is puzzled about its future. Should it be a playground, a haven for retired people, and an agricultural county, or should it become industrialised? Areas of Cornwall are, of course, already industrialised . . . china clay around St Austell, engineering in Camborne, the ship repairing docks at Falmouth, the developing tin industry; and there are factories for light industries, often subsidised by the Government, on the outskirts of many other towns. But there are those who would like to see such industrialisation substantially increased pointing out that this is the only way that the young of Cornwall will be able to find work in the county. There are others who argue that the native young, like their forebears, consider it adventurous to leave home; and that although some will want to stay, there will be a negligible number to staff the new industries. Hence labour will have to be imported with all its attendant social problems; and values, which hitherto have provided the Cornish with happiness, will be destroyed.

Propagandists for more industrialisation also make capital out of the unemployment figures which are above the national average. These figures were increased by SET, and by higher basic national wage rates; for no local employer can now afford to keep a person on his staff who does not give his maximum effort in return. Nevertheless the figures give a misleading impression of the true situation. Cornwall is so pleasant a place to live in that there are unemployed who are quite content to remain unemployed. There are also the seasonal unemployed. Fishermen who sign on as unemployed when the weather is unsuitable for their vessels to go to sea, those who work in the holiday trade during the summer, then take a holiday themselves during the winter.

All these inflate the unemployment figures. Few of them, I fancy, would exchange their present way of living for a life in a factory. For better or for worse they believe, deep within themselves, that they have a sounder philosophy than those who live in industrial centres; and when every summer the roar of the holidaymaker comes to Cornwall, the wisdom of this belief seems to be confirmed. Holidaymakers do not suggest that those who earn high wages in monotonous conditions are to be envied. A sophisticated society, it appears, has to lose its soul as a price for the transient rewards it worships.

The policy makers of Cornwall, meanwhile, are pressing for a trunk road (a spine road they call it) through Cornwall to Penzance. The prospect of a bonanza of motor cars being able to speed to this end of Britain excites them. Faith in communications, in the form of motorways and trunk roads, is the vogue; and a trunk road to Penzance therefore suits the age. But those of us who live in West Cornwall wonder what is to happen to the traffic when it reaches Penzance. For ten months in the year there is not enough traffic to cause any trouble, but in high summer the town is already a bottleneck. There is a talk of a by-pass round the town, and that poses another problem. What happens to the traffic when it reaches the few narrow roads and lanes on the other side of the town in the wild, rural district of West Penwith? But perhaps the prospective chaos does not matter. Perhaps the object of spending vast sums on a trunk road is to make industrialisation inevitable. Factories, and new housing estates, will have to line the route to justify the expense. Materialism accompanied by its vandalism, will be victorious.

Sometimes I lightheartedly wonder whether the small though influential pressure for industrialisation stems from the stark religious convictions of the Cornish past, when pleasure was considered a sin. All those grim services in draughty chapels, all those heady revivalist meetings where sinners suddenly saw the light, perhaps still echo down the years. Everywhere there are reminders of those days. Small chapels isolated in the corners of fields, great barn-like chapels in main streets, even posters on noticeboards still exhort the passersby to behave according to the scriptures. 'Steer clear of alcohol and you will steer clear of trouble.' 'Keep to the narrow path and you will do no wrong.' And there are too, along with this haunting religious fervour, reminders of the industrial times that belonged to it. Desolate mine stacks are scattered around West Cornwall, prodding into the sky like headstones in a cemetery, a constant reminder to every Cornishman that in the nineteenth century the Cornish mining and engineering traditions were known throughout the world.

Perhaps this is the reason why local dignitaries, from time to time, refer to the holiday trade in terms that suggest they are almost ashamed of it, as if it were a trade of immoral earnings. You can also hear disparaging remarks about the ageing population of retired people with which Cornwall is allegedly burdened. This is a viewpoint I can never understand. People are going to retire somewhere after working hard all their lives, and Cornwall is lucky to attract so many. They bring their savings with them and, most importantly, they spend their income in the county. Retired people, a holiday industry . . . this impression of a lotus land is offensive to some. Yet the holiday industry is already worth £42 million a year, and future expansion could be enormous, particularly if it set out to attract people from abroad. It needs, however, just as much practical encouragement from the Government of the day as the Government now gives to build factories.

Meanwhile the Cornwall County Council is giving a lead. It is trying to centralise all aspects of the holiday trade under its advisory control; and in taking this action it is following the example of such holiday areas as Bermuda and the Bahamas. Both are geographically part of the West Indies, just as Cornwall is geographically part of the South West; but such are their individual attractions they prefer to operate each on their own. Cornwall, too, with its special attractions, must act on its own.

The County Council, therefore, will supply the driving force behind such essentials of the holiday business as publicity, tours by travel agents from abroad, and other aspects of business promotion that can best be developed by a centralised Cornish organisation. It is also compiling a register of high standard accommodation in hotels, guest houses and farms throughout Cornwall and the Scilly Islands for distribution among potential holidaymakers at home and abroad. Support will have to be given to the Council if it is to carry out its programme, and here is the rub. Until the success of the Council's plans are proven, those in the holiday industry are loth to subscribe towards the expense; and if they dither and do nothing, the enthusiasm of the County Council may wane; and instead of the holiday playground it aims to create, the earth moving machines will proceed to eat up the rich agricultural lands, destroying the countryside and the magic of Cornwall. Then the holiday industry will fade away, and the inhabitants will remember with nostalgia their present spirit of independence as they trudge towards the factory gates. Those in the holiday trade may be edgy in early July time, but such edginess does not last long. Soon the visitors begin to arrive who are free spending, and business begins to boom, and Cornwall is giving pleasure to tens of thousands of people. Surely such an industry imaginatively developed is worth far more to the Cornish both financially and spiritually, then a multitude of factories.

Jeannie and I, meanwhile, remain in our private world. We discuss solemn problems, argue about them with others, but are happiest when we pretend they do not exist. It is easy to pretend when we are up on the bridge. Each day, each hour, each minute the scene is different in the kingdom around us. This is the glory of living in the present, of having the time to marvel at the grace of a buzzard, at the sight of a Peacock butterfly, first of the summer, settling for a second on a leaf of the escallonia beside us, at the shape of a cloud above the Lizard; and relishing sudden excitements like watching the perambulations of Whitepants, the fox who lived on the other side of the shallow valley in the copse where the magpies had their cumbersome nest.

He was a fine dog fox with a splendid red-brown coat and brush. He looked, in fact, quite a normal fox until you saw his haunches, and these were a light fawn colour like a tropical khaki. He was a comical sight, half noble, half a

114

clown; and he had an unusual temperament for a fox. He was clearly an easy going, placid character who had faith in the good nature of everyone in the neighbourhood; and as a result he courted danger unnecessarily. He was also a punctual fox. He used to appear, this July, from his hideout in the copse at six every evening on the dot; and so when I saw him I did not have to look at my watch to know it was news time. Whitepants and the time signal coincided.

He would then proceed to potter in the field beside the copse, a field in which potatoes had been grown until a month before and where the dried up tops of potato plants still strewed the ground, and where the jackdaws and the crows pecked at the potatoes that had been left behind after the harvesting. Jeannie and I would sit on the bridge, evening drinks beside us, with our field-glasses trained on him, watching his every move and observing his intelligent face. Occasionally he would turn his attention to the hedge, and like a cat he would poise himself to pounce on some mysterious rustle, and after a tantalising minute of waiting he would leap forward. There he would be, spreadeagled, motionless. 'He's missed it,' one of us would say.

He would move on through the gap to the big field of green grass opposite us, and there the young rabbits of summer would see him coming; and they would stop nibbling, and those who were close would scurry away, and others would sit upright like begging dogs, half afraid, half curious. Sometimes he would make a dart at one of them, a half-hearted rush which suggested he had made the move because it was expected of him, not because he wanted a rabbit for his supper. Indeed this was what puzzled us about Whitepants. Why set off on a journey when there were still hours of daylight to provide danger?

It was, too, the time of day when a young man or two would be out with their guns; and from over the brow of the hill we would hear a shot, and we would glance at an unperturbed Whitepants nosing in the grass, and we were the ones who were afraid. Then a few minutes later we would see a young man silhouetted against the skyline, advancing towards the field, and we were aware that he would be able to hide on the other side of the hedge at the top; and both

Whitepants and the rabbits would be in view. You cannot blame a farmer for shooting a fox when his chickens have been repeatedly raided. You can understand him being furious with someone like myself who scares the fox away just as the shot is about to be fired; and thus scares the rabbits away too.

However, after a while, after becoming so accustomed to Whitepants that I felt it my duty to protect an interfering nuisance, I could not stand the tension any longer; and when, one evening, I saw the young man advancing again, I left the bridge, ran down the lane, and up the slope to the field towards him. I was trespassing. I had no right to be there. Nor, as it turned out, had I any need to be there.

I was out of breath when I reached him.

'Please,' I managed to gasp. 'Please don't shoot the fox you see down here very evening . . . it's a fox we know very well and we're very fond of him.'

I felt foolish. I realised I sounded a little hysterical; and that it would have been so much more dignified had I walked slowly, nonchalantly up the field, and conveyed my feelings after a few casual words of introduction.

'I won't harm him,' said the young man, and he looked at me good humouredly, the same sort of way that an indulgent father might look at an over eager son, 'I don't shoot foxes anyway.'

Whitepants had a neighbour in his copse, a dog fox who lolloped around on three legs; the fourth, although not completely useless, barely touched the ground when he was moving. We did not see him often, and we certainly never saw him in the company of Whitepants; but from time to time we noticed him edging along the shelter of the hedge, then into the copse and out of sight. He may, of course, have been on passage to the cliff and the route through the copse was a convenient one to take. He may, on the other hand, have been a relation that Whitepants did not like, or a visitor that had outstayed his welcome, or just an old fox whose time was up. All I can say is that one late afternoon, about half an hour before Whitepants was due to make his customary appearance, a hyena-like sound came shrieking from the copse, accompanied by fox barks, and a general

116

thunderous noise of battle. Once before I had heard such a din. We were bunching daffodils late one night when there was a terrible cacophony up the lane; and it went on so long that finally I went with a torch to have a look. Half way up the light shone on a fox in the ditch. It was dying. An old fox killed by a young one.

On this occasion I took no steps to investigate. I had a good view from where I was standing on the bridge, and so I just stared at the copse, and waited. The noise stopped just as suddenly as it started. Then a second or two later I caught sight of the three-legged fox emerging from the copse into the field, and he was slinking along as if he were ashamed of something which had just happened. Then I saw him stop, and sit down and lick himself . . . onwards a few yards and the same anxious licking. Otherwise, although I was looking at him through my field-glasses, I could see no sign of any wound on him. He reached a broken down part of the hedge, and hopped through it into the green carpet of bracken, and disappeared from my sight. I never saw him again.

Half an hour later, punctually at six o'clock, Whitepants appeared. A suave, unperturbed Whitepants. No detective observing his serene manner, would have guessed he had so recently been guilty of violent assault. Or had he been guilty? My thoughts may have been maligning him all the while. Perhaps he had been sound asleep in his earth. Perhaps he was just waking up when he heard this noise up above. A third fox, face to face with my three-legged fox on the track through the copse to the cliff, may have been the attacker. I will never know. This is the maddening, delicious part of living in the country close to nature . . . there are so many unanswered questions. One does not have the mind of a scientist, ponderously seeking logical explanations, or coldly coming to confident conclusions which in a few years are proved to be wrong.

I do not know, for instance, what happened to Whitepants. Throughout that summer he continued to follow his routine, and it was a routine as I have said that had its dangers. A fox, if he is wise, does not wander out on a summer's evening, then follow a route which takes him straight past farms where milking is just finishing, where tired, even irritable, farmers are about to have their supper. It is something a sensible fox, a fox always alert to fear, simply would not do. Whitepants acted otherwise.

After he had made his gestures at pursuing the rabbits, after he had no doubt watched me making my out of breath pleas for his safety, he continued his dangerous way. He quietly, ruminatively, sniffed around the field, then jumped the hedge into a no man's land of gorse and brambles, and became hidden from my sight. Not quite. The magpies followed him when he hopped that hedge, after I had been watching him, the magpies took over the watch. I stood on the bridge listening to them chattering as they displayed his secret whereabouts from above. Every evening the same disclosures were made. Were others aware of them as well?'

A fox has a fascination for a magpie. I have seen so often a magpie hopping about in a field where a fox is roaming, baiting the fox, cackling insults at it. A pair of magpies had always made a special point of baiting Whitepants who continued his perambulations without taking notice. Indeed a family of magpies used to dance around him. No doubt they came from the cumbersome nest above his earth; and I wonder what they thought when one day, later in the summer, he did not appear. I know that Jeannie and I missed him as we sat on the bridge. Poor Whitepants. He should never have begun his nocturnal adventures in daylight.

TWELVE

We seldom leave Minack during the summer even for a
day. Once a week Jeannie shops to fill the larder; and as we
have a refrigerator with a small deep freeze compartment,
such weekly shopping presents no problem. Nor do we have
to worry about fresh bread because Jeannie bakes it herself,
or milk which we have from Jack's farm at the top of the
lane (from the milk Jeannie makes her own Cornish cream),
or about vegetables because we grow our own. Nor do we
have to queue at the laundry. We have an automatic washing machine which merrily does its work while Jeannie per-
forms some task of her own; and the contents are then hung
on the washing line, up above the well, and when they are
dry they have the salty scent of sea air.

There is still, however, shopping to do; and every Friday morning Jeannie drives up the lane on her way to call at Ted Chappel's in St Buryan, or Jackson's in Sennen, or Jim Veal in Newlyn where she buys fish landed that morning, or Reg Stevens the butcher whose shop faces the river beside Newlyn Bridge. All these have the pleasant atmosphere associated with small shops, where as you make your choice, national events of the past week are discussed and local gossip exchanged. No one is in a hurry. Care is taken that you have exactly what you require. The mood is conveyed that shopping is to be enjoyed and not to be anxious about. You leave looking forward to your return, despite the fact that prices next week will have risen again.

In Penzance Jeannie parks the car in the car park behind the Greenmarket. Penzance is still a charming old market town although one wonders how long it can maintain its character. A monstrous skyscraper, housing government departments, now looms above the rooftops in the centre of the town. The route of a new road round the harbour will, if the plan is implemented, demolish many old houses including perhaps the one in Chapel Street from which Maria Branwell set off for Yorkshire to meet and Marry Patrick Brontë. The entry into Penzance along Eastern Green is already a conglomeration of utility factory buildings, a garish petrol station, and a caravan site that looks like a shanty town. More significantly, long established shops are one by one closing down unable to compete with SET and the invasion of supermarket chain stores; and thus old buildings disappear and Market Jew Street, the main street of Penzance, is becoming like any suburban High Street. But what value has antiquity in this age of landings on the moon.

The latest plan to hasten on the changing face of Penzance is a diabolical one . . . the Central Electricity Generating Board propose to transport huge transformers through the town from the harbour on giant trailers destined for various booster power stations in Cornwall. The Board has intimated that on sections of the route where it is too narrow for the trailers, the offendings buildings will be compulsorily purchased; and pulled down. The fact that the buildings contain shops, that people will lose their livelihood does not seem to matter. For the moment the buildings have been reprieved, but one wonders for how long. Whatever happens, the fact that the proposal was made is an example of what planners are prepared to do in the name of progress.

There is still, however, the friendliness of Penzance to be grateful for, the pleasure of watching people strolling instead of hurrying; and there are the sudden moments of beauty when you catch sight of the sea through the slit of a street, one of the narrow streets falling downhill towards the harbour and Mount's Bay; or you may be stirred by a glimpse of St Michael's Mount away in the distance by Marazion; or you may see the Scillonian, white and elegant like a tiny cruising liner, setting off for the islands; or you may notice a ship anchored in the Bay which is a stranger, and you are momentarily puzzled as to why she is there. The emotions are stirred too by the small Regency houses that you find in odd corners of the town, and by the Morrab Gardens where near-tropical plants blossom, even by the promenade which stretches from the harbour to Newlyn, rebuilt after the great storm of 1962, and now the finest in the west country. There is still much to delight in Penzance.

Jeannie's weekly visit, however, does not last long, and this not because she does not enjoy it. It is simply that shops she used to go to have disappeared; and now her regular visits are limited to friends like Mrs Michell who keeps the newspaper shop up the steps from the terrace of Market Jew Street, and the staff at Peasgoods, Neil James of Davy's, and the girls at Leroy; and there are occasional visits to see Mr Simpson about buying a shirt for me, and to Mr Nicholls the ironmonger, to Mr Dunne of the photography shop, to Gerry of the Post Office at the bottom of the town, to Mr Cousins in Alexandra Road, and to the remarkable Michells the jewellers who seem to repair any watch, any small piece of jewellery for kindness instead of for profit; and on the way home she may look in at the Queens Hotel on the front where she used to go as a child before sailing to the Scillies; and where Frank the barman and Billy the porter are still there to fuss over her. The Queens is our headquarters in Penzance. Jeannie always goes there, as I do, whenever she has to make a long distance telephone call.

She will also have seen Charlie Brockway during her visit. Charlie Brockway is a black and white cat of substantial stature, a notorious personality in the town, whom you meet sometimes striding along the terrace in Market Jew Street, or lurking in Morrab Gardens, or sauntering along the West Parade between Alexandra Road and the car park behind the Greenmarket.

It is in the car park, however, where you will generally find him. This is his patch. This is where he will stretch himself on the bonnet of a car and refuse to move when the owner is wishing to leave. He has a particular fondness for vans, large vans; and it is fortunate for him that only local vans use the car park, and the drivers, knowing his eccentricities, look out for him, both inside and outside their vans, before they move off. Even so I have seen a van move off with Charlie curled on the bonnet, and the driver laughing, and tooting his horn, ready to stop as soon as Charlie woke up.

His home is the shoe shop from which he takes his name. The front faces Chapel Street, the back the car park; and the wall which separates the back from the car park is where Charlie holds court, where he washes in leisurely confidence, pretending to be indifferent to the noises of praise from his admirers, who pause by him, hoping for recognition, shopping bags in hand. There are many like Jeannie who look forward to seeing Charlie Brockway, and when he is not there on the wall or on the bonnet of a car, the car park attendant will be questioned: 'Where's Charlie?' The attendant, himself an admirer, will reply inconsequentially: 'Yesterday that Charlie caused some trouble . . . ' and he will tell another of Charlie's adventures.

He was a stray before he came into his world of shoes. He was looking through the door of the shop one day when a lady assistant showed an interest in him. This alerted his instinct of self-preservation; and he proceeded to behave in that irresistible, beguiling fashion that strays adopt once they have decided on the home that suits them. The shoe shop would be his home, he decided, and nothing would stop him. Of course, the assistants were only too happy to

122

oblige, and so too were the customers. They were delighted that such a beautiful cat should take such an interest in their stockinged feet; and so Charlie wandered at will during the day, but was sure to be home by closing time. He had a job to do. He was night custodian of the shoes; and he clearly enjoyed this role. But on one occasion he was faced with a situation that all night watchmen hope will never occur. A thief broke into the shop. Nothing serious was stolen. Perhaps the sight of Charlie advancing towards him, claws at the ready, frightened the man off. Whatever may have happened, the reaction of both staff and customers next morning when the theft was discovered was the same. 'What about Charlie?' was the cry instead of 'What has been stolen?' . . . 'Was Charlie frightened? Poor Charlie!' There has been a touch of glamour about Charlie ever since.

One day before the end of July we went to the Scillies to see Jane. A day away from Minack always requires serious preparation, for it upsets the peaceful routine. Thus it was arranged that Geoffrey would do work close to the cottage, would stay on after his normal time, then lock the gate near Monty's Leap when he left. He would keep a close eye on Boris, feed him with his favourite digestive biscuits, and shut him inside his house at the end of the day. The donkeys, meanwhile, would be kept in the stable field because they would be sure to hoot if any strangers came up towards the cottage from the big field; and thus Geoffrey would be alerted if he had not seen the strangers himself. Lama, of course, would be well fed before we set out, but a window would be kept open for her; and Geoffrey would try and keep track of her peregrinations during the day, and would make sure that she was inside the cottage, and the window shut, when he departed. The gulls were provided for by a plate of Jeannie's home-made bread, so Geoffrey would toss them a piece whenever their squawks became too prolonged; and the small birds of the bird table had a Michael Truscott designed pottery dish full of grain from which Geoffrey could feed them. All this organisation because of a day away from the premises. An example of what happens when your life becomes so pleasantly parochial that you deem such matters of high importance.

The purpose of the visit was to attend the christening of Jane's daughter Sylvia. We were godparents and it is understandable that we were pleased. Jane had been part of a turbulent period of our life at Minack. I remember her arriving with her mother, a fey woman of indomitable courage to live in the middle cottage of the three at Pentewan, her mother having taken up the job of herdswoman at the farm; and they brought with them a caravanserai of animals. Lamb, the sheep who was given a hut in the garden, Siamese Sim, and Val the white Persian, Eva the griffon, half blind and personal dog to Jane, a parrot who once belonged to Jane's great-grandmother, and Acid, a brindle bull terrier, who was to play for hours every day in the fields above the sea with Jane's young brother Jeremy.

Jane was at boarding school at the time, but within a few months she would be fifteen, and when she learnt about our flower farm, she decided she would like to work for us; although her headmistress had high ambitions for her future, pressing her to stay on at school, Jane was adamant; and after she had won her mother over to her view, she arrived one day at Minack. We did not need her help, we could not even afford her. But there she was and she became a part of our lives . . . and I can see her now with fair hair falling over her shoulders arriving across the fields from her cottage with a puzzled Boris in her arms after an admirer had brought him for her dinner; and coming up from the cliff in a storm of rain, basket of daffodils in either hand, her face hidden by a black sou'wester much too big for her; and sharing the excitement with Jeannie as they prepared the flowers for the Penzance Show (the prize cards we won line the oak beam above me as I write); and then her moment of triumph after she had left us and gone to Tresco Gardens, when she won the Prince of Wales' Cup at the Show, the most important cup for any grower to win, and she was the youngest ever to do so. Understandable, therefore, that there was a special pleasure in this visit to the Scillies.

She lived now on the island of Bryher, her mother had

died, Dick, her husband, worked on one of the small flower farms, and in his spare time was a craftsman in woodwork. He met us in St Mary's after we had flown from Penzance in the helicopter, and he had a launch ready to take us to Bryher. I had never been to any of the outer islands before, and as the launch splashed through the sun-sparkled water, I suppose it was inevitable that I should begin thinking of my time in the South Seas. Small yachts, some flying foreign flags, lay anchored around us as we passed, reminding me of those I watched from my hotel window in Papeete, conveying the impression of adventure, snugness, hot days, danger, all in one. There was the island of St Martins to my right in the distance, heaving out of the sea like Bora Bora, and everywhere were the small, uninhabited rocks of islands which were like the coral reefs of the Tuomotus. Samson was to my left with its white beach like Toopua, and opposite Bryher was the green land of Tresco, lush like the hinterland of Tahiti. And when the launch hove-to off the long beach of Bryher, and we jumped into a rowing boat to be rowed ashore, and the keel of the rowing boat crunched against the sand, this primitive arrival took the years away from me; and my senses, if not my eyes, at that moment belonged to other arrivals, other islands.

Jeannie used to come to Bryher when she was a young girl. Her father, although he never stayed there, had a passion for it; and when he built a house in St Albans at the top of the hill in Avenue Road, he called it Bryher Lodge; and if that was not enough to prove his affection for the island, he called a week-end cottage at East Mersea, Bryher Cottage. The family used to holiday at the Atlantic Hotel on St Mary's, then make frequent picnic expeditions to Bryher; and on one of them they bought a set of exquisite lace mats, crocheted by a very old lady called Aunt Sarah. Aunt Sarah caught Jeannie's imagination, partly because her hands were crippled with arthritis and Jeannie marvelled how she did her delicate work, partly because she had lived all her life on the island. A Hans Andersen character, Jeannie thought, and she used to talk to me about her until I was tired of the telling. We have the mats now at Minack. And we walked by the cottage where she used to live, on the way to Jane on the other side of the island.

'Jane!' called Dick as he opened the door of their home, 'Jane!'

The christening, of course, was an important event in the island, and so it was the hostess Jane who greeted us, not the Jane who preferred to walk about barefooted on hot summer days, who cared nothing for the urban ways of living. For a day such moods were forgotten, and it was an absurdly young looking Jane in a cyclamen pink dress who showed us the baby in the cot; and then went on preparing the delicacies for those who were coming back after the service. Jeannie, in due course, said the cake might have been produced by Fortnums; and Jane then explained that she had taken the precaution of first making another one, a trial run over the target; and it had been a disaster. There were delicious canapes and sandwiches and wine; and all the more pleasant to enjoy because of the knowledge that the feast had to be planned far ahead. In Bryher you cannot say you will have a party, then go into the High Street to buy what you want.

But these pleasures came after the service in the church built in the eighteenth century, close to the beach, the oldest church in use in the Scillies, to which we walked, Sylvia in a carry-cot between her parents. I am no church-goer although the ambience of churches, of whatever denomination, have a deep significance for me. Here among the stone arches, altars, painted glass windows, ancient fonts, and musty smells, the mood of timelessness reaches into your secret depths; but for me this is not achieved when I worship in the mass. I find myself instead looking forward to the end of a hymn, or a sermon, or the service itself. My mind wanders, I am a spectator and not a participant. Perhaps this is because religion was made into a weapon of punishment when I was a schoolboy at Harrow; and instead of the Bible being an adventure to read, for instance, it became a menace. Copying out verses of the Bible, several times over, was frequently the fate of those boys who had erred; and the memory of this tedious task has remained with me for ever. Nor were the services any more enjoyable. They were a bore, in fact, until the last verse of the last hymn when we knew there were only minutes left before we were released.

I prefer, therefore, to be alone in a church instead of being one of a congregation, although there are other times, at services for special occasions, when I am easily emotionally involved. For me, indeed, there must be a reason for churchgoing; and that reason will involve an individual . . . a wedding, a funeral, or a christening. But the conventional service has little meaning for me. I feel closer to God when I am in some beautiful corner of Minack without anyone in sight.

We walked back to the cottage after the service. Friends strung out along the path, the sea in sight, the parson whose first christening on Bryher it had been, strolling along with us . . . living on Tresco he had come by boat for the occasion. There are of course no cars on Bryher, and when Jane was married she travelled in her bridal dress to the church on a tractor. Thus we wandered along, a happy, unselfconscious procession; and I am glad we have a memento of the day.

I had admired the many examples of Dick's craftsmanship in the cottage, beautiful woodwork which communicated the patience and skill of those who worked wood long ago; and when I happened to say that I admired one piece of craftsmanship, I did not expect he had noted what I said. 'You must sell these beautiful things,' I had urged, 'the tourists would love them surely.' His reply was noncommittal. Or perhaps he was being modest. Or he felt the tourists wouldn't pay the price to cover the time, labour, and material expense of the work. Whatever went through his mind, he did however realise that we admired his talent; and so he thought he would like to give us some pleasure. The following Christmas a small oak jewellery box arrived at Minack, lined with red baize, and inscribed: 'Made from materials from S. S. *Mando* wrecked Golden Ball, Scilly, 1955.'

THIRTEEN

High summer, and the end is beginning. The elder flowers
have turned into berries, the apples are fattening, the tomato
plants have only the top trusses to ripen, the air sing with
insect sounds, flies bother the donkeys, convolvulus is
winding up the camellia bush beside the rose garden, up
the fuchsia and the honeysuckle in front of the cottage,
up any plant or bush it can find; bees fill themselves with
honey from the mignonette on the bridge, multi-coloured
nasturtiums tumble over rocks, night-scented stock and
tobacco plants romanticise the evenings. There still seems
much of summer ahead . . . but the swifts are gathering,
briefest of our bird visitors, and any evening they will be
spiralling into the sky above Minack, calling their shrill cry

128

of farewell, higher and higher, until they disappear in the fading light.

I no longer hear the cuckoo. I was walking with Jeannie and the donkeys along the path towards Lamorna when I saw the last cuckoo of summer, three of them in fact; a before-breakfast walk, and the fishing boats were passing below us, hastening to Newlyn fish market. I saw them perched on the rocks of Carn Barges and for a moment I thought they were woodpigeons. Then I realised my mistake and I called softly to Jeannie and we stopped; and as I did so Fred nudged me in the back, so I put a hand over his muzzle which he knows to be a signal for quiet. We stood there and watched, then away the cuckoos went, flying south. 'Jeannie!' I had called, in a fit of sadness as they took off, 'hold on to their tails!' And we both laughed at my nonsense.

The swallows remained. Our brood still flew gaily together around Minack, playing their games in the sky, chasing each other high above the stable field and away over the green tops of the elm trees, out of sight, and back again, swerving, dipping, twisting; and suddenly they would be tired and they would swoop down on the electricity cable connecting the cottage, and settle side by side twittering for a minute or two; then off again. At night they still roosted in the barn, clustering together on a beam, but they were not to be there for much longer. Their parents shooed them off. The eggs of the second brood had been laid in the same nest, three of them; and when they were hatched, the barn was a nursery again.

There was another nest, a greenfinch nest, in the fork of the elm above Boris's pond. Jeannie, for some reason, has a special fondness for greenfinches. She loves their plaintive call, but although we hear this call off and on throughout the summer, they never seem to nest with us until late in the season. Once, in an August, a pair of greenfinches had a nest in the same fork of the same tree above Boris's pond. It was a cold, wet August, and I remember that when the brood of four were about ready to fly a vicious easterly gale blew up. It was so fierce that it was a marvel that the nest was not blown away, and the brood with it; but during the second day of the gale, orders were given to abandon ship. The nest that evening was empty.

The following morning was sunny and still and we heard the plaintive greenfinch cries in the wood, and thought all was well; but as Jeannie was walking to the small greenhouse to weigh tomatoes, she saw a movement in the grass, and there near the foot of the elm was a baby greenfinch. It was sick. Its eyes were half closed, and its head nodded, and it had all the signs of a bird that had not long to live. Jeannie picked it up and placed it in a box full of hay in the greenhouse, then managed to put a few drops of Exultation of Flowers down its throat by gently holding its beak open with her fingers. The vet happened to call that morning, and so she asked his advice; and he told her that her treatment was correct, except that he had never heard of Exultation of Flowers (it is a secret blending of flower juices and it comes from Nairn in Scotland); and he added that as the sun was now shining, it would be a good idea to leave the invalid and its box outside the greenhouse during the day so that the parents would be able to feed it naturally.

This we did. There was no risk of Lama attacking it although the box was on the ground. Lama, never in her life, has shown any greed for catching birds; like Monty before her. Boris would have been more of a danger; but Boris at the time was having a love affair with a patch of ground near his hut which meant he would not be waddling towards the small greenhouse. Boris was like that. A patch of ground was sacrosanct for a while, then on to another.

So during the day the parents fussed over the invalid, and at night we carried it into the greenhouse out of the evening damp air. Then one afternoon we saw the invalid hop out of the box, and we had to retrieve it. The next day it flew up on to the low wall close to Boris's pool; and we retrieved it again. Another day and we couldn't find it anywhere.

This story might have been forgotten by us but for the outcome three weeks later. Jeannie was sitting on the white seat beside the verbena bush when she heard a surge of plaintive cries coming from the elder tree which is next to the verbena. She looked up and saw six greenfinches within a few feet of her. Two grown up, and four young all in a row, facing her. Jeannie has a fanciful mind, but I believe her assertion that they were singing her a song of thank you.

There was no such incident this summer. No gale to disturb the nest. No sign of any touble among the fledgelings. We kept watch, of course, and we would point out the nest to visitors, and the children among the visitors would listen gravely as we told the story of the young greenfinch of another year. And then I would tell them other stories like that of one-eyed Billy the robin who, after being in the neighbourhood for a couple of years and a regular at the bird table, had a fight with another robin; and received the worst of it. He found his way to the door of the cottage, and I nearly stepped on him as I came out of the cottage, a crumpled handful of feathers. He too was taken to the small greenhouse; and we kept him in an óld chicken coop with a wire front until we thought he was well enough to live on his own again. Unfortunately we were too hasty. No sooner was one-eyed Billy set free than his enemy pounced on him again; and had I not been there to see the attack, Billy certainly would have been killed. His enemy was vicious, pinning him to the ground, and pecking furiously at him. So I rescued him again, and this time he was in the coop until he was as strong as any rival except for his one eye; and when I took him to the greenhouse door and let him go, he flew off merrily into the wood. We saw him from time to time for several months afterwards; but there came a very cold spring, and we never saw him again.

We had a nest of hedgehogs also this summer. I had never seen a hedgehog in the neighbourhood before, and I had no knowledge of their habits; and when one night I heard squeaks from under the floorboards of our spare room, I called out to Jeannie in alarm: 'Rats! We've got rats!'

Our spare room is unusual. It was designed as a chicken house, but it is now connected with the cottage at one end, and with the bathroom at the other. When we bought it we were advised to erect it on some kind of base so that the floor was off the ground, thus keeping it safe from damp. We, therefore, collected a number of large stones or small

131

rocks, built six blocks from them, three for each side, then levelled the floor of the chicken house upon them. There has always been, therefore, a gap between floor and earth; and it was from within this gap that there came the squeaks.

In such a situation one hopes the problem will solve itself. The rats, I prayed, were only temporary visitors, and they would soon run off elsewhere; but the noise persisted and I began to be worried. On the second night the squeaks were louder than ever though without doubt they seemed to be happy squeaks, game playing squeaks, and Jeannie and I wondered whether our rat theory might possibly be wrong. But what other animal *would* make such a noise in such a place? It was obvious that I would have to investigate in the morning.

In the morning we were woken up by a piercing scream. It sounded like a child reacting to a moment of terror. Silence for a second, then the scream again. We hastened outside, half thinking it might be the scream of a rabbit caught by a stoat; but such a scream does not last long, the rabbit dies too quickly. Scream! There it was again.

The donkeys who had spent the night in the field beside the cottage were now as interested in the scream as we were; and when I saw Fred, ears alert, staring intently at a spot outside the bathroom I hurried towards him. 'What's up, Fred?' I asked, 'have you found out?'

He had. Outside the bathroom was a drain, and this drain was hidden from sight by a wooden cover. Scream! The sound came from under the cover. I bent down and lifted it up. To my astonishment, trapped in the drain's basin was a baby hedgehog.

So we no longer had to worry about the squeaks from under the spare room; and at night we would go out with a torch and catch sight of the hedgehog family drinking the milk from the saucer placed there by Jeannie. They were nervous creatures. They scampered back to their nest within a second of the torch lighting upon them. Then later, as I sat in my bath, I would hear their squeaks again as they played.

Every day, now that the holiday season was at its height, we were greeting strangers. This aspect of our life now played so dominant a part in the daily curriculum that we could make no plans without considering it. We would expect to be on our own up to eleven o'clock in the morning, but after that hour we were likely to have callers any time to dusk. There was no question of taking a couple of hours off together and going down to the sea for a bathe, or having a picnic on the rocks; for Geoffrey would soon be shouting from the top of the cliff that someone was waiting to see us. Nor could we pursue any particular task for long. Once upon a time we would have been helping Geoffrey dig the bulbs at this period of the year or taking part in some other acitivity on the land, but this was impossible when interruptions were regular throughout the day. We had to be on duty. We were always half listening for a car coming down the lane, or half watching for a figure coming up to the cottage door. Yet if we had not remained always available, those who had come considerable distances would have found the place empty; and we had had enough experience to know that this could cause disappointment.

The question is, however, why bother in any case? It was far too demanding a routine for the reason to be that of vanity. Naturally we were pleased that people should want to meet us, should make the effort to plan their holidays so that they could come and discuss subjects they believed provided a common interest; but it was not the kind of fleeting flattery that a film star receives when asked for his autograph. We were involved with these people who came; and so we had an acute sense of our own inadequacy. If someone had come a long way, had to search for our where-abouts, who knew all about us though we knew nothing about them, who was prepared to accept a rebuff after walking down the long lane in the event of us not reacting in the way it was hoped . . . it was natural we should feel inadequate. Years ago I had discovered that life is sad rather than funny; and that, when a stranger wants to meet you, one should always remember this. Hence, when a stranger came advancing towards me, rather shyly and apologising for the intrusion, I was aware of other occasions in other years when I myself wanted a welcome.

The gain, however, is mutual. Jeannie and I have met a

far larger cross-section of people than ever would have been the case had we lived in a city; and as a consequence we have had the opportunity to listen to views and experiences that otherwise would have been denied us. In a week taken at random during the summer, there were among the strangers who came down the lane: a computer designer, a young prison warder, a matron of a hospital, a parson, three schoolmasters, the head of an advertising firm, a sixteen year old schoolboy from Kingston in Surrey, a professional organist, several children, a hat manufacturer, two nuns from a convent, four girl secretaries, the head of a shipping firm, a Q.C., a bank manager, an Australian couple, two Mary Quant assistants, the storeman of an I.C.I. factory, and a member of a pop group. You can understand why the gain is mutual.

Unfortunately an author is not able to live on attention alone. Hence the time we have spent with callers, pleasant and informative as it may have been, has not proved to be a practical way of earning a living. Perhaps we should set up a stall for books, and another stall for Jeannie's paintings and drawings and treat this side of our lives in strict commercial fashion. Such a prospect, however, does not please us. Neither of us enjoys selling our wares. We are poor at doing so. Jeannie, this summer, arranged a number of her paintings in her hut in the wood, but we never succeeded in persuading anyone to look at them. We failed because we adopted the soft sell technique, not the hard sell. We preferred it that way. We therefore hinted that Jeannie had pictures to sell . . . but nobody took the hint; and the only picture she sold was one that I bought myself at the end of the summer. A captivating oil of Lama.

Nor did I do much better. I also hinted. I hinted that I had hard cover copies of my books (not paperbacks) which I would be happy to sign, murmuring that such books would make as good a holiday present as any Midland-made Cornish memento in one of the 'Gifte Shoppes'. Sometimes the information was welcome, at other times there was dead silence. More often I never hinted anything at all. I felt it was out of place to do so. I would instead listen to remarks like: 'It takes so long to get your books from the library,

Mr Tangye . . . I always have to wait *six months* at least.'
Or: 'When I get your books from the library, I spend
hours copying out those passages I like best, before returning
them.' Or: 'When does your new book come out in paperback? I'm *so* looking forward to reading it.' A paperback
earns me 2d a copy. A single hardcover copy in a library
may be read by scores of people, but the author is only paid
the royalty for that one copy.

Yes, despite these financial disadvantages, there are
rewards beyond price. An author who writes about his own
way of life will only have response from those who are on
the same wavelength. It is similar to direct contact with
people. Some you like immediately, some you cannot abide;
some instinctively understand you, some obviously have
nothing in common with you. I cannot abide, for instance,
languid people who are devoid of enthusiasm, people who
avoid facts which interfere with their preconceived opinions,
and people who are ruled by their intellects instead of their
hearts. Nor, for that matter, can I abide professional critics
in any sphere who, like tired roués, no longer find an interest
in anything normal. Such people are unlikely to visit Minack.
Instead, those who have come here have in many instances
kept in touch with us afterwards, and our lives have been
enriched by their friendship.

We were now also in the season of Fêtes, Carnivals, and
Galas; and our special interest, of course, concerned the
festivities of St Buryan and Lamorna. St Buryan has a
splendid village Playing Field, founded and developed by
the local people; and every summer there are two days of
sports and gaieties to celebrate their achievement. Penny
and Fred have a standing invitation to attend, and it is a
pity that they have never done so; but the three-mile road
to the village is narrow and winding, and cars travel fast
along it, and the donkeys, even in our lane, have the habit
of turning broadside on when they see a car approaching.
Thus a journey to St Buryan entailed a risk. There was no
such risk in going to the Gala at Lamorna. We would be able
to reach the field where it was taking place without walking
on a busy road except for a few yards. Or that is what we
thought.

The Gala was in aid of the Lamorna Village Hall Fund; and yellow posters had for some days been displayed in the area, pasted on barn doors, garden walls and the trunks of trees, proclaiming that Jeannie and I were opening the Gala at 2.30 p.m. 'Accompanied by PENNY AND FRED THE DONKEYS.' It sounded easy. All the four of us had to do was to arrive punctually at the appointed place, and the Gala could proceed. All four of us. But supposing two of us chose to be obstinate? Supposing, on the afternoon concerned, two of us wanted to go elsewhere? Or roll in the dust just before we were due to leave? Or supposing, given the good luck of arriving at the Gala, two of us decided to be temperamental? And brayed during the speeches?

Jeannie and I were apprehensive. True the donkeys had always behaved in exemplary fashion at Fred's birthday parties, but these had taken place in the security of Minack, where they were the hosts in a familiar meadow. Even so, such occasions could cause us concern. Anyone, I think, would feel concern if they saw children happily and fearlessly playing around the legs of a donkey. Yet both Penny and Fred accepted such games quite calmly. We were only concerned in case at some stage their patience might be momentarily exhausted. When children were about, therefore, we were always on watch, asking the children to move away whenever necessary. It would be more difficult to watch them at the Gala; and it would be the first time they had ever appeared together in so public a place. The Gala, therefore, would be both an adventure and a test. Their reputations would be at stake.

This also meant that their appearance had to be elegant, and it was fortunate that their coats were now in full summer glory. It is strange how long it takes a donkey to rid itself of a winter coat . . . all through May, June and July, there were woolly patches on both Penny and Fred, giving them both a moth eaten look; and it was to no avail that I combed and groomed them. But the patches had gone now, and the coats were in magnificent condition, Penny a shining black, Fred a glossy chestnut; and all that was now necessary to have them ready for the Gala was a pedicure.

A pedicure suggests a gentle event, and so it should be if the donkeys are in an amiable mood. The hoof of a donkey grows quickly and during the summer a pedicure is necessary every six weeks. A neglected hoof is a sad sight. When Penny first came to Minack, each hoof was elongated and curved upwards at the end, so that she could only walk on her heels. This one-time neglect has made her scared whenever her turn for a pedicure comes round; and although she is normally the most docile of donkeys she will, if in particular nervous mood, behave badly when our blacksmith tries to perform his task.

Our blacksmith, Kenny Male from St Buryan, is a patient man, an expert in handling horses and donkeys, and we are lucky to have such a person who is understanding enough to cope with Penny's tantrums. On this occasion Penny was calm as he dealt with each front hoof, cutting and filing them until they both looked trim; but she became highly excited when he tried to catch hold of a back leg. It is not a job I would at any time like to do myself. Penny was wildly lashing out while Geoffrey struggled to hold her by the halter, and while Kenny waited coolly for the moment when he had a chance of seizing a leg. This, in due course, he succeeded in doing. First one leg, then the other, each hoof receiving its trimming; and when at last the task was completed and Penny realised her ordeal was over, she looked as happy as someone who had finished a tough session at the dentist. We rewarded her with a large carrot.

It was at this precise moment while Penny was munching and I was leading Fred by the halter towards Kenny, that a party of teenagers appeared, headed by a schoolteacher. They came from London and were exploring this part of Cornwall; and the timing of their arrival at Minack was heaven-sent. For Fred had been observing the tantrums of his mother; and had no doubt been saying to himself, 'what she can do I can do better.' The sight of the audience, however, quite changed his mind. Fred responds to an audience as a film star responds to a mob of fans; and although, a moment before, he may have been prepared to be mischievous, he now saw the opportunity of showing off his sweet nature. This is the role he most enjoys playing. The role which provokes people to murmur: 'Oh, isn't he a dear!' and: 'Such a darling, your Fred,' and: 'He's so handsome!'

Hence Kenny had no trouble at all. The audience gathered along the small fence which separated them from the spot where the pedicure was about to take place, made flattering remarks as Fred quietly advanced, led on the halter by me, and watched admiringly as Fred put on his act. An act which received praise from all of us.

'Do you want my right hoof first, or my left?'

Kenny wanted neither.

'Oh, you're starting with my back left . . . Don't worry . . . I'll keep still.'

The performance was soon over, and Fred accepted the applause. He had been admired once again, and now he shared with his mother the smartest hooves in the district. The donkeys were ready for the Gala.

We had allowed three quarters of an hour to reach the field. It was a hot summer's day, and the lane was dusty, and we would have been wearing casual summer clothes had we been taking the donkeys for a normal walk. The occasion, however, required formality. We had to look as smart as the donkeys for whom we had bought two white halters; and so I was wearing a grey suit and well polished shoes, and Jeannie a pale yellow sleeveless dress with gloves to match. She had, however, taken the precaution of asking Geoffrey to go ahead in the car, taking her pair of Raynes shoes and matching handbag with him; and thus along the lane she wore ordinary shoes which she would change in the car park. A good idea. She would look at herself in the car mirror, and arrive at the Gala cool and collected, having joined me and the donkeys again at the gate.

First, however, we had to reach the car park; and after coming to the end of the dusty lane, we turned right, not on to the main road but on to a narrow lane which led to two farms, a Methodist Chapel, and the Menwinnion Hotel which was once the home of my dear friend Jimmy Williams, the remarkable Elephant Bill. His book about the elephants of the Fourteenth Army in Burma is an immortal one. He and the animals in his life shared an intuition

138

for each other; and he was a man, if you were suffering from animal grief, whom you would dearly love to meet; and I remember that the day after Monty died Jeannie met him in Penzance. She returned calmer to Minack.

The four of us were approaching Menwinnion when Geoffrey appeared in the lane with Philip and Julie his children. They had walked up from the car park to meet us. This was a relief. The donkeys were now in virgin land as far as they were concerned; and they were showing signs of excitement. *What* was the Chapel building? *Who* lived in the two cottages? *Why* can't we go up that turning which is signposted to Tregurno, or that other one to Boleigh? The sight of Geoffrey, therefore, gave us confidence; and the sight of Julie in a pretty pink checked dress with a bow in her hair, and Philip in white shirt and shorts gave us the atmosphere of the Gala to come. We began to rid ourselves of the anxiety which always attacks some of those who feature in such an activity; and, as I walked beside him, I gave Fred a pat. 'You'll enjoy this,' I said.

We passed Menwinnion, where the tarmac lane ended, and then on we went down the south side of Lamorna Valley, down a narrow footpath called Rocky Lane until the car park came into view on our left. 'We've timed it perfectly,' I said to Jeannie, looking at my watch, 'you go ahead and change your shoes. We're due in five minutes. Geoffrey will lead Penny.'

Five minutes later we were in trouble.

I should, of course, have foreseen the situation. I should have made a reconnaisance of the Gala field beforehand, and noted that to reach the field surrounded by Lamorna woods, a wooden ridge had to be crossed. A wooden bridge! As soon as I saw it I knew what would happen . . . the donkeys reached it, looked at it, and came to a full stop.

'Donkeys,' I cried out in anguish, 'please, please don't let us down!'

Nothing I said, nothing we did would make them budge. We cajoled, we tugged, we pushed. The Gala visitors laughed, the organisers looked serious, and Jeannie and I were distraught.

'Donkeys,' I implored them again, 'everyone is waiting

for you. For goodness sake MOVE!'

They never did.

We had instead to turn back ignominiously, and make a detour round by the main road, then across two fields, and over a bramble-covered patch of waste land. Jeannie in her smart shoes. The donkeys revelling in such a new and interesting walk.

I began my speech thirty-five minutes late.

FOURTEEN

The behaviour of the donkeys at the Gala was impeccable.
They listened attentively to my speech. They were unperturbed by the noise and the games played around them. They
politely walked round the field time after time, with children
on their backs. They posed for photographs with the
patience of professional models. They were friendly towards a fine horse called Neptune and a little pony called
Tucker who were also helping everyone to enjoy the afternoon. There was no trouble at all at the Gala. Only the
wooden bridge caused trouble. Once again, when we left,
they refused to cross it; and back across the fields to the
main road we had to go.

I was, therefore, relieved when finally we returned to

Minack, so relieved that I rewarded the donkeys by taking a shovel to the kitchen garden and digging half a basket of carrots. This was an excessive amount, enough for a week, but there was sense behind my extravagance. I had reason to believe that they would be restless after such an afternoon of excitement, that they would be expecting us to pay them further attention; and that unless I did something drastic they would hee-haw their way through the evening. Such a prospect I could not bear. I had had enough of donkeys for the day. I wanted peace; and I reckoned that half a basket of carrots would provide it. I was correct.

I do not enjoy making speeches, and I make very few. Some people, however, delight to stand on a platform with upturned faces in front of them. Such an occasion offers a pleasant illusion of power and self-importance, and as the time of the speech draws near they experience excitement instead of dread. Let me not deprive such people, I usually say to myself when I am invited to open this or that, of their pleasure. Let one of them endure that moment after the speech when one yearns to ask: 'Was it all right?' Let one of them suffer lugubrious comment, fortunately not often overheard by the speaker concerned: 'He was not as good as so-and-so last year.' Let one of them open this or that, not me.

Speechmaking, except for the confident, is a painful business; and Jeannie shares my view. One summer she was invited to open a swimming Gala at Mousehole and, like the rest of us, she was kept awake at night worrying over the speech she would make. The morning of the Gala arrived, a hot August morning, and she went down to the rocks for a bathe. Once there she used the sea as an audience and she stood, a slim sylph-like figure, on a boulder close to the waves repeating the speech over and over again until she had learnt it by heart. Unfortunately the speech was never heard by anyone else, and her agony of the past few weeks was wasted. The microphone at the Gala went dead as soon as she began.

As for myself, as for my speech at the Lamorna Gala, I hurried through it oblivious that during the course of it I made a bloomer. I had urged that the Cornish should resist big business interests from across the Tamar, that Lamorna Vally must remain for all time a true example of old Cornwall. Inoffensive rhetoric, I thought, until a kindly resident of the valley approached me after I had finished. 'You have forgotten,' he said with a smile, 'that eighty per cent of us who live in Lamorna are "foreigners".' Yes, I had forgotten. Perhaps the reason is that the 'foreigners' concerned are so pleasant that they appear to belong to the valley.

It is no use believing, however, that life in the country spares you discordancy with others. We have the usual problems of human relationships; and though we may be on happy terms with most, there will always be occasional times when we may have misunderstandings with one person or another. I had, for instance, such a misunderstanding with the elderly gentleman who bought the neighbouring farm, including the cottage where Jane once lived. The gentleman came from the north, and he had a determined manner. The previous owner, a Cornishman, had a herd of Guernseys, and grew potatoes and daffodils; and from him we once rented the two acres of cliff land. The new owner did not follow this pattern of farming. He had a fine herd of beef cattle instead. He also kept the three cottages of Pentewan, empty.

The first misunderstanding I had with him concerned half a ton of Magnificence daffodil bulbs which were still in one of the meadows of my old tenancy of the Pentewan cliff I has foolishly believed that I would be able to dig them in my own good time and transfer them to Minack land. Legally, however, they were no longer mine. My new neighbour had bought them along with the farm. Hence all Jeannie and I could do, daffodil season after daffodil season, was to watch them bust into yellow from our side of the hedge (the blooms were never picked commercially). It was an infuriating experience, and costly too; for they were worth £30 or more a year. But the elderly gentleman has left the area now, and the bulbs are back at Minack.

The second misunderstanding I had with him concerned the coastal footpath. There has always been confusion about the footpath along this part of the coast; and even today there is no official one. True the authorities have drawn up

143

its route and have legal powers to enforce it; but such powers are not easily enforced when a landlord is determined to resist them. This means delay and the coastal path in this area has been delayed for years. Hikers could cross Minack land along a path I had marked, but there was no marked path on my neighbour's land; and hikers there were not welcome.

I had, however, a certain sympathy with his attitude. Hikers once left a gate open, and his herd of beef cattle nearly went over the cliff as a result; and he was also subjected to the tactless manners of footpath propagandists. Footpath propagandists are inclined to behave like little dictators. They sally forth from the towns, armed with maps, aiming to trace long forgotten footpaths. These forgotten footpaths were used in bygone days by a farm-worker, perhaps, walking from his cottage to the farm, or by a family going to church, or by the postman. Such paths have no place in these modern days of hikers. A footpath propagandist, therefore, who bossily tells a farmer that a public footpath of long ago passes through his farm-yard or, across a field which is cropped with broccoli, or where a stone hedge keeps cattle from straying, is certain to be unpopular. Indeed the footpath propagandist is only doing a disservice to his cause. He is encouraging the farmer to be awkward. The farmer, after all, is trying to earn a living on his land. The hiker is only passing by.

The manner of mapping footpaths should be brought up-to-date. Too much goodwill is being lost by this emphasis on old footpaths. Indeed, a farmer or landlord, should be invited when necessary to suggest a path over his land. The planning should be done in a spirit of co-operation. Hikers would then be able to enjoy their walks, footpath propagandists would stop looking for trouble, and farmers would have their privacy.

The coastal path that I have marked over Minack land proves this point. Hikers obediently follow it, do not stray away from it, and are glad that it is there. Not that there are many hikers . . . perhaps ten a week during the summer. But this marked path meant also that I was encouraging the hikers to walk across my neighbour's land; and this, in fact, meant encouragement to trespass. I fear my neighbour did not approve of such behaviour, and so this was the cause of our second misunderstanding. Yet I do not believe that the fault was his. Had he been asked, not ordered, to co-operate with the footpath planners, he would have done so.

There was also the complication of the lighthouse. The lighthouse had been erected on his land soon after the wreck of a Spanish ship, the *Juan Ferrer*, a mile or so up the coast; a five hundred ton vessel on passage from Bordeaux to Cardiff with a mixed cargo of onions, cedar plywood, and thousands of chestnut stakes, which went on the rocks one early foggy morning. Minack was chosen as the head-quarters of the rescue parties, and so we saw at first hand the chaos which ensued. At first there was only the vaguest idea as to where the vessel had run aground, hours indeed went by between the time the faint May Day signal had been picked up, and the time the vessel was finally dis-covered. In the meantime eleven sailors had been drowned.

There was no public enquiry afterwards such as takes place after a train or airliner disaster, as to why matters had gone so awry; but it was decided to declare that the lack of a lighthouse was the cause. It focused public opinion on something tangible. It diverted people from asking questions.

It is called an automatic lighthouse, but it is only auto-matic in the sense that no one is stationed on the premises. The fog signal, for instance, still requires someone to push a button to start it; and this is performed by an officer of Trinity House five miles *down* the coast at Penzance ... on the advice of a coastguard five miles *up* the coast at Tol Pedn at Gwennap Head. Hence fog at Tol Pedn results in the fog signal sounding, although visibility in the lighthouse area may be so clear that the Lizard is visible. This is irk-some for those of us who have to listen to it ashore. More-over the site of the lighthouse is ill chosen. The site is so far within Mount's Bay that the fog signal is often driven inland instead of out to sea, because foggy weather almost always comes in from the south; and so when a wind is blowing, a sea rushing noisily against a boat, the fog signal isn't heard by a boat a mile or so up the coast. The fog signal, indeed, is an anachronism in this age of electronics; and our particular fog signal exists only as a reminder of eleven Spanish seamen whose lives might have been saved.

Meanwhile the lighthouse has provided an indirect obstacle to the coastal path. Trinity House put up a notice-board on my neighbour's land close to our boundary, at the spot where the coastal path would normally run; and the notice on the board was deceptive. It read: THE PUBLIC IS PROHIBITED FROM ENTERING THE LIGHTHOUSE OR ANY PART OF THE LAND ADJOINING THE LIGHT-HOUSE. BY ORDER OF THE CORPORATION OF TRINITY HOUSE.

This suggested that Trinity House had some control of the land when, in fact, it only owns a strip of land on either side of the lighthouse which is some distance from the notice-board. Confusion, as a result, among coastal path hikers who often came to me to complain; and complain too about the strands of barbed wire that run along the boundary, and which my neighbour had fixed as a protection against straying cattle. Or straying donkeys for that matter. Penny and Fred often grazed in the adjoining meadow and once, after a footpath propagandist had cut the wire, they ended up by the gate at Pentewan cottages.

Occasionally the complaints were made aggressively. One day two men and a woman arrived at the door of the cottage saying they had torn their pants on the barbed wire, that this must be my fault, that I was one of those who tried to stop the enjoyment of the public, and that when they returned home after their holiday they would lodge a complaint with the hiker association to which they belonged. All this without asking me what the true situation might be. I would have been happy to explain the reason for the barbed wire, the Trinity House notice and so on; but they were determined to vent their feelings on someone, and so they chose me. I knew, however, their type, and so I didn't argue. They belonged to that intellectual race who are so burdened with the knowledge of other people's rights, so supposedly liberal in their thinking, that they have no room in their minds for truth.

The same evening I was on the bridge and saw Daisy for

146

the first time for some weeks. She was in the stable meadow near to the hedge bordering the lane, a small grey figure intent on some activity in the couch grass; and when her interest waned she looked up at me, too far away for me to see her eyes, just her head facing towards me; and then she began to walk across the meadow, a slow walk towards the cemetery field. And then I forgot about her because Jeannie came to me and said that Boris was squatting on the grass by his pond, and he didn't appear to want to move; and she was frightened that something was wrong.

He had been outside the cottage door for most of the day. Normally he would only come up to the door to receive some special delight from Jeannie or me, stay ten minutes or so, then plod away down the path of grey chippings; and during his brief stay we would make our customary remarks to him.

'Boris, old boy, what are you up to?'

'Now, Boris dear, you've had *plenty*.'

'Dear Boris I'll walk back with you . . .'

But for the past few days he had been staying close to the door as if he had special reasons to want our company; and he annoyed Lama by doing so. Lama was always on guard in case, as she passed him, he had a nip at her tail; and she would eye him warily as she approached the door, then rush past him at speed. It was imagination on her part, of course, that he would harm her; or perhaps it was only a game that she was playing, a ruse to enliven for a minute or so old Boris's day. There they were, the two strays who had come into our lives; the one who had been scheduled to provide a dinner, the other who might have been wild for ever. Both had had a decisive effect on our future. And I wanted neither when first they arrived on the scene.

I went down to the pond with Jeannie, but Boris was no longer squatting there. He was on his way to his house, and there seemed to be nothing wrong with him because he was pausing occasionally and pushing his beak into the new mown grass. We waited until he reached the door, then we bade him good night and shut it.

Back in the cottage Jeannie went to turn the bath on and

I heard her call out that there wasn't any water. This was a routine happening now that summer was ending, the springs low. A. P. Herbert was staying with us once at this time of the year, and I remember an occasion when he advanced towards me, pretending to be a sailor marching across the quarter deck.

'I have to report, sir,' he said, saluting, 'that the pumps are sucking.'

Usually the electric pump turns on automatically when the water has reached a certain low in the tank, a hundred-gallon tank which stands beside the well and the pump; and up comes the water from thirty feet down. When the springs are low, however, the bottom of the well only holds forty gallons, and even this small amount takes five hours to gather. Hence I have to switch on the pump manually, and wait four minutes or so beside the tank until the water starts to splutter out of the pipe, and I know the well is empty. Sometimes I walk away after I have started the pump, day-dreaming about some matter; and I proceed to forget all about it until ten, twenty, thirty minutes later I suddenly shout: 'The pump!' . . . and I race away to switch it off. By then it is pumping air, and so a tedious task is the penalty of my forgetfulness. I have to prime the pump when I next use it; and this means using a watering can and labouriously pouring the water down the pipe until its level also fills the pump, and the air is driven out, and the pump can operate again.

That summer evening I had no need to prime it. I switched on, and stood there waiting until the water splashed into the tank. It was dark now, and the stars had come into their own, and I saw above me the bunched cluster of the Pleiades. I first consciously observed them when I lived on my South Sea island of Toopua; and they were directly above me then, as they were now at Minack. I hadn't changed much, I found myself thinking. I did not feel any older, any wiser. I still had self-doubt which would lead me into making a move which was against my interest. I still believed you were a lucky person if you could be happy on your own; and that such people were able to hear the whispers as well as the shouts. I still believed, therefore, that peace of mind could only come from within yourself; and that no outside agency would ever be able to provide it for you.

Nor did my views on people differ much. The sophisticated in London still lived lives of perpetual unfulfilment. I was still surprised by the ease with which people made promises without any intention of carrying them out. I still marvelled at the conceit of those who seemed always certain their opinions were correct. My instinct was still to like everyone at the first meeting. I still believed that courage and kindness lay beneath the surface of the majority. I still admired those with good manners. I was still saddened at the way people were forced to sacrifice their integrity in the cause of self-preservation.

But there were new factors in my life since those days in Toopua, and obviously they must have affected me in other ways. A war had come and gone, and I had survived, and every day of my life I was grateful. Awareness of the luck of it came to me in sudden moments, reminding me that I was one of those who lived on borrowed time. Such moments offered other thoughts as well. I remember a pretty secretary in my office who fell in love with a Dane serving in the R.A.F.; and within a month of their being married he was killed. Of course such an incident was repeated a thousand, thousand times during the war so that it became a normality. Yet there are moments, and this was one of them as I stood there up by the well, that I reflected about that girl, and those who suffered like her, wondering whether the intensity of her love all those years ago has ever been quelled. So I was grateful too for this . . . for the fact that I hadn't carried that kind of desolate memory through my life.

And since that night I first became aware of the Pleiades, Jeannie had come into my life; and I had learnt there were no rules to follow in a happy marriage. Only that both of you must feel that you have freedom and that you are not chained to a conventional routine. Habit is what must be avoided. Every day must bring the unexpected so that, in a way, you remain strangers anxious to discover each other. All my years with Jeannie have been an adventure; the frivolous, glamorous times of London . . . or the first night at Minack when we slept on a mattress on the floor while the rain dripped through a hole in the roof. The companionship I have had with her has had its warmth through the unexpected. I am unable to take her for granted. She is elusive, provocative, feminine, always ready to make a sacrifice, showing faith in reality by not running away from it, yet always on the verge of chasing wild, imaginative Celtic dreams. No dullness with Jeannie.

The water in the pipe began to splutter, and I switched off the pump; and as I did so a flight of curlews flew over the wood uttering their sad, romantic cries. An owl answered from somewhere near Boris's house; and from across the valley I heard a fox barking. Lights of houses speckled at intervals along the coastline of the Lizard, and close to those of Porthleven, I could see the red lights of helicopters hovering like fireflies above the naval air station of Culdrose. It was warm, and the night air was fragrant with the night-scented stock and the tobacco plants. I could hear the hum of a trawler, and then I saw her starboard light rounding Carn Barges; and far out on the horizon there was a tiny smudge of light, a liner no doubt though there was no telling which way she was sailing. I went back to the cottage and saw the shadow of Lama waiting for me at the corner by the water butt. I bent down to stroke her but before I was able to touch her she dashed away towards the porch. Bedtime, she had decided.

Next morning I went in my usual casual way to open the door of Boris's house; and I gave him my customary greeting: 'Good morning, old boy. Have you had a good night?' I noted him in the corner, and took no more notice because in recent weeks he had been slow to move out. Not like the old days when he behaved like a greyhound waiting to be released from a race trap . . . then he would bounce out of his house in a flurry of wagging tail feathers, accompanied by a cacophony of hisses. He was eager to take part in the day.

Breakfast was to be on the bridge, and I went up there and waited for Jeannie to bring me two boiled eggs and coffee; and she brought them on a tray with a saucer of milk for Lama who was sitting close to my feet, gently purring. Two of the gulls were on the roof, and when they saw

Jeannie with the tray they began to squawk for their breakfast; and so she had to go back and cut them some bread. I thought it was going to be an ordinary day, and I revelled in the prospect of it. The tomatoes were virtually finished; and so there was no work for me to do in that direction. Perhaps, I said to Jeannie, we might take the donkeys for a walk along the cliff towards Lamorna; and she thought this a good idea because there would be blackberries to pick, and she would be able to make her first jar or two of jam.

I finished my breakfast and went over to talk to the donkeys who were quietly grazing in the big field above the cottage; and as I reached them Fred thought I had come for a game, and suddenly sprinted away. I was about to chase him when I heard Jeannie shouting, and her voice was so urgent that I started to run back across the field; and this, Fred thought, was also part of the game, and as I ran, he was close behind me.

I found Jeannie in front of the cottage by the rose garden with Boris beside her swaying, as if he were unable to keep his balance. As I reached them, Boris stumbled away towards his pond, plunged into it, and began beating his wings on the water. After a minute he flapped his way out, and collapsed on the grass. I thought as I watched him, that I was watching him die. Then he got to his feet again and before we had time to stop him, he half flew across the grey chippings towards the corner of the cottage, then up the short steep path to the water butt, and right to the door. The route he had taken every day of his life with us at Minack. There he was in his favourite place, waiting for something that only instinct made him expect.

We carried him to the small greenhouse, and made a nest for him in a bundle of hay; and we had a vet out to see him; and we watched over him and cared for him during the following two nights and days.

Then quietly at midday on a Tuesday, he died.

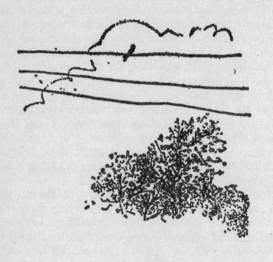

FIFTEEN

The swallows were leaving. The electricity cable which ran
from pole to pole through a gap in the wood, up the valley
to the farms at the top, provided the resting place of the
travellers from up country. Long lines of swallows would
settle for a while, cleaning themselves, twittering, dashing
away to skim the fields and moorland, then back again.
They would stay for a few hours or so, longer sometimes,
and then off towards Lands End and, if the wind was fair,
straight on across the sea to France or the Basque country,
even a long flight to Portugal. What parts of this country had
they come from, what old houses of England had been their
homes during the summer? I was saddened by the gay manner with which they were leaving. No British winter for us.

152

We want the sun of South Africa. Let's fly away as soon as possible.

Our second brood, however, were still in the barn; and I had observed that, as always, there was one more advanced than the others, a bossy young swallow with white shirt front rimming the nest, seizing the best flies brought by his parents. We called him Pip, and the other two shy ones, Squeak and Wilfred. Any day now they would be learning to fly, and they had not much time to spare if they were to be strong enough to start on their journeys before the autumn gales began.

From the bridge we watched other travellers, the spotted flycatchers and the warblers, training our field-glasses upon them so that their bright eyes were so close that it seemed we were watching their minds at work. The spotted flycatchers were easy to recognise. They would choose a branch of a tree, perch there quite still, a perky little bird with the shape of a robin, then suddenly dart at a passing fly twisting and turning to catch it, and then back to his perch, to await another. Sometimes we had a dozen or more around Minack, waiting for a wind to help them on their way to Africa.

I am at a loss, however, when trying to identify the warblers. I have various bird books, and I scan them closely, and notice how confidently the writers discriminate between a Garden Warbler, a Chiff Chaff, a Wood Warbler, a Willow Warbler, and other kinds of warblers . . . but they all look the same to me. I can recognise a Chiff Chaff, that's easy. I just listen to his chiff chaff call, then observe the busy hopping of the bird from branch to branch of a tree. Others of the warbler family, however, just baffle me. I have observed them from the bridge darting among the leaves of the apple tree which I planted years ago in the grass in front of the bridge; and among the leaves of the blackthorn in the three-cornered meadow to the right of the bridge. Secretive birds, always on the move, and I have to be smart to keep them in view as they skip around picking up grubs from the leaves; and then after a week or two they are gone again, setting course for the savanna country around the Congo forests three thousand miles away. But to

153

what branches of the warbler family did they belong? Alas, Jeannie and I gave up trying to find out. We just watched them and marvelled, and in so doing I remembered my father's advice.

My father, when I was a child, warned me never to ask questions about sights that were naturally beautiful. Accept them, he used to say, as a means of exciting your emotions but do not try to analyse why. I do not suppose he expected me to take this advice too literally, but I have learnt to understand what he was trying to tell me. Those who were guided by the heart, he used to argue, were closer to the truth than sceptics who were always trying to satisfy their intellects. Pleasure, in fact, should be for enjoyment and not for critical investigation. An out of date view, of course, in this technological age. Yet it is a view that still has substance for some of us.

I was aware, on the other hand, that an idle time of staring and contemplation and living in the present, could only be justified if you had earned it. I knew, for instance, that our own pleasure this summer had been derived from experiences of things past, by efforts laboriously made, by all the failures, by successes which had suddenly pushed us forward without pushing us too far. Thus we had been able to pause, and live a dream without being so far from reality to deceive ourselves that it could last forever.

We still had to earn a living in professions, for instance, which had no means of countering rising costs by obtaining rising returns. Booksellers were closing down in many parts of the country. As flower growers and tomato growers we could not agitate like farmers for increased controlled prices in the annual government price review. The prices we received were half what they were ten years ago, and yet we were enforced by law to pay the rising costs imposed upon us. No wonder there is a drift of labour from the land. There isn't the money available to pay the wages.

Thus the summer had nearly ended, and our basic problems remained as real as ever though I did not allow myself to be concerned by them. There were the September pleasures still to enjoy, and I sat on the bridge indulging in such minor delights as the aroma of blackberries stewing. Most days we went blackberrying accompanied by the donkeys; and sometimes there was rivalry when one of them tried to reach a juicy clump before we had noticed it ourselves. Jam was the main object of our blackberrying. Jeannie aimed to make twenty pounds.

There were, too, such minor delights as watching the young green woodpecker devouring the ants that crawled by the wall where we fed the donkeys in the field above the cottage. Or listening to the hum of the bees among the brilliant red flowers of the fuchsia and among the honeysuckle opposite the cottage door. Or watching Daisy pass across the stable meadow. Or seeing the swallows still tirelessly diving in and out of the barn door. Or being deceived by a patch of red brown bracken into thinking it was a fox sunning itself. Or seeing an oil rig being towed across the horizon towards the Lizard, the size of a vast city office block, scaringly incongruous in a shipping lane. I shouted to Geoffrey when I saw it, and after looking through his field-glasses, he said with a Cornish-man's native sense: '*That* would make a good wreck.'

We continued to have visitors, all kinds of visitors. A young man arrived who was a male nurse in a London hospital, and he enthused us with the account of his dedication. Another was a young musician from Chester who had come to see us in other summers. Then there was an Australian who called, bringing with her messages from her neighbours in Melbourne. A Canadian family on a world tour arrived in a Daimler, and when I first saw it coming down the lane I thought to myself that it was too wide to get over Monty's Leap. It survived . . . but an American couple in a Rolls-Royce a couple of days later became stuck. The sharp dip into the water bed of the Leap was too much for the exhaust pipe. It became wedged against the lane surface, and it required cunning work on Geoffrey's part to free it.

People came and asked for Boris, and when we told them what had happened, there was a silence, and a child who had come with her parents inquired: 'Did he just fly far away?' We could not bear to see his empty pond after he had died, so we emptied it and broke up the cement of the basin, and buried him there; and we planted the London

Pride on the surface, the same London Pride which edged the rose garden and upon which he liked to doze. And there were two girls who came, and they were so concerned that they went away, unknown to us, to search the area for another muscovy drake to take his place. They returned in due course with a baby drake in a box; and we had to explain to them that their kindly thought was misplaced. We did not want a substitute for Boris.

Lama had special visitors of her own. She has, in the past, even had cats brought along by holidaymakers to visit her. I admire the nerve of such people who take their cats on holiday. I have a recurring nightmare of taking Lama to London by car, and the height of the nightmare is when I am in a traffic jam in Shaftesbury Avenue, and Lama manages to escape from the car and then disappears into the side streets of Soho. I wake up moaning. This September a fine tabby called Sammy came to Minack with his owner who was a district nurse in Croydon. She and her husband were holidaymaking in a tent near Lands End, and Sammy took his unnatural surroundings quite for granted. Sammy was an experienced traveller. He daily accompanied the district nurse on her busy rounds back home.

Then there was a charming elderly French lady called Madame Madeleine Boniface who came specially on a two-day visit to Penzance from Paris in order to meet Lama. A great admirer of Colette she considered that both Monty and Lama were in the tradition of the cats of Colette; and so she felt impelled to make Lama's acquaintance.

On the morning she called I had looked through the window of the lane side of the barn and I had seen that Pip for the first time had left the nest, and was perched on an old windbreak which was leaning against the inside barn wall. This indeed was a sign of summer's end. Squeak and Wilfred would soon follow, and after fluttering around in the nursery for a day or two, they would be flying outside, and soon after, they would be joining the great concourse on the way to the south. All these months of watching the swallows behaving as if they owned Minack; and now the sky around the barn would be empty. At least the donkeys would have the place for themselves again.

It is not easy, from the bridge, to see a figure in the lane near Monty's Leap for it is hidden by the low leafy branches of the elms bordering the lane, and this means it is also in the shadow. If, therefore, someone is standing there hesitantly, my attention to the presence is first drawn by the movement of feet. Madame Boniface, in this case, had come by bus from Penzance to the end of the lane, walked the mile distance to the Leap; and then had lost her nerve. She was about to return when I observed her shuffling feet, and went down from the bridge to ask her whether I could be of any help. She thereupon confessed her mission.

Unfortunately Lama, as the summer months passed by, had become increasingly indifferent to adulation. At first, in the spring there was a freshness in being told how beautiful she looked. The flattery was stimulating, enhanced the pleasure of her days, and indeed there was excitement as to who might be arriving next to pay the praise which was her due. Of course she had her disappointments, occasions when she sauntered nonchalantly towards a visitor who, unknown to her, disliked cats; and who had come to see the donkeys, even ourselves, instead. Such moments of embarrassment, however, were quickly covered up by swift action on the part of Jeannie or myself. Acutely sensing the atmosphere, we would gather up Lama in our arms and hurry her indoors.

These occasions, nonetheless, were rare. She was, in fact, so much in demand, so repeatedly photographed, picked up, hugged, stroked, played with, innocently teased by children, and generally made a fuss of, that by August a blasé mood could be noted in her behaviour. By September this mood had become glaringly apparent. Some admirer would approach her with suitable friendly noises and she would forthwith turn her black silky posterior towards the admirer and march away, leaving us to make the excuses. Sometimes, however, I felt she had good reasons for such rudeness. There was an inclination on the part of many of her admirers to inquire her age. There she would be in the most obliging fashion coping with the hugging, the clicking cameras, and the contrived games when suddenly the remark would be made: 'She must be getting on . . . how old is she now?' Our own tart reply was to say that it was not good manners to ask a lady her age. But this Lama did not think was good enough. Indeed I believe that the frequency of this question throughout the summer was one of the chief causes of her September impatience. What did age matter? Why was everyone so self-conscious about age?

In September she became increasingly inclined to hide. She had nests in various spots around Minack, each of them securing her favour for a while; and although we believed we had mapped them all she was always able to fool us. There was a nest on the wall close to the bridge, a curved cavity of pressed dry grass, a most favourite spot from which, as we sat letting the time go by, we would hear a quiet heave-ho of gentle snores. There was another up by the well, and another by the stream at the bottom of our small orchard, and another high up on the wall which framed our old wooden potato house. This nest was within the territory of the stable meadow which the donkeys used; and Fred knew about it though he was aggravated by the fact it was just out of reach of his enquiring nose.

But it was remarkable how often she was in none of these nests we knew; and we would vainly call her and rush from nest to nest, becoming increasingly irritated, our calls even louder, until at last in our exhaustion we would have to admit to the admirer who had come to see her that she was unavailable. And this is what happened when Madame Boniface called. There was not a sign of her. We spent an hour and a half charging round Minack and there wasn't a miaow in response. Every foot of land we examined. Every section echoed with our calls. She was no longer my favourite cat. I became angry. For after all how often does a one-time wild cat receive a visitor from Paris?

Half an hour after Madame Boniface's departure, Lama appeared. All purrs. So there was only one thing I could do. We shut her in the bedroom. Then I drove to Penzance, found the hotel where Madame Boniface was staying, and brought her back. No trouble this time. Lama was charming.

Three days later I saw Squeak and Wilfred caught in the cobwebs of the alcove by the barn window. Pip was already flying on his own outside, then returning to the barn; but Squeak and Wilfred were just out of the nest. I picked each up in my hand, removed the cobwebs clinging to their wings, then took them to the barn door and let them free. It was the first time they had seen the space of the world, and they left my hand unafraid, and soared into the sky and, though watching them for some clumsy aerobatics, I saw them flying around the stable meadow with the ease of veterans. Two more swallows ready for South Africa.

The sun was still warm, and the school holidays were over, and two days would go by without anyone calling; and Jeannie and I found our minds were at ease, so that, as in the spring, we felt able to picnic on the rocks with a bottle of wine and sandwiches of home-made bread; and feel free of anyone wanting us. The gulls, of course, were still annoyed when they saw us appear. They rose from the rocks, uttering raucous epithets, and we were sorry that we were disturbing them; but the sea and the sky were their kingdom, time too, and there was no reason to feel guilty as they drifted away from Minack rocks.

At night I took a torch to the barn to check the swallows which were roosting there. The parents were the first to go. Pip went next, five days later. Then Squeak four days after him.

I was never happy as to what happened to Wilfred. He was always the weakest. He still came back to the nest a week after Squeak had gone.

Then he too disappeared; and the summer was ended.

END

COTTAGE ON A CLIFF

To Caroline Oliver

CHAPTER ONE

Michaelmas Day is the beginning of winter. The day when retiring farmers hand over to their successors, when beefy lifeguards have departed from now deserted beaches and holiday hotels have closed till another summer, when sea-shore car parks are empty and pampered gulls wonder what has happened, when ice cream kiosks are shuttered and the winds begin to blow, when some will grumble that life has become too quiet and others will be glad the holiday season is over: 'Cornwall belongs to Cornwall again.' The visitors have gone.

There are sleepy flies on the last blackberries, spider webs stretch across narrow paths, I flush the first woodcock from a patch of battered bracken as I walk towards Carn Barges, a fieldfare in the stable meadow below the cottage looks surprised to be in a strange country, a late wasp buzzes dozily against a window of the porch, blue-tits have returned to the bird-table after being self-sufficient during the summer, faded honeysuckle still blooms in odd places down the cliff a hundred yards away, ivy leaves are yellow-green and leaves of the brambles have turned a robin-red. Wild violets are in clusters. Winter gorse is in flower.

I pull up an imaginary drawbridge at Monty's Leap when winter comes. I play a game that Jeannie and I live in a fortress with a deep moat surrounding us. We have no part in the busy, fractious, unsatisfied outside world, and nothing can disturb the easy motion of the day. Strikes, inflation, unemployment, violence, greed, envy, all these I pretend play no part in our lives. I have passing fantasies that peace of mind has been permanently obtained by looking after our own lives instead of interfering in the lives of others. I am therefore immune, I pretend, from the tedious troubles of the herd. I live in a world where time is mine. I am a countryman living in a remote place with the chance to keep my own identity. I am as simply happy as the uncomplicated peasant of a hundred years ago who never left his parish. Such a game I may play for a day, for two, for three: and then some incident will occur which wakes me up to reality.

'Ian has killed himself,' I said.

The post had arrived a few minutes before, brought by Roger on a bicycle from the village post office of St Buryan. I had opened a couple of letters, then this third one from a journalist friend in London. Jeannie was standing by the fireplace.

'I can't believe it!' And she put her hands to her face. 'Oh no. What happened? Why? Why should he have done it?'

Why, why. Always the same question. One can understand the causes of tragedy, seldom explain them.

'Read the letter,' I said, and handed it to her.

Ian was English, divorced and around forty. He had had exceptional success as a film scriptwriter; and also as co-producer of three films which have become classics. He was, and this I particularly remembered in the light of what had happened, a comfortable person to be with, an easy-going person with a wish to please, a good friend, and generous. We used to see a good deal of him in London, and he was one of those who regularly came to our Boat Race parties when we lived at Thames Cottage overlooking the finishing post at Mortlake. After we left for Cornwall our reunions necessarily became fewer. He stayed with us here at Minack once, and by that time his circumstances had begun to change. The film group with whom he worked had broken up, and he was on his own operating as a free-lance with see-saw success. Then his luck began to run out and money to be short, and pub sandwiches took the place of expensive lunches, and a bedsitter in Fulham the place of a flat off Berkeley Square. Nevertheless he remained one of those people whose success seems always to be near if only the chance came their way; and he was on the verge of such a success when he took an overdose of sleeping tablets.

What had happened was this. He had adapted a well-known novel for a film, and his shooting script had been warmly accepted by a film company. A contract had been drafted, a famous actor had agreed to play the leading role, and so six months' hard work was about to receive its reward. The actor, however, was an international star in a position to state his own terms. He was delighted to play the star part, he said, but he didn't like the shooting script . . . and he demanded that a friend of his should rewrite it. The news reached Ian in a telephone call near midnight on a Saturday. On Sunday morning he was found dead.

Part of me wants to believe in the myth that we are masters of our fates. There are occasions, no doubt, when we are in command, those occasions when we make a firm decision determining the pattern of a day, a year, and for that matter the rest of our lives. In this respect we can be masters of our fates. We are powerless, however, when it comes to the multitude of incidents that even with hind-sight we know we could not have controlled. The chance meeting, coincidences, the galaxy of times when luck plays the dominant part. We are then at the mercy of fortune and William Henley's cry, 'I am master of my fate,' becomes a mocking one. Ian, for instance, could not have controlled the timing of that telephone call. If he had received it in the morning, he would have been more resilient. Might he not have been alive today?

I still marvel at the luck that brought Jeannie and me to Minack. There are legions of people who yearn to pack up their jobs, and find some patch of land where they can create their earthly Nirvana. Jeannie and I were among that number who have succeeded in turning that dream into reality, but this was not achieved simply by exercising cold reason. We needed many unexpected circumstances to be on our side.

We both, for instance, had to share the wish to leave London, for failure would have been certain had one been dragging the other; and it would have been understandable if Jeannie had hesitated about leaving the fun she had as publicity head of the Savoy, Claridges and Berkeley. There were, too, the circumstances surrounding the discovery of Minack. The name, Lamorna, captured my imagination when I was a boy, but I never paid a visit to this lovely valley until one day in London I had a sudden urge to spend a few days' holiday there. Thus it was that Jeannie and I took a walk along the track above the harbour, then through chest-high bracken above the rocks and the sea until we climbed up the cliff to the point called Carn Barges. It was then that we saw the grey cottage inland, half hidden on the edge of a wood; and we knew from that instant we were going to live there. This intuition proved to be correct, but here again an odd circumstance helped it to be so.

At the particular time when we started to negotiate for a lease, there was a squatter scare in the area. Squatters were threatening to take possession of any cottages they found empty; and Minack was empty. It was in a desolate condition, rain leaking through the roof, rat holes in the boards that covered the earthen floor; and yet obviously it would prove to be quite satisfactory for any squatters. A potential squatter group was also nearby, living in the moorland near Lamorna; and their presence caused considerable concern to the farmer who was responsible for Minack. The group was harmless and pleasant enough, living out their theory that sharing was the secret of happiness; but the farmer was apprehensive.

Hence when we came along offering to rent the cottage, we had this luck on our side. True the farmer took time to make up his mind, but he would never have decided in our favour had it not been for the presence of the squatters. We were his answer to the squatters. He didn't really want anyone in the cottage, but there was no harm in letting it to us for a few months ... We looked respectable, I was Cornish, and our presence would keep the squatters at bay. In due course the squatters would leave the area, and also, he was sure, would we ... after all the girl would be certain to return to her glittering life at the Savoy. To his credit, when he realised his judgement about us was wrong, he did

10

everything possible to help us; and he became a great friend.

We depended on luck, therefore, to come here. And we have needed luck also to stay. Hence we have learnt not to take any day for granted. We are on guard. I may pull up an imaginary drawbridge at Monty's Leap when winter comes and pretend that we have no part in the fractious, outside world; but I only have to have a letter to remind me that I still belong to it.

For wherever one lives and whatever one does, contentment will always be illusive. It just happens, however, that contentment is less illusive when one lives in a place which is far from the crowd.

Ian, I know, would have liked this kind of life if he had had the luck to live it.

CHAPTER TWO

'The donkeys are hooting.'

'I heard.'

The hoots came from a distance, from the meadows overlooking the sea of Mount's Bay, bordering the track which leads to the onion meadow at the boundary of Minack land.

'What's happening?' said Jeannie.

'Usual thing, I expect. Just wanting attention.'

'Fred was sounding his alarm note ... it's the poacher again.'

'Perhaps.'

Fred was born at Minack beside a rock that grows out of the ground in the big field which was called the cemetery field because cattle used to be buried there; and which is now called Fred's field. He is a splendid-looking donkey with a fine intelligent head and a coat of chocolate-brown which is thick in winter like a moorland pony. We had bought Penny, his mother, at a pub near Redruth a month before he was born ... a black donkey with sad eyes and a coat which was in a moth-eaten condition. The publican said she had no future. He explained that after her foal was born she was to be sent to the knacker's yard while the foal was scheduled to go to a travelling circus. Such talk was

11

good salesmanship. It was persuasive enough for Jeannie to say that she wouldn't leave the pub unless Penny came with us; and that was that. Penny returned with us to Minack in the back of the Land Rover.

'You had better go and see what's happening,' said Jeannie.

It was a lovely morning. A morning that belonged to summer. A still sea, soft salty scents, a quiet sky. I could have believed it was a June morning except there were no swallows dancing in the sky or darting in and out of the barn door; and the bracken swathing the moorland was a red-brown instead of a rich green, and spider webs shimmered on the hedges, and the leaves of the elms had begun to fall in the wood, and buds were plumply showing on the December-flowering camellia bush. The year was lying about its age. It had produced this Indian summer to fool the Red Admiral butterfly that fluttered from leaf to leaf on the escallonia opposite the entrance to the cottage, and the blackbird which sang a spring song in the blackthorn near the well, and the fox I saw basking in a corner of the field on the other side of the shallow valley . . . fooling also myself, as I walked off to see the donkeys, into pretending no winter lay ahead, no storms to prove again the omnipotence of the elements, no misadventures.

The donkeys were reliable watchmen, and their hearing was as acute as their eyesight. I have seen them many a time look up from the grass they were grazing, then stare intently into the distance with ears pricked; and in a minute or so I would find someone coming down the lane, or observe a figure moving in the moorland far away.

Penny did not, however, sound the alarm in the manner of Fred. Her voice was simply not good enough. She croaked a bray, wheezed it, producing nothing better than a strangled cry, a kind of banshee wail. Poor Penny, it was always painful to watch her frustration as she tried to compete with her son.

Fred, on the other hand, could bray so heartily that he could be heard in the next parish and beyond. Obviously this could be embarrassing when the weather was quiet, for not everyone enjoys the sound of a donkey in full cry. And so Jeannie or I would rush to him as fast as possible begging him to stop, shoving into his mouth, if we had time to collect it, a large piece of bread as a gag.

At night both were usually silent. They were undisturbed by the badgers, foxes and rabbits who roamed around them on nocturnal duties. They remained sleepily serene. Yet I was sure that they would always raise the alarm if there was a stranger about, or some activity which puzzled them. I had had evidence of this a month previously.

On that occasion, a dark though clear August night, I was woken up around three in the morning by bellows from Fred. It was very still and I squirmed at the thought of the people in the neighbourhood roused by him. It was a terrible noise, and it went on and on, until I realised that something very unusual was bothering him. Then he stopped . . . and I heard voices.

On still nights we often hear the voices of the crews of passing fishing boats, sometimes the sound of voluble French from the crabbers on the way to and from Newlyn, but they soon fade away into the distance. On this night they did not fade away. And as I lay in my bed realising they had persisted for too long a time to belong to a moving boat, I knew I had to get up and investigate.

I pulled on some clothes, went outside, and shone my torch into the stable meadow below the cottage where I had left the donkeys. The light shone on Fred who was standing with his head facing towards the sea, ears upright like a V sign, displaying so intense an interest as to what was mysteriously happening that I felt like saying to him: 'Here, take the torch, go and find out what it's all about.'

Jeannie had now joined me, and we went down the path and through the white gate into Fred's field. At this moment there was a thunder of hooves behind us. The donkeys, of course, wanted to come with us, and when they found the gate shut on them Fred began trumpeting again.

'Shut up!' I said, 'shut up!' He took no notice.

At the point in the field where we were standing, we were able to look down on the sea and the shadows of the rocks below . . . and over to the left at the bottom of a castle of rocks known as Carn Barges I saw lights. I had brought my field-glasses with me, and I peered through the darkness and saw perhaps three or four moving pin-points of lights which I guessed were torches. But there were also two bright lights like those that lampers use when hunting

13

rabbits at night with their whippets. As I watched, these lights went out for a second, then on again, then out. They seemed to be signalling.

'A boat's run aground,' said Jeannie. We knew every inch of this part of the coast, and dark though it was, I could visualise in my mind the position of these lights. They came from a spur of rocks jutting out into the sea, deep water at high tide.

'It couldn't be a boat in this weather,' I said, 'there's no fog and no sea.' Then I added: 'If you stay here and calm the donkeys, I'll go ahead along the cliff path and see whether I can make contact.'

The cliff path was a rough one even in daytime. We used to keep it open for hikers by regularly walking along it with the donkeys. The donkeys loved this walk, and they would nibble the straying brambles that crossed the path, helping me therefore as I cut back brambles and gorse.

At night, however, the path was hazardous, especially if you were half running as I was doing. There were boulders on the path, and trip wires of bramble roots. Hence at one moment I missed my hold on a boulder and fell into a forest of stinging nettles, and the next I was tripped into a prickly hive of brambles and gorse. There was, too, at one point a section of low-lying elders. I hit the top of my head on one of the branches, and cut it.

By this time I was growing impatient. Who could these people be who had so aroused us! The waves, rolling on to the rocks, were surprisingly noisy; and though the torches were now several hundred yards away, I realised they might have difficulty in hearing me.

'Hello, hello,' I shouted, 'do you need help?'

There was no question of a boat being aground. The lights were on the rocks. I was quite certain of this. But I persisted with my call because I thought of no other.

'Do you need help?' I bellowed again.

No reply.

It was at this moment that I found myself in the law-abiding citizen's perennial problem. How seriously should I treat the situation? It was now half past three in the morning, and if I were to call the police or the coastguard I would have to return to the cottage, get into the car and drive to a telephone box three miles away; and what would I report?

Fred's suspicions? My own doubtful ones that illegal immigrants were being landed? Or gun-runners loading a dingy? I had already scanned the sea with my field-glasses and, although seeing the lights of two vessels sailing the normal route across Mount's Bay to the Lizard, I observed no vessel close to shore. So wouldn't I be making a fool of myself if I reported curious goings on at four in the morning?

Felons galore have escaped with their sins because of doubts like mine. Once, however, when I was living in Richmond in a house facing the river just below the bridge, I acted upon my suspicions with embarrassing results.

One early morning I heard an unusual noise downstairs which seemed to come from the hall leading into the dining-room. I crept to an upstairs telephone, and informed the police that I thought the house was being burgled. Could they send a constable to investigate?

I waited for his arrival, watching for him from the bed-room window; and within ten minutes I wished I had kept my mouth shut. I suddenly realised that the house was being surrounded by a legion of dimmed torch lights. A major police attack had been mounted. And my suspicions were soon to be proved wrong.

The noise proved to be a rat gnawing a hole in the wain-scoting.

The memory of this experience has always haunted me. Hence as I stood on the cliff path staring down at the strangers below me, I said to myself that I had better play safe. The men down there were probably night fishermen. It was a reasonable explanation to believe. And by believing it I would spare myself from appearing as an interfering busybody.

So I returned along the path to Jeannie and the donkeys, and to bed. Next day I learnt they were indeed fishermen . . . taking part in the Mount's Bay night fishing championship.

Fred had also given me a warning about the poacher.

One evening during the summer just before dusk, he had let out a great bellow while we were having supper. He and Penny were in the same meadow as they were now on this lovely morning; and when I had hurried down to see what was happening I found the donkeys in one meadow and a man with his back to me, shotgun raised to his shoulder, in another.

I had known the poacher had been around for some weeks because I kept finding spent cartridges at various points of the cliff. I knew, too, where he came from. He was not local though he was temporarily working in the district. And yet I had never been able to catch him in the act. Until that moment.

'May I ask,' I said gently, 'whether you have permission to shoot on this land?'

He had been about to fire, and when he swung round towards me he still kept the gun on his shoulder. He was enraged by the interruption. Indeed for a brief second I thought he was going to press the trigger. Then he turned and ran, murmuring incoherently as he did so.

On this lovely morning, however, there was no poacher. Fred's alarm note had been due to a hiker who was passing by; and by the time I arrived the hiker had unhitched his haversack and, to the donkeys' delight, was offering them buns.

'You don't mind, I hope,' he said. He was middle-aged, a round merry face, a ginger beard, and stocky. He was dressed in the manner of a hiker of all seasons. Anorak, rain-proof trousers, tough boots.

'Of course not,' I said. 'Going far?'

'Penberth, Porthgwarra, Land's End ... I may stay at Sennen Cove or go on to St Just.'

'There's a first-class hostel near St Just overlooking Cot Valley.'

'Is there? I'm a member of the Association, but if the weather isn't too bad I prefer to sleep out. I carry a tent, you see.'

'You'll find it rough going until you reach Penberth. There's no clear path yet.'

'I don't mind about that. Part of the pleasure is trying to find the way.'

Fred was wanting another bun. He was pushing his nose into the haversack, so I put out my hand and shoved him away. Then Penny tried to do the same, and I shoved her away too.

'Where did you start today?'

I am naturally inquisitive. I find life too short to follow the dour Englishman's policy of never asking a stranger a question. You can miss a great deal by such silence. I therefore believe the risk of a rebuff worth-while; and I was quite prepared, when I once asked a hiker a similar question, to receive the reply: 'Mind your own business.'

This time there was no hint of a rebuff.

'I got to Penzance last night, then walked through Newlyn and Mousehole and around about dusk I found myself in a kind of quarry overlooking Lamorna Cove.'

'That's the quarry which was worked at the beginning of the century and produced the stone for the Victoria Embankment in London.'

'Anyhow, it seemed isolated so I pitched my tent.'

The donkeys, aware that the haversack was out of bounds, were now a few yards off. They had found something to eat in the hedge.

'They would do well in the Pyrenees,' said the hiker, watching them, 'that's where I should be, walking along the narrow paths meeting donkeys like them. I started off from Bradford to do just that, then I got to Southampton and found myself suddenly saying I don't want to go there after all, I want to go to the far west of Cornwall where I've never been, instead.'

'Are you pleased,' I asked, 'with what you've seen so far?' I heard myself ask the question and was amused. I was putting a leading question to satisfy the ingrained wish for approval.

'Beautiful, beautiful,' he said, 'for many years I have walked all over Europe, but every year the tracks which once I knew were wild are becoming more civilised. The cult of hiking is becoming too rationalised. It has become so easy that the real pleasure of hiking is lost. You should see Austria in the summer. Tracks which I used to follow for miles on my own are now highways ... filled with perspiring holidaymakers from all over Europe. You understand, now, why I enjoyed this morning.'

'What else do you do?'

He had picked up a strand of grass and was chewing it.

'I'm a heating engineer by profession. I advise on the heating equipment for factories mostly. As you know the

17

law came in a year or two back requiring standard heat conditions for workers. That meant a lot of opportunities for someone like myself.... and I took them up to a point.'

He paused. He was watching a French crabber with a bright green hull that had just come into view.

'But I wasn't going to let these opportunities,' he went on, 'interfere with my basic philosophy of life.'

'What is that?'

'To be free to be myself.'

I laughed.

'Those of us who feel like that are antisocial. We are told it's wrong to isolate one's personal whims from the destiny of the human race.'

'Perhaps that's today's conventional view, but it doesn't have to be the right one, and you don't have to follow it.'

'In theory you are no doubt right,' I said, 'but in practice it is hard not to be conventional if you have to earn a living.'

'Oh yes, you have to compromise.' Fred had come up to him again. He enjoyed taking part in a conversation, or rather to appear to take part. 'I compromise for that matter,' the man went on, 'though, of course, it is easier for me because I am not married and have no family responsibilities. So I stay long enough in one job to live on my savings for a year. I'm starting such a year at this moment. Thus this month I am in Cornwall, next month maybe in the Dordogne, the next in the Camargue. I'm thinking of Mexico later on. Just me and my tent, so it's cheap.' He paused for a moment, still stroking Fred's white nose. 'And what do *you* do?'

I may be adventurous myself in asking people personal questions, but I am surprised when someone asks *me* such a question. This man, however, stimulated me. He belonged to a kind of life I did not know. It is strange how often, on this wild section of the Cornish coast, I meet people who have sheered away from standard values.

'Jeannie, my wife, and I have a flower farm,' I answered, 'or perhaps I should be more accurate and say it used to be a flower farm. At one time we grew violets, wall-flowers, anemones, winter-flowering stocks, forget-me-nots and so on. Those were in our optimistic days, but one by one we had to give them up because they became too expensive to grow for the prices we received. We were quite ignorant

18

about commerical horticulture when we came here. Jeannie had been press officer of the Savoy Hotel group, and I was in MI 5, and for a long time we had to live very primitively compared to our previous kind of life. No electric light in the cottage, no running water, and the land was a wilderness, and we made many, many mistakes. At last we settled upon growing daffodils which we start picking at the end of January, and tomatoes during the summer ... those apparently empty meadows you are looking at, for instance, will be producing thousands of daffodils in February and early March.'

The BEA helicopter, bound for the Scilly Islands, came clattering along off shore a few hundred feet above the sea. It normally flew the inland route above the A.30 and Land's End. It only flew along the coast in foggy weather and so I half wondered why, on this fine day, it had come this way.

'I also write books about our life here,' I added. 'Jeannie writes too, and also draws and paints. She sells her drawings and pictures.'

'Sounds ideal.'

'Yes.'

Fred had moved away, and was staring out to sea at a passing stone boat, one of those which weekly load from the quarry at Newlyn.

'Are you apprehensive about the future?' the man asked.

'Of course. Everyone is at one time or another.'

'I didn't mean in a personal way. I meant apprehensive about the future of the environment you live in. Somewhere like Cornwall seems totally at the mercy of the advancing motorways and the millions of people who will invade you as a result.'

I did not contradict him.

'I read the other day,' the man went on, 'that seventeen million city people will be within three hours' motoring distance of Dartmoor when the scheduled motorways have been completed in a year or two. Soon after, they will be descending on Cornwall.'

'This is progress.'

'Progress to what? Nobody ever mentions that.' He paused, and then added: 'The trouble is that the population is encouraged to breed like rabbits, and the result is bound to be a plague of human beings.'

19

I smiled.

'Perhaps then,' I said, 'you will agree with the solution I have for Cornwall.'

'What's that?'

'You've heard of the lost lands of Lyonesse, the land which is supposed to have been swamped by the sea between Land's End and the Scillies many centuries ago? My idea is to have a vast sign planted in the sea with the notice WELCOME TO LYONESSE ... the drivers of the cars pouring down the motorway will see the sign, and drive on over the cliffs.'

The man laughed.

'I don't suppose the planners have ever thought what happens when the motorway reaches Land's End.'

'They haven't, nor what happens when it reaches Penzance, nor what happens to the surrounding country and coast. Cornwall is a narrow county, and there is no room for millions. But it is an age of motorway mania ...'

'And people are brainwashed into accepting it.'

'Yes,' I said.

The donkeys had returned to us. It was the haversack which appealed to them, and when the hiker picked it up and began fastening it on his back, Fred's nose once again had to be pushed away. The hiker was ready to go.

'Goodbye,' he said, and held out his hand. 'I'll think of you sometimes on my wanderings facing these problems. These problems are the same all over Europe. But you are one of the lucky ones to have privacy. Privacy is becoming the most precious commodity in the world.'

'I agree.'

'Mind you, your life wouldn't suit *me*. I wouldn't like to be anchored in one place however beautiful the surroundings.' Then he added casually, 'What do you do in the winter? Don't you find it lonely? Don't you get tired of the wind and the rain? Don't you want change?'

He was not requiring a reply. His mind was already on the next stage of his journey. He patted the donkeys, bade me goodbye, then strode away.

The haversack was irresistible. The donkeys moved away with him.

CHAPTER THREE

A girl, a secretary from Nottingham, came to the door a few days after I saw the hiker. She said she was making a sentimental journey to find Jane's cottage ... *Jane who once worked for us, then went away to live in the Scilly Isles. The girl said she admired Jane's attitude to life, the unselfconscious way she lived close to nature, her gaiety and determination. There was indeed much about Jane to admire ... only fifteen when she came to us, fair hair falling over her shoulders, a rebel against conventional schooling, wandering barefoot about her work, always sure of the standards which she wished to maintain, an elfish charm of a vagabond ... these qualities have attracted people. There had been others, before this girl, who had asked about Jane.

'She used to use those two granite steps leading to that field,' I said, pointing to a field close to the cottage, 'then over that hedge which is now covered by brambles, then across another field, over another hedge and across a further field. That way it didn't take her five minutes.'

We came that way ourselves once upon a time when there was no lane to Minack fit for a car. We turned left after

* Jane of *A Drake At The Door*.

21

passing the stone circle known as the Merry Maidens, if we had been coming from Penzance, then on past farm buildings on our left, down a narrow lane to the three cottages, all in one building, that stood high above the sea facing Boscawen Point and Logan Rock in the distance, then we drove across a grass field to our boundary hedge. We left the car there.

Jane's cottage was the middle one of the three, and she used to live with her mother, young brother, two cats, an ancient parrot, a griffin, a bull terrier, and a sheep. Once she kept a muscovy drake in her bedroom but this proved too much for her tolerant mother, and the drake was offered to Jeannie and me. I did not want it myself. I had enough responsibilities at the time without taking on any more; and so the sight of Jane arriving for work one morning with the large drake in her arms, filled me with dismay. I protested, but neither Jane nor Jeannie took any notice. They were in league together. The drake, they knew, was scheduled for the pot if it didn't find a home at Minack. So I had to be ignored; and how glad I am that they acted as they did. Boris, though only a muscovy drake, gave us much pleasure during the eight years he imposed his character upon Minack.

'It'll be easier for you to go round by the cliff,' I said to the girl, and I proceeded to explain to her the way.

The meadows she would pass, the Pentewan meadows I called them, had brought despair to us during the time we had rented them. They had been offered to us by a neighbouring farmer, and although we were occupied enough by the Minack meadows, we believed that this extra land would give us the opportunity to assure our future. Nothing of the sort. Our enterprise was to prove disastrous. We grew anemones, and the hottest late summer in years shrivelled them into dust. We grew spring onions, and twenty-four hours after the seed was in the ground a torrential downpour washed them out of the ground. We grew wallflowers, winter stocks and violets. None of them prospered; and every year, of course, we grew potatoes, potatoes which with remorseless regularity were blasted by terrible gales before harvesting time. One might have thought we would have hated these Pentewan meadows as a result, but we didn't. They provided our education in growing, made us

22

realise that the elements were always supreme however smart the human race might think itself to be, and showed us the way that if we were to be happy in this environment we had chosen, it was necessary for us to be an integral part of it. An onlooker would never belong.

The girl came back an hour or so later, and said she was surprised to find the cottages, all three of them, empty; and she wondered why they had been allowed to become so dilapidated. They did indeed look forlorn. The cottages had been built in the first part of the century for workers on the farm, but they were too remote and primitive for modern standards except for those kind of people who were refreshed by a contrast to their normal style of living; and when Jane lived there, the other two cottages were used by a schoolteacher during the holidays and a small-part actor when he was out of work. Then the Cornish farmer for whom Jane's mother worked as herds-woman sold the farm and the cottages; and the buyer was an elderly gentleman from outside the county who decided he might want the cottages for his own purposes. Hence Jane and her mother went to the Scillies, and the schoolteacher and actor found somewhere else to which they could retreat.

The cottages were, in fact, never occupied except for the rats and the mice and the occasional wanderer who sought a temporary shelter; and now a window or two were broken, and slates had been blown off the roof, and the front doors were worm-eaten and unpainted. The elderly gentleman had been forced by circumstances outside his control to change his plans; and the cottages had suffered.

There was now, however, a change to their fortunes likely to take place. The elderly gentleman had in his turn retired, and sold both the farm and the cottages. In his place there had come a modern young farmer with a keen business sense. He lived on another of his farms and needed the land, not the buildings. Thus he was prepared to sell to outsiders the farmhouse and cottages, even the old stone cowsheds as potential holiday flatlets as well. In the dreary necessity of today he had to look upon this beautiful farm as a factory, not a home.

'I met a black cat on my way,' said the girl casually, 'in fact it looked starving. It followed me to the cottages and

23

then back ... it suddenly disappeared into nowhere just by the quarry where I first saw it.'

Such information interested Jeannie and me.

'Was it fully grown?'

'Oh yes, but it was terribly skinny.'

The small quarry had been out of use for many years. Its stone once provided the base for the lanes in the area.

'It looked like Lama,' said the girl, 'except for its skinniness.'

I glanced at Lama who was lying like a miniature Trafalgar lion on a yellow cushion in the porch. A black, silky, plush figure, utterly at peace with the world she lived in. A serene example of a contented cat who was sure of the safety of each day, of a regular, well filled plate, of immediate obedience to her whims. A cat who appeared to have no reason to expect that the comfortable progress of her life would ever be rudely disturbed.

She was wild when we first knew her. She roamed the meadows around Minack one daffodil harvest time, watching us from afar, sizing us up I suppose. Ten months before, Monty, the ginger cat who came from London to Minack with us, had died; and I had then sworn, such was my sadness, that I would never have another cat. But some strange, compelling instinct forced me to hedge against this declaration, and I said to Jeannie that I would make an exception if a black cat whose home we never could trace, came crying to our door in a storm.

The cause of my unwillingness to have another cat was not, however, only due to my sadness. I had been for much of my life an anti-cat man, and although Monty was able to make me a slave my devotion was to him and not to his breed. I did not want to become involved again. I certainly did not want some kind-hearted person offering me a replacement. Monty was unique in my life, and that was that. Hence my seemingly impossible condition about a black cat coming to the door of the cottage in a storm. Hence my bewilderment when my condition was in fact fulfilled and Lama came to the door and we heard her miaow above the roar of the southerly gale and the rain.

There was, however, another condition to be fulfilled. Had she a home? Was she just a lost little black cat whose owner somewhere was grieving for her? The vet who came to see her declared she was about three months old, and at that age she could not have travelled very far. It was therefore comparatively easy to carry out our investigations, and we soon discovered that no one in the area had lost such a little black cat. Where, then, had she come from? We had our suspicions, but no reason to believe these suspicions had a base until an incident took place nearly five years later.

We had made a distant acquaintance, long before Lama appeared on the scene, with a small grey cat who wandered from time to time across Minack land. She displayed no desire to be friendly, and ran away into the undergrowth as soon as we approached her. Yet she had a strong personality, and we found ourselves taking an interest in her movements, and we would call to each other if, after an absence of a month or two, we suddenly saw her again. Jeannie gave her the name of Daisy and so, if I saw her, I would say, 'I saw Daisy this morning crossing the stable meadow.' Indeed on the morning of the day the girl called to see Jane's cottage, I had seen the compact little figure of Daisy slowly making her way up the lane. She was old now, of course, but she was still very pretty ... and her compactness, the shape of her little head, the texture of her grey coat, all of these added up to an uncanny resemblance to Lama. Was she Lama's mother? We were sure that she was. Apart from the resemblance, there was this incident which took place nearly five years after Lama appeared in Minack meadows.

We were planting daffodil bulbs down the cliff at the time, in a meadow where we have a palm tree growing in one corner. Geoffrey was with us. Geoffrey who worked at Minack when Jane and Shelagh were here, then had to leave after a bad season when we had no money left to pay him. Then later he returned, and became a corner stone of our life; and there he was now, close to the palm tree using his shovel to plant the bulbs when he suddenly saw at the top of the meadow near the entrance of a small cave ... a black kitten.

It was, of course, as wild as a rabbit and it darted out of sight as soon as Geoffrey approached. But we kept watch for the next few days and saw it from time to time, and we saw Daisy several times close to the cave; and there was one early morning when Jeannie crept down the cliff on her own and discovered the kitten curled asleep in the cave on a bed of dried leaves.

We had never, however, seen Lama and Daisy together. We had seen Lama *observing* Daisy on her peregrinations, but only observing. They were always at a polite distance as far as we knew ... until one evening at dusk when I had gone out to shut Boris in his house in the wood, I surprised Lama and Daisy halfway up an elm near the flower shed. They were close together, and to my astonishment there was no sign of any animosity. They seemed like two old friends having a gossip.

The following morning Jeannie asked me to fetch an onion from a string that hung in the stables, the ancient stone building in front of the cottage. I reached the doorway, the door had been left half open, and suddenly I saw on an old sack in the middle of the cobblestone floor, the little black kitten of the cliff. It was sound asleep, but such was its wild instinct that it immediately woke up to the danger of my presence and dashed to hide among a pile of old bric-à-brac at one end of the stables. There was no doubt that it was the double of Lama when she was young; and for the following ten days we had more opportunities to observe it. We used to put saucers of milk and scraps on the cobblestone floor, then watch through the window which faced the lane as the kitten cautiously emerged from its hiding place and proceeded to have its fill. The situation was certainly extraordinary ... two black kittens who had mysteriously appeared at Minack, both the same shape, both the same shape as Daisy. I think, therefore, we had good reason to believe that Daisy was Lama's mother; and that Lama had also been born down the cliff.

Then the kitten disappeared, and we never saw it again. We of course searched everywhere in the immediate area, but there was no trace of it. Nor was there any sign of Daisy, and indeed it was two months or more before we saw her pass through Minack again. We could only guess what had happened; and our guess was that Daisy had wanted to introduce her kitten into a larger world than the cliff. First, therefore, she had asked Lama in special feline fashion, if she would mind the kitten staying a while within her territory. Lama raised no objection, and indeed it had been strange to find Lama taking no interest in the stable while the kitten was there. Then, when the kitten was strong enough, Daisy decided it was time to move on. Where to?

This tantalising question remained unanswered, but it was always there at the back of our minds; and so when the girl who had gone to Jane's cottage spoke of the starving black cat she had met, we immediately wondered whether it might be the kitten grown up.

That evening Jeannie went to the quarry to investigate, and found nothing. We went together the next day, and the next, and still found nothing. I began to think the girl had imagined the incident, and decided to give up the search. Jeannie, however, remained persistent. There was a full moon the following night, and just before going to bed, while I had my bath, she announced that she was going to walk once again over to the quarry. I was lying in the bath when twenty minutes later I heard her call: 'Come here, quick!' I clambered out, wrapped myself in a towel and went into the sitting-room just in time to see Jeannie walking out of the door with a saucer in either hand. She had found the black cat, it had followed her back, and she was now about to feed it in the garden outside the porch.

I looked round for Lama and found her curled on the sofa in a tight ball. She was in a deep sleep, making a little clicking noise as she breathed, a strange little noise which was often her habit as she slept. She was therefore oblivious to what was going on outside, and I felt safe to join Jeannie in her unfaithfulness. She had already given the cat a name. Felix.

'He is starving,' she said, looking at Felix as he gulped the John Dory which had been scheduled for Lama's break-fast, 'and look at his eyes, they are glazed, he is literally dying of hunger!'

The moonlight was bright, bright enough to bathe the ancient granite rocks of the garden in an ethereal shine, though hardly enough for me to verify Jeannie's diagnosis. This was Jeannie in her exaggerating mood, I felt sure. The black cat, as far as I could see, had a long body, a bony head, a thin tail, and obviously a healthy appetite. But hardly a starving cat. If it had been it would not have jauntily followed Jeannie back from the quarry, a good ten minutes away. In any case there were plenty of rabbits for

27

it to catch on the cliffs. It was either a wild cat, or a domestic cat which had been deserted by its owner.

'Anyhow,' I said, as the cat licked the now empty plate, 'I am certain this is not a Daisy cat. It has no resemblance to her or to Lama. Far too long and leggy.'

'He is very friendly,' said Jeannie, stooping to stroke him.

There was always this fundamental difference of attitude between Jeannie and me about cats. Jeannie, from a child, had been ready to gather any cat under her protection. She represents the true cat lover, the music-hall version of the lady who will happily fill her home to overflowing with cats. I, on the other hand, was born a cat hater; and although I have now been converted by the charms of the race, I still have no wish to have more than one cat in my home. I am, in fact, still a one cat man.

I am, therefore, not a true cat lover. The true cat lover is ready to be obsequious towards any cat just in the hope of one purr in reward. The true cat lover takes no notice of those angry outbursts, those abusive remarks, that a cat makes when he is unwillingly picked up. The true cat lover queerly approaches a cat with childish cooings, and is undaunted when the cat reacts with a baleful stare. The true cat lover enjoys blissful confidence that he has a profound understanding of cats, an unfailing way with them . . . and is unabashed when a cat spits at him. The true cat lover by nature fawns upon cats.

Lama hated this cat lover's attitude. She was not influenced by flattery. If someone was mature enough to treat her as an equal, she would play fair on her part. She would respond to politeness. She would respond to admiration if conventionally conveyed. But she detested the way some cat lovers treated her as if she were an eccentric. Why do they have to gurgle like babies? Why can't they behave with normality? Poor fools.

'What are you going to do?' I asked Jeannie.

Felix was rubbing his bony head against her hand, and purring loudly. 'We can't have him staying around here.'

'You don't expect me to take the poor thing back to the quarry, do you?'

The poor thing was clearly enjoying himself. He was pushing his head against Jeannie's ankles, flattering her by his attention, and spurred on by his intuition that he had a cat lover on the run.

'He's not going to stay here,' I said firmly, 'we'll shut the door on him and hope he disappears by morning.'

Next morning when I awoke, I prayed that the cat had disappeared. Lama was on the bed still asleep, stretched out by my side like a black ribbon. I lay there stroking her silky back waiting for the return of Jeannie who had gone to investigate. My prayer was unanswered.

'Felix is still here,' she called from the porch, 'he's a clever cat. He made himself a nest in the shelter on an old cushion wedged between the paraffin tank and the wall.'

At this moment Lama stirred and sat up. Her day had begun. It was time for her to partake of a fish breakfast then enjoy a perambulation around the cottage. She stretched, and jumped off the bed.

'They're going to meet!' I said anxiously.

'Perhaps they'll like each other,' said Jeannie hopefully. 'Wouldn't it be fun if they did?'

'No,' I replied.

Jeannie, of course, was as anxious as I was not to upset Lama. Both of us were her slaves in a way that logical minds would disapprove of. We never went away, for instance, unless circumstances forced us to do so. The donkeys, though expecting our constant attention, had each other. Lama had Geoffrey during the day, but from five o'clock onwards was on her own. Was it our silly imagination that made us believe she might be unhappy during those long hours? And did this matter in any case? I suppose the answer lies in your valuation of trust. An animal possesses the original innocence, and is guileless in his trust. A human being, full of inhibitions, self-conscious education, and envy, is often incapable of trust; and so some pour ridicule upon those of us who love an animal. It is their loss that they do. They will never be aware of the subtle rewards we receive. The trust of an animal provides an anchor in life.

Lama had her breakfast, stretched again, then nonchalantly strolled to the porch door, wishing to be let out.

At the same moment I saw Felix at the window. His black, bony face was staring into the sitting-room.

'Heavens,' I said, 'we're in trouble.'

My voice was a moan. I sensed that if the cat was too appealing I might weaken. The pull of divided loyalties, one of the most bewitching of emotions, showed signs of twisting my judgement. I had begun to feel sorry for Felix. I remained devoted to Lama. But how was I brutally to turn away a lonely creature like this cat? I longed for it to go. I needed it to go to save me embarrassment. It *had* to go if Lama's life was to be normal.

'Hop it!' I shouted to the face in the window; and it took no notice.

Such a reaction would never have come from a truly wild cat. Lama, for instance, when she was wild, never came to the window and stared into the sitting-room. This was a cat who clearly knew of the comforts a home would bring.

'If you hold Lama for five minutes,' said Jeannie, 'I'll give Felix a good feed out of sight of the cottage. That'll keep him quiet. He'll go off afterwards for a sleep.'

Lama did not want to be held for five minutes. She wanted to get out of the cottage. Quick.

'Now Lama it's for your own good . . .'

Jeannie had gone out by the back door. One, two, three minutes, and I could hold Lama back no longer. I opened the porch door and Lama stalked out, paused for a second to sniff the October air, then wandered off round the corner by the water-butt, intending no doubt to stroll slowly and peacefully down the lane to Monty's Leap where she would have a drink from the little stream which came from the wood.

Felix, however, had failed to co-operate with Jeannie. She had carried his breakfast to a spot behind the flower shed where he had eaten it, purred a little, then to show his appreciation still further he proceeded to skip his way back to the cottage. He had no wish to sleep. He wanted to rejoice at his good fortune. A home again! Someone to care for him! This was no time to waste in sleep.

And so the confrontation took place.

Plushy Lama found herself nose to nose with long-legged, skinny body, bony-faced Felix . . . and ran away in terror.

The rest of the day, it was a Sunday, was tense. Felix refused to sleep, and kept peering gleefully through the window. His charms, he seemed to think, were irresistible, and so why couldn't he be allowed inside? This was a cat of character, I regretfully realised, a cat who would be difficult to be rid of, a cat who still had confidence in the human race whatever shocks he had had in the past.

But Lama . . . Lama skulked under my desk, moved to the bed in the spare room, slept fitfully, roamed the sitting-room, refused to eat, jumped on the table in the porch, stared through the glass, found Felix staring back, then uttered a frightened little cry before she jumped down and into hiding again.

By the end of the day I knew that such a situation could not be allowed to continue.

'Tomorrow morning,' I announced to Jeannie, 'the cat must go. We'll set out and find where he comes from.'

On Monday morning, therefore, we drove to our village of St Buryan and asked our friend the grocer, who had a round in the area, if he could help us. Yes, he said, he remembered a black cat at the elderly gentleman's farm which had recently been sold. The cat may have been left behind; and as the farmhouse was empty, it may have set out to find a new home. He suggested we asked the farmer who lived next door; and twenty minutes later we had the information we needed. Felix had, in fact, been left behind. The next door farmer had been feeding him, and was ready to continue to do so.

So we returned to Minack, collected Felix, put him in the car where he sat on Jeannie's lap looking alertly at the passing scene, and deposited him at his empty farmhouse, a couple of miles away as the crow flies. Then we saw the next door farmer again and he assured us that he would feed Felix every day. A kind thing to do in view of the fact he had a number of cats of his own. We were now thankful that the drama seemed to have ended, and later in the morning we went for a stroll with Lama around our meadows. She was at ease again, mistress of her own property, and the sight of her contentment gave us much pleasure.

By Tuesday midday Felix was back.

I had some trouble with the pump of our well which is some yards away from the cottage, and as I was returning after repairing it I suddenly saw Lama on the cottage roof. She was lashing her tail and looking downwards, and was plainly very angry indeed. Below her a happy Felix was waiting at the porch door.

'Felix,' I said coldly, 'buzz off.' And he promptly hastened towards me.

Once again we picked him up, and drove him back to the farm.

Wednesday he returned to Minack again at midday. This time Lama didn't see him; and he was away in the car while she was still sleeping on a chair in my office.

There was no sign of him on Thursday.

But on Friday morning, just as I was about to photograph some visiting friends, one of them holding Lama in her arms, another figure suddenly appeared in the view-finder.

Felix.

The maddening thing was his cocky behaviour. He was undaunted by our obvious desire to be rid of him. He felt completely at home with us. He moved around with aplomb. He was affectionate. He was certain he had a passport to stay at Minack. And so it must have been very bewildering for him why we were repeatedly picking him up, putting him in the car, and taking him back to his empty home. After all he had proved his wish to be with us. An insincere cat would not have crossed fields, and jumped over hedges, to be with us.

'Only one thing we can do,' said Jeannie, that Friday morning, 'we'll find out the telephone number of the old gentleman who had the farm, and tell him about Felix.'

The old gentleman, now retired, had moved to a house in another part of Cornwall.

'Then we can take Felix over to him.'

Once again we had Felix in the car. This time we drove to a huddle of cottages called Sparnon where there was a telephone koisk at the cross-roads. We never minded these excursions to telephone. It was a small price to pay for the pleasure of never hearing a telephone suddenly ringing in the cottage. Once upon a time each of us believed a telephone was indispensable to our lives. We now knew better. We were, for instance, now spared trivial invitations. If someone really wanted to contact us urgently they sent a telegram; and we replied by going out and ringing them up.

'You talk to him,' I said to Jeannie, when we reached Sparnon, 'you'll be more persuasive.'

One of her special charms has always been her speaking voice. It is soft and clear, and when she was at the Savoy

32

Danny Kaye wrote a song in praise of it, and sang it at the Palladium. I believed, therefore, that the old man would succumb to her description of Felix's plight. But she failed. I saw her in the kiosk wildly gesticulating with one hand as she talked into the receiver; and I guessed that the old man was saying that he could not have Felix with him again. His new home was no doubt too small.

'We can do what we like with him.'

She had come out of the kiosk and confirmed my guess. 'Poor Felix.'

He had been on my lap while Jeannie had been telephoning; and he had been purring away as his future had been discussed. I felt very sad for him. I felt sad for myself and for Lama. I foresaw the awful prospect of having to keep him. I could not let him be abandoned. Jeannie, I knew, would want to look after him. How on earth could I reconcile this with my loyalty to Lama?

At this precise moment a tractor and trailer came along the road we had just travelled to Sparnon; and driving the tractor was the modern young farmer who had bought

the old man's farm. A miraculous timing. Here was the new owner of Felix's old home appearing on the scene at the exact instant that Felix's future was being determined.

And within five minutes the future of Felix was settled. The young farmer was as co-operative as could be. He had no real cause to show any responsibility towards an abandoned cat, but he was prepared to be kind, and helpful, and anxious to solve the predicament in which we found ourselves.

'I'll take him,' he said, 'and as I bought his home I suppose I ought to look after him. We have enough cats as it is mind, but I reckon my wife will put up with another. The children will, anyhow.'

In this way the future of Felix was solved. I have never seen him again, but I gather he goes walks with the children, and on summer days he plays with them on the sands.

I wonder what would have happened to him if the girl from Nottingham had never come to Minack to find Jane's cottage.

CHAPTER FOUR

I have a dream, a muddled dream, that I live in a city again. I dream that I live in a featureless room above a car-filled street tied to a job I do not enjoy, enduring the day instead of living it. I press buttons on a cunning machine which I do not understand; and I am confused because at one moment I am obeying the orders of my company, the next of my union. Then suddenly in my dream I become affluent. I find myself imprisoned within conventional success, an important executive who is living expensively, winning applause from superiors, experiencing temporary triumphs, finding macabre fun in playing with power. A glossy, restless, hard-working, sophisticated life which provides the spur for beginners.

Then comes the end of my dream, and I am frightened.

I suddenly see myself as a disembodied person who is observing, and taking no part in the action. And I see a countryside as it was many, many years ago when it was free from man's calculated interference. There are crooked fields with the hedges still intact, and lanes sided by an

34

abundance of wild, useless beauty, lush vegetation, butter-flies, weeds, insects, no sprays or insecticides to kill them. Horses plough the fields, and foxes and badgers roam wooded valleys living in earths and setts which are only known to a local or two. New motorways do not threaten them, nor the giant, roaring, clawing machines intent on laying waste the land for the benefit of the factories and beehive housing estates. The sea is clean, and rivers are crystal clear. There is no sour sight in this romantic dream. And yet at the end of it I am frightened.

For this paradise is beckoning me, trying to seduce me away from my featureless room or my conventional success. It is trying to take away from me my resolve to remain steadfast to the present. A machine operator or a glossy executive, I do not want to be tempted. It is necessary for me to remain blind to any alternative way of living. I must not allow myself to be charmed towards an existence which is out of my reach. I must serve my sentence. I must avoid any prospect of escape because I have insurances and mort-gages and pension schemes, and next week I might be promoted, and I might be able to move to a house which will lead me upwards in the social scale. Thus I do not wish to be distracted. I do not want to recognise the glimmer of my inner self which yearns for truth in living. I cannot afford to do so. And so I am frightened. My romantic dream points to a way of life that I crave, and the chances of having it are slipping by, and I am chained. I am conventional. I talk myself out of taking risks. I am scared of appearing foolish.

Then the release comes, and I wake up, and the romantic dream is over. The great ball of the rising sun is over the Lizard, and through the bedroom window I watch it edge upwards inch by inch until it is out of sight, and the day has begun. But the dream has left me with a hang-over of disquiet. What is there for me to worry about today? Not much. There is no great chasm for me to leap as in my dream. I am under no pressure to hurry through the day, no bus or train to catch, or traffic jams to infuriate me. I have no awkward meetings to attend, and no wish to be anywhere except in the environment of Minack. Thus the day stretches happily before me, an ideal prospect of a day, the perfect example of contentment that anyone seeks.

And yet there are worries to nag me. They may be trivial compared to those of other people but, because Jeannie and I live life slowly, it is remarkable how they magnify themselves into worries of irritating importance. In any case I have a temperament which is inclined to worry. I see imaginary shadows. I am unable to take happiness for granted.

There is always, for instance, the basic problem of how to earn an income from the land we have. The land is not our own. We now rent it, twenty acres all told, from an enlightened landlord who cares for the still wild stretches of the Cornish coast as much as we do; and he permits us, within reason, to be free to do what we like with the land. We have therefore been able to develop it without interference. Moreover the landlord, who comes from one of the oldest of Cornish families with large estates in various parts of the country, has thereby given us the sense of ownership without its responsibility. We never could have afforded to buy it when we first came. Indeed, like people in other spheres, we have always suffered from lack of capital; and the lack of it has been expensive.

We started out life at Minack believing that we could live on £3 a week, and expecting that stamina for hard work would alone look after our future. This naïve optimism was our salvation. Had we foreseen that our expectations were as impossible to fulfil as a cart-horse winning the Derby, we would have had second thoughts about leaving London. As it was we truly believed that we could earn enough from the land to give us a living. I do not remember what long term prospects we had in mind; for neither of us had any particular ambitions. We were not setting out to become big business flower farmers, nor had either of us any intention of writing about our experiences. We came to Minack in a mood of impractical happiness. Minack offered the roots we knew we needed, and that was enough. Minack, the most beautiful possible home we had ever found, would take care of our future. I suppose the luckiest people in the world can be the Celts who have no patience with reason.

Our beginning was also complicated by the manner with which we acquired our tenancy, for we had in fact no tenancy agreement at all. The farmer had only let us occupy the cottage so as to keep out the squatters in the area; and he was not in a position to offer us a legal agreement because he was only a tenant himself. We had to wait seven years before our position was legalised; and then at last we became a direct tenant of the owner, and our security of tenure was assured. Moreover we were also allocated extra land under this agreement, cultivated land close to the cottage, and so very different from the scrub and moorland which we carved into cultivation during our first years at Minack. The land was flat, so now we also had the chance to have greenhouses.

But during the first years we had no chance of having greenhouses even had we been able to afford them. Our land was then so rough and full of boulders, and so steep, that it was impossible to find a site where the ground would be level for a greenhouse. Thus we struggled along, once we had hacked the meadows out of the under-growth, growing potatoes for May lifting; and flowers cheap to grow from seed, like wallflowers, calendulas, violets, forget-me-nots, de Caen anemones and Beauty of Nice stocks, for picking and sending to market during the winter.

These flowers, however, were not so easy to grow as one might think. Wallflowers, forget-me-nots and stocks had first to be grown in seedbeds, and then transplanted into the meadows we had prepared for them; and as the transplanting took place in mid-summer when there was frequently a period of drought, we used to find ourselves sticking the roots of the small plants in dust. Then in dismay we would watch them wilting and dying, and in panicky efforts to save them I would fill an old milk churn with water from the well up the lane (our own well water provided hardly enough for ourselves), and then proceed to dip a cup in the churn, and empty it around a plant. Of course the result was a fiasco. The dust absorbed my drop of water. The plant never had a sip.

In due course the rains came, and the surviving plants began to grow, along with the weeds. By early September the weeds were growing ferociously faster than the plants, and Jeannie and I tried hard to dispose of them in the time we could spare. At this stage of our flower farming career, however, we were often hampered by the appearance of London friends who, being on holiday themselves, thought it would be pleasant to see us again. The circumstances were now quite different. Instead of a scene in the Savoy American Bar with language like: 'What will you have?' they found us grubbing in the soil on our knees, a large basket beside each of us stuffed with weeds, in old clothes, and a desperate look on our faces which, had they correctly interpreted it, said: 'Oh, hell, the last kind of people we want to see!'

Some of these people, of course, came out of curiosity. I remember one lady whom Jeannie had always tried to avoid in London, cooing sweetly as she observed our earthy condition: 'Darlings, I'm told you're starving ... is it really worth it?' There was another occasion when an old acquaintance of mine arrived at the cottage door after bursting the exhaust pipe of his car on the way down the lane. 'Derek,' he said, admonishing me, 'you must make your entrance *civilised*.' And there was the couple, a delightful couple in the London surroundings we had known so well, who came one day and told us to wake up. We were throwing away opportunities, they said, and the man, a politician, who had been flatteringly enthusiastic over a long book I had written about the British Commonwealth, urged that I ought to stand for Parliament. Then he added, glancing at Jeannie in a flattering mood again: 'You could take Camborne in the next election ... Jeannie would win you the votes.'

Jeannie, however, was more anxious to clear the weeds and so provide the plants with the chance to produce flowers which would give us an income during the winter. But the avalanche of friends and relations continued to hinder us. Our predicament, we found, was difficult to solve. Anyone who came to see us, or wrote beforehand saying that they intended to see us, viewed themselves in isolation. Hence when they arrived to disturb us, they did not believe anyone had come before them nor did they foresee that anyone would come after them Jeannie and I proceeded to abet their self-deception by confiding in them our predicament. This, of course, was a fatal move. Our predicament, as a result, did not apply to *them*. They were the privileged few who did *not* interfere with our weeding; and so, inevitably, we were given advice. We had it often. '*Don't*,' ran this advice, 'see anyone who interferes with your work. Just tell them to *go away*.' We took this advice on one occasion, told one couple to go away along with their two noisy children; and heard echoes of our ruthlessness for a long time afterwards.

There were also those who decided to use our cottage as a base for their holiday. Our spare accommodation, of course, was very limited. Indeed it consisted at the time of a converted chicken house to which we had added a bathroom after we had sunk a well and excavated a cesspit. It stood separate from the cottage, and we used it as a depository for our clothes, as a writing and reading room (Jeannie wrote *Meet me at the Savoy* there), and as a place to bunch violets by paraffin lamp on winter evenings. Each corner of the chicken house was perched on rocks to keep it clear of the earth, and so when you moved around the room there was a hollow sound apart from the creaking floor boards. Nevertheless it offered a haven to those who wanted a contrast to their life in London; and so from time to time we would receive a pleading letter from some nerve-shattered friend who yearned for the healing qualities of the quiet Cornish cliffs.

Thereupon there was great household activity on the part of Jeannie. The weeds were left to grow except for my own lonely efforts to paw them out of the ground, while she did her best to change the chicken house into a bedroom. The red check gingham curtains were washed, the rush mats were beaten, a white cloth was placed on the trestle table to make it appear like a dressing table, and the cupboard was emptied of our clothes. If one person was coming, a narrow settee was made ready; if there were a couple, Jeannie also produced a canvas camp-bed which her father used during World War One. Then at last the tired out visitors arrived, and the cooking began.

In retrospect I marvel at our weak-mindedness. There we were struggling to survive, having to watch every shilling we spent, vividly aware that the weeds were getting the better of our plants and that the prospects of our winter income were, therefore, being remorselessly diminished ... and yet we acted as if the visitors were welcome. Good middle-class manners, I suppose. Equal good manners were displayed when we waxed over-enthusiastically about the small chicken which was contributed to the larder, or the

39

bottle which was largely consumed by the donors. Anything, for a peaceful life, it seemed. Our household bills might be quadrupled, Jeannie as unpaid maid of all work might be exhausted, my own good intentions to continue with the weeding might evaporate ... we were prepared to make all these sacrifices in order to be bored by the brittle world we had come to Minack to forget.

'I *must* tell you about Angela. You remember how she and Robert parted ... well, the most *fascinating* incident has brought them together again, for the moment *at least*. It seems ...'

'George had this fabulous success at the Court, and that was that as far as Jenny was concerned. He's gone off to New York and she, poor dear, is languishing in that dreadful flat off Sloane Ave.'

'Toby was *quite sure* he was to become editor. The proprietor after all was practically having a loving affair with him. Toby was down in Sussex every week-end ... and then of all things the *northern* editor was appointed!'

'Did you see that review of Gareth's last book in one of the Sundays? I can't remember which. It was pretty awful and Gareth was furious about it. Now he has got positive proof that Sullivan Smith who wrote it never read the book at all. He only had time for the blurb ... and *that* came from Sullivan's girl friend who told Gareth's sister.'

'Did you hear about Caesar Downes? He stopped writing his daily column and people began to wonder whether he had been fired. But he had gone to Switzerland for one of those curious operations ... and now he only goes out with friends of his grand-daughter!'

'We want to talk to you both seriously. Haven't you made a mistake? The Savoy are longing to have you back, Jeannie, we know that. You're a legend, people come from all over the world asking for you. Doesn't that mean something special to you? People wanting you like that!'

Certainly. She was wanted now. She had to decide how many loaves she had to bake, what there was for lunch, and how she was going to satisfy her visitors at dinner. Then there was the silver to clean, the dusting to do and because we had no electricity for a vacuum cleaner, hand brushing of the carpet. We were quite mad to put up with it.

'We've had a marvellous time. Can we come again next year?'

'NO!' I shouted in reply. I almost believed I had spoken aloud.

Good manners and truth are often enemies. One is always meeting people who boast about their frankness, and the traditional blunt Yorkshireman has established himself as a folk hero. Is he a pleasant hero? It may suit him to speak his instant thoughts without worrying about the effect they may have on the person addressed, and I even admire his moral courage, but I do not really like such bluntness. Truth, in certain circumstances, should remain hidden; and a convenient place for it to hide is behind good manners. Time is thereby gained to make more measured assessments, and these may produce more kindly results. On the other hand, as in the case of Jeannie and myself in the role of unwilling hostess and host, they confirmed the fact that we had allowed ourselves to be conned. And by midwinter we knew the price we were having to pay.

In these days various herbicides and chemical sprays keep the weeds at bay; and the saving in labour is naturally enormous. But the advantage thus gained is now often off-set by overproduction, both of vegetables and flowers, and the prices obtained in the wholesale markets sometimes do not warrant the sending of the produce. This past year I have seen fields of uncut broccoli and cabbage; and acres of potatoes were only cleared because the fields were needed for another crop. The prices in the shops, meanwhile, are unaffected. The retailer has his own overheads to worry about, and he is in a position to dictate his prices. But the grower, especially the small grower, who nurtures a crop along for six months, then finds that harvest time coincides with a glut, is faced unfortunately with financial disaster. He has spent capital on producing the crop, more money on boxes or crates, and more money still on the always increasing transport costs. A retailer, or wholesaler, may have a bad week but he has the chance of recovering his losses in the following week. A grower has to wait for a year.

But when we began at Minack overproduction and consequent gluts were comparatively rare; and this particularly applied to the kind of annuals we were growing. We could rely on steady prices, high enough to cover the

41

cost of our living expenses; and there was always the chance of a bonanza if the weather up country was severe, or if there was a shortage of flowers around Mothering Sunday time. But these flowers still had to be well grown, and this was why we suffered when visitors stole our time. Plants, which for a period had been choked with weeds, could not be expected to prosper when the winds began to blow. The wallflowers were spindly, the violets small, the forget-me-nots too soft. And all because we had not had the strength of character to tell our friends to leave us alone.

We had, too, in those early days, another misfortune; and this concerned the daffodil bulbs we first bought. Clearly it was of great importance for us to stock with bulbs which would produce daffodils popular with the public. We knew nothing about the fashion in bulbs, how some varieties lose their appeal after a few years so that their blooms are practically unsaleable; and we were not aware that, as the possessors of land which had never grown bulbs before, we enjoyed a huge advantage. The land, being newly broken in, was clean of all disease; and so the chance was ours to build up a stock of bulbs which would be the envy of other growers whose land, because of years of use, had become infected with one of the bulb diseases. If, therefore, we bought clean stock of commercially popular varieties we could, even with the small amount of money we had to spare, build a foundation of bulbs which would provide us with an income for many years to come. For bulbs increase every year if they are healthy; and every so often, every two or three years is the ideal, the bulbs are dug up, sterilised, and planted again. So, like a good share, the original investment is increasing.

We asked advice from a family acquaintance who was a specialist bulb grower; and we blessed our luck that such an expert was available. It meant that we would be able to rely on him to let us have disease-free bulbs at a favoured price; and that the varieties concerned would be those most in demand in the markets. In due course the bulbs arrived. He had sent us several with charming names like Bernardino, Lucifer, Sunrise, Campanella and so on; and when they came to bloom in the spring they were as delightful as their names. Unfortunately Covent Garden did not share our pleasure. We despatched the first boxes in high expectation, and indulged in the inevitable calculations as to what price they would fetch. I thought each bunch might earn us around two shillings of the old currency; and I was appalled when we received the returns and found none of the varieties had fetched more than sixpence.

We had a kindly salesman at the time called Bobby Page, who also had a club off Covent Garden which, during the war, was a home for RAF crew. These crew, when they had leave between missions, would crowd into his club, drink hard to forget, and be sure that Bobby was all the while watching over them. Bobby would find them a place to sleep, took care to see that their festivities did not stop them from returning to base, and allowed countless drinks on the slate which eventually never could be paid. Bobby was plump, and enthusiastic, and jovial, one of those who had the chance to make the lives of other people easier; and took it. But even Bobby could not be enthusiastic about the Bernardino, Lucifer, Sunrise, Campanella and so on.

'They're out of date, Derek old friend,' he wrote, 'the market long ago lost interest in them. But you can rely on me to do my best . . .'

I have a suspicion now, Bobby died some years ago, that even at sixpence of the old currency he was paying us more than the bunches were worth. He had an avuncular interest in our activities, his natural desire to help other people; and I am glad that we did not entirely let him down. Our King Alfred, the bulbs had come with the others, were superb, for instance; and we also by chance invented Cornish posies.

We began the posies because our neglected wallflowers, anemones and forget-me-nots were not good enough to send on their own. The blooms were also scarce, and so we were at our wit's end to know what to do. One day Jeannie fashioned a dozen bunches from all the odds and ends, and sent them off in a box to Bobby, identifying them as Cornish posies. They were such a success that we were asked to send as many as possible, which was, of course, very frustrating. We just did not have the flowers to meet the demand. The following season we had more flowers available, we grew them specially with the posies in mind, and the success continued. Each posy was about the size of my fist, and Jeannie took great trouble in arranging

43

the colouring; and she used any flower that was available from November onwards. It was slow work, but the rewards were good. Then, inevitably, the posies were copied, though other growers were not the case of the competition. The florist shops were our problem. They found it cheaper to buy different flowers in the market, and then fashion their own posies. The price began to drop, and we gradually realised that the posies were taking up too much of our time and so the flower packing shed ceased to have row upon row of Cornish posies waiting to be packed. London posies had taken their place.

We were, however, left with the daffodils which nobody wanted; and this was a burden we had to carry for a long time to come. These bulbs took up space in the ground we could not spare. There was a stretch of them, for instance, down one side of the big field that ran towards the cliff; and this stretch we had created by our own hand labour from brambles and undergrowth. Hence these useless bulbs occupied favoured places; and although they were not going to earn their keep, we did not have the time to remove them. Hand digging of bulbs is a slow, lengthy business; and there always seemed something better to do than hack them out of the ground and get rid of them. So they stayed, displaying their pretty blooms each spring, bringing us financial disappointment, and so causing us much useless picking, bunching, and packing. We disposed of them in the end. My mother died, and with money she left me I financed the removal of the bulbs. They didn't go far. We scattered them all over Minack, in hedgerows and in the wood, in grassy banks close to the sea, and along the lane which leads down the hill to the cottage; and they have repaid the disappointment they caused us by the yearly, breathtaking display of their beauty; for now they are not daffodils which have to be hurried away to a distant market like Covent Garden three hundred miles away, from where they are taken to a shop, then a vase, then a dust-bin. They live out their lives now naturally, jostling side by side in unruliness; and of course my aesthetic sense is much moved.

But I cannot help wondering how much for the better our lives might have been, had we never had the need to see the sight of them. Had we been more professional, had we had capital to spare, we would not have had to rely on

44

family acquaintances; and our virgin land would have been stocked with bulbs which could have assured us a financial future. Instead, at the very beginning of our careers as flower farmers, we moved backwards.

Did it matter? Probably not. Had we been successful at the beginning, we might have developed business ambitions. We might have become a large unit with all the worries that this entails.

As it is, if anything ever goes wrong, we will still be able to continue on our own. We hope so, at any rate.

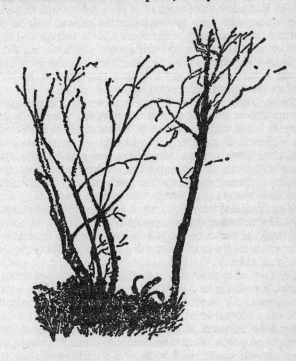

CHAPTER FIVE

We have a porch now at Minack where we sit when the cold winds blow, catching the warmth of the winter sun. It faces the small front garden and the steps that lead to the gate of the donkey field; and beyond you can see the privet hedge which hides the storage tank of the well. On the left is the door, the top half of glass, which is in fact the front door; and there are rocks in the ground outside it, making an uneven path to the corner of the cottage and the blue-painted water-butt. At this corner you look out first on to the moorland, then the sea, then the sweep of the Lizard peninsula. At night it is here that you can see the light of the Lizard lighthouse winking at you.

On the right, with its evergreen leaves and blue-mauve flowers almost pressing against the glass, is a giant veronica bush. It is too big for the small corner in which it stands, and experienced gardeners tells us that we should remove it but we leave it there for sentimental reasons. Shelagh brought it to us as a young plant, digging it up from the garden of the cottage where she lived, close to the grocer's shop in St Buryan . . . Shelagh who worked here at the same time as Jane, and who died a week after her twentieth birthday. The veronica bush therefore, reminds us of these two, and the part they played in our lives at a time when their enthusiasm was of more value than any wage we could have paid them.

Geoffrey, able as always to turn his hand to any practical job, built the foundation of the porch, first prising and inching large rocks which were in the way with the inbred skill of a Cornishman who understands stone; and his father Ken Semmens, a craftsman carpenter, designed and created the porch itself. His task was difficult because of the awkward shape, and because the framework had to be moulded securely against the old stones of the cottage around the original front door. Another carpenter had warned us, for instance, that this could not be done successfully unless the old stones were faced with a layer of cement twelve inches deep; and we both hated the sight of cement.

We were hoping for an old-fashioned porch which, when completed, would look as if it had been there for years. Ken Semmens created our hopes into reality, and the old stones of the cottage remained as they had always been since the cottage had been built by some crofter over five hundred years before; but Ken Semmens took his time. I was irked by his apparent lack of activity.

'How is your father getting on?' I would ask Geoffrey hopefully during the course of a day, aware that fashioning the framework would be done at home, then brought to Minack to be assembled.

'Dunno,' came the answer.

Dunno is a word that Geoffrey often uses. He delivers it in a forbidding tone on some occasions, in an impatient one on others when he considers my question a foolish one, and gently when he knows that I am seeking his help but considers, rightly, that it is not his business to become involved.

Two weeks would go by, then I would ask again.

'Any news of your father?'

I am sometimes devious in putting my questions, too devious. I desire people to catch the significance of a question without my putting it bluntly; and the result is I get no answer at all. I display the same weakness when I want some task to be performed. I am loath to give orders. I prefer to coax the person to carry out my wishes, letting his intelligence interpret my words; and so preserve a form of partnership between myself and the person concerned. Unfortunately my good intentions go astray if I make the mistake of expecting too much intelligence. I then appear to talk in riddles; and it is then that I realise that the command, 'Do this or do that', can provide a relationship sounder than that of partnership.

Another week or two.

'I expect we'll be seeing your father soon?'

Afterwards, when the porch had been completed, I was ashamed of my impatience. I had succumbed to the contemporary mood of expecting instant results. I was chivvying a craftsman, a Cornish craftsman at that, to hurry his work. I was behaving like a brash city newcomer with no experience of country life; and I was startled that an attitude which I thought I had long buried, had popped up again.

'I was thinking,' I persisted, 'that the porch might be ready by Christmas.'

Geoffrey was having his croust, the Cornish equivalent of a tea break, in the shed which we once used for bunching and packing daffodils. He was sitting in a canvas chair with a chaffinch at his feet, a tom tit, and a couple of blue tits. These birds and others waited impatiently for his croust breaks, and at week-ends when he was at home, they fluttered in annoyance beside the closed door.

'Is there any chance?' I added.

He looked at me as if I were a spoilt child, took a bite at the cake he was holding in his hand, and replied, mouth full:

'None at all.'

Unlike myself, Geoffrey was usually direct in his speech. I might disagree with him but I always knew that he was speaking the truth as he viewed it. I therefore could not feel offended when he was blunt. He saw no purpose in wasting time in *finesse*. He saw a problem in black or white, a solution in the same colour. He did not allow his judgement to be cluttered by a permutation of pros and cons. And I envied him this quality.

'Oh,' I said doubtfully, 'I'm sorry about that.'

I was naturally curious to find out why, but there again my timidity got the better of me. I did not dare intrude into the world of Geoffrey and his father. I was prepared to prod but was too apprehensive to do more; but to my surprise, Geoffrey on this occasion showed none of the reticence I expected of him; and without requiring any urging from me proceeded to explain the reason for the delay. The explanation was so simple that I marvelled at my stupidity for not extracting it before.

Condition of the timber was the reason. I had imagined that the necessary timber had only to be bought at the timber yard for the carpentry to begin; and this is the case in many sections of the carpentry trade. But Geoffrey's father had different ideas. He was suspicious of all timber for sale, and when he went to the yard he would poke around for hours, looking at this piece of wood and that, feeling it, dismissing it, taking as much care before making his choice as a jeweller sorting out gems.

Nor was he content with his choice once it was made;

and hence the delay to our porch. He sought perfection, and although the timber he had chosen was in his opinion the best available, it still had to be *dried*. Present day timber is in so much demand that it is scarcely out of the forest before it is in the workshop. And so it is immature, green and sappy, and no good for a master craftsman.

Thus I learnt that the timber Ken Semmens had chosen for our porch was in a workshop where a paraffin heater was burning day and night, a slow method of drying I would have thought, but the only method which was possible; and the timber was shifted this way and that, so all parts of it had the benefit of being close to the heater at one time or another. Such dedication to perfection is the route to a masterpiece; and though a humble porch could never enter the rating of masterpieces, Ken Semmens's porch certainly has one claim to fame. No part of it has ever leaked despite the battering it has had from the rain and the gales. The wood had been dried. The joints, as a result, have never shrunk. The craftsmanship had been perfect.

So although we had hoped for the porch by Christmas, it was worth waiting . . . till after Easter.

We sit often in the porch in daytime during the winter. A banquette runs the length of the little garden side. Opposite, between the door into the sitting-room and the end where the veronica bush presses against the glass, there is a small settee made of bamboo and cane. It is placed alongside a small natural wood table, the shape of a miniature refectory table though large enough to seat five; two on the settee, two on the banquette, one on a bamboo chair facing the veronica bush. Jeannie, when we are alone, generally sits on the banquette, and up above her through the glass roof, she can see Philip the gull passing time on the chimney. Or he will flap his wings and stare imperiously at her so that she is impelled to fetch a piece of bread and throw it up to him. I, on the settee, meanwhile am forced into awareness that the donkeys are demanding my attention. There they will be in the corner of their field just above the little garden, head beside head, white nose beside white nose, two pairs of solemn eyes watching my every move, driving me in the end to exclaim: 'For goodness sake, donkeys, do look at something else!' It is at such a moment that they know they have won. Penny will nudge Fred, and Fred will paw the ground. They know that it will be only a matter of minutes before I will leave the porch and attend to their wants. Move to another field? No. Chocolate biscuits? Yes. Well here you are. Anything for quiet.

We were to have another creature that winter, staring at us through the glass. A racing pigeon who had tired of racing. At first we took little notice of it as it hung around the neighbourhood of the cottage, sometimes huddled on the roof, sometimes perched on a jutting stone in the building we call a garage, sometimes squatting on the grey chippings while Lama watched it from a distance. For the temporary presence of a racing pigeon was not unusual. Racing pigeons, wayward racing pigeons, like to pause at comfortable homesteads if they find themselves in the mood. Maybe a young bird has lost its way, and needs a rest to regain its nerve; or perhaps it is an old bird, now cynical about the purpose of racing and expending so much effort. In either case they do not normally stay long, a week or two at the most. Then off, refreshed, flies the young bird to search for his distant loft; and the old bird, resignedly, sets off for his.

Neither, alas, are likely to be welcomed on their return. Pigeon fanciers require sensible, obedient birds, conventional birds, who will hurry back to their timing clocks without taking a holiday on the way. Pigeons, therefore, who pause at Minack are asking for disgrace; and, indeed, on two occasions when we traced the owners of errant pigeons by the identification ring a pigeon carries on its leg, we were told we could keep them. On a third occasion we traced the owner to Dublin; and were informed that although it is in order for a pigeon to fly direct to Ireland from the despatch point, it cannot be imported in a normal manner for fear of it carrying the germs of foot and mouth disease. Hence our offer to return the bird by rail and boat was misguided. The owner would have to bear the expense of quarantine, and he had no intention of doing so. He told us to kill the bird. We didn't of course, and one day, a week or two after we had received the letter, it flew away. Back to Dublin? I hope not.

We had learnt, therefore, to keep secret the presence of a

racing pigeon at Minack. Not that it was ever easy to discover its identity, because a pigeon is so elusive, as elusive as any bird, if there is no loft. Indeed when we decided that we would never again try to trace the owner we were relieved our chasing days were over. Our contribution to a pigeon's welfare was now limited to scattering grain periodically on the ground and making sure it had water available. Thus is could rest with us, feed, and fly away when it felt inclined.

Lama, meanwhile, viewed each visitor with interest; and although the phrase 'cat among the pigeons' has a fearsome ring about it, Lama's interest was not fearsome. She would settle a few yards from a visitor, crouching on the ground and staring, while the visitor unconcernedly pecked for the grain. The visitor was never in any danger of attack. Lama, except once when she swiped with her paw at a chaffinch which was annoying her with its monotonous call a foot away from where she was trying to sleep, has never attacked any bird. It is one of her charms that she has no inclination to do so. One of the charms, too, of Monty who was her predecessor. Neither wished to kill birds. I am sure I would have had a different attitude to both of them if they had.

Sometimes one of the visitors would be fascinated by Lama instead of Lama being fascinated by the visitor. There was one heavily-built racing pigeon with the colouring of a wood-pigeon who was so intrigued by Lama that he would keep following her about as if she was a guide in the strange place in which he found himself. Lama would set off on a philosophical stroll down the lane towards Monty's Leap, and this heavyweight pigeon would promptly swoop off the cottage roof where he had been perched, fly imperiously for a moment or two overhead, then land a few feet in front of a startled Lama who, until that instant, was only intrigued by rustling noises suggesting possible mice in the grass on either side of the lane. This pigeon would then strut self-importantly in front of her, cooing; and when Lama failed to do whatever it was he expected her to do, he took to the air again but with such a noise that his wings sounded like castanets in the sky. Lama continued her stroll unperturbed.

Once I found a racing pigeon lying near Monty's Leap

51

in the lane, and at first I thought it had broken its leg. I picked it up and carried it to the coop we had for injured birds and which we kept in the small greenhouse. We soon realised that its legs were uninjured, and that instead it was suffering from concussion. It had been a foggy morning and so, I presume, its in-built radar system must have gone astray and it had crashed into a tree when it believed it was flying in the open sky. I was told later that this was not unusual; and that if, in a cross Channel race, the leader of a group of racing pigeons lost its sense of direction in a fog and flew into the sea, all the other pigeons would follow.

Anyhow our concussed pigeon slowly recovered its balance, staying for over three weeks in the coop before we considered it was well enough to be let out; and even then we still kept it within the confines of the greenhouse for another week or so. It was now, of course, very tame, and we naturally became fond of it, so by that time we had given it a name and, guessing it was a male, we called him Percy.

Percy, in pigeon fancier's parlance, was a blue chequer which is very similar to a rock-dove, ancestor of the racing pigeon. We have rock-doves in our neighbourhood, and a pair has from time to time nested insecurely on a ledge in a cave which leads from the pool where we swim in summer time. I say insecurely because the ledge is safe when the weather is normal and the sea below is quiet ... but if a gale blows up the cave becomes a cauldron of huge waves and spray. Moreover this pair of rock-doves had the habit of nesting late, and I used to see young in the nest as late as October when the great gales of the autumn were due. Poor foolish rock-doves. The young never survived those gales.

Nor, I am afraid, did Percy survive his stay at Minack. When we let him out of the greenhouse, let him be free, he had completely recovered and the opportunity was his to fly away to any destination he wished. Instead he decided to stay in the neighbourhood, and though occasionally during the day he would fly off on a voyage of investigation, he spent most of his time close to the cottage; and at night, the door of the greenhouse left open for him, he would go inside to roost. After a few weeks we were so accustomed to his presence, so accustomed to the complete trust he seemed to have in us, in Geoffrey, in Lama, and even in the strangers who called that we began to take it for granted that he would be staying with us forever. Then one day there was no sign of him, nor the next day nor the next.

A week later I was in one of our meadows overlooking the sea. It was a pleasant morning, hazy, and the *Scillonian* which was passing on the way to the islands, crowded with holidaymakers, hummed through the quiet water like an elegant yacht. This was a trip I thought, that the holiday-makers would enjoy. No seasickness today. A voyage so unlike those turbulent voyages of winter, a southerly gale sweeping across Mount's Bay, bigger vessels than the *Scillonian* hurrying for shelter, yet the *Scillonian* herself always keeping to schedule, lurching and plunging, making me thankful to be on land as I watch her pass.

I was in this meadow, wondering what we could grow in it. The meadow had always been unsatisfactory. Over the years we had tried potatoes, anemones, stocks, wall-flowers, lettuce, and more recently daffodils; and none of them had produced crops which were worth the work involved. I had had the soil analysed, and there had been no sickly revelations. Pundits had suggested this and that to no avail, and I had reluctantly come to the conclusion that the only course I could take was to leave it fallow. It was a pity because it was a pleasant meadow facing south, and large by our standards; and I felt frustrated by my conclusion. Hence I would wander off to the meadow from time to time to stand and wonder, an idle, fruitless game of imagining lush crops which might bring in the cash.

As I stood there I suddenly saw a scattering of feathers beside a rock in the corner of the meadow. It was not unusual, however, to see such feathers. A hawk may have pounced on a blackbird or a thrush, or it may have been the peregrine falcon which haunts this coast which had made the attack, or was it a fox who had had a meal? I looked at the feathers from a distance, sadly but without involvement, when some instinct urged me to go closer. I reached the rock, knelt down and picked up a feather, holding it for a moment in my fingers. I will never know the truth of what had happened. That is the trouble when one lives close to nature. There are always so many unanswered question marks. It is impossible, as in urban societies to pretend to be knowing.

All I can say is that the scattered feathers were blue and white; and we never saw Percy again.

The new pigeon had arrived at Minack later than usual, in the middle of October, long after the racing pigeon season had ended. There was the customary identification ring on one leg, and a second ring, denoting that at some time in the previous weeks it had been taking part in a race. It was a very pretty pigeon, more delicately built than the previous ones we had known. Officially it would have been called a red pied pigeon; and a red pied pigeon is one whose colouring is partly brick-red, partly white. Of course there are many variations, and I have since seen a red pied which was more white than red, and another which would have been all red except for a streak or two of white. But the colours of our new pigeon were nicely balanced, and its general appearance was admirable. Its only fault, if this was a fault, was a patch of white on its head which made it look comic. So comic, in fact, that Jeannie was reminded of the old-time music-hall performer called Nellie Wallace. Nellie Wallace had a bird-like face and made a habit of wearing funny small hats; and this patch of white on the pigeon's head looked, to Jeannie, like one of those hats. Our new pigeon now had a name. Nellie.

Nellie, at first, was just another pigeon who would soon be off and away, and we paid no more attention to her than was our habit towards intinerant pigeons. We gave her grain and water, made some remark when we passed her, and waited for the day when she would no longer be with us. Gradually, however, as the weeks went by she began to impose her personality upon us, and impose it on others as well . . . Lama, the gulls on the roof, our local chaffinch, robin, blue tits, and the dim little dunnocks. All of us became aware that we were in the company of a Presence. I began to find myself, for instance, stopping to talk to her, instead of passing her by with a casual remark. I felt she expected me to do so, and I did not want her disapproval. Her attitude towards Lama was equally compelling. Lama, who at first treated her with polite curiosity, was startled to find Nellie behaving in a bold, challenging fashion towards her. Lama, curled in a niche of rock sheltered from the wind by the porch, dozing, would suddenly wake up to find Nellie advancing towards her ejaculating: 'Coo,

coo, coo!' ... as if she was meaning: 'Boo, boo, boo!' The small birds received similar provocative attention, and they soon found it unwise to attempt to snatch a grain or two from the handful we had scattered on the ground for Nellie; for she would dart at them in greedy fury. As for the gulls on the roof, their lazy dignity was made to look foolish when Nellie, in a dashing sweep from the sky, decided to join them. For no valid reason she would jostle them away from the spot they had chosen to survey the scene below them; and, except for Philip, they would surrender their positions without argument. Philip, our oldest gull on the roof, would never budge. He would stare at Nellie, then open his wide beak. Nellie never made the mistake of testing his intentions.

Her favourite place, we soon learnt, was the glass roof of the porch. Why it should have been so appealing to her I do not know but whenever it was fine there she would be, sitting on the glass directly over our heads. Presumably she wanted companionship. Or perhaps it amused her to keep an inquisitive eye upon us. In any case while I, from my seat, would look up and see her squashed, feathery underparts, Jeannie on the other side of the table faced the funny, Nellie Wallace head . . . and a beady eye. She was often to watch us from this vantage point during the winter months.

CHAPTER SIX

The rains came in November. They came roaring in from the south, grey skies, grey seas, water-butt overflowing flushing a channel in the grey chippings, pools on the stone path outside the door, donkeys with heads down and backs to the weather when they could be dry in the stable, land soggy, noisy restless trees, birds sheltering in the escallonia by the terrace we call the bridge, a gull clinging in the wind to the roof, all nature accepting the first punishment of winter.

Then suddenly a day, and the sky is blue brushed by fluffy white clouds, and it is unexpectedly warm, and I forget. Momentarily yesterday's storm is only in the imagination. We have a day lent. The Indian summer continues.

On such a day I began the annual inquest into our efforts. I was sitting at the table in the porch, Nellie on the glass above, invoices and price returns around me, in a serious mood, prepared to study details which my lazy nature would have preferred to avoid, expecting Jeannie to join me; and there was no sign of her.

'Jeannie!'

No reply.

I become mildly irritable when, after deciding to perform some task which I do not wish to perform, some factor hinders me from immediately starting it. I may have decided, for instance, to pay bills and I am ready to carry out the unpleasant task, my cheque book at hand, the bills staring at me; and then I discover I have run out of envelopes. Or

I may have decided to spend the morning writing, locked in the old stable which is my office, quite undisturbed, determined to concentrate on my work instead of letting my mind wander; and an overnight telegram is delivered with the post . . . will I ring so-and-so by midday?

'Jeannie!' I called again. 'What are you doing? I've got everything ready.'

My voice, from the porch, carries easily through the cottage. There is only the sitting-room, the kitchen, our tiny bedroom with its windows facing Mount's Bay, the spare-room which we bought as a chicken house, and the bathroom. All on the ground floor.

The sitting-room is thirty-five feet long. On the left, as you look into it from the porch, is the end wall on which hangs a wistful portrait of Jeannie by the Polish artist Kanelba. Below, to the left, is the gap prised out of the three-foot-thick stone wall which leads to the converted chicken house. Here at this end is the widest part of the sitting-room, fifteen feet wide. It is here that I have my veneered walnut kidney-shaped Regency desk which was given to me by my father and mother as a wedding present; and here, too, is the small, oak gate-legged table where we eat when it is too cold to be out in the porch, sitting on Windsor chairs which we brought with us from London. Beside my desk beneath the window is a storage heater which has solved the damp problem from which old Cornish cottages suffer; and then comes the hi-fi radio and record player, and next to it is an eight-drawer mahogany tallboy which had been for many years in Jeannie's family, then bookshelves. There are other bookshelves beneath Jeannie's portrait behind me to my right as I sit at my desk: and directly behind me is a corner oak cupboard, top half with three shelves and a glass door, which came from my old family home of Glendorgal near Newquay on the other side of Cornwall. I remember this cupboard as a little boy. It is of Dutch origin, and there used to be kept in the top half a weird collection of Indian doll-like figures which my father had brought back with him after touring the world as a young man . . . a sepoy in Indian Mutiny uniform, a turbaned Sikh, a Pathan with a magnificent flowing black moustache, a Ghandi-like figure naked except for a loin cloth, an extravagantly dressed figure which

I believed to be a Maharajah. They were all gaily coloured, very small and beautifully made, and yet they seemed to me to be slightly menacing. I can only guess why I felt like this; I suppose it was a childish fear of the unknown. But the cupboard, in contrast, gave me a sense of security. It was a simple design without frills, and it caught my imagination, and this is the reason why it is at Minack today. Known as Derek's cupboard, it came inevitably into my possession after my parents died.

At the other end of the sitting-room there is a black enamel stove, to the right of an old oak dresser, which provides an open fire if you pull up the mica-covered front; and it is set in an alcove. A black enamel pipe climbs from the stove up the back of the alcove and disappears into the ancient chimney, and it looks unusual. So unusual that I explain to those who remark upon it that the stove is Swedish ... and immediately there are knowing murmurs of appreciation. It does, in fact, look as if it might be Scandinavian, one of those sturdy, practical stoves which conjure up a picture of cosiness on snow-filled winter nights ... but it is an ordinary British stove. Nothing, except for the pipe, unusual about it at all.

The alcove is our own creation, or rather we have re-created it because there is no doubt it existed there before. In those days the alcove would have served as an open fireplace, and the crofter who lived in the cottage would have kept the fire burning with furze from the surrounding moorland, and quantities of bog turf. Here then was his hearth, and where his family cooked with the aid of those strange utensils like the Cornish kettle, not the customary kettle but an iron bowl with three legs in which stews and vegetables were cooked by the heat of the furze flames. I found such an iron bowl not long ago half-buried in a hedge nearby.

But when we first came to the cottage the hearth had been filled in and faced with plaster; and a battered, rusty Cornish range showed that the old-time method of cooking had been given up years ago. The Cornish range was far too decrepit to use, and we took it out and substituted an inexpensive cooking stove we bought in Penzance. Then later we took that out, too, and had an Esse instead; and it was when we were installing this Esse that we discovered the 'cloam' oven.

This oven was, of course, as old as the crofter's hearth and it would have been in use since the days the cottage was built. It was shoulder-high on the right of the hearth, and had a slab of granite as its floor, then a dome made up of small stones ... thus making a circular space like the inside of an upturned cup. The entrance, on the hearth side, was less than two-foot square, and when the oven was in use this was blocked by large stones kept handy on a ledge. First, however, the oven was stuffed with furze and wood and set ablaze; then when it was judged to be hot enough, the embers were swept out into the hearth, the food placed inside, and the entrance tightly fitted with the large stones. In this way centuries of baking took place in this oven.

News of the discovery of this Minack antiquity quickly circulated. The mason who made the find came from Mouse-hole, and from Mousehole the news was carried to Newlyn, and within a few days I was having a haircut in Penzance when I was startled to hear the barber remark: 'Congratulations ... I understand you have found a cloam oven at your place.' Such is the interest of the Cornish in things ancient.

Then one day we saw the vicar coming up from Monty's Leap towards the cottage. He was an old man, much respected in the district, and known in a wider sphere as an authority on West Cornwall ancient monuments. We ourselves, when we saw him through the window, believed he was making an evangelical call upon us; and there was a flurry of picking up magazines and newspapers, shaking of cushions, and other activities that take place when an unexpected visitor suddenly descends upon one. He arrived panting at the door, he had had a long walk, and I greeted him warmly.

'How nice to see you, Vicar,' I said, still blind to the reason for his visit, 'do come in. We were just making ready a cup of tea.' My mind, meanwhile, was wondering how to explain to him that solitude in a meadow overlooking an ungovernable sea was more spiritually uplifting to me than a disciplined service shared by a duty-bound congregation.

I had no reason to concern myself.

'I have come,' said the vicar gasping, 'to see your oven.'

In due course electricity was brought to the cottage; and it was then that Jeannie decided she no longer wanted a fuel stove to cook by; and so the Esse was removed and the new stove, the Scandinavian pretending stove, was substituted. Meanwhile she had designed, after much research into the kind of kitchen she was looking for, a kitchen which was like the galley of a yacht. It had to be like a galley, because there was no room for anything else.

It faces the sitting-room door into the porch, an oak chest on one side of the door, a large settee with its far end close to the alcove on the other. It is seven foot long, and there is only a two-foot space between the cooker, sink and refrigerator, all set against the wall ... and the table-high top of a cupboard where Jeannie prepares her dishes. Cupboards are a remarkable feature of the kitchen. There are, indeed, thirty-six cupboard doors, and the carpenter who made them, a boatbuilder from Newlyn, jokingly said afterwards that he would never forget the experience. They are in natural wood with black hinges, and they range in size from a comparatively large one which holds such things as a mop and a long-handled duster, to the small ones which climb up the ceiling in which china, glass and stores are kept. Every inch, therefore, of the kitchen is made use of, yet crowded though it may sound, there is an attractive airiness about it. One end is open to the sitting-room, except for a waist-high door like the bottom half of a stable-door; and then there is a special feature, a large window-like frame without glass, which was Jeannie's brightest idea. This window is set in the centre of the kitchen, facing the porch. So if you are standing in the porch, or in that part of the sitting-room, you can see into the kitchen; but you will do so through the contents of a bowl of flowers. For it was part of Jeannie's idea that a window frame containing a bowl of flowers would help to make the kitchen a part of the sitting-room without it having the severity of an open-plan kitchen; and the idea has been much admired. Thus there is the kitchen and its cupboards and its equipment on one side of the window, while on the other there are pictures hanging on the wall and two rows of bookshelves below them.

Our bedroom, our box-like bedroom, is only a yard from the kitchen. It is so small that the one who lies on the far side of the bed has difficulty in getting there, and usually climbs over the other to do so. But tiny though the bedroom is, it is a very beautiful one. The walls are of the original rough stone painted white and the ceiling is papered with a Werner Graaf design of pink dianthus and lime-green leaves. There is just enough space for a William-and-Mary chest of drawers, and a little walnut desk, like a school desk, where Jeannie keeps her papers. The two windows are curtained with material of the same pattern as the wallpaper. One window looks down the lane towards Monty's Leap, and in winter when the elms are bare of leaves I look out on the fields on the other side of the shallow valley; and as I lie there, head on pillow, I sometimes watch a fox at first light trudging back to his earth on the cliff after a night's hunting. The other window faces east to the Lizard, and when the visibility is right a flick of light every few seconds comes blinking across the thirty miles of Mount's Bay. I count these flicks, if I am trying to sleep, as other people count sheep.

The spare-room, the converted chicken house, is also papered with a Werner Graaf design, both ceilings and walls; and so, too, is the bathroom, with all the windows curtained to match. There are table-high fitted cupboards along one side of the spare-room; and on the other side, the three windows, through which the chickens were expected to look out, are still there, though the frames themselves are, of course, different. A tall, old-fashioned wardrobe is also still there, one which we managed to squeeze through the door of the chicken house when we first erected it ... but, because of the transformation, it is now impossible to move out. You would not now think it had ever been a chicken house; and the outside is disguised by the cedarwood tiles which cover the roof and the walls.

The cottage, therefore, is small enough for a shout easily to be heard. And yet Jeannie didn't reply.

'Jeannie!' I called once again, then began impatiently to gather up my papers, the invoices and the price returns. If *she* wasn't interested, I wasn't either. This unreasonable action on my part was accompanied by a coo above my head. Nellie, still squatting on the glass roof, was perkily looking about her. I scarcely took notice of her. Let her coo. I was too concerned with the destruction of my good intentions.

Then suddenly Jeannie appeared. From *outside* the cottage, not inside. And Nellie stopped her cooing.

'Where on earth have you been?' I said crossly. 'I have been waiting for you all this time . . .'

My harshness was misplaced. I was making a fool of myself. I could see it in the way she looked at me.

'The water has gone again!'

This was something more vexing than wrecked good intentions.

'Oh hell,' I said.

'There's nothing coming into the washing-machine.'

She had slipped out of the back-door, while I had been waiting for her, with a bundle of washing, taken it down to the hut where we keep the machine, then waited for the tub to fill. It hadn't.

We are not on the mains. The mains were brought a few years ago to the farm buildings a quarter of a mile away up the hill; and we had the chance of having it brought down to Minack. We did not take it because, apart from the expense involved, we preferred the flavour of our own well water. The well, thirty feet deep and sunk on our behalf by two miners from St Just, provided water which had the freshness of a mountain stream.

Unfortunately the well was not deep enough. The dowser prophesied we would have plenty of water at fifteen feet. It wasn't there. Nor at twenty, nor at twenty-five; but at thirty a great shout went up from all concerned when water began gushing into the splendid base of the hole which had taken so much of our money to reach. So much money, in fact, that there wasn't any left that year to pay for a pump to pump it up.

In retrospect, I realise, I should have asked the miners to go still deeper, or alternatively to widen the base so that it became a small reservoir catching the seeping veins of water around it. Hindsight, however, can be deceptive. Hindsight is inclined to ignore the mood and circumstances of the time concerned, dwelling instead on the logical steps one might have taken. Hindsight relies on the evidence of memory, and memory often forgets the influence of emotion.

Thus, when the miners struck water, we had become so emotionally exhausted by the weeks of waiting, of collecting and returning them to and from St Just, of the periodic explosions as they blasted the rock, of the laborious hand drilling, of the slow clearance of the debris, and our anxious efforts to find the money to pay them, that we were only too thankful to say goodbye to them, kind and enthusiastic though they had been. Water had been found . . . so next year, we hoped, we would have the money to pump it into the cottage.

And we did. The following year the water came flowing into the cottage, and we had the same pleasure of turning on a tap as some primitive couple who had never seen one before. Washing up became conventional. Hot water, heated by calor gas gave us the experience of baths again and we wallowed in them instead of washing in sea water among our rocks, or trying to manage in an old-fashioned hip-bath helped by a couple of kettles warmed on the stove. We were now as comfortable as if we were in one of those Savoy suites we knew, glorious deep baths after full days, and made the more pleasurable after the Spartan past. Unfortunately at the beginning of October the water in the well began to disappear. Gasping, air-locked pipes took the place of rushing water. The storage tank was empty. The pump which filled it had nothing to offer.

The situation is repeated annually. Wet or dry summers make no difference. Wells, it seems, are compelled at that time of year to take a holiday; and as they show the signs of becoming lower and lower, well-owners share a comradeship with each other like old soldiers.

'How's your well?' I will ask another well-owner; and immediately feel comforted when he confides that he is greatly concerned.

Or I would put a feeler in a more devious way.

'My well is doing very nicely this year. Hardly any trouble as yet.'

'You're damned lucky,' I would gleefully hear in reply, 'mine has never been lower.'

I have mitigated some of the inconvenience by making use of another well several hundred yards away up the lane, a well from which previous inhabitants of the cottage used to fetch their water in pails, and lead their cattle to drink in a neighbouring trough. It is a surface well, about three foot deep, and it was shared by us for some years with our friend Bill who keeps one of the farms at the top of the lane. He needed it both for his cattle and domestic purposes while I, in the summer, used it to water the tomato plants. It was not, however, a vigorous well. It never went dry but it was very slow to fill; and so if I used too much for the tomato plants, Bill was put to considerable inconvenience; or, alternatively, if he obtained the water his house and cattle required, the tomato plants went thirsty.

Bill is now on the mains, which means we have full use of the well; and we do so in two ways. The overflow, for instance, takes a winding route in a ditch, underneath the lane in a pipe, through a copse and along the top of the greenhouse field and down the side bordering the wood, then through a gap close by the small orchard and continuing secretly some yards among boulders until it enters the lane at the spot known as Monty's Leap. Then it crosses into a patch of ground which we are always intending to make into a water garden, though a hole in the hedge until it finally reaches the reservoir . . . a small reservoir which we dug out with shovels so as to provide a plentiful supply of water for the tomatoes.

Now this may appear to be an ideal arrangement; and so it would be, both for the tomatoes and as a reserve supply for ourselves, were it not for the fact that this lane well can also become so weak that only a trickle overflows, only a trickle runs along the ditch and into the reservoir which, in a rainless period, is barely covered by more than a foot or so of water. Nor is the water as clear as it might be; and it is certainly not suitable for a washing-machine.

Hence we have another method of tapping the well. We syphon it. You can do this if the well is higher than where you want the water delivered; and so we have an alkathene pipe with an end stuck in the well, carrying the water down hill to the tap at the other end. Thus the overflow water moves day and night into the reservoir, while the piped water is used on special occasions.

One special occasion is when the cottage well begins to fail, and is only able to pump thirty or forty gallons a day. There upon we move a hundred gallon tank alongside the reservoir, fill it with clean water through the alkathene pipe, then use the reservoir pump to pump it up the hill to the fixed tank adjoining the cottage well. This sounds complicated, and it is. I have to keep a cool head.

We still use, for instance, the cottage well for drinking water, switching the electric pump on and filling a couple of large jugs direct from the pipe that rises from the bottom of the thirty foot hole . . . but we used the fixed tank for the supply of all household needs, including the washing-machine. It is therefore my duty to see we have drinking water from one source, and that one tank fills the other for our household needs. But how do I remember to do this?

I don't. I may remember in the morning to fill the first tank, the tank by the reservoir, then see that the contents are pumped into the second tank, the tank by the cottage well . . . but I don't remember to keep a check on the situation during the day. Suddenly, therefore, I hear a cry from Jeannie, a cry like the one I heard as I was mooding over the invoices and price returns.

'The water has gone again!'

In civilised places one becomes so soothed by the availability of necessary services that one takes them for granted, like wearing trousers or a skirt. And when there is a breakdown in the conventional routine, the failure of a loaf to be delivered or the morning newspaper, or the daily bottle of milk, there is such astonishment that the mishap is certain to attract the attention of newspapers and radio. Highly paid ladies and gentlemen will interview housewives whose world has been turned upside down by the striking breadmakers or milkmen or delivery vans; and millions of people, either seeing the news or reading it, will devote their minds for a minute or two to the disaster which has befallen this section of the supermarket civilisation.

'The water has gone!' said Jeannie again.

'I heard . . .'

It was maddening that in November, after such a deluge of the last few days, we should be thirsty for water. Water was everywhere, and mud . . .

It was strange, too, that Jeannie, who has such intelligence, who held the top girl job of her time in London, who has written two books including *Hotel Regina* which a critic described as better than Vicki Baum's *Grand Hotel* . . . was mentally incapable of understanding the sequence of actions which filled first the reservoir tank then the cottage tank, then the washing-machine or anything else. For years I had tried to explain the position . . . then long ago I gave up. I always did the job myself.

'All right, darling,' I said on this occasion, meekly, 'I'll see what I can do '

I walked down to the tank by the reservoir and turned on the tap of the alkathene pipe, then I came back to the cottage waiting for it to fill Syphoning was not a quick job. The water flowed at the rate of seventy gallons an hour.

'Remind me,' I said to Jeannie, 'that I've turned it on.'

'I'll get the buzzer.'

The time buzzer, the lifebelt of forgetful people.

'How long?' she asked.

'An hour.'

Inconveniences, however, can enhance the pleasure of living. We have never bemoaned our isolation because we are cut off from much of the floss of civilisation. Indeed the contrary is true. As civilisation becomes more rarefied, more dependent on watching instant history, more influenced by media personalities offering instant opinions of doubtful sincerity, there is an increasing delight in being primitive.

Yet you cannot live in a dream world, you cannot escape from reality; and the reality, always with us, was that the long costly struggle to put our plans into effect, the plans so hopefully made when we first came to Minack, were not receiving the material reward we had expected. Truth, we had discovered, was always changing.

Had I foreseen, for instance, years ago the array of equipment, glasshouses and bulbs by the ton we now possessed, I would have had no doubt that our future would be secure. That was the truth of the time. Certainly we still lived in the environment we loved, and every day, every moment of the day, we rejoiced in our good luck; but we never foresaw that conditions, fundamental to our livelihood, would change. We were like the majority. We had been living in a period when it was normal to believe that the world stood still. Our world at any rate. We therefore had believed that if one aimed at creating a happy situation which suited the present, the present would still be there when this happy situation had been attained. A naïve mistake to make. For when we had achieved our aim, the present as we had known it was no longer there. A tougher, vastly more expensive present was in its place.

Our experience during the past tomato season was an example. Tomatoes have been for years the breadwinner for growers, especially for those like ourselves who have a holiday trade on the doorstep, and no rail expenses in consequence. True it is a crop which requires an immense amount of tedious, hand labour to grow, and over a long period of time, but in normal circumstances the financial rewards were worth this trouble. It was certainly worth the trouble when Jeannie and I were planning our greenhouses. It seemed worth it, too, when later we decided to install automatic air heating, a heating method of oil-fired heaters with fans which blow the warm air through the greenhouse in polythene ductings. Indeed, at the time when we were poring over the catalogues first of the greenhouses and then of the heaters, we were sure that only lack of nerve on our part separated us from a summer income which would give us security. We needed nerve to raise capital. And when, after many adventures, the capital in each case was obtained, I said to Jeannie that the worst part of our endeavours was over. On both occasions I said this. First, after I had raised the money for the greenhouses; then again after I had raised the money for the heaters.

But I did not foresee, needless to say, the wage explosion and the consequent jump in our annual costs. Nothing unusual about this of course, though it does seem to me that market garden growers were affected more than most. Unlike farmers, for instance, growers are not cushioned by guaranteed prices. All their produce is sold on the open market and the prices obtained are dependent on supply and demand which in turn is controlled by the vagaries of the weather. A cold spell in summer means frustration for the lettuce grower; and we have sent splendid daffodils in January to Covent Garden, only to receive a poor price because the London area was snowbound.

Growers, therefore, are unable to raise their prices to balance their costs. Florists and greengrocers who receive the produce can do so, but growers can do nothing to

67

counter the leap in oil charges, and freight, and fertilisers, and packaging, and all the necessities of growing. They also come under the control of the Agricultural Wages Board. When the Board decrees an increase in wages, farmers can be largely reimbursed when their annual Price Review is negotiated. But growers do not have this good fortune. Wage increases have to come out of their own pockets, irrespective of the financial state of their businesses. They are forced inevitably to cut down on staff, for only the cheerful, keen, experienced workers are worth-while retaining. These, in any case, will have wages above the legal minimum. Unfortunately, as the minimum wage rises, differentials are slowly erased; and yet the grower, however generous he may wish to be, cannot help any more. The decrees of the Agricultural Wages Board have seen to this. No wonder workers on the land become fewer and fewer every year.

This past tomato season was a bad one in any case. The June prices for tomatoes throughout the country (June being the month when growers with heated greenhouses rely on receiving high prices) were the lowest ever recorded for that time of year. Leaders of the tomato industry held an inquest to discover the cause; and they came to the conclusion that the great god efficiency had been up to his mischief again.

For growers, particularly the large growers, had set out to defeat costs by increasing their output of tomatoes. They had been aided by the army of research workers who operate in the background of the horticultural industry, both Government and private company research workers. These people have been so skilled in their researches, so persuasive in putting over their ideas to growers that the primary object of the grower to make money has been defeated. There are now too many greenhouses, too many skilled workers using precision methods of controlled environment growing, too many tomatoes. Efficiency had taken its toll again. Overproduction had killed the market. Growers, like their counterparts in other industries, were the victims.

So there I was sitting in the porch, invoices and price returns on the table, Jeannie now beside me, Nellie still above, probing our problems without coming to any conclusions, when the buzzer startled us with its alarm note. Startled Nellie also.

As I hurried down to the tank, I saw her flighting beautifully into the distance.

CHAPTER SEVEN

A week later the springs rose. I peered into the depths of the well, shining a torch on water that reached a jagged rock in the well wall; and the rock, I knew, was ten feet above the bottom. I now could dispense with my complicated arrangements. The automatic pump could be switched on. We were back on our personal mains.

'You mean I can use as much as I like?'

'Yes. No rationing.'

Down at Monty's Leap, the dribble of a stream had

widened and hastened. Car tyres, after crossing it, traced their damp marks for thirty yards instead of twenty. Stones no longer checked its flow, nor drooping weeds. The stream was gathering strength. Another week and it would be gushing into the reservoir, reaching the overflow gap, then into the undergrowth beyond, seeping down the valley until it found its course of previous winters, through brambles, beaten down bracken, wild mint, reeds, grasses, down, down, down, to the smooth rock of the cliff's face, and into the sea.

Winter had now become a companion. In the wood I found nests which I had not seen in summer. The bushes and trees were bare, and I suddenly discovered the tiny nest of the goldfinches who had haunted me in June and July with their bell-like chirruping, and darting red and gold. There it was in the hawthorn, just above me as I passed by Boris the drake's old hut, clusters of red berries now around it. A few yards away, within touching distance of the path, was a thrush's nest hidden in summer by the green leaves of the blackthorn; and cupped in the fork of another hawthorn was the nest of a chaffinch, and in the bank close to a magnolia was that of a robin and in the ivy that greedily climbed an ash-tree was a bundle of moss belonging to a wren, and in the branch of a willow were the dried sticks of a wood-pigeon's nest, and in one of the elms was the perfectly rounded hole of a green wood-pecker who never stayed to use it.

Winter unmasked summer. Summer had hidden the various things I had forgotten I had left in odd corners of the wood where I had left them year after year, each year intending to remove them until the year had gone and summer had returned, and I had done nothing. Discarded pieces of wire-netting now matted into the ground. Rusty sections of cloche frames. A battered, galvanised water trough for chickens. Jam jars now filled with compost from old leaves. The rotting roof of the chicken house, covered by ground ivy, in which Queen Mary, the Rhode Island Red who came with us from Mortlake, hatched her only chick. The bottom half of a broken hoe. A strand of barbed-wire. More wire-netting, and the stretch was still there against which Lama dashed hysterically when she was a wild kitten, trying to escape from the chicken run while I ponderously attempted to catch her. I touched her then, for the first time; and then away she ran, up a tree, on to the hut roof, a leap to a branch, down to the ground again, and out of sight. The wire-netting served no purpose now. We gave up the chickens long ago, and the hut, since Boris died, had only been used for the storing of fertilisers and other cumbersome goods. This winter, I said to myself, the wire-netting must be removed, so, too, the other tangible memories of the past. I must not be fooled by the lush greenery of another summer.

I walked further into the wood, scrambling over the barrier placed across a gap to stop the donkeys roaming further than their own donkey land. The big field to my left was theirs, and they were allowed into the remaining part of the wood because the trees were mostly elder, and they didn't fancy the bark of elder. But they were forbidden to enter the big meadow in front of me. Elms and hawthorns bordered three sides of it, and no elm or hawthorn was safe if the donkeys had a chance to reach it. The bark was a delicacy. That of the hawthorn they just gnawed, but they peeled off a strip of an elm, a softer bark, then gently ate it in the manner of someone enjoying asparagus. No tree could survive such attention, for as soon as the full circle of bark has been removed from a tree, however narrow it may be, the tree is certain to die.

The big meadow, the wood meadow, as it is called by us, was a jungle of undergrowth in summer when it came into our possession, and a bog in winter. We slashed the undergrowth away easily enough, but the bog tested our patience. Nothing could be grown in it until it had been drained, and yet it remained obstinately undrainable. We dug a ditch down the middle during the dry period of summer hoping that the water either side would drain into it when the springs rose. The ditch filled with water true enough, but the land still remained a bog. So the next summer we dug several ditches at angles to the main one, then waited for the winter to find out whether we had solved the problem. Once again we were disappointed. So the following summer we dug more ditches, until the meadow was littered with ditches. And when winter came we had the satisfaction of watching water in all of them merrily running to the main ditch which, with the gush of a small stream, took the water away from the meadow along a route leading to the ditch from the lane, then to Monty's Leap, the reservoir and beyond. The next step was to lay pipes in all the ditches, shovel in the earth, taking care there was a tiny gap between each pipe to drain the land water, together with a few stones to prevent soil blocking the gap ... and then to plan the crop which would justify our persistence and our financial outlay.

We decided it would be an ideal meadow for bulbs, and it was just a question of what variety of daffodils we should choose. Unfortunately I was not feeling bold at the time. I was not in the mood to spend money, or take any kind of risk. Periodically in my life I have had this miserly attitude, a loss of nerve just when flamboyance was needed. Nor does this only concern money. I have found myself at some gathering where a show of personality might do me some good, or on some other occasion where it would be useful to give a good impression, and suddenly I am suffering from a load of inhibitions; and instead of being at ease, letting myself be myself, I talk too much, over-emphasise, make remarks that I later regret. Or I can be too serious, appearing to strain. In either case there is an inner-self watching detachedly, as if it were a tape recorder providing me with the evidence to contemplate upon afterwards. Usually my conclusion is that I lacked self-discipline to control my mood. Yet, although I accept that this may be true, I argue with myself that there are often extenuating circumstances. Dull people, for instance, people who look at you, glass in hand, but do not speak, bring out the worst in me. Intellectuals who belong to small, mutual admiring cliques, do so too. Also gun-happy gentry who rely on ancestors to justify their boisterousness. No need for self-blame when I fail with such people. But I would prefer, when I need confidence, that I kept my nerve. Just as I needed to keep my nerve when I had to decide what bulbs I should plant in the meadow.

Perhaps I was greedy. Or perhaps I was influenced by Jeannie who, in Scottish fashion, can be too generous at one moment and too careful at the next, in coming to the decision I did. I know now, in any case, that I regret the decision.

The previous year we had grown two tons of bulbs in the greenhouses. The venture had been partly provoked by the example of the Lincolnshire growers. If they could produce what amounted to *ersatz* spring daffodils under unnatural forced conditions and thereby capture a large part of the early market hitherto the preserve of Cornish and Scilly growers, why should we not try to have a pinch of the market? We would not force unnaturally however. We would not use heat, nor would the bulbs be pre-cooled. The daffodils would grow naturally except for the protection of the greenhouses against wind and excessive cold. Thus our daffodils, we felt, would qualify for that mystical attraction created by true spring daffodils.

Our pigmy effort against the big battalions had some success. We at any rate shared with them the prices prevailing in January; and we were certainly the only growers in our area who had daffodils to send away at that particular time of the year. Nevertheless the prices were not as high as we had expected, and in due course we decided we would not repeat the venture another year.

We still, however, had the bulbs and they all belonged to a variety called Golden Harvest, representing a capital investment of about £300. We had earned from them a little over £400, and so we had made a profit of £100. This was far too small a margin as far as we were concerned because, apart from the normal picking, bunching and sending away, there were the labour costs of planting them (the long greenhouse in front of the cottage had the bulbs in whalehide pots which had to be filled, planted and then transported) and then there were the labour costs of removing the bulbs after the daffodils had been harvested.

Yet if we could keep the bulbs, as we kept bulbs bought for the open fields, we would be earning a return on our investment for year after year; and it would seem obvious to do this. Forced bulbs, however, have to have time to recover; and the big growers with all the machines and facilities available to them will plant out their forced bulbs in the fields, lift them after a year, and then plant them again; and they reckon that in the third year the bulbs will be flowering again as normal. Some other growers, on the other hand, find the cost, time, and space involved not worth it; and they throw the bulbs away. We were advised by a master bulb grower to do this ourselves.

We did not agree with him. We considered our case

quite different. After all, we argued, we had not really *forced* our bulbs, not at any rate in the manner of the Lincolnshire growers. We had only provided protection during the growing period, protection which could be likened to an exceptionally warm and calm spring. We believed, therefore, that we could keep our bulbs, plant them again, and reap the harvest.

I had, on the other hand, doubts. The master bulb grower was so firm in his advice, so adamant that his opinion was the right one, that I would have been foolish not to doubt. Jeannie, however, thought otherwise ... the bulbs were a tangible asset, the master grower had no experience of our method of forcing, and we just could not afford to throw away £300 worth of bulbs. Obviously we couldn't. But irritatingly my doubts remained. Old growers, men who, over many years, have experienced the permutation of harvest results, have the knack of producing the right conclusions, however unpalatable they may be. And the man gave another reason to justify his advice. Golden Harvest, he said, was a tricky bulb.

Golden Harvest has been the rage in the markets for the past few years. It is a beautiful golden yellow daffodil with a light yellow perianth, and there is no doubt that it deserves to be greatly admired. But I see no reason why it mesmerises the salesmen in the markets and the florists to such an extent that equally beautiful daffodils like Joseph MacLeod and King Alfred are looked upon as inferior. The public, I am sure, cannot tell the difference between them. Yet sleepy-eyed florists disgorge from their vans at the markets in the early hours of each weekday morning, murmuring Golden Harvest to the waiting salesmen who of course are only too happy to oblige. Golden Harvest, therefore, has the power of a well publicised brand name; and growers naturally hasten to cater for the demand.

It happens, however, that the bulk of the Golden Harvest suffers in certain conditions from a fungus disease called basal rot. The disease causes a brown decay of the bulbs starting at the roots, and before long the bulb becomes a squishy mess beyond the hope of any recovery. Severe attacks, therefore, can decimate a meadow of bulbs within a couple of years, and those that are left will produce only short stemmed, weakly blooms, and it will be only a matter of another year or two before they also disappear. And to add to the menace of basal rot, the fungus remains alive in the soil after the bulbs have rotted.

Nevertheless Golden Harvest thrives in ground it likes, and in such conditions shows no sign of disease. The only difficulty is to know which is the right ground and which is the wrong ground; and, at the time of our Golden Harvest, knowledge was incomplete because no one in our area had grown the bulbs. The knowledge is available today. I met the other day a doyen of daffodil growers who for many years has flower farmed the eastern slopes of Lamorna valley. He, too, had been axious to satisfy the demands of the sleepy-eyed florists. 'Golden Harvest?' he said to me, eyes under grey eyebrows giving the impression of contempt, 'they're no good for us. They're not happy on our cliffs.'

How right he was. How right, too, the master bulb grower who advised us to dispense with those greenhouse bulbs. We acted, ignoring his advice, ignoring the doubts I felt myself, by transporting the bulbs to the wood meadow; and planting them. We had even a sense of triumph when the planting was completed. Geoffrey in control, extra labour engaged; and the day when we looked upon the brown earth, sheltered all around by the elms and the hawthorn, was a day we felt was an achievement in our life here at Minack. It proved we were bold, and tenacious, and able to defy fuddy-duddy traditional caution like that of the master grower.

Inexperience, and the consequences, belong to any age. It is not exclusive to youth. But the youth has one great advantage because, in defeat, it is soothed by the notion that there are an everlasting number of years ahead in which to follow mistakes with victories. I still am soothed by this notion. I refuse to accept the fact, except when in a sad mood, that the options are becoming fewer.

This is just as well. There was an anaemic look about the Golden Harvest in the wood meadow from the moment they showed a few inches above the ground. They were in four-foot-wide beds, an eighteen-inch path between each bed, and they looked as if they required a good tonic. No, not even that, I realised, would help them. I watched them, pointing their weak, pale green foliage to the sky, a few accompanied by buds, and knew that we had made a major mistake. We had handed over a virgin meadow to a couple of tons of bulbs which hated the ground. Bulbs would rot there, spread their disease, and deny us the reward of the work and expense we had expended. Moreover I was aware that there was nothing we could do about it. Digging up bulbs was a far more laborious performance than planting them and we would never be able to spare the time to do so. Thus the decaying bulbs have remained there. Some still push up foliage, a few even produce daffodils. But I know now that I should have accepted the advice of the master grower. We were greedy. We did not want advice. Another option had gone.

So there I was staring at the wood meadow when I saw a movement in the far corner to the right, on the hedge built long ago of stones, now covered by grass, with an umbrella of hawthorn above it. First I thought the breeze was blowing a patch of tired bracken to and fro, then an instant later I saw quite clearly the head of a fox. I was not at first unduly surprised by the sight of it because foxes over the years have passed around Minack with nonchalant confidence. They would bolt, of course, if they came face to face with one of us, silently gliding away into the nearest undergrowth, but they never gave the impression of being on guard as they nosed around Minack. We were part of their landscape, and so they took us for granted. There were no dogs to chase them, no guns to frighten them. Only the donkeys to watch. Fred, looking for a diversion to help pass the time, would prick his ears when he saw a fox in his field, then advance towards it, first slowly, then at a canter, then at a gallop though the fox would long have disappeared over the hedge before he could reach it. Then Fred would stand balefully looking at the hedge, snorting.

But the fox I saw in the wood meadow was behaving in a most unusual manner. It was standing on the hedge, as if poised to jump down into the meadow; and swaying. Foxes are so quick in their movements, so decisive in carrying out what they want to do, that the sight of this fox behaving as if it was intoxicated was momentarily funny. Then suddenly it made up its mind to jump, and promptly sprawled flat on the ground.

I now started to walk quietly towards it. I could see it was a fine dog fox though not one I recognised as being recently in the neighbourhood. The coat was a paler bracken-red than usual, so, too, the head, though the sun shining upon it may have caused this impression. I was continuing to walk towards him, and was within twenty yards when he struggled to his feet, frightened obviously by my approach, and proceeded to run, not away from me but past me in the direction of that part of the wood which surrounded Boris's hut. He had not travelled far, not even out of the wood meadow, before he collapsed again. A moment later he was up, started to move forward, but only went round in a circle.

I thought at first he might have an injured leg, but the way he ran past me didn't suggest this. Clearly something was seriously wrong and, after seeing him desperately floundering around in a circle, then flop down again, it seemed likely that he was suffering from some kind of brain damage. He now lay not many yards from me with head stretched out on the soil, eyes nevertheless alert, and watching me.

I was sad enough not to move forward. Animals, like some human beings, prefer to be invalids on their own without people fussing; and I realised that whatever was wrong, there was nothing I could do to help. This fox was dying, so let him die on his own.

I thereupon retreated from where he was sprawled, stepped over the hedge where I first saw him, then pushed my way through some undergrowth, over another hedge and across a field to the lane which led down to the cottage. By taking this roundabout route, I had avoided advancing upon him, and so frightening him once again. I also had avoided any responsibilities that I might have had towards him, any second thoughts that it might have perhaps been my duty to be his executioner which, without a gun, could only have been clumsily achieved. Thus I returned to the cottage and Jeannie, unhappy of course, but consoled that I was letting nature take its course, letting a wild animal die a wild animal quite on its own.

Then suddenly half an hour later, I saw him at Monty's Leap, gulping from the stream. He was lying down as he did so.

'Jeannie!'

I was only at the corner of the cottage when I saw him, and I dashed back to tell her. She was hoovering the sitting-room carpet, and she didn't hear me above the whining hum of the machine.

'Jeannie!' I shouted.

The power was flicked off. There was silence.

'The fox!' I said urgently, 'the fox is down at the Leap!'

Immediately she came with me. The stone chippings would have sounded the alarm, had we moved quickly, and so we crept towards the Leap, taking advantage of stepping on the grass by the white seat and the verbena bush, then on the patch of grass opposite the old stable, and on the grass beside the lane until we were within a few yards of the fox. Poor soul, he had had his drink now and lay panting, a beautiful fox, helpless, years of roaming and hunting behind him; and being hunted.

'He's been poisoned,' said Jeannie softly.

'You can't know,' I said.

He moved then. He struggled to his feet, swayed, and turned his back on us; and tottered into the bushes of the little valley which took the stream from Monty's Leap. I suppose he was on his way back to his earth on the cliffs. I never saw him again. Later I searched the bushes and undergrowth of the valley, but there was no sign of him.

'He had been poisoned,' said Jeannie again.

'Why do you say that?'

'I just feel it.'

'Foxes have to die sometime. We just happened to be here to watch the end of a life. Young cub, mating fox, finish.'

'I still think he was poisoned.'

I had read about foxes being deliberately poisoned, but I had never heard of anyone in our area setting a bait of poison. But this fox could have come from afar. He could have been travelling over many miles, obeying this instinct which is strong in some foxes of going home when they are in trouble, going home to the earth where they were reared as young cubs. Or he may have picked up some poison by mistake. If he had been nosing about a farmyard, where rat poison had been laid, he might have done so. Strangely, Lama also was poisoned a week or two later.

We knew Lama was not well when she lost her purr; and we were immediately concerned one afternoon as we amused ourselves by courting her, by performing such delicate gestures as stroking her silky black head with a finger, when we were met by silence. Lama was always generous with her purrs, though she was equally generous with her squeaky growls if she considered we were being unduly attentive; and so when there was total silence, we were mildly alarmed.

'Did she eat her breakfast?'

'Only a little, now I come to think of it.'

'But she had it late, didn't she? I let her out before we listened to the news, and she was out for some time.'

'She came in about eleven.'

I am amused sometimes, in retrospect, by my tendency to be over-anxious. I am faced by a problem or an emergency, and promptly prepare for the worst so that I will not be shaken if it occurs. This attitude also means I am elated if my imaginary fears do not mature. My emotions, therefore, when trouble looms, are on a see-saw.

But if I was now showing over-anxiety, without any tangible reason as yet, it was because Lama was growing old; and I was haunted, always had been haunted, by the last weeks of Monty's life until the vet came and said he could do no more for him. This pain, universal though it is among those who love, remains unique to oneself. A personal agony which leaves an observer, however sympathetic, untouched; and only the cold never experience it.

Later that afternoon Lama showed the signs that our fears had a basis. She tried to be sick, and when we took her outside she slowly set off down the lane towards the stream, and when she reached it she crouched beside it drinking for minutes on end, just as Monty did when he was ill. Then she went into the grass and lay there although it had begun to rain.

That evening I went out and rang up the vet. Vets, I find, are so quick to respond to a call for help that sometimes I wish I was registered with a vet instead of a doctor. Our own vet, a Scotsman, was particularly zealous in this respect; and when he arrived in his large white car, from the moment in fact we saw it turn the corner in the lane beyond Monty's Leap, we felt reassured. He was merry, and sensible, and kind both to our anxious selves and to the patient whether a cat or a donkey. Thus when I rang up and found he had gone away for the night, and that both his partners were out on urgent missions, I was abruptly surprised. I had taken it so for granted that he would be out to see Lama within the hour instead of in the morning that I felt like someone who had suddenly been given the sack. Over-confidence, as always, had exacted its price.

Every now and then throughout the night I would wake up, my mind pleasantly clear of trouble for a few seconds, then blanketed with gloom as I remembered Lama. In reality I was remembering Monty. I was thinking of the years in between, from the time of Monty's death, Lama's strange arrival, and now; and I was angry, and puzzled and sad, that the years had run away so fast, and that I had so soon to feel again emotions I once thought would always be unique.

Lama was worse in the morning. She ignored the fish, a portion of her favourite ling, which Jeannie had poached for her; and drank instead a quantity of water. We were always amused by her manner of drinking water, because she would not have it in a saucer, as she would have milk. She insisted on drinking from an old-fashioned lemonade mug, of pink pottery decorated with flowers, which once was used by Jeannie's mother; and we had to keep it topped up because the water was out of her reach whenever it was a couple of inches from the rim of the mug. We topped it up a couple of times that morning, then carried her outside, put her down on the flower-bed close to the escallonia, and proceeded to watch her wobble to a patch of wet grass where she crouched as if the grass was cooling her tummy.

A few minutes later I heard the sound of a car. Our ears are tuned in to the grating of tyres on stone chippings and, if the weather is quiet, I can sometimes hear a car passing the farm buildings at the top of our lane; and then I follow the sound as it turns the bend until at last I see the bonnet as it comes into the final stretch towards Monty's Leap. The car I saw now, was white.

'He's arrived!'

The sight of the vet was enough to make us believe our fears were over. Without him saying a word, without any logical reason, we suddenly felt confident. The vet would never let Lama die. The vet had mysterious powers like those of a witch doctor; and we felt, now that he had arrived, as child-like as those who believed in witch doctors.

Came the usual questions.

'What were the first signs?'

'Has she cried?'

'Could she have come into contact with any poison?'

Jeannie and I, of course, had already conducted an inquest into Lama's immediate past. We could find no clue as a reason for her illness. We kept no poison on the premises. Some growers, on the other hand, stock pesticides and various forms of weed-killers because they insist it is necessary to do so. Such aids to profitable growing can be deadly dangerous; and I know one chemical product used for the sterilisation of bulbs which killed a grower's dog. A drop of the product had fallen into a puddle outside the house, and the dog drank from the puddle, and he died. Strange how the desire for efficiency blinds a person.

The vet sat on the sofa listening to our answers. Lama was on Jeannie's lap, held there, waiting for inspection. I was standing, puffing at my pipe.

'I wouldn't say she looks too bad,' said the vet, 'her coat's bright, so are her eyes. Think back once again. Can't you think of any clue at all? What about Geoffrey? Perhaps he has an idea.'

We had discussed the matter with Geoffrey. It is easy to talk to Geoffrey about animals and birds. We will waste time, for instance, during the day because we have seen an unusual migrant, or he may call to us that he has seen a hare, and we will leave whatever we are doing, and join him, watching. Pleasant intervals during the day's work are provided by such observations.

'Now, Lama,' said the vet, 'let's have a look at you.'

I left then. I had a sudden wish to talk to Geoffrey again, an instinct he might now remember some incident that would help. Clues are not always remembered immediately. Often they come into one's mind a long time after one has first sought them.

I found him having his croust, munching a slice of cake with his usual companions; a chaffinch, a pair of blue tits, a tom tit with one leg, waiting for crumbs to be thrown to them.

'We're still looking for clues,' I said; 'the vet seems to think she has picked up poison from somewhere.'

'I've been thinking,' he answered, 'I've got an idea.'

I listened as he told me his theory, then hurried back into the cottage.

'I think I have the answer!'

Lama had just received an injection, and she had wandered off across the carpet to beneath my desk, angry no doubt.

'I'm sure I have,' I said, then went on: 'When Geoffrey arrived yesterday morning, he found one of the dust-bins had been upset, lid off, and contents partly out. Half asleep he lifted it upright, and thought no more about it. He's suggesting that a fox must have tried to scavenge the contents during the night. Some of the contents had been there for nearly a week because dust-bin collecting day isn't till tomorrow. So Lama could have eaten something which had gone bad . . .'

'She couldn't be so greedy,' interrupted Jeannie.

'Well she was out long before Geoffrey arrived so she had plenty of time.'

'And you know how curious cats can be,' said the vet.

'Lama,' said Jeannie, addressing her across the room, 'I'm ashamed of you!'

Relief mingled with the shame. The injection, coupled with the medicine we gave her during the following twenty-four hours, changed our tottering Lama into a normal cat. Then came the happiest moment of all.

'Come here quickly,' Jeannie called to me, 'come and listen. Lama has found her purr!'

CHAPTER EIGHT

I saw Daisy, Lama's mother, the following morning in the stable meadow, slowly taking her usual route across it towards the cliff; a grey, compact little figure, seemingly unaware of the gale which was blowing up. She had some business in hand which she intended to complete; and the gale, and the salt which came with it, dampening her fur, sticky, was not going to deter her from fulfilling her secret task.

'Going to be rough,' I said to Geoffrey.

'Didn't hear the forecast.'

'Forecast said sunny periods and light winds.'

He laughed.

'Wrong again.'

Black clouds emptying their rain, were scurrying across the bay like upside-down mushrooms. At intervals the sun broke through, shining like a brilliant dagger on the sea. This was a sea that was glad of the turbulence to come, waves were slapping each other, leaving trails of foam in their wake, and watery pits; and above, yet so close that they seemed to be playing their own idea of Russian roulette, were the gulls. They dived at the waves, and swept through the spray; and settled, settled on the surging mass, bobbing spots defying the mountains which seemed at any moment to smother them. This was the beginning of the storm, the limbering up; and in an hour or so the gulls would have gone, gathered on sheltered rocks or inland fields, heads crouched in feathers, facing the wind, leaving the sea to rage.

'Better check that the greenhouses are all right,' I said.

I had greenhouse neurosis when they were first erected. I could not believe that they could withstand the gales which bashed them; and I would lie in bed listening to the roar outside, imagining the flying glass and the destruction of the crops inside, until I forced myself to get up, wrap myself in an oiler and, with a torch in my hand, set off to see the damage.

'Be careful,' Jeannie would say, 'do be careful.'

83

It was a long time before I rid myself of this neurosis, before I realised that greenhouses can be as tough as any building; and that although the glass may rattle like the sound of a thousand tin cans, making it a fearsome experience to be inside the greenhouse while the gale blew, it would need a whirlwind to destroy them.

But there was an occasion, the occasion of the worst gale in the Penzance area this century, when it seemed a whirlwind had anchored itself at Minack. The storm began the day before the famous Spring Show in Penzance; and Jane had come over from the Scillies where she worked at the Tresco Gardens, going there with her mother after she left working for us. She had brought with her a beautiful array of daffodils which she was entering for the Prince of Wales's Cup, the most coveted cup in the Show.

The weather was calm when she arrived, and she asked me whether I would mind her putting the daffodils in pails in the greenhouse, the long one in front of the cottage, because the blooms were backward and the warmth of the greenhouse would bring them out. That was a Tuesday afternoon, and entries for the Show had to be in their places by nine o'clock on Wednesday evening. Early on Wednesday morning the storm began; and by midday it was so fierce that the greenhouse was swaying like a drunken man, and the roof was leaping up and down. It appeared that any minute the whole structure would collapse ... and Jane's precious daffodils were still inside.

I told her that it was far too dangerous to open the door and fetch them. An open door would provide the funnel for the wind to rush in, and that would mean the end of the greenhouse for certain, and the risk was obvious that she might be lacerated by glass. Better, therefore, to leave the daffodils where they were.

Jane, however, had an ally in Jeannie. I was being too imaginative. My greenhouse neurosis had warped my judgement. It was absurd that I should dictate such orders just because I was scared of an open door. And so they plotted together that when I took our normal consignment of daffodils to catch the train at Penzance, they would act on their own. Just as well that they did. Jane won the coveted Prince of Wales's Cup, the youngest competitor ever to do so.

'All the vents are closed,' said Geoffrey after his inspection, 'and I've tried the doors.'

There was nothing in the greenhouse at the time. The tomato plants had been pulled up during October and the process of sterilising the soil set in motion. We never sterilised by steam, partly because of the initial expense of buying the equipment, mainly because of the lack of water at the time we had to do the steaming. We used a chemical instead, a powder which was rotovated into the soil. The soil was then lightly watered so that the fumes let off by the powder were sealed in the earth; and then for six weeks the greenhouses were kept closed while the germ and fungus destruction took place. No chance, therefore, to grow a winter crop; and so, whether we liked it or not, we had to depend on tomatoes to warrant the existence of the greenhouses. The past season's poor prices had to be forgotten. Optimism had to be drawn upon once again, and the plans laid for next summer.

'I've ordered the Maascross,' I said to Geoffrey.

I had been late in ordering the plants. Here it was the beginning of December, and the seeds had to be sown by the middle of the month. Sometimes we had considered growing our own plants, but we always checked from doing so because we realised that at the time they would need most attention, pricking out and so on, we would be immersed in the daffodil season; and the daffodils left us no time to spare. Thus at first I used to have the plants from the Land Settlement Association at Newent in Gloucestershire; and they were brought in a vast van which, on one occasion, half toppled over into the ditch as it came down our narrow lane. They were excellent plants but became too expensive; and now we have them from a Cornish grower at Truro called Hitchens who brings them to us early in March, a foot high, for planting out. As for the reason why we have the variety Maascross, the answer is that it likes our soil. We have tried others such as Eurocross, Moneymaker, Ailsa Craig, but none grows so well as does Maascross. The tomatoes also have a very fine flavour although this factor is now considered unimportant. Bulk sellers of tomatoes require only tomatoes of uniform shape. They must all be of exactly the same size. The pre-pack mentality demands this. It does not demand any flavour. But in Cornwall during the holiday season, old-fashioned pleasures are enjoyed again; and our tomatoes with the slogan, 'Tomatoes Grown for Flavour', stamped on the side of the containers, are always in demand.

The rain was now falling on Minack; and the sound of it as it swept through the trees, and the sound of the gale pausing, rushing, shouting as if in argument, produced in me a sudden sense of exultation. I left Geoffrey in the hut which was his office, the hut where we first bunched daffodils, where I constantly knocked my head against the cross-bar in the middle, sometimes cutting it, until Jane and Shelagh covered the bar with foam rubber . . . and went outside into the storm. I glanced at the primitive building which acts as a garage, and noticed Nellie sheltering, perched on one of the rocks jutting out of the bank which serves as one side of the building. Nellie was safe there, and comfortable, and happy so it seemed. Why therefore did she always fly away when dusk fell? And where? I was to find out one day, yet even the answer puzzled me.

I went out and braced myself against the rain and the gale, and strode to the gate of the stable meadow, a chewed, wooden gate, made so by the donkeys when they were bored by the absence of attention; and I passed through the gate, passed the donkeys themselves as they stood, bottoms to the hedge, heads down, tolerating the storm with a dopey attitude of patience. Yet the barn door was open for them. They had only to move there and be out of the wind and the rain, but no. They desired to indulge in donkey masochism. They preferred to maintain the donkey tradition that they were a persecuted race.

On I went along the path, across Fred's field, down to the little gate at the top of the cliff, down the steps, down through the pocket meadows, past the palm tree which I planted when my mother died, through the narrow gap between two hedges of blackthorn and into the bottom daffodil meadow of all, then down again to the point where the grass ended and the grey rocks began. Here was my journey's end. Here I stood with the grandeur of a Cornish sea just below me, watching it foaming the rocks where we lazed on summer days, watching the great waves mounting their assault, coming nearer and nearer, and growing, and the tops curving and sharpening so that for a split second the tops resembled a knife's edge before they thundered down on the rocks which halted them. This was a scene which belonged to immortality. I was seeing the same waves, hearing the same roar, wet with the same spray, nothing had changed throughout the centuries. This was the universe. This was the back-drop to all history, to all conflicts between nations or individuals, to impatient ambitions, to the passing fashions of each age, to the vanity of man. This was continuity which some ignore, some deride; and in which some find comfort. Man's conceit as he overpopulates, drowns the countryside in concrete, pollutes the sky and the rivers, will surely wither. One day he will learn the universe is master.

A seal was in the teaspoon of a bay to my left, the tiny bay where once Jeannie and I tried to solve our fish supply by having a trammel net stretching across from a galvanised ring cemented in a rock to a buoy forty yards out. The trammel net had two ropes, one to pull out the net, one to pull it in; and for a few weeks we had much excitement as we harvested the fish. Most were wrasse and uneatable, but we caught some pollack, a mackerel or two, and even a conger-eel. But a gale came and took away our net; and instead of cheap fish, we realised we had the most expensive fish we have ever eaten. One day, perhaps, we will try again; for it is always a minor triumph if one corrects a past mistake.

I was not surprised by the sight of the seal, for I had seen one there before in a storm. On that occasion I first thought it was a piece of wood, then it might be the body of a drowned person, then I realised it was a seal which seemed to be relishing in its defiance of the storm. So now. This seal I was watching, insolently awaited the curving waves; and when they crashed down on the rocks, they appeared to crash down on him, so close was he himself to the rocks. Then the waves, splintering their white, rushing froth into crevices and high points which were dry except in the great storms, which gulls themselves normally believed to be high ground, reluctantly receded and I saw the seal again, head and whiskers above water, a grey knowing face, amused that he had defeated, as he always would defeat, the rage of a storm.

Our coast is not usually seal country. I have never, for

instance, seen a seal basking on a rock, nor have I ever seen more than one seal at a time. Seals prefer the north coast, places like the island of rocks called The Carracks near St Ives, or Hell's Mouth between Hayle and Portreath, or St Agnes where there is a seal sanctuary soon to move to Perranporth. But there is another stretch of the coast nearer to us, a stretch we sometimes walk and which is one of the most beautiful walks in the world, where a seal once gave us a magical experience.

We had left the car at Porthgwarra, a hamlet at the end of a valley with a slipway between rugged rocks leading to sand and the sea. It is the last hamlet on the south coast of Cornwall, and it lies sheltered from the westerlies by the massive promontory of Gwennap Head, on the fierce cliffs on which marine commandos train to climb. Tol Pedn coastguard station stands at the top, a box of a building manned day and night, where every passing vessel is recorded, where the *Torrey Canyon* was observed as she sailed towards the Seven Stones reef in the distance.

Below the station are the coastguard dwellings, solid homes huddled together, resembling a fort; and they edge a vast area of barren land, barren except for the heathery ling and stunted gorse which covers it like a giant cushion. Here pause the migrant birds; and here, from time to time, we have flushed a quail, and seen a grey shrike, small to be so fierce, and watched wheatears bobbing their tails, displaying their white rumps, listened to the rattle of grasshopper warblers without any sign of them, observed cuckoos scouting for rock pipit nests; and always, of course, there are the swallows, resting on the telephone lines running down the valley after arrival, resting again before departure. Reasonable enough that this is a place for birdwatchers.

But there are seals, too, to watch. The coastal path leads away from the coastguard dwellings, around the rim of Porth Loe Cove, and upwards, until it levels out on the edge of the cliff high above the sea. From here, on clear days, you can see the shadowy outline of the Scilly Islands; and, in the morning, you will see the white speck of the *Scillonian* on the way there from the mainland, passing the lonely Wolf Rock lighthouse where a keeper was swept away not long ago as he fished from its base. On your right, if you are facing the sea, and four miles away, is the Longship lighthouse, most photographed lighthouse in Britain; and, as if adjoining it though there is a mile of sea in between, is the tourist mecca of Land's End. It is fashionable to condemn the ugliness of this mecca, but I do not find it as ugly as its reputation. There are only five shops, all low-roofed, and the hotel with its magnificent views has none of the offensive, utility coldness of modern hotel buildings. There is the car park, of course, and the crush of people in summer, disgorging from coaches, wearing funny hats; but go there in spring, and autumn, and winter, and you will experience the loneliness of the place. It is at the village of Sennen, a mile away, where man flaunts his ability to destroy beauty; for here is a site of permanent, crude caravans, so situated that, from afar, the lovely centuries old-church seems to be surrounded by them. Nor has any satisfactory attempt been made, although the site has been there for many years, to screen it within a shelter of trees. It remains, unashamed, a monument to man's vandalism

Below Tol Pedn coastguard station are the rocks where seals gather, and it is at the point on the coastal path above Porth Loe Cove that you can observe them. There is nothing secretive about them, and we have often watched them slithering on and off the rocks, playing games with each other, sometimes immobile, ruminating, two or three grey-black seals, perhaps a couple which are creamy-coloured. Sometimes, also, we have heard them singing, but their sound was raucous compared to the song of the seal which provided us with the magical experience.

We were following our usual route, past Folly Cove, along Ardensaweth Cliff, aiming for Nanjizal Bay. It is a little bay and in some summers it has a beach of sand; in others, if the weather has been stormy, it has a beach of boulders. We never, as it happens, go down to the beach ourselves, but it serves as a terminal. We reach the cliff above it, look down, remark upon its state, then return the way we have come.

On this occasion we had reached a steep dip in the walk, between Ardensaweth Cliff and Nanjizal Bay, which opens on another bay called Pendower Coves. Down you then walk into the narrow valley, then across a little stream where wild cotton grows alongside in summer; and then up the other steep track towards Carn Les Boel, and Nanjizal. It is pleasant on such a walk to have no human being in sight; and it is remarkable how often such freedom from distraction is obtained. In solitude one becomes part of the grandeur of the scenery, and involved in its rugged past. One does not want to be reminded of today. One wishes to enjoy illogical emotions, like the irrational awareness that one has been there before, and that one's spirit will always be there. Thus, when Jeannie and I see somebody on the horizon coming towards us, we plan avoiding action. Others, we have found, take similar action if they see us. A local lady, a dedicated lover of this walk for many years, stopped me in Penzance one day. 'I hope,' she said, 'you don't take it personally when I hide from you on the Porthgwarra walk.' 'Of course not,' I said, 'while you are hiding behind one rock, we are hiding behind another.'

We had reached the dip, Jeannie and I, had almost reached the stream, when we heard from across the still water a sound like a flute being played.

'Listen,' I said, 'a seal is singing.'

No movement. No speech between us. It was a sighing, ethereal sound; and it was coming from inside a great cave that burrows into the cliffs.

'Mary Rose,' said Jeannie, 'it is like the song of the fairies in Mary Rose.'

I left the other seal, the seal in our teaspoon of a bay, and started back up the cliff. I did not hurry. I am by inclination a stroller, not a walker; and I have often irritated Jeannie by my dawdling. I prefer to pause, and look around, and contemplate. Jeannie likes to reach her destination. I prefer to delay doing so . . . even in a storm.

I paused, therefore, by the palm tree, sheltering below its sword-shaped leaves, the trunk swaying, the leaves cackling as the gale rushed by; and I stood facing the gale and the sea, spray mingling with the rain on my face, elated by this fury of nature, clouds lowering, and the roar so loud that no one would have heard me had I shouted across the meadow. I saw a fishing boat heading for Newlyn, one of the Stevenson trawler fleet I realised; and then another, a smaller one; and closer inshore there was a French crabber with an all white hull, and as it heaved between the waves, then momentarily riding one like a surfer, I could see the crew in the stern, matchsticks of bright orange-red. Bigger vessels would be coming soon; and almost immediately I caught sight in the dropping visibility of the outline of a small coaster, foreign no doubt, whose captain had decided that the shelter of inner Mount's Bay was a wiser place to be than rounding the corner of Land's End. By nightfall, I was sure, there would be several boats riding at anchor within sight of Penzance's promenade.

I moved from the palm tree and went up the cliff, pausing again just before I reached the little gate which led to Fred's field. I was staring downwards now, down at the turbulence of the sea, down at the fishing boats and the French crabber, down at the coaster and another one which had just come into view. And down, I realised, at my past.

For this cliff was the lure which led us away from our London lives; and on that day, sickle and scythe in our hands, when we began to slash order into the cliff, opening up again long-forgotten meadows and creating new ones, we truly believed that the world stood still. Machines? Horticultural industrialisation? We were so naïve that we never considered such things would interfere with our future, never considered the possibility of man-made over-production. Only the elements, we thought, would be our enemy; and when in due course we endured gales which pulverised our crops, or a sudden frost which destroyed six months' income in a night, we were comforted by the knowledge that nature had been the architect of our defeat, not man. Nature represented freedom, and could be forgiven; man, in contrast, offered chains, and more chains. Man's mistake is to believe that freedom is orderly.

Hence we relished the earthy philosophy of our neighbours and of those who helped us. Their words were shouts of defiance against the trends of civilisation.

'I've lost my waistcoat, boy,' said a farmer as he surveyed a field of potatoes, haulms blackened by a gale. 'And where am I going to find my waistcoat again? Why, right here ... next year!'

We had helping us, during our beginning, a tall, lean, eccentric Cornishman called Tommy Williams who lived alone in a caravan not far away. He was middle-aged, believed women a nuisance, would suddenly burst into hymn singing as he was digging a meadow, ate only out of tins, and prided himself on being a collector of *objets d'art*. These were of a varied nature. I remember him arriving one Monday morning with the news that on the previous Saturday in Penzance he had bought a Rembrandt. On another occasion he announced that he had discovered in a junkshop a Stradivarius violin. He spoke of his finds in such authoritative fashion that I never dared question their genuineness; and for weeks afterwards, as I pursued some earthy task in his company, I would have to listen to his future plans for them. The Rembrandt, I remember, was understandably scheduled for Christies. The Stradivarius, on the other hand, was to be kept.

'I've always had a mind to play the violin,' he explained to me.

Tommy had many qualities. He was adept at moving rocks, and there were many rocks at the time to move. He would often work overtime, then refuse any pay for it. He was a good shoveller, and it was he who taught me to use the long-handled Cornish shovel. And he was constantly presenting me with ingenious ideas, few of which proved practical. Once, for instance, during a rainy period which was causing him to be behindhand in the task of turning ground for the coming potato season, he proposed that I should buy him a tent. He would turn the ground while sheltering in the tent. A praiseworthy idea, no doubt, but unfortunately he had not taken into account the wind which came with the rain.

But as I stood, looking down at the meadows, looking down at the sea pounding the rocks, looking down at the boats making for the shelter of Newlyn, I could see Tommy again. There he was in that meadow to the right, having discovered a tiny spring, and already a grandiose plan was forming in his mind. He would harness this spring, build a dam, build a reservoir ... henceforth there would be no water problems on the cliff. No drought would ever again spoil a potato crop. More important still he would have the edge on others in the neighbourhood, men with whom he had grown up, men he had worked for ... *their* potatoes would be like pebbles. Only Minack cliff potatoes would be large. Alas, the spring died when summer came.

Tommy wearing a Panama hat in summer, a peak cap in winter. Once I found him on his knees groping in the grass around the edge of a meadow, and I asked him what he was doing.

'An unusual insect. A very unusual insect. I'm trying to catch it.'

And there were other times when I would sit beside him in one of the meadows of the cliff, listening to comical stories which I had no means of knowing whether they were true. I was then still a Londoner. I was learning to be a countryman.

'Chickens,' he would say, 'fly up into a tree when they sense a fox is about ... so what does the fox do? He will walk round and round the tree, for half an hour or more, and the chicken will be watching him until it becomes dizzy and falls to the ground.'

'Dirty animals, foxes,' he would explain, 'badgers won't have anything to do with them ... badgers are real house-proud. But there's one thing I can say in favour of foxes. They can't stand fleas. If a fox has fleas he will go looking for a stream or a pond, pull a tuft of hair from his coat, then stand in the water still holding the tuft in his mouth. He will go on standing until the fleas, to escape drowning, have all collected on the tuft. Then he lets it go.'

I slowed down with Tommy. I was like a schoolboy who, at a formative time, has the luck to have a teacher who reflects, but with experience, the boy's own feelings. I became aware of small pleasures. I learnt that to enjoy such pleasures I had to have patience. They are not revealed to those who hurry. I learnt, and years later this lesson is much sharper, that many of us are like puddings in our reaction towards the senses.

For this is a visual age. Our eyes are satiated by pictures which capture our admiration, or our weakness for gaping, but which do not capture our involvement. We travel the world and space in our armchairs, marvelling at the photography as we land on the moon, explore the Nile, study land-crabs on some island in the Indian ocean, watch a soldier on guard against a sniper's bullet at a modern city's street corner, climb the vertical face of a mountain, participate in an Asian flood disaster, observe white horses galloping in the Camargue, round the Horn in a boat too small for survival to be expected. Every evening of our lives we seem to be acting as observers. A new generation is growing up which even considers this observer way of life as normal. These people watch a storm, and do not feel the wind and the rain. They are in a pine wood and do not smell the pines. They look at danger but do not experience it. Emotion is missing. Only the eyes count. Only curiosity is satisfied.

But how can anyone be blamed for reacting like this? Few people have the chance to live life slowly, to live amidst beautiful surroundings. You have to have luck to be able to do so. You have to have luck to avoid living life second-hand. You have to have luck to be able to enjoy the small pleasures.

Small pleasures like the spread of a red admiral butterfly on an ivy leaf in autumn. A green woodpecker with crimson head, clasped to the trunk of a bare tree. Golden plover in a ploughed field on a December afternoon. Red berries of hawthorn. Woodsmoke curling away from your own hearth. Piping of a snipe as it zig-zags like a flying firecracker away from you, safe because you have no gun. A December primrose, and you bend down, and the frail scent touches you, turning away your worldly cynicism. The daffodil spikes showing in the meadows where the donkeys enjoy their winter roaming. Time now to ban them because their hooves will crush the spikes. Small excitements . . . like the heron who slowly dropped into our reservoir one morning, floating down with legs hanging, like the wheels of an aircraft. I hurried to tell Jeannie, hiding the sound of my footsteps by walking where possible on grass. But the gull on the roof had also seen the heron, and was screeching, urging other gulls to screech too, until the heron floated up again from the reservoir, sedately climbing into the sky, ignoring the common people who were bawling at him.

Jeannie once imagined a joke method of measuring happiness. She invented in her mind an instrument called a happometer, designed on the same principle as a car milometer or a walker's pedometer, except that it was operated manually. Her idea was to measure each moment of happiness during the day by pressing a button on this happometer; a touch for a flash of happiness, a long touch for some out of the ordinary happiness. Thus a business tycoon might push long and hard at the button after a successful takeover bid, a politician perform the same after rousing an audience to hail a policy which gives him some personal kudos, and Jeannie would celebrate in the same fashion because, perhaps, she had been thrilled by the dying evening light on winter bracken, the sea beyond; or she had experienced delight in some small pleasure like an unsolicited purr from Lama. Her use of the happometer, therefore, displayed no practical appreciation of the sensible world we live in. Yet her reactions were of the kind which can bring another dimension to living ... if we are patient, cease sometimes to be community minded, if we allow emotion occasionally to govern us, instead of intellect. Then occur moments which can take us away from conventional reality. Aloneness, we discover, can be more rewarding than being part of a herd.

It was time to go. The storm had ended its skirmishing, ended its first flush of magnificence, and now had begun the hours of solid battering. There would be no work to do outdoors today. Geoffrey could saw logs, I thought, but first we had better go together to have a look at the ditch that ran down the hill beside the lane. A blockage, and the water would gush over into the lane itself, turning it into a river-bed, seering still further the already rough surface. Many occasions I had forgotten to check the ditch in time. And then I would take the donkeys into the stable whether they wanted to go or not. They themselves would be prepared to stand bottoms to a hedge throughout the storm, but I could not bear the lugubrious sight of them. So much more comforting as I sat indoors before the fire, to know that the donkeys were away from the gale and the rain.

I turned to go up the few steps and through the little gate to the big field when suddenly I had a feeling that I was being watched. A second later I saw Daisy, ten yards away, crouched at the foot of a bank of brambles.

'Daisy!' I called out, 'this is a mad place for you to be in such weather.'

She stared back at me, and I am sure she was thinking to herself that I, too, was mad. I had a home to go to where I could be dry and warm, so why wasn't I there? She belonged to the storms. She had been a part of them all her life, and she knew how to cope with them. She had hiding places, clefts in rocks, and earthy corners, an umbrella of undergrowth overhead. Yet why was she watching

95

me? She had always had this habit of watching, watching, watching. It seemed she wanted to involve herself with us but on the terms of her complete independence.

'Daisy,' I said, 'you are a funny cat the way you never ask for anything.'

Just a stare.

'And the way you never come within touching distance.'

Still a stare.

'Yet you behave as if you belong here. I wonder what goes on in that mind of yours.'

I left her where she was, not a sign of her wishing to come with me.

But she did come to us in the end. We touched her too.

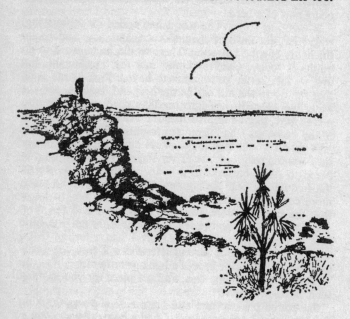

CHAPTER NINE

We had acquired during the summer a squirrel attitude towards the winter. We had decided to hoard. We aimed to create a supply situation whereby we could withstand a siege.

A caller first set me on this policy. We have many callers during the course of a year, and we learn much from them. One caller advised me to buy shares in the company he worked for because there was soon to be a takeover bid. The bid took place, the shares shot up, and I was left with a groan: 'Why didn't I take his advice?' Another caller was an expert at field mushroom growing, something which Jeannie had always wanted to do, and promised he would send us a bagful of the spawn at the appropriate time of the year. It never arrived, and this has left Jeannie with another groan: 'All Minack would now be littered with mushrooms if he had remembered to send it.' Other callers have been more productive. From university students one learns that the basic aspirations of youth are no different from one's own, years later in age. From others one discovers that solitude, in contrast to loneliness, is still considered by the sensitive to be a prize. Again and again one marvels at the courage that is shown by the sick and blind, and those that are victims of bad luck or great sadness; and always, surprisingly perhaps, one is aware of the happiness that most people have in each other's company.

There was, however, this caller, who put forward to us a very practical idea. She had brought her daughter to Minack to meet the donkeys; and while the girl was feeding Penny and Fred with the carrots she had brought, the mother began extolling to us the virtues of the deep freeze she had at home. I listened sceptically. I had heard other stories which did not measure up to her enthusiasm; and these stories had substantiated my instinctive distrust towards the machine, if a deep freeze can be called a machine. One friend described a luncheon party at which Dover sole from a deep freeze had been served with unfortunate results. Another described how, because of the box-like design of a deep freeze, one never reaches the frozen food stacked at the bottom. Another that meat from a deep freeze was always tough. There were also the usual accounts of frozen food possessing no flavour. Indeed, as far as I was concerned, frozen food was synonymous with tastlessness.

Our visitor now proceeded to correct this attitude of mine and, further, also proceeded to enlighten Jeannie as to the time and expense which she would be able to save if we possessed a deep freeze. It was at this moment that I realised that deep freeze addicts, like rally drivers, race-goers, football fans, and everyone else who is devoted to some particular hobby, are apt to overwhelm their listeners with their technical enthusiasm. Our visitor certainly overwhelmed me. She departed with her daughter leaving me in a haze; and I only wish I could have met her again to tell her that when I came out of the haze, Jeannie and I had become deep freeze addicts ourselves.

Thus when now I meet someone whom I believe would benefit from a deep freeze I immediately launch into the attack, ignoring the fact that it is none of my business.

'A deep freeze will change your life,' I cry, 'and the money you'll save will be enormous. Fish and meat wholesale! All those peas and runner beans which run to seed in your vegetable garden because there are too many to eat when they are ready . . . all these will be in the deep freeze. Then the fruit! Raspberries, strawberries and blackberries. And the ready cooked dishes like steak and kidney pie, and goulashes, and stews . . . Jeannie prepares a dozen at a time, a dozen meals which only have to be warmed up!'

At this stage, in true addict fashion, my enthusiasm has grown out of hand. I have adopted a missionary zeal. I am like a hot gospeller wishing to spread the good news that I have seen the light. My listener looks apprehensive. My listener, especially if he scarcely knows me, wonders how he can change the subject But I relentlessly continue to drive my points home . . .

This behaviour of mine, however, has often been prompted by the desire to find a subject of conversation. I am thrust into the company of someone with whom I seem to have little in common, find my sentences reaching nowhere, and so resort to the deep freeze. Thus I sometimes use the deep freeze as a ploy; and recently I used it as a ploy of minor revenge against a charming lady whom I sat next to at a luncheon party. This lady, as soon as she had sat down, and having no clue to my past or present, straight away shot this question at me.

'What *practical* things do you do?' she demanded.

I have learnt since, that this is a familiar question at diplomatic gatherings. It is a question that helps to bring a diplomat alive. You are in a crowded room, champagne glass in your hand, saddled with a diplomat from some new country you have never heard of, and you hurtle at him the question: 'What *practical* things do you do?' The answer is sure to be informative. It will give you an idea of the part of the world he comes from. He will be flattered that you are interested in such a personal way; and his attention will be held long enough for you to catch the eye of a friend who will come and rescue you.

I, however, failed to satisfy my luncheon companion with my answer, She had, in fact, taken me so much by surprise that my answer was a garbled sentence.

'Well, er . . .' I said, 'well, I write. I write books.'

This clearly did not fit in with diplomatic form. She had no notion of what books I had written, and my answer had given her no clue. So she repeated the question, this time with even greater emphasis on the word *practical*.

At this point I caught sight of Jeannie looking at me across the table with amusement. She had guessed I was having difficulties. I was in even greater difficulties a minute or two later.

My companion, casting a charming glance around the table, but still managing to make it seem she was waiting expectantly for my answer, now received an answer which even surprised myself.

'I also cook,' I said.

This indeed was a remark of desperation. It was certainly a foolish remark. It was not original. Had I been a diplomat from an undeveloped country it would have had no chance of bringing a light to the eye of a sophisticated official of the United Nations. There would have been no chance of a quietly taken note: 'Met an intelligent chap at the Mauretania party tonight. Must see what we can do for this new country of his.' No positive thought would come out of a remark like mine. I would have failed my new country. What United Nations official could possibly be interested in my cooking?

Clearly I was off balance. My companion had succeeded in unnerving me; and I believe the reason lay in the sweeping fashion that people, accustomed to meeting countless strangers, are sometimes inclined to appear superior as a means of personal defence. They cannot know everyone with affection, even though they might like to; and so they gush on with words that have no meaning. Or ask questions out of habit. As my delightful luncheon companion proceeded to do.

'Cook?' she said, toying with her smoked salmon, 'that's practical . . .' I thought at this moment that I had successfully dealt with the situation when she added: 'And *what* do you cook?'

This, of course, added to my confusion. I would have liked to have replied: 'Bangers!' . . . and left it at that. But my companion had succeeded in imposing her personality upon me; and I was now a little frightened of her. My muddled mind even wanted to impress her; and so a second or so afterwards I heard myself murmuring: 'I cook special dishes . . . very special dishes.' Just as if I was Robert Carrier.

It was a disastrous moment. My companion suddenly turned her full attention upon me, as if at last she considered I was a person of consequence.

'Special dishes?' she exclaimed, her voice throatily charming. '*Do* tell me . . . *what* special dishes do you cook?'

She had floored me, and I threw in my towel. I didn't even attempt a reply. I just looked at her and asked:

'Have you a deep freeze?'

Then launched my counter-attack.

I will now, however, quell my over-enthusiasm. I want to be serious about our deep freeze, and explain how its installation has influenced our daily lives. The daily life of Lama, for instance.

Lama turns up her nose at normal cat foods. She may consume the first spoonful of a newly opened tin, but that is enough. She walks away with her tail in the air if we offer her a second. Hence we have always tried to keep her supplied with fresh food; and when this has run out, so anxious have we been to please her that we have broken away from our work to drive the five miles to Newlyn and the butcher or the fishmonger. Not any longer. Not any longer are we faced by a bare larder, not any longer do we have to waste petrol and time catering for a cat. Nor do we have to pay the high prices of winter when storms have kept the fishing boats in harbour. At the end of September we bought 70 lbs of ling, a favourite Lama fish, at a glut price of ten new pence a pound, each pound in a polythene packet of its own; and for a change of diet packets of minced beef await to delight her.

Penny and Fred, on the other hand, gain no benefit at all. Nothing on their diet needs a deep freeze. Their carrots are stored in net bags, hay in bales, and the pony pellets for which they have a passion, in bags. But the gulls benefit in a roundabout way.

There are the five regulars. A pair who fly up from the Lamorna direction, a pair who come from our own rocks; and Philip, who usually comes when the others are absent. Philip is a sedate old boy, a contemplative gull, and he never shouts for his dinner. The others, however, bawl their heads off, and there has been many a time when I have been compelled to go out and bawl back at them: 'Shut up! Shut up!'

Earlier gulls of ours like old Hubert, Squeaker, Knocker, and Peter, certainly were raucous at times but never were they so persistently noisy as the present four. But they may have a reason.

These gulls used to have Jeannie's home-made wholemeal bread; but only Philip has it now as a kind of old age pension. The reason is that Jeannie found she was spending more time baking bread for the gulls than she was for ourselves, and so she rightly said the gulls would have to put up with shop bread. Unfortunately, up to this time, the gulls had shown no interest in shop bread. We had thrown pieces up on the roof but after a peck or two they had left the jackdaws to swoop on the roof and carry the pieces away. Therefore it took a while for the gulls to realise that they were living under a new regime; and that they were now obliged to eat the bread consumed by the majority of people in this country.

They did, of course, have changes of diet. Odd bits of

fat, fish skin, discarded pastry; and there were the occasions when we had eggs and bacon for breakfast. All of them seemed to know what we were having within a few minutes of the bacon sizzling in the frying-pan. They were after the rinds; and we tried to distribute them fairly, though we were always biased towards Philip. He was so much the more intelligent. Hence, on these occasions, he refused as always to mix with the others on the roof, but stood instead on a grey rock at the edge of the donkey field just above the cottage. Sometimes the donkeys were within nose touching distance of him; and when we threw a rind at him, he would catch it in his beak, then sail away into the sky, leaving the donkeys watching him.

The others, the noisy ones, have their shop bread in slices from packets; and before the arrival of the deep freeze the contents of these packets used quickly to go mouldy. Thus, although the gulls may desire Jeannie's bread, they at least now have their shop bread fresh.

Now this bread of Jeannie's is of remarkable quality. It *tastes* of bread; and I quite understand why the gulls preferred it to any other. It puzzles me sometimes why the bakery trade cannot offer bread of similar quality. They have the flour. They have the knowledge. But it seems the bakery trade has suffered more than most for the sake of efficiency and the cutting down of costs. Brilliant methods have been devised to produce their products with economy but without flavour; and a generation has grown up which expects no better.

When I was a Billy Bunter schoolboy I revelled in doughnuts, chocolate eclairs, Bourbon chocolate biscuits, various cream buns, and particularly a marvellous walnut cake with soft powdery icing on the top. But doughnuts do not taste like doughnuts any more, nor eclairs like eclairs, nor Bourbon biscuits like Bourbon biscuits; and the biggest disappointment of all is the walnut cake. It still has the same proprietary brand name as the cake with which my mother consoled me before my return after the holidays to school, a last present which she thrust into my hands while I wondered how much of it I would have to share with my schoolboy companions. Then it was a marvellous cake. Today the contents of the cake have the texture of froth. Mass production has ruined my schoolboy cake.

Jeannie's bread, of course, also now goes into the deep freeze. This is of special help to her because the bread requires an effort to make, even a manual effort, and she now can bake twice as much at a time. She used to bake four pounds a week, but by the end of the week the last loaf, though not stale, had certainly lost its newness. Now she wraps each loaf in a polythene bag, puts it in the deep freeze, and by the end of a fortnight the last loaf is as new as the first. Nor does a loaf take long to thaw out. A loaf brought from the deep freeze after breakfast is ready by lunchtime. And here is the recipe she uses. It is an old one and comes from her mother's family.

Out of three pounds of wholemeal flour and three teaspoonfuls of dried yeast, you can make four one-pound loaves. While the yeast is dissolving in a cup of warm water, you mix half the flour, a tablespoonful of brown sugar and one of coarse salt in a warmed basin. To this you add about one and a half pints of warm water mixing it all into a batter; then add the dissolved yeast, mix it in, and leave in a warm place for fifteen minutes or so. The rest of the flour is then emptied into the mixture and kneaded for five or ten minutes until the dough is firm and does not stick to your hands. After this the dough is cut into four sections, put into warmed, greased bread tins and left to rise in a warm place until the dough has doubled in size. Finally the tins are put in a very hot oven for about three-quarters of an hour; and after they are baked let them cool before putting them into the deep freeze.

Yet it is necessary to admit that the deep freeze, convenient though it may be, demands a great deal of Jeannie. It stands white and gleaming, an orange light at floor level denoting the motor is operating, constantly reminding her of the uses to which it can be put. Hence there are times when she appears to be the servant of the deep freeze rather than the other way round.

'I must spend the morning,' I will hear her say, 'making steak and kidney pies. We have only one left.'

Or:

'It's bread day tomorrow.'

Or:

'I have a whole basket of tomatoes which I must make into purée.'

The tomato purée is a basic content of the deep freeze; and there is the added appeal that we are no longer wasting the tomatoes which for one reason and another are not suitable for market, over-ripe tomatoes or misshapen. These we used to dump in a pile near the compost heap, giving delight to the blackbirds who considered them a delicacy, but causing distress to ourselves. The tomato purée, therefore, stored in one pint containers, has solved this problem of waste. There it is waiting, from one tomato season to another, to enrich a Provençale Bourguignonne or a Bolognaise sauce, or any other meat recipe which is enhanced by it.

Tomato purée, in any case, has a significance for me. This remark is not as absurd as it seems. Its significance is due to a freak period of my life when I founded a 'carry home a cooked meal' restaurant at Kingston-on-Thames, soon after the end of the war, one of the first of its kind.

The idea behind it seemed a good one. Food rationing was still stringent. Restaurant menus were limited and monotonous. Entertaining was very difficult; and I thought I had hit on an idea which would bring me a fortune. I foresaw a string of such restaurants. I imagined myself touring the sites and collecting the takings; and when, after a period, the success of the venture had become renowned, I would sell.

'Foolish,' a Savoy director warned Jeannie when she told him of the plans, 'your husband is very foolish.'

She repeated the comment to me, and I of course disregarded it. Business history is, after all, littered with Jonah-like warnings which have been proved false by those with initiative. Anyhow I was carried away by the enthusiasm which is my nature. I see no fun in life being told I am wrong even before I have made the effort to be right. Thus I launched the first restaurant, christened it The Larder, and looked forward to the bonanza.

It is soothing to look back upon a dismal period of one's life, and be able to say that at least one learnt something useful from it. It is a consolation prize for a time one otherwise wishes to forget. The consolation prize I had from The Larder was in the persons of two chefs, Bunny Pessione and Adam Almeida. Pessione was rotund, short and dark with black hair though in his late sixties; and an air about him of a man who had failed to fulfill his ambitions. Almeida was shorter, always clasping his stomach as if in pain, always talking about his retirement one day to his native Portugal, always with smudges of flour on his face. Both were artists in their way. Both belonged to the pre-war age. Both possessed a sense of service which would now be considered archaic. Both were wasted at The Larder. Both joined with me at riling at some of the customers.

I quickly discovered that my image of myself as an observer-manager, rather than a direct participant, was a silly dream. This was very annoying. I was involved in other, far more important tasks, and I considered that the sort of things I ought to do in helping The Larder were the sort of things I least wanted to do. Yet I realised that the money I had invested, and the little I had to keep the business running, would soon disappear unless I undertook a personal interest in its every day affairs. For one thing Pessione and Almeida would lose heart; and for another it was impossible to expect any manageress both to deal with the customers over the counter and also cope with the stores which the chefs required for their kitchen.

Thus I found myself embroiled in a kind of life which I quickly detested. Loyal people were doing all they could to help my idea to become a success, yet I sensed it was already a failure. Money was running out. Dreams of my becoming a temporary tycoon and gaining the capital which would have given us independence ... these dreams were quickly disappearing. I was now working to save what I could of my investment. I had to face the fact that the only thing I could do was to cut my losses, and pray for a buyer to come along and save me from greater trouble.

But waiting for a buyer in any circumstances is an unnerving experience. You dare not leave the house, you rush to the telephone only to find the caller has the wrong number, and you spend hours of your time determining in your mind whether the couple who appeared so keen would ever come back with a firm offer. If, however, you are trying to sell a failing business, the experience is still more unnerving. You greet the first prospective buyer with a forced jauntiness as you are aware the asking price is far above the true value of the business. You greet another prospective buyer, then another, and another, though there are often intervals when no one shows any interest at all, until at last you would be happy to give the place away so as to relieve you of the strain. That's what I practically did with The Larder.

Meanwhile, as I waited, the two chefs gave me their support. Almeida would clutch a rolling pin, wave it in the air, crying: 'Fools, what fools! All this good food, and the damned public pass us by!'

I remember my increasing irritation with the public during this nerve-wracking time. I had dispensed with the manageress and had taken her place behind the counter. I was now in the front line. I had to keep calm as a customer stared at a hamburger, then asked if I would sell half of it. I had to put up with sadistic customers who complained that our delicious chicken *vol au vent* had no flavour. I had to cope with the superior tone of a lady, holding a white pekingese on a lead who after buying one of our special Cornish pasties, remarked: '*If* I like it, you will see me again.' We didn't.

I had to offer fake laughs to customers who made jokes. One looked at my new sports jacket, made a wry smile, and said: 'Hardly the right coat to wear here!' 'Why?' I asked. 'It looks horsey,' came the hearty reply. I had to try to be pleasant when a fat lady, overdressed, over bejewelled, demanded: 'One sausage roll, please.' 'Sorry, madam,' came my answer, 'there are no sausage rolls today.' 'What else is there then . . .?' A pause, then she added: 'There is nothing!' Yet there were ten dishes on the menu.

Then there were the obsequious remarks I found myself making: 'And what can I tempt you with today, madam?' Or: 'Change in the weather, madam . . . well, we mustn't grumble after a wonderful summer.' (This was repeated *ad nauseam*.) There were comments from customers, some of them bewildered. 'Can you tell us where to sit down?' Or: 'What a marvellous idea!' Or: 'It smells like heaven in here!' Or there was the old journalist who ruminated: 'Kingston is a town of visitors. After half past five in the evening the town shuts down and divides itself into four parishes . . . St Luke's, St Mark's, St John's, and All Saints. They are like four pieces of cheese in silver packets. They look very nice together in a box, but they do not belong to each other. And that is Kingston.'

The kitchens were within easy sight of the customers. That was one of the best ideas of The Larder. Everybody could see what was happening. Everybody could see where the dishes they were taking home had been prepared. They could see the chefs, and the chefs could see them, and listen.

Thus Pessione would hear me say to a customer who had bought fried fish: 'Would you like a portion of Sauce Tartare to go with it? The sauce is specially made by the chef.' And Passione would hear the reply. 'Heavens, no. I don't like those made up sauces, nor does my husband. We prefer our sauces out of a bottle.'

Pessione, for the most part, appeared to be a phlegmatic person, keeping his temperament under control; but there were occasions, and this was such an occasion, when he rivalled in temperament a great French chef called Vatel under whom he had worked before the First World War at the old Carlton in the Haymarket. Vatel was preparing a banquet for a company of notables; and when the fish from the fishmonger failed to arrive in time, he became so upset that he stabbed himself to death in a corner of the kitchens. Pessione used to tell this story as proof that great chefs were also great artists with passionate souls. He loved this story. He would tell it often; and I am sure that while at The Larder he imagined himself sometimes emulating his hero. But for a different reason.

'Sauce Tartare!' I heard him cry out after the customer had disappeared into the street, 'so she prefers a sauce out of a bottle to my Sauce Tartare!' I now saw he was brandishing a carving knife in the air. 'Criminal! Typical of the people today. Sauces out of bottles and mackintoshes. That's all they think of!' He was not, as it happens, referring to Mr Wilson. Mr Wilson was unknown at the time. 'Yes,' Pessione went on, his voice rising, Almeida with flour on his nose watching him, smiling, 'the days of great chefs are over. Nobody has standards any more. Me? I am lucky. I am finished' . . . then turning to me, 'Ah, Mr Tangye, I am sorry. These customers with their dull minds drive me crazy. You want your lunch? I will give you again Spaghetti Bolognaise. My speciality. You will enjoy it but . . .' and he grinned at me, 'the base of the sauce will have to come out of a bottle!' I well remember that bottle, and the others like it. A concentrate of tomato purée which Pessione despised;

but we could not possibly afford to make purée from fresh tomatoes, and I am sure the customers would not have known the difference in any case. Pessione, therefore, would have appreciated Jeannie s purée, 'Ah,' I can hear him saying, no longer brandishing a carving knife, 'here is something good. Here is an ingredient which would have pleased the great chefs of the past!'

The deep freeze was at its most demanding during the late summer. Always, of course, during the winter there had to be the bread days, the stew and goulash days, the steak and kidney days; but it was in late summer that the basic stores were laid down for the imaginary siege we were pretending to withstand.

Vegetables, for instance. I had already in the spring perused my Suttons catalogue, and consulted our old friend Percy Potter, who has a parson as a son, and who himself is in charge of the Sutton Trial Grounds at Gulval on the Hayle side of Penzance. We have known Percy, who later this winter was to help us plan next year's cottage garden, since we first came to Minack; and whenever we were in particular distress, when gales or frost or gluts had hit us badly, we used to go to Percy for comfort. He is an instinctive gardener. Though able to talk detachedly about his work, he was so at one with the mystical side of growing, the growing which has nothing to do with laboratory-inspired theory, that you felt while listening to him that you were in the company of a missionary. Growing, you realised, can never be a wholly scientific exercise. Growing will always require the instinct of a Percy Potter if a garden is to flourish.

We had, of course, the usual array of lettuces, beetroots, parsley, chives, carrots, marrows, and so on during the summer; and for the winter we would be planting out brussels sprouts and cauliflower. Our quest, therefore, when we visited Percy, was to discover which varieties of peas, broad beans, and runner beans we should grow that were suitable for deep freezing; and the results were Enorma runner beans, Early Onward peas, Green Giant Longpod broad beans, and Gullivert petit pois. We grew seventy-foot rows of each of them, and wondered whether we had grown enough. Late summer showed that we had done so. More than enough.

For when we came to preparing them for the deep freeze, we were faced with a task we had not foreseen. We had baskets and baskets to shell or shred. We had them up on the bridge, and we sat there during the summer day, side by side like two old maids, gossiping, breaking off every now and then to greet a caller, picking up a pea pod, opening it, watching the peas shoot into the basin.

'It's almost full. I'll go and weigh them.'

'Not on your own,' I would protest. 'I'll help. You're not going to leave me alone with these baskets.'

The peas weighed, polythene packets of a pound each taken to the deep freeze, we would return to our work. A pea pod picked up, opened, thrown away into another basket. The routine became therapeutic. A warm day, a chaffinch cheeping, two gulls on the roof, Fred pawing at the gate, boats passing, Lama in her nest gently snoring . . . I found it a peaceful occupation shelling Early Onward peas.

The broad beans, too, were peaceful, even more peaceful because being larger they filled the basin quicker. We began to run into trouble, however, when we started on the runner beans because we had only one shredder and we argued as to who should use it. Runner beans have to be shredded first before they are put into the deep freeze; and we had searched Penzance for another shredder. No luck.

'You use it,' I would say to Jeannie, as if I was offering her out of good manners the first glass from a bottle of champagne, 'do use it. I can manage with a knife.'

'I wouldn't dream of doing so. I am perfectly happy as I am.'

Our polite conversation was clearly a little unreal. Our mundane task had affected us. We were like anyone who operates within a very small world. We were making private jokes. We found it mildly amusing to talk in stilted language.

The language, on the other hand, was not stilted when we came to the Gullivert petit pois. These have always been a special favourite of mine; and I remember answering an advertisement in a newspaper once which offered those special tins of Belgian petit pois at a considerable discount; and I remember my anger when, after sending the money, I did not receive the tins. These petit pois did not make me angry. They made me exhausted. The deep freeze was already stuffed with broad beans, runner beans, and conventional peas ... yet we were up on the bridge, side by side, trying to fill the basin with the miserable, tiny petit pois. Hour after hour we popped the little things into the basin while the basin showed little sign of filling. Hour after hour. And now, months after their pods tested our patience, I have become doubtful that we were wise to grow them in the first place. Those we have had from the deep freeze do not seem to have the magical flavour I had expected from those Belgian tins which never arrived.

They are there, though, in the deep freeze, along with the others. Not only the peas, and the broad beans and the runner beans. We have also the blackberries picked by ourselves and any friends we could persuade to help us; and we have apple purée made from our own apples, and strawberries, and raspberries.

We have, therefore, the supplies with which to withstand our imaginary siege. We are independent.

And that, after all, is what we have sought since we came to Minack.

Yet how permanent can be independence?

110

CHAPTER TEN

Nellie had her independence.

When the rains came day after day, when the cold winds blew, when snipe rose, zigzagging in front of us as we walked up the lane to fetch our milk from Walter and Jack's farm at the top, when owls in the wood hooted messages on frosty nights, when fluttering flocks of linnets, finches and starlings raided a field then another, when summer snails were asleep in crevices, when the donkeys preferred to shelter in the stables, and we ourselves were glad to be indoors beside the fire, Nellie behaved as if she was impervious to the weather.

She continued to settle on the glass roof of the porch from time to time during the day; and when we threw grain to her on the ground, she was as bossy as ever towards the blue tits who tried to have a share. She was vociferous towards them. She burbled insults and threats, then she would make a dash at one who was proving to be too bold; and when the grain had gone, she would follow us as we walked by, expecting more. She was attached to us, that was clear. She liked our companionship, liked to observe the comings and goings of Minack, liked the way we took care of her; but she remained aloof. She had no intention of becoming a pet bird. We were a convenience, no more. She had no wish for us to touch her; and she was expert in evading our attempts to do so. And even in the stormiest weather, she always flew away at dusk.

'We must find out where she goes,' I said to Jeannie. I often said this.

I would say it at some point during the day with the intention that in the late afternoon I would put myself on sentry duty; and watch.

'If we went to Carn Barges,' I would add, 'and took our field-glasses, we could see her leave and the direction she takes.'

It seemed so easy. I had the time.

'Yes,' Jeannie would answer, 'let's do that.'

It was surprising, therefore, how the days and weeks

went by without putting our good intentions into practice. Something trivial was always enough to stop us. Brussels sprouts had to be picked for dinner, or the donkeys required attention, or I had to fetch coal or logs, or Lama wanted to have a stroll up the lane, expecting me to go with her. Then by the time these small tasks had been completed, I would find that Nellie had already gone. Or, if I was near her, I would hear the warning she always gave when she was about to go. She would coo a determined kind of coo, reminding me of a roll of drums heralding a great event.

Our behaviour on these winter evenings, this lack of will-power to follow up our wish to discover where Nellie flew away to, is evidence of the pleasant form of corruption which had engulfed us. We knew we had the time to amble through the day, and we were allowing ourselves to do so. The daffodil spikes were only beginning to show in rows, and blooms could not be expected until the middle of January; and I was not writing a book. This was the between times of the year, between summer and spring harvests, and we were at liberty to do what we liked with our time. Thus we found ourselves putting off making decisions, however small. We relaxed; and enjoyed this particular form of corruption.

Yet there were moments when we had a sense of guilt that we were content. After all it is unfashionable to be content. It is an age of protest, and of injustice real or imaginary, and of violence, and of haste, and of the cynic who knocks the pleasant aspects of life. Any good cause, or person of integrity, is a potential victim of the cynic. It is so easy to win sniggering laughs by knocking. I listened not long ago to one of the professional cynics making witty comments about King George VI. The King, he inferred, had been a nonentity, a colourless figurehead, someone whom the present generation should laugh at. But those of us who lived through his times, through the war period when surrender would have been inevitable unless there had been a man like the King upon whom to focus our loyalty, will always remember him with great admiration. And I will also always remember a sentence from the speech he made on V.E. Day.

'Let none of us,' said the King, 'do anything unworthy of what those who have died would have expected of us, or let our children ever do anything unworthy of what was sacrificed for them.'

But Jeannie and I did not allow our fleeting moments of guilt to interfere with the enjoyment of each day. We were now experiencing the kind of life we had always wanted to experience. We were not rushed. We had no need to see people. We had comforts around us. We had worked hard, and thus this idleness was a holiday. We were aware of our luck, and neither of us took it for granted.

'What shall we do today?' I would say to Jeannie as I lit my pipe after breakfast. I smoke a mixture called Down the Road which comes from the old family firm of Simmons in Burlington Arcade. I have smoked the same mixture for years; and soon after I met Jeannie we were walking together down the Arcade and I pointed out the shop to her. 'That's my tobacco shop,' I said, 'and where I get my pipes.' She said afterwards that she thought I was giving her a hint. She insists that I also added: 'Every girl should know the whereabouts of her man friend's tobacco shop.' I am sure she is imagining this. I have to admit, though, that she gave me a pipe soon after that walk down the Arcade.

'What shall we do?'

First there were the mundane tasks which had to be done, like tidying the cottage and washing up. We do not have anyone to help inside the cottage; and though there would be obvious advantages if there was such a person, we both relish the freedom we have as a result of being on our own. We do not have to do any cajoling, or wondering why extra presents are not appreciated, or any soothing of mysterious, ruffled tempers. True we have been lucky in those who have helped in the past but we prefer to be free. And on those occasions when Jeannie momentarily regrets the tasks she has to do, I pick up a Bristol glass hand-bell which I bought long ago, and which is known by us as the Freedom Bell. I pick it up and ring it.

'We ought to move the wine,' said Jeannie

'That won't take long.'

'We've been meaning to move it for ages.'

'All right,' I said, with sudden decisiveness, 'before I do anything else I'll carry the cases to the donkey house.'

The donkey house was another name for the stables where the donkeys had the opportunity to spend the rough winter nights; and because the walls were arm-length thick, it was a warm place to be; and suitable for the storage of the wine Jeannie had made. The cases were of cardboard.

'Only hope,' I added, 'that the donkeys won't eat the cardboard.'

'If they do,' said Jeannie, 'they are unlikely to pull out the corks.'

'But supposing they suddenly lash out and kick the bottles and break them?'

'Isn't this where it all began,' asked Jeannie mildly, 'isn't this why we haven't moved the cases? . . . all because we waste our time wondering what the donkeys might do?'

I laughed.

'Agreed.'

We used to despise home-made wine. We used to consider it a concoction devised by worthy people who needed a hobby. Then a couple of years ago we experimented, produced a few bottles of elderberry champagne and elderberry claret, and found them delicious. Then we looked at our wine bills, and asked ourselves why we were wasting money. We had the opportunity on our doorstep to make all the *vin ordinaire* we needed; and we calculated, without allowing for the labour involved, that it would cost little more than five new pence a bottle.

We are now aware, of course, that home wine-making is rapidly becoming a profession, and not just a hobby. The economical reasons for this are obvious; and those who take their wine-making seriously can organise a cellar of very high quality. I am not, of course, referring to instant wine made out of packets which you can buy at a chemist. The old recipes are the ones to follow, the same that have been used by countrymen for generations; and based on ingredients which abound in the countryside.

In due course Jeannie and I intend to experiment still further. We have a list of old recipes given to Jeannie by her aunt who is an expert; and they include wines from marigolds, primroses, cowslips, rose petals, clover, dandelions and hawthorn blossom. Then you can make wine from beetroots, carrots, celery, pea pods, and old potatoes. Potato wine, we are assured, tastes like dry sherry after letting it stand for three months, and like old brandy if left for over a year. Gorse petal wine is another good one; and so is blackberry which matures like a kind of *vin rosé*. I would not believe the claims made for any of these wines, were it not for the success we have had with our elderberries.

The elderberry champagne is made from the flowers of the elder-tree, picked during June; and the claret from the berries picked in September and October. The elder-tree itself plays a large part in folk lore, particularly in regard to its healing qualities. The flowers once upon a time were used as the base for a healing ointment for cuts and burns. The freshly gathered leaves, warmed in an oven, are supposed to relieve headaches when pressed against the head. The berries, when green and stewed in camphorated oil, become a medicine for coughs and bronchitis. Then there are the superstitions which haunt the tree. An unhappy home will become a happy one if a tree is coaxed to flourish in the garden; and such a tree will ward off wickedness, so that anyone advancing with evil thoughts on the house and its occupants finds himself powerless. Such a legendary background enhances the pleasure of drinking the wine. We are put in a virtuous mood. We are benefiting our bodies as well as stimulating our minds. No wonder we had made several cases both of the champagne and the claret which I now had to move to the donkey house.

The move was no distance. Our wine-making centre was in one half of the small greenhouse where we bunch daffodils in the spring, and weigh tomatoes in the summer. It was a convenient place for the equipment because there was a bench for the jars and buckets, and a cement floor where the messy side of wine-making could be done. It need not, however, be all that messy. It is just a question of trying to avoid spilling the contents of the bucket when transferring these contents to the jars; and of trying to avoid spilling the contents of the jars when transferring them to the bottles. Having said this, let me explain how we achieved this cellar of wines from which we will be drinking next summer.

We picked the elder flowers on sunny days when they were scenting, and when they were fully opened and the petals were beginning to fall. We picked them from the many elders we have at Minack, some bordering the lane, some down the cliff where they act as hedges around the daffodil meadows. In summer, of course, the daffodil leaves have died back and the meadows are covered by lush grass and vegetation; and this gives pleasure and feed for the donkeys. The donkeys usually accompanied us on these expeditions, and they would watch puzzled as I climbed up to a branch to collect a handful of flowers. Is he doing it for us? He's filling that yellow bucket, let's put our noses into it. They would then advance on me, and I had to push them away, thinking nevertheless that it was pleasant to be accompanied by donkeys in one's own vineyard so close to the sea.

We had to measure the quantity of the flowers, and we did this by gently pressing the flowers into a quart jug until it was full. This we did when we returned to the greenhouse, putting them back afterwards into the plastic bucket. Then, for each quart jug of flowers, we brought a gallon of water to the boil in a preserving pan containing a pound of seedless raisins and two and a half pounds of preserving sugar, letting it simmer for half an hour and removing the scum. We next poured this through a sieve over the flowers in the bucket; and when it had cooled, we added the strained juice of a lemon and an ounce of dried yeast scattered on the surface. We then left this to brew for a fortnight, stirring each day with a wooden spoon (never a metal one); and then strained all the contents though a piece of butter muslin and a funnel into a gallon glass jar. The jar has a special stopper which enables the brew to ferment without bursting the jar; and there followed the pleasantest part of wine-making. We were able to watch the brew at work, bubbling, until several weeks later when there was no more bubbling to be seen and the wine was ready to go into bottles.

The method of making claret was similar. We picked the berries, shredding them from the stalks, then went through the same routine as for the champagne except we used demerara sugar instead of preserving sugar and did not add raisins. As for the pleasure the wine will give, I can only say that last year's vintage was magnificent. The champagne had a soft effervescence, and a flavour like the true scent of elderberry flowers on sunny days; and the claret had a body to it, and a style, that deceived a guest, an expert on wine, into asking who shipped the claret. Unfortunately, although we had this summer many more bottles than we had for the first year of experiment, there was still not enough. They had all gone by the time I was moving the cases of the new vintage; and we now have to wait till next summer before we taste this new vintage. Jeannie believes it will be finer than ever before.

My grandfather, Sir Richard Tangye, disapproved of alcohol in any form; beer, spirits or wine. He claimed that his total abstinence was a basic reason for his successful life, and he never ceased telling his friends, work associates, and his children to follow his example. The children were loth to do so. My aunt Elsie told me that she so rebelled against his fanatical attitude that she used to slip into the bar of Snow Hill station in Birmingham, and have a quick one; and she gulped the drink as a gesture of defiance. Nor was my father teetotal, though he believed that neither myself nor my two brothers should drink alcohol before we were twenty-one. He therefore offered us each £100 if we did not do so, and put us on our honour to keep our side of the bargain. My two elder brothers collected their money but I, alas, was out of luck. At the age of twenty my father, one of the most generous men I have ever known, explained to me that his funds were low, that he would not be able to give the £100, and so I could do what I liked. Even then I never went into a pub until I was nearly twenty-two, but that perhaps was for a snobbish reason. My Harrovian education had led me to believe that pubs were vulgar, and not the happy, friendly places I later found them to be.

My grandfather was a remarkable man. He was born at Illogan near Redruth, one of five brothers. His own grandfather came from St Columb near Newquay where he worked as a boy on a farm. He was still a boy when he decided to set out for the tin mines of west Cornwall, and he walked on his own, except for his small dog, all the way to Illogan carrying on his back his only possession, a saddle. There he obtained a night job in the mines, and shortly after some rough land of rocks and gorse, and this he worked at during the day. He lived to his nineties, and Richard describes in one of his books how the old man died. A Citizen Kane kind of end ... for he relived that walk from St Columb to Illogan and his last words were: 'Has the little dog come in yet?' Richard himself a dog lover delighted in this sentimental story. He also described it as a lesson in loyalty.

117

His father had a shop in Broad Lane, Illogan, and also ten acres of land which he used to plough in Quaker dress and broad-brimmed hat. The sons, however, had no intention of following this quiet profession; and in any case four of them had the qualities of genius. Richard and George were the ones with a business flair; Joseph and James, particularly James, were the inventors. So in due course these four left Illogan to find fortune in the Midlands and within twenty years they had founded the Cornwall Works in Birmingham where two thousand people were to be employed, and had also made the name of Tangye world famous for its engineering products.

Often their inventions came before their time. A bicycle proved a failure because it seemed to be so unusual; and the 'road locomotive' was a failure because the landed gentry were afraid that their horses would take flight at the sight and the sound of it. But the road locomotive was a remarkable achievement. The Tangye brothers called it the Cornubia; and it could travel at twenty miles an hour, and could carry ten people. The first Cornubia was on the road in the early 1860's and created enormous public interest; and the brothers were right to believe they were about to make their fortune. But the landed gentry had powerful friends in Parliament; and as a consequence an Act was passed forbidding any machine to proceed along the highway at more than four miles an hour, and even then it had to have a man walking in front holding a red flag. This did not deter the Tangye brothers. They scrapped the Cornubia, and set about developing other inventions.

They had already had one major success; and this was an improved version of the hydraulic jack which on a day in January 1858 was to create a legend. Isambard Brunel had built his steamship the *Great Eastern*, and found he was unable to launch his ship down the slipway into the Thames. The jacks he was using would not budge her. Having heard of the Tangye invention, he told his agent to contact the brothers. They still at that time had only a small workshop in Birmingham which was down an entry behind a baker's shop (the baker's oven saved the expense of heating the workshop); and when the agent one dark evening rang the bell, he was sure he had come to the wrong place. He apologised for his mistake when Richard opened the door. 'I'm looking for Tangye's,' the man explained, 'Mr Brunel needs their jacks to launch the *Great Eastern*!' Forever afterwards Richard used to say: 'We launched the *Great Eastern*, and the *Great Eastern* launched us.' Twenty years later Tangye jacks gained further fame when they hoisted Cleopatra's Needle into position on the Victoria Embankment; and one of the jacks was placed in a recess of the base where it still lies, along with worthy companions including a map of the London of the time, the book of Genesis in Arabic and Hebrew, copies of the newspaper of the day, weights and measures, and copies of the Bible in various languages. I have often walked along the Embankment, or looked down upon the obelisk from one of the Savoy windows, and felt proud that my family played a leading part in placing it there.

Richard, apart from his business acumen, was a man of liberal ideas. He was a great philanthropist, kept to strict rules of honour throughout his life, believed his work people were as good as himself and that they should always receive a fair reward for their work. He expected their loyalty as a result (there were never any strikes at the Cornwall Works), and was convinced that a job of a great industrialist was to be paternal. His paternalism certainly produced reforms. He was the first industrialist in this country to introduce the nine-hour day, the first to give a half-day on Saturday, the first to pay wages on a Friday, the first to provide a canteen for the workers, and the first to provide a free health service. These reforms were strongly supported by all the brothers, especially George, but they caused displeasure among other industrialists; for the reforms were taking place towards the end of the nineteenth century, and the industrial barons resented the Tangye brothers weakening their power by a liberal example.

Richard, in fact, could have become a politician of note. He was repeatedly asked to stand for Parliament and Gladstone urged him to stand for Birmingham. Lord Rosebery, too, was anxious that he should enter political life. But my grandfather seemed to consider a political career of little appeal because he believed a successful industrialist could serve the community more usefully by retaining his freedom. Nor did he believe in honours. A peerage did not interest him, and he only in the end accepted his knighthood because he truly considered it as a compliment to the people of the Cornwall Works.

He was also a collector, and a great traveller. He was a frail man, small with a flowing beard, and I marvel at his energy and his boldness in carrying out his travels. America, Australia, New Zealand . . . he made journeys to such places in little boats, unperturbed by the discomfort. He and his brother George gathered together the finest private collection of Wedgwood pottery in the world, then presented it to the City of Birmingham (a few pieces were kept in the family and Jeannie has a brooch from a medallion); and he also became one of the great authorities on Cromwell, writing a notable book called *The Two Protectors—Oliver and Richard Cromwell.*

My mother, however, did not like him. 'A funny little man,' she used to say, dismissing him in a feminine way; and I have often wondered why. My mother was a darling person who devoted herself completely to the bringing up of us three boys. She was prepared happily to make any sacrifice if it had the likelihood of advancing the happiness of myself or that of my two brothers; and I have never had any doubt that she possessed a selfless and generous nature. Yet she disliked my grandfather; or perhaps she was frightened of him. I think also it is likely that she failed to impose her personality upon my grandfather; and this nettled her. At the time she married Gilbert my father, Richard was a dying man; and I can understand that he might have been suspicious of my mother's flirtatious ways. She intended by her manners to show him the warmth she had for the Tangye family; but he, I guess, interpreted her youthful enthusiasm as being an affront to his Cromwellian principles. In any case, my mother's rebuff, if she did indeed receive a deliberate rebuff, resulted in my never realising my grandfather's true worth until years after I should have done.

I wonder, too, why my father did not enlighten me. My father was a successful barrister before the 1914 war when he volunteered and entered Intelligence. After it was over he decided to stay in the army instead of returning to the law; and I believe it was a decision he always regretted. There were, however, compensations, not the least being able to satisfy his love of music. The England of that time had a philistine attitude towards music while in Germany, in Cologne and Wiesbaden where we lived, the opera houses were playing to enraptured audiences; and legendary singers were appearing like Lotte Lehmann and Frederick Schorr, and conductors such as Bruno Walter and Otto Klemperer. Such performers provided emotional experiences for myself and my brothers; and my father helped us in every way to indulge in them. In my holidays from my English preparatory school, I would spend three or four nights a week at the opera house and, because evening dress was obligatory, I would wear an Eton collar, the uncomfortable starched Eton collar, as I sat through four hours of *The Mastersingers*. My taste was catholic. I loved Puccini, and was undaunted by *The Ring*, was thrilled equally by Richard and Johann Strauss, delighted in Mozart, and was specially excited when on an advance poster I saw that an obscure opera like *Die Toten Augen* by d'Albert was to be performed. I am in everlasting debt to my father that he awoke me to music; and now, years later, as I sit sometimes in the cottage at Minack, listening for a whole evening, for instance, to *Karajan* and the *Gotterdamerung*, and at moments becoming as emotional as I became when I first listened to the music as a small boy, I return in my mind to my seat in the dress circle of the Cologne opera house, and I am wearing again my Eton collar.

When my father returned from Germany, he soon became Joint Chairman of the Cornwall Quarter Sessions, and then, until he died during the Second World War he performed, endlessly, various public duties. He was also for a period, chairman of Tangyes though it was now a very different business from that of my grandfather's day. The business was struggling to survive. For more than thirty years it never paid a dividend though the employees continued to be looked after in a benevolent manner. The origin of this debacle was due to praiseworthy high-mindedness during the First World War years, when engineering firms were making huge profits out of munitions and war materials. Tangyes, however, refused to make a penny profit; and when the war ended and the slump came, they did not have the reserves to cope with the situation. There is no Tangye in the firm now and it belongs to a combine.

Glendorgal was my father's home as it had been Richard's.

It had a glorious position above its own inlet of a bay at Porth near Newquay; and it faced up the north coast, the high jagged coastline of Watergate Bay, Bedruthan Steps and in the far distance Trevose Head. It was here that my grandfather kept his unique collection of Cromwellian relics which later became part of the Wallace Collection in Stafford Place after the Tangye family had given it to the nation. It was housed at Glendorgal in a large room with a glass roof, and which I knew as the billiard-room when I was a boy. I used to play billiards by the hour either by myself or with my father; and occasionally with my brothers. My brothers, then, were remote people to me; and years later they told me that they didn't even notice my existence until I went to Harrow. We had left Germany by then. Later on, when we began bringing girls to Glendorgal, the billiard-room became a party room; and after dinner we would adjourn with our girls to the party room while our parents sedately read their papers. We used to listen to the *Welte*, a superior kind of pianola or automatic piano, which my father had brought back from Germany, or to a record player, or to the piano itself being played by one of ourselves. We used to sit in an alcove of the billiard-room on a long curved seat covered by worn leather, with the huge window behind us facing up the north coast I have described; and at night, when we looked through it, we could watch the winking of Trevose lighthouse just as today I can watch from Minack the winking of the Lizard light. My father, for some reason, always called the Trevose light Becky's Eye. The girls we brought to Glendorgal lived in London, for we knew no local girls. The girls were young actresses, and models, and some who had nothing else to do except to be debs; and we used to bring them for long weekends, hastening to and from Cornwall in our cars. I wonder what has happened to some of them, what they did with their lives. When we sat in that alcove we believed life stretched without end in front of us, only momentary problems to solve, like the young in any age, the same outlook except for the fashions of the time. But within a year or two these pretty things were in uniform, or in love with a pilot in the Battle of Britain, or driving ambulances as the bombs fell on London.

I loved Glendorgal in the same way I now love Minack. I belonged. I knew every part of it, every incline, every rock;

and I was emotionally involved in the place so that there was hardly a corner of it which did not share with me some secret, personal experience. When I went to Glendorgal I never wanted to leave its environment, just as now I never want to leave Minack. Both belong in my mind to a world which is untamed; and therefore true and unselfconscious. I never knew an unhappy moment at Glendorgal.

My father was an example to me for the love of roots. His public duties took him often away from his home but, whereas others would have stretched a visit to three days, my father would hurry back to Glendorgal within two. He loved my mother. That was one reason; and in forty odd years of their marriage there was not a day, even during the wars, that he did not write to her if they had not seen each other; and yet Glendorgal was in a way even more important to him than my mother. Glendorgal gave him a mystical sense of security. He was, like all the Cornish, inspired in the final instance by Cornish magic. The Cornish, and this is their secret, are aware that the senses provide happiness. Materialism doesn't, except that it helps. Only a fool would say it doesn't help.

My father, therefore, awakened in me the emotional side of living yet, erudite man though he was, failed to educate me. I do not remember him ever extolling the virtues of 'the little man' who was his father. Probably this was my fault. He may have tried, and I had shown no interest. I have often been amazed in retrospect at the periods in my life when I have been blind to the advantages which were staring me in the face. If someone is prepared to unfold his experience and knowledge, the listener must be in the mood to be receptive; and there have been many times in my life when I was not in the mood. Thus I do not blame my father for my failure to benefit from what he could have offered me. I am thankful enough that I inherited from him his love of Cornwall.

Snow fell before Christmas, and Nellie continued to fly away from Minack at dusk. Geoffrey had made a loft for her out of an old box and fixed it high up on the wall in the barn, a cosy home in such weather, but though she would sit there during the day, she did not like it as a bedroom. She had a better place to go. Where?

We do not often have snow. Once, in our time here, there was a day-long blizzard which blocked our road into St

Buryan, and it remained blocked for a week; and there was a legendary blizzard at the end of the last century which isolated many of the farms for six weeks. On the present occasion the snow was thick enough in the lane to prevent a car driving up the hill; and so I was glad that I had taken heed of the snow warnings and taken the car up to the top by the farm buildings, and left it there. When the snow ceased falling, the wind had gone round to the east, and it was bitter cold.

We do not mind snow, now that we do not grow crops, like violets, which can be hurt by it; and we even like it because there is amusement in tracing the spoors . . . the V sign of rabbits, the straight line of a fox, the spread of a badger, the petals of a cat. A simple pleasure, but sometimes illuminating; and we were following at dusk the fresh spoor of a fox, along the path towards the onion meadow and the Pentewan meadows, and we had reached the boundary which divides them when a pigeon skimmed our heads. It had disappeared within a second into the cold greyness, but not before we saw the direction it was taking.

We had found at last the whereabouts of Nellie's sleeping quarters.

CHAPTER ELEVEN

Nellie's sleeping quarters, we now realised, were close to the lighthouse. Nobody lives at the lighthouse. It is half a mile away on the Pentewan cliff, and is hidden from our sight by the hill behind us. Nor do we see it from any other part of our land, save from a couple of meadows that lie below the onion meadow. Strange, however, for Nellie to choose such a place. There was a flashing light that might have been expected to disturb her, and the sound of the fog signal known as Howard's Howl.

Some people consider Howard's Howl a romantic sound, a reminder of the wildness of this coast, conjuring up a picture of small boats fighting great seas. One person thought it a reassuring sound. 'Isn't it company for you in that lonely place of yours?' he asked.

Such cosy impressions however, are not shared by Jeannie and me. We know too much about Howard's Howl. We have heard it too often howling away when the visibility around us is clear. On such occasions I sometimes jump in the car and drive to the nearest telephone box and telephone the duty officer of the Trinity headquarters in Penzance.

'You can see right across the bay,' I will say in desperation, 'can't you turn the damn thing off?'

He can't. He has to obey the Trinity House regulations; and these regulations decree that if there is less than three miles visibility at Tol Pedn coastguard station five miles up the coast from the lighthouse, the fog signal must be switched on; and also the same situation exists at Penzance five miles down the coast; and most curious of all, if there is fog thirty miles away across the bay at the lighthouse on the Lizard.

Thus, although our lighthouse is described as automatic by Trinity House, it is only automatic as far as the light is concerned. This turns on as soon as dusk falls, but Howard's Howl? A report comes in from Tol Pedn or the Lizard, and the controller at Penzance presses the button. Five miles away we hear the result.

'Blast it!' I cry, 'Howard's Howl is at it again, and I can count six ships on the distant horizon!'

The irritation we feel is, of course, insignificant compared with others who have noise problems. We have no whine of aircraft to disturb our days and nights. We have no drills roaring on a building site. We have no traffic to shatter us into taking its thunder for granted. We are lucky therefore. We are only irritated.

We are particularly irritated because Howard's Howl is an unreliable warning system. Its effectiveness depends upon which way the wind is blowing. We can tell, because when the wind is blowing up the coast away from us, we can scarcely hear Howard's Howl. But if the wind is blowing from the south towards us, the sound can be heard on the road halfway to Penzance; and if this is at night, sleeping countrymen are awakened by the sound far inland.

Thus Howard's Howl is of dubious value, for if it is a rough sea, a strong wind blowing, only boats sailing against the wind will hear it. There is a good reason, therefore, why some people argue that its cost could have been better spent elsewhere . . . helping to eliminate black spots on the road for instance. Motorists are far more in need of help than some occasional sailor who has carelessly strayed off course.

Weeks go by, however, when the weather is clear all round the coast, and Howard's Howl is silent, and we find ourselves forgetting that its electronic note exists. This was the case this Christmas. All through December it had kept quiet, and neither ourselves nor Nellie had been disturbed. Not that we knew until now that Nellie was sleeping her nights so close to it.

'Let's find out this evening,' I said to Jeannie next day, 'exactly where she's going to. If we're by the lighthouse steps a quarter of an hour before dusk we'll be able to see her flying in from Minack.'

It is one of the luxuries of having time to spare that we could indulge in such a frivolous quest. These minor moments of pleasure are repeated all through the year, pointless moments perhaps, but helping to provide a depth to living.

'It's time,' Jeannie replied, 'that we did so. Silly Nellie, flying away from the comfort we offer her.'

We were, I suppose, a little put out by her behaviour. Geoffrey had made her a splendid box in which she could shelter from the weather, and yet she ignored it. She preferred to desert us at the very moment when the temperature was swiftly dropping, flying away from the comfort of Minack, in favour of some ledge on a cliff.

It was bitterly cold when we set off. It had been bitterly cold all day; and the water-butt by the corner of the cottage had remained frozen over; so, too, the donkeys' water trough, once the china kitchen sink, but now wedged in the hedge of the field above the cottage, a pipe connecting it with the tank by the well. The pipe was frozen also; and I reckoned we were lucky that the main pipe to the cottage was still running.

Blackbirds and redwings clucked their warning notes as we walked along the grass path towards the onion meadow and the Pentewan boundary. Redwings distress me. I have watched them in many winters when the cold comes, foraging in the banks after the sun of the morning has melted the snow and softened the earth; and there is always a mood of desperation about their efforts. They belong to the thrush family, and nest in the far north of Scandinavia so that you would have expected they were immune to cold. At the first sign of winter they fly across the North Sea in their thousands, settle in the north until Britain, too, begins its winter, then start to fly south. They now seem to panic. They fly south, south, south, just ahead of the frost and the snow, across Dorset, Somerset, Devon until they reach the north coast of Cornwall, then down the coast to Land's End, round the corner, and up again in their thousands, lemming like, along the cliffs of Mount's Bay, up the south coast into the very cold again. I have picked up dozens of casualties in some winters, some I have tried to save, taking them into the warmth, but I have never succeeded. They are easy victims of pneumonia, and no care can help them.

We reached the boundary between our land and the Pentewan meadows, climbed over the stone stile we have built there, went past the Trinity House notice declaring that no one was allowed in the vicinity of the lighthouse, then crossed the thirty lace meadow. A lace is the Cornish means of measuring a meadow. A lace is, in fact, six yards by six yards; and in our potato days we used to follow the custom of our neighbours by judging the extent of our crop by the quantity extracted from each lace. Hence if in some meadow we dug half a hundredweight of potatoes per lace, it was a very bad crop. If it was two hundredweight, it was a very good one. The thirty lace meadow, however, when we worked the Pentewan meadows, unfailingly produced a bad crop. The potatoes were always the size of marbles.

We went on past the Dairyman's Meadow where seventy years ago a donkey used to graze. An elderly lady came to Minack the other day who lived as a child in the same Pentewan cottage where Jane used to live when she was working for us. She told us how her father used to use this donkey to carry the potatoes up from the lower meadows on the cliff; and how she herself, as a child, was taught to drive the donkey in a trap, driving it regularly into St Buryan. Naturally she asked if Penny and Fred did any work; and I replied that they didn't, only gave pleasure. I half expected her to snort a reply that I wasn't making proper use of them but to my surprise she said how wise I was to let them live their life in this way. 'Our donkey,' she explained, 'had the usual donkey fate of being asked to do more than he was capable of doing. One morning he was carrying up a load of potatoes from where the lighthouse now stands, and it was too heavy for him. Just as he reached the path that leads to the cottage, he slipped. And he broke his fetlock. Father killed him then, there was nothing else he could do . . . and he buried him in one of the meadows by the path.'

Just past the Dairyman's Meadow is a hut, known as the Pink Hut. It was a hut built of corrugated iron before the First World War, painted red, and now faded into a dirty pink. Here we used to 'shoot' our seed potatoes, remorselessly picking each one from the sack in which they had travelled from Scotland, and setting it side by side with the others, eyes of the potatoes facing upwards. It was here, too, that we helped save a badger caught in a gin trap, which had been released by the trapper who had taken pity on it. For weeks we fed it with bread and milk. And then one day we arrived at the Pink Hut, and found, it seemed, that a pick axe had been at work on the wood based floor. It was, however, only the badger. He had recovered. He was well enough to leave. He had dug his way to freedom.

We now reached the site of the lighthouse. There was an old quarry biting into the side of a hill above it, the stone of which, in the middle of the last century, built the lanes of St

Buryan. The site itself was a narrow strip of land diving down to the sea with the lighthouse at the bottom. A number of cemented steps led downwards, and on either side of them was a cemented ramp designed to take the Trinity House Land Rover. It was a steep ride for the driver, not one that I would enjoy.

A grey-painted gate was at the head of the steps, and along-side a notice-board, black lettering on white, similar to the one on our boundary: THE PUBLIC IS PROHIBITED . . . etc. A threatening, authoritative notice, incongruous on such a beautiful coast, but necessary. An unattended, well publi-cised, lighthouse begged the attention of vandals.

Jeannie and I were not vandals, but we felt apprehensive. We were trespassers; and as we started down the steps I wondered what I would say if some official suddenly appeared and demanded an explanation. 'I'm looking for the sleeping quarters of a pigeon,' I heard myself replying. An unconvinc-ing reply at a time of day when dusk was falling and the temperature was well below zero.

We were halfway down when we caught sight of Nellie in the sky. She came flying from the direction of the onion meadow and Minack, swerved round the lighthouse, and then plummeted out of sight beneath the edge of the cliff. The light was falling quickly, and the lamp was already sweeping the sea as we hurried down the remainder of the steps, ran round the side of the lighthouse, and peered over the point where she had disappeared.

The sea was fifty feet below us, grey against the snow on the land, and still as on a quiet day in summer. A company of gulls glided above our heads, and I saw a cormorant beating its wings a few feet above the water flying towards Lamorna. The rocks looked black though in daylight you can see the blue in them . . . blue elvin rock it is called; and, as if we were in the far north, I saw icicles on the rocks formed by seeping land springs.

An old stone hedge lined this section of the cliff, a relic of a once used meadow; and I put my hands on it and leant over. I saw Nellie quite clearly. She was crouched on a small ledge, close enough to the sea, I would have thought, for her to be in danger when the winds blew. Foolish Nellie to have preferred a bed like this, when she could have been snug and safe in Geoffrey's box. But she was acting like the rest of us who want to be free. We do not want to be told by others who pretend to know what is wise for us to do. We want to make our own choice, untrammeled by the views of busybodies. She had no wish to become a racing pigeon, and now she had revolted, and returned to nature. A symbol for all of us who have been brainwashed by society into behaving like robots.

Jeannie was now leaning over the wall. Dusk had fallen and it was only by the periodic flash of the light that she could see Nellie.

'She's not alone,' Jeannie said suddenly, 'there's another pigeon there.'

I didn't see it myself. When I looked over, I could only see a hump of rock that might appear to be the shape of a pigeon.

'I've never seen another one around,' I said.

'Nor have I. But I'm sure it *was* a pigeon.'

Nellie was with us again the following day. She was with us every day for several weeks afterwards, and always alone. Then one morning . . .

Meanwhile there was Christmas; and the early days of January when we had time on our hands and we went on expeditions to other parts of Cornwall; and the middle days of January when first one daffodil was ready to pick, then another and another; and apart from the beauty and the excitement of another early spring, there were the dour calculations as to what the harvest might earn.

But first there was Christmas.

On Christmas Eve we gave the donkeys their mince-pies. We always give Penny and Fred mince-pies on Christmas Eve. It is a solemn custom.

We go down to the old stables below the cottage half an hour before midnight, and we call them in from the field if they are not already there. I then light a candle and its flickering light brushes the rafters and the rough, lime-washed walls; and I hold the candle high above the white noses of the donkeys. They think it is a prize they are seeking, and they push their noses upwards towards it, but it is Jeannie who holds the prize. On a plate, also held above their heads, are the mince-pies.

Every year it is the same except for minor variations. This year a wren was puzzled by the light and the commotion we

130

were causing, and it flew out of a crevice where it had intended to spend the night; and its sudden movement surprised Fred into pricking his ears like a V sign. Only momentarily.

'Fred!' Jeannie called, a mince-pie in her hand, 'Happy Christmas!'

Then again.

'Penny! Happy Christmas!'

Fortunately I am not fond of mince-pies. I find them an exaggerated part of the Christmas fare, but this does not prevent Jeannie painstakingly making her own mincemeat. Delicious it may be . . . but I do not compete for it with the donkeys.

First one mince-pie, then another; and a pause for munching.

Their coats by this time of the year were as thick as a woolly rug. Fred's was even thicker than his mother's, and around his head and eyes it was so thick that it appeared that he was wearing a muffler. There was the scent of the sea in their coats too. A salty scent mingled with a donkey aroma may not have sophisticated appeal, but it has charm; and it has a particular charm on Christmas Eve when you are with two donkeys in an old stable, straw on the cobble floor, the light of a candle; and, before long, an empty plate of mince-pies.

We did not stay long. The woollies, as we often refer to them during winter, had a traditional task to perform; and this task had to be performed in secret. Tradition has it that all donkeys in every part of the world fall to their knees as the clock strikes midnight on Christmas Eve. I have met an old Cornishman, living Nanceldra way between Penzance and St Ives, who has kept donkeys all his life; and he swears that they kneel. I have no evidence myself. I have never dared to watch Penny and Fred for fear they might disappoint me. Jeannie and I therefore leave them several minutes before midnight, leave them with the flavour of mince-pies in their mouths. Yet perhaps they do kneel. I like to pretend that they do so. After all, no other animal can boast that Jesus rode on its back into Jerusalem; no other animal has been so jealously maligned through the centuries by such an insulting epithet as ass. The loyal, intelligent, stubborn, sturdy, patient, loving donkey deserves to be on his own as he kneels at midnight on Christmas Eve; and so preserving the romantic illusion that this Christmas tale is true.

On Christmas morning we awoke to our usual morning. Its beginning never varies throughout the year. Lama, who had been sleeping on the bed, jumped off and started to pound up and down, and rubbing her head against the door, demanding breakfast. Then the gulls began to cry on the roof raucously and impatiently; and there was a blue tit tapping his beak on the window informing us there was no grain on the bird table; and from the stable meadow below the cottage came a hee-haw. First the wheezy, unfulfilled hee-haw of Penny, like the tuning up of a violin before a concert; and followed by the more musical notes of Fred. A soft flute, as a beginning, then changed into a warbling note growing louder and louder, until it burst into the flamboyance of a Kneller Hall trumpeter proclaiming a fanfare in St Paul's Cathedral. A moment of glory and it started to soften, slowly losing its impetus, fading gradually away until it ended in a resigned groan, suggesting a thought was going through his head: What's the use of my song if nobody cares for me?'

We cared enough, however, to leave our warm bed, and dress, and take out a bunch of washed carrots which an admirer had sent them as a Christmas present; and to attend to the others. Swoop for the small birds, bread for the gulls, a saucer of ling for Lama. Nellie also was there after her night on the cliff, and we scattered grain on a flat rock and she pecked at it as if she was starving.

Time now for our breakfast, and the opening of the presents; and afterwards we set out on a stroll around our land, crumbs in our pockets as a Christmas diversion for any chaffinch which might pay us attention, or any robin; and in particular for a robin of character which was the boss of the meadows down the cliff. It flew to us when we were halfway to the bottom, and perched on a blackthorn; and I threw the crumbs among the daffodil spikes. The snow had melted in the sun, and it only lay in patches under the hedges, or hung like strands of cotton wool among the brambles and blackthorn. But far away across the water we could see the snow lying on the hills behind Prah Sands, a curving heap of white, as if part of the sky. We were warm here down the cliff, another world.

We stood staring at the sea for a few minutes. I could see only one ship heading west; and I wondered what festivities were being planned on her, or whether she might be manned by a crew from some country which had never heard of Christmas. Only the sea murmured. What more could a human being seek than to be in such a place, feeling carelessly happy, gulls ruminating on the rocks, all the freedom of the sea before us, and the purity of nature as a companion?

We turned and started back up the path. We had reached the meadow where grow the California daffodils which have a bright yellow cup and a sweet scent and come into bloom after the Magnificence and Joseph MacLeod; and we paused for a moment, looking at their six-inch-high spikes, guessing how long it would be before we would be harvesting them. I expected Jeannie to speak aloud her guess. Instead she said quietly: 'There's Daisy . . . over there by the far end.'

She was watching us, as always, detachedly. Beside her was a badger track which led into the undergrowth towards a series of setts. A most desirable badger residence, sheltered, hidden, and with a view over the sea; and it was into one of these setts that Lama disappeared one anxious afternoon when she was young. When at last she came out again she was quite unconcerned; and I realised that badgers had been her normal companions when Daisy brought her up the cliff.

Yet I had often wondered how Daisy had survived all these years. A rogue badger could have come her way and attacked her, or a rogue fox. It seemed a miracle that a rogue fox had never sneaked up while she was sleeping in some corner of the undergrowth. There had been several examples of foxes killing cats in the district, especially during the period of myxomatosis.

This terrible rabbit disease, however, performed a service to Daisy. At a time when she was young enough to be roaming far and wide there were no rabbits alive in the area; and hence there were no gin traps. Then, by the time rabbits had grown immune to the disease and were annoying farmers once again, the gin traps had been banned by law. We rejoiced when this law was passed. We celebrated.

The celebration was a little too soon. We were lulled, like others, into believing that mass cruelty of this kind had ended. I knew that snares were to be allowed, and I was

133

prepared to tolerate them because I appreciated that farmers had to safeguard their crops. Multiple stores took care to stop pilfering, and so it was reasonable to allow farmers to guard against pilfering rabbits. Unfortunately I was mistaken as to the way that snares were allowed to be used. It took me some time to realise what was happening.

I had thought the law declared that a snare could only be set at the entrance of a hole, a rabbit hole or the hole of a run entering the undergrowth. I also believed in my innocence that the snares were so set that a rabbit was instantly strangled when it put its head through the noose. The prospect of this killing of a rabbit, did not please me; and yet I had to agree that the rabbit population must be controlled. Rabbits might not affect my living, but they hurt that of my neighbours.

I was to find, however, in due course that my conception of snare setting was quite wrong. The various rabbit clearance societies, then backed by the Government of the day, had complete freedom to set their snares where they wished. It was not a question of being obliged to set them in a hole. The operator who acted for them was permitted to set them by the score in an open field, or along-side a path. No warning to the public was required either by a notice for the benefit of strangers walking with a dog in the district, or by verbal notification of householders who might have wandering cats. However we knew our trapper and he always warned us when he was at work; and so we kept Lama indoors during the week he performed his task.

I have now awakened to what the task involves. In many ways the results are far worse than what happened in the days of the gin trap. In those times, a trapper used often to make his rounds during the night, and pick up the rabbits which had been caught. Today the job of the trapper is a nine to five job. If a rabbit is caught in a snare at five past five, and it's alive, or if a cat is caught, it is there until work begins in the morning.

I have learnt, also, that snares do not necessarily kill. They catch. They catch a foot, or if it is a widely set snare they rim the body. I have now witnessed enough horrors caused by a snare to believe that the gin trap days, when a foot or a paw only were at stake, gave a better chance for non-rabbit victims to survive. Gin traps were seldom set in the open.

'I don't like snares,' a trapper said to me, 'but they're part of my job . . . mind you I lose a lot of rabbits to foxes and badgers. They see them caught, and pounce on them. They get caught themselves sometimes but they usually get away taking the snare with them. Cats are a problem. They struggle like mad . . . but I always try to free them.'

I accept that rabbits have to be controlled, just as I believe the population of the world should be controlled . . . none of our environmental problems can be solved until this is recognised. Cruelty, however, need not be a weapon of such control. Yet at the very moment you are reading this there will be rabbits, and other small animals, in fields and pastures throughout the country experiencing the organised cruelty legally imposed by man. It is sad that man, as civilisation grows older, does not become kinder.

Daisy, therefore, had been running a risk. She had been lucky. Many a time she must have been hunting in an area where snares had been set in profusion, and yet had escaped. She was a wise old cat. She had learnt by experience which route to take, which place to hunt; and perhaps this was the reason we saw her in the meadows of the cliff. She was safe there. She could stare at us without fear. Vulnerable, tantalising Daisy. She was like some human beings who long to yield affection, but whose inhibitions check them.

'Daisy,' I called, boldly, hopefully, 'it's Christmas. Come and share it with us.'

I took a step towards her; and she promptly set off along the sodden track towards the desirable residence of the badgers.

CHAPTER TWELVE

Grey seas and skies. Bare trees. Snipe piping. The screech of a water-rail from the marsh near the reservoir. The pile of logs lessening. Yellow patches of winter gorse amid battered brown bracken, shining like lamps. Gunshots. Plovers rising into the sky, wailing. Winter heliotrope scenting by Monty's Leap. Puddles outside the porch door now that the snow had gone. Nellie as hungry as ever. The tits, a chaffinch or two, the dunnocks, and the family of house-sparrows clinging together like gypsies, all begging for the bird table to be filled. Majestic gannets flying south a mile off shore. The hum of a distant tractor. White camellias on the bush by the rose garden. The mauve scented flowers of the veronica.

January has no urgency. The day passes and there is no sign of a human being except Roger the young postman, and Geoffrey. Geoffrey is happy on his own. He is in tune with us. He belongs to the cliffs. He has worked within the sound of the sea all his life. His first job as a boy was to turn potato ground at a place called St er Dellon, a couple of miles up the coast. 'Early land,' I have heard him say a dozen times, 'we always lifted Mayqueen by Buryan Feast.' Some countrymen may yearn for a factory worker's wage, while others realise they have compensations. They do not live artificial lives. They are close to the true pleasures of life. If wages were costed according to the satisfaction a man obtains from his job; a countryman would be far wealthier than many city dwellers. But countrymen are in retreat. Theory boys with city standards are imposing their ideas on the country-side; and before long a way of life which gave happiness to all of us who lived it, will disappear. Or can the theory boys be brought to their senses in time?

We do not, for instance, require a motorway in Cornwall, bringing a concourse of caravans and tents to smother the coves and villages. This will not result in economic advantages because the owners of caravans and tents are low spenders. They largely bring their own food, and spend their days taking advantage of the free sand and free sea, the free walks and the free views. One of course has sympathy for them. If they are able easily to have such a holiday, one cannot blame them for taking it. But it is foolish to pretend that they are helping the economy of Cornwall. They are in fact a hinderance to it. They will drive away those people, including an increasing number of Europeans, Americans, Canadians, who seek in Cornwall the wilderness and mysticism it has been celebrated for. These are the spenders. These are the people who sustain the Cornish holiday economy. They will not come if they find that Cornwall has been developed into a holiday camp. Perhaps a solution is to charge an entry fee into Cornwall.

We have to be on guard, too, against farming industrialisation. Certain areas of Britain may be suitable for prairie size farms with no hedges in sight, but not Cornwall. Cornwall will lose its character if it loses its hedges, and the cost of this will be far greater than any temporary gain of being able to use a machine that little bit faster. Yet the hedges are being bulldozed away, aided by a government subsidy. Near Sennen, entrance to Land's End, old established farms have been bought by a farming company at high prices; and the hedges have been swept away. True that wise old farmers foretell that the farming company will regret the day they did so because the gales will erode the soil, but you have to accept the damage has been done. There will never be stone hedges in this area again.

Ugly farm buildings are just as much a threat. Farmers require no planning permission for the erection of any farm building of 5000 sq. ft. or less; and they do not seem to have much difficulty in obtaining planning permission for buildings that are much larger. The Sennen area is a case in point. Permission was granted to erect on a hill a conglomeration of buildings one of which appears to be the size of a jumbo aircraft hanger. This movement to up-country enterprise infuriates the local population, and saddens those who have come to Land's End to escape the signs of industrialisation.

But pressure on planning officers is severe. That on local planning officers is particularly severe because they are often, without choice, socially involved with planning applicants. Yet they are the people who hold the future of the countryside in their hands, for although they have local council

137

committees to help them on occasions, these committees are greatly influenced by the views of the planning officer. Apart from withstanding pressure, planning officers have also to deal with tricks played on them. A farmer, for instance, will apply to build a bungalow on his farm, an application which, if it had been made by a non-farmer, would be immediately refused. But the farmer maintains that he requires it for a workman, or for his son or his daughter who is shortly to be married and who will continue to work on the farm. The application is therefore granted. The bungalow is then built, a crude box-like affair of brieze blocks and plaster savagely out of keeping with the surrounding old buildings and scenery, and a year later is up for sale. The workman never materialised, and the son or daughter has gone to live elsewhere.

Cornwall has also had to cope with the Concorde. One can understand the euphoria surrounding this aircraft. A magnificent technical achievement, providing jobs for thousands, politically important for Anglo-French co-operation, there appears to be no logical justification to criticise . . . just as there was no logical reason to criticise the products of the world's chemical industries which are now polluting the oceans.

But those of us who have acted as guinea pigs for the flight tests believe we have good reason to criticise. Jeannie and I were sitting peacefully on the bridge, Lama on my lap, the donkeys grazing in their field, when the first Concorde came over Minack. There was a double thunderclap so loud that Lama jumped off me and ran terrified away, the donkeys raced across the field towards the wood, while Jeannie and I were left shaking our fists at the sky shouting 'Damn progress!'

A later test was more dramatic; and it demonstrated the unruly behaviour, similar to bomb blasts, of supersonic shock waves.

Jeannie was in the spare bedroom when the Concorde produced its supersonic bang. A second later there was a crash in the sitting-room, and she ran to find out what had happened. It was an astonishing sight. An old Victorian lamp of heavy brass with a clouded glass shade had performed extraordinary antics. It had been on a small table by the sofa, next to the sitting-room door which opened on

138

to the porch; and both this door and that of the porch had been left wide open.

The lamp had jumped a couple of feet from the table and now lay on the sofa where anyone might have been sitting; and the glass shade had separated from the lamp, though it had admittedly only been held loosely by screws to the lamp. Moreover the small mat on which the lamp was placed was now at right angles both to the table and the lamp; and was lying on the carpet.

This experience, and other Concorde experiences, poses a question in our minds. Has anyone the right to protest against its technical success? If lamps leap, if historic buildings like Trerice Manor near Newquay display signs of cumulative damage, if nervous people suffer . . . does it matter? At first we were assured that the Concorde would never fly commercially overland, but already this assurance is creaking. The glib aircraft salesmen are now saying that the Concorde *has* to fly overland if it is to be commercially viable; and add, as a sop to the millions in the cities, that *it will only fly overland in sparsely populated areas*. One of these could be Cornwall.

The world is divided between the sensitive and the insensitive, just as it is divided between those who have a musical ear and those who have not. I know people who do not mind the Concorde bang, just as they seem not to mind the traffic roaring past their door. 'You'll get used to it,' they say to me, passing on this twentieth-century phrase of despair. Perhaps their attitude is due to the fact they do not live in a sparsely populated area. We hear the bang against the background of silence. Obviously we suffer more. Sometimes, on the other hand, I admit the bang has been muffled, but this is because of the low cloud cover which has acted as a barrier to the bang. If, however, permission for overland flying is weaved out of the politicians, the days and nights in a few years' time will be punctuated by bangs; and probably then, too late, the sensitive will be proven right. The supersonic value of carrying people in small numbers to destinations where they need a long time to recover, will be miserably outweighed by the distress caused to those they pass over. Chemical waste pollution will have Concorde pollution as a companion.

Meanwhile we pursue life in our small world. This January it was momentarily enhanced by lemons on our small lemon tree. The tree had begun as a pip stuck in a small earthenware pot by Jeannie's mother when she was living in London; and when she died a few years ago Jeannie brought the pot to Minack. It grew, like Jack's beanstalk, until we had to take it out of the pot and plant it in a corner of the small unheated greenhouse where we bunch the daffodils and weigh the tomatoes. It then developed voluminous dark green foliage from spiky branches, but it was only some months previously that at last it produced a flower. Several more flowers proceeded to appear, and these one by one turned into green pebbles, fattening slowly until they became the size of a conventional lemon. They took a long time to ripen, but a dozen yellow lemons in due course decorated the tree; and we were able to enjoy a social one-upmanship.

We had a friend to lunch and offered him a gin and tonic.

'Would you like a slice of lemon?' I asked casually.

'If you have it . . . yes, please.'

'Come with me then,' I replied, and led him outside to the greenhouse.

'There,' I said, pointing to the tree, 'pick your own lemon.'

On another occasion I took a lemon to a party. The hostess lived in one of Cornwall's great houses with a garden famous for its magnolias, camellias, and dozens of rare plants from all over the world.

'Have you a lemon tree?' I enquired.

'Oh, no,' she replied, 'you can't grow them in Cornwall.'

I took my lemon from my pocket.

'Please accept this,' I said graciously, '. . . a Cornish lemon.'

Jeannie is the gardener at Minack. I feel myself quite competent to plan the work, and perform it. But my plans are inclined to differ from those of Jeannie. Moreover when I take it upon myself to hoe and to weed, some devil in me persuades me to mistake a newly installed rockery plant for groundsel; and on those occasions when I have decided to prune the roses I manage to cut out the main shoots instead of the suckers. It seems that I lose my nerve when I garden. I am like an actor fluffing his lines. Jeannie has such excellent ideas as to what we should grow, and where, and when, that I would be far wiser to leave the whole performance to her.

I have, however, a gift of knowing where to plant shrubs. It is a gift which only comes with a far seeing mind. Thus on those occasions when we have bought a new shrub, I have put forward my views that the spot which Jeannie has chosen will prove to be unsuitable in a couple of years' time when the shrub has properly established itself. I will quietly point out that it is too close to another shrub, or too exposed to the wind, or that it is perhaps too near a path or the lane, and that it will in due course overlap.

My misfortune is that my far seeing thoughts take such a time to materialise. There I am pouring out wisdom which is promptly discarded because there is no tangible evidence to prove I am right. A hole is dug for the shrub, the shrub is planted; and I wait. I wait one year, two years, three years until the evidence is clear. I *was* right. Two shrubs which should be well separated from each other, are in fact embracing each other. The lace hydrangea which was planted beside the lane on the cottage side of Monty's Leap has so expanded that vehicles have to dodge it. The syringa opposite our bedroom window is entangled with the branches of the apple tree. Another syringa is obviously sick because the wind has blasted it. My contribution to the garden, therefore, is negative; and even when proved right, the evidence comes too late to give me any satisfaction.

There is, too, a conflict of opinion over the use of weed-killers. I have always been deeply suspicious of weed-killers, and as far as insecticides are concerned I share Jeannie's determination never to have a tin of one of them on the place. But I have been persuaded that a proprietary brand of weed-killer spread from a watering-can over the path is perfectly safe; and that it will keep away grass and other weeds for a whole season. Jeannie, however, remains suspicious. She has a basic lack of faith in the claims of any scientists, believing that they have one-track laboratory minds which stop them from considering the general effects of their chemical inventions. I do not, however, agree with her in respect of this particular weed-killer. Nor does Geoffrey. He and I, therefore, act together as conspirators. We wait until she has set off for Penzance. Then out comes the watering-can and the weed-killer; and the paths are spread with it and for the whole year we are free of those irritating grasses and weeds. Jeannie is pleased with the result. She remains suspicious, however, even claims when a young plant mysteriously dies that the weed-killer is responsible, but she

141

accepts that hours of tedious labour have been saved.

Our garden has never been a show garden. It is very small, truly a cottage garden. For a long while we neglected it because we were so busy growing flowers and produce to send away to the markets that we did not have the time to pay attention to a simple garden. We therefore allowed it to behave as it wished; and out of its soil blossomed primroses, wild daffodils, lilac blue periwinkle, white convulvuli in profusion, a variety of ferns, clumps of alstroemeria and mombretia which once in a garden obstinately stay forever, and bushes of wild hypericum, and fuchsia, violet petals turning purple with drooping flowers reminding me of decorations on a Christmas tree.

But now we have put sense into the garden. The beds have been given shape by moving rocks from one place to another, and new beds have been created so that form has been given to the garden. Yet it is still unruly. It appears to be part of the landscape. It is not one of those neat gardens meticulously maintained which would please a gardening expert. The aim of our garden is to be full of colour and sweet scents, and natural.

Geoffrey has performed the heavy work; and with his feel for stone he created the walls like that of the bridge where on summer days we sit and ruminate; and built the steps that climb up from the front garden to the gate of the donkey field. Geoffrey is as interested in the appearance of the garden as we are ourselves.

Jeannie, though, is the organiser. Her special quality is the stamina of her enthusiasm. I am inclined to start on a job with flourish, then find an excuse to do something else when the job becomes tedious. Jeannie, on the other hand, will refuse to be diverted if she has a hundred wall flowers to plant, or a basket of bulbs. I lazily observe her, bending over the soil stabbing it with a trowel, ferociously attacking her task until the wallflowers are in rows or the basket empty. Jeannie, therefore, is the creator of our cottage garden. She chooses the plants, decides where they should go . . . and does the work.

Yet I have my moments. I produce ideas which sometimes are greeted by Jeannie with pleasurable surprise. I had noticed, for instance, that Jeannie had often been thwarted in obtaining the annuals she required. The cause was the big business interests from across the Tamar, that Lamorna Valley must remain for all time a true example of old Cornwall. Inoffensive rhetoric, I thought, until a kindly resident of the valley approached me after I had finished. 'You have forgotten,' he said with a smile, 'that eighty per cent of us who live in Lamorna are "foreigners".' Yes, I had forgotten. Perhaps the reason is that the 'foreigners' concerned are so pleasant that they appear to belong to the valley.

It is no use believing, however, that life in the country spares you discordancy with others. We have the usual problems of human relationships; and though we may be on happy terms with most, there will always be occasional times when we may have misunderstandings with one person or another. I had, for instance, such a misunderstanding with the elderly gentleman who bought the neighbouring farm, including the cottage where Jane once lived. The gentleman came from the north, and he had a determined manner. The previous owner, a Cornishman, had a herd of Guernseys, and grew potatoes and daffodils; and from him we once rented the two acres of cliff land. The new owner did not follow this pattern of farming. He had a fine herd of beef cattle instead. He also kept the three cottages of Pentewan, empty.

The first misunderstanding I had with him concerned half a ton of Magnificence daffodil bulbs which were still in one of the meadows of my old tenancy of the Pentewan cliff I has foolishly believed that I would be able to dig them in my own good time and transfer them to Minack land. Legally, however, they were no longer mine. My new neighbour had bought them along with the farm. Hence all Jeannie and I could do, daffodil season after daffodil season, was to watch them bust into yellow from our side of the hedge (the blooms were never picked commercially). It was an infuriating experience, and costly too; for they were worth £30 or more a year. But the elderly gentleman has left the area now, and the bulbs are back at Minack.

The second misunderstanding I had with him concerned the coastal footpath. There has always been confusion about the footpath along this part of the coast; and even today there is no official one. True the authorities have drawn up waiting, have arrived at the moment of reality. I am like a trainer watching his horse go down to the post. Everything possible has been done to ensure success; and now luck was required.

'Pity Cornwall doesn't have the early market to itself,' Percy added, 'like in the old days.'

'Damn those growers of forced daffodils and their great hangers of greenhouses,' I said.

One gossips with Percy. One listens. One suddenly finds oneself discussing a subject far removed from the one in hand. One often darts off at a tangent.

'Percy,' I said, 'can you ever get hold of Sharpe's Express for me?'

'Not now I couldn't. But next year perhaps.'

'I think they're the best flavoured new potato of all,' I said, 'we never grew them commercially but Elephant Bill used to swear by them. We had them at a lunch he gave us. I have never forgotten them.'

Jeannie smiled.

'He's more interested in the kitchen garden, Percy.'

The Sutton Trial Grounds are on the right as you come into Penzance. Since a child I have been aware of Suttons because I used to look out of the window as the train rushed past Reading; and fleetingly be aware of the multi-coloured strips of flowers waiting to become seeds. Their Gulval Trial Ground is much smaller, but in summer it is a marvellous kaleidoscope of colour. It provides the prettiest part of Gulval. Gulval used to be known for its character, and for its church. The church is still there but the character has mostly gone. The village no longer enjoys pure views of Mount's Bay with St Michael's Mount to the left, fields in the foreground. The village now looks down on the heliport and listens to the revving of the helicopter engines. And beside the heliport is the conglomeration of caravans, light industry factories, and holiday flatlets which represent the personification of how men of little taste can ruin a district. Only the church and Percy's corner of beautiful flowers save Gulval.

'What ideas have you got for us then, Percy?'

I handed him a box of matches as I spoke. He had filled his pipe some minutes before and as he had not lit it I thought perhaps he had no matches.

summer taking short cuts. And all I would say to our garden admirers would be, pointing to the appropriate flower: 'Delphinium . . . pansy . . . marigold . . . aster . . . dianthus.' I would be wise enough not to become involved.

Nellie and Wallace came back later in the day. They both settled on the roof, and it was amusing to watch Wallace's embarrassment. He reminded me of a young man who had been brought by a girl to meet her parents for the first time. He was restless, fidgety, and awkward. He was so much bigger than Nellie. There she was on the roof beside him a delicate bird; and, if I speak truthfully, a lucky bird. At a time of crisis we were there to help her.

If we had not been prepared to help, feed her, and give her water, she would never have met Wallace.

He took her away next day. We never saw either of them again.

CHAPTER THIRTEEN

Daisy was changing her routine. I was taking a daffodil basket to the cliff when I found her lying on the path just at the top of Fred's field. Usually she would have darted away as soon as she heard me coming but, although it was a quiet

147

day, she did not move until I called her when I was only a few yards away.

Jeannie reported other changes in her routine. She had always from time to time offered her delicacies, though Daisy would never dream of showing that she appreciated these delicacies in front of Jeannie. The delicacies had to be left, Jeannie had to retreat; and then an hour or two later they would be gone.

One winter there was competition between Daisy and a fox for these delicacies; and the competition put Jeannie in a quandary. The fox was once a cub whom we nursed back to health after it had been caught in a gin trap. The trapper himself had brought it to us, providing proof that trappers are not ruthless men just because they have to earn a living in the way they do; and at first we thought it was a male and called it Sam. Then we discovered it was a female, and so we changed the name to Samantha.

We cared for her in the small greenhouse for several weeks until her leg had healed from the effects of the gin trap; and then one morning we opened the door and set her free. For a while afterwards we used to see her from time to time, occasionally for several weeks on end. I would see her at the far corner of the meadow, and I would call to Jeannie that Samantha was wanting her dinner. On cold nights in the winter she used to share the shelter of the stables with the donkeys. I kept a small pile of hay on one side, hemmed in against the wall by a lathe fence; and so she was able to slip into the hay without fear of the donkeys nosing her out.

Jeannie's quandary was when both Daisy and Samantha were hoping for a meal at the same time; and it amused me to observe Jeannie's concern.

Jeannie, in the setting of the Savoy, Claridges or the Berkeley had been at ease in dealing with sophisticated social problems. She was a natural hostess. Elegant restaurant managers like Vercelli of the Savoy Grill, or Luigi of Claridges or Gino of the Berkeley, enjoyed fussing over her, seeing her wants were cared for; and how many times I have watched admiringly as she presided at a table, distinguished people as her guests, and behaving as if it were simple to make them feel content.

This aplomb was missing when it came to coping with Daisy and Samantha. Who was to have the left-over lamb chop? Where shall I leave the liver Lama doesn't want? On the path on the way to the onion meadow? Daisy is likely to find it there, but what can I give Samantha?

Her concern, I always considered, was unnecessary. She had no need to be in such a flutter because neither Daisy nor Samantha gave me the impression that they depended upon her. They were self-sufficient. They did not require the help of a human to feed them. Nevertheless if a human was prepared to be so foolish as to drop delicacies at unexpected places, each would try to get there first.

Daisy, however, was now acting differently. She still kept well away from the cottage, still made it quite clear she wanted to maintain her independence, but instead of seeing her occasionally we now saw her every day. She was always in the neighbourhood. She used to sit for hours, for instance, on a rock which showed like the tip of an iceberg out of the ground in the lane corner of the greenhouse field. It was a sunny corner, even until late into the afternoon, and Daisy would rest there; and when I put my glasses on to her, I would see her eyes gazing towards the cottage. Jeannie romantically explained her behaviour.

'She's thinking,' Jeannie said, 'of her daughter who was born out in the wild, but who made her way up in the world.'

I laughed.

'Look at her daughter now.'

She was in a round ball, sound asleep on the sofa.

Daisy also began hovering around the donkey field above the cottage. She never wandered to the cottage half of the field, but she seemed happy and confident enough to roam the other half near the wood. Nor was she frightened by the donkeys; and with good reason. The donkeys knew her better than we did. They took her for granted, not an oddity to chase, but a fellow companion who lived as they did in freedom on a Cornish cliff.

We made remarks to each other.

'I saw Daisy curled up asleep in the grass a few yards out from the corner where Geoffrey has stacked the wood.'

'Daisy was fifty yards away and never ran. She just watched as I left the saucer in the gap.'

'I saw Daisy in the lane, and walked slowly towards her, calling . . . but she ran away.'

149

'Daisy was in the California meadow just now. She was walking up between the beds.'

The daffodil season had begun to hasten. The flush of the first daffodils, the Magnificence, was over; and the meadows of the cliff were now bare of blooms save for the odd ones which had bloomed late. We were now picking the Golden Harvest, and the Oblivaris which resemble miniature King Alfreds, and our favourite daffodil, the beautiful Joseph MacLeod. The other day I learnt from a Dutch bulb grower how it came to be called Joseph MacLeod.

A neighbour of his, a fellow bulb grower, bred the seedling during the war when Holland was under German occupation. He was proud of it, and believed it would develop into a great daffodil. The process of developing a seedling into a bulb product of commercial value takes time and in any case, with the war in progress he was in no hurry. But he did want to give it a name.

The man was a member of the Dutch resistance, and one of his jobs was to listen secretly to the news broadcasts from London. It was one of the worst periods of the war. The British Army had been in retreat for three years, and his own resistance unit had been penetrated by the Germans and he was expecting arrest at any moment.

His radio was under the floorboards of his sitting-room, and the particular floorboard was covered by a rug. He moved the rug, then the floorboard one evening just before the nine o'clock news, and lay listening. It was the evening that the break through at El Alamein was announced. A victory at last! The Dutchman listened to the details, and at the end he heard the words of the announcer: 'That was the news, and this was Joseph MacLeod reading it.'

'Ah,' said the Dutchman to himself, 'a celebration . . . in honour of this day I give the name Joseph MacLeod to my seedling!'

After the Golden Harvest and the Oblivaris and the Joseph MacLeod came the California, masses of them, then the Sulphur whose name we had changed to Lamorna because nobody wanted to buy a daffodil with a name like Sulphur. This was the height of the daffodil season. Basket upon basket was brought by Geoffrey on the tractor, and bunched, and packed in the cardboard boxes, and loaded into the Volvo to be taken by me to the station.

'How many today?'

'Eighty.'

'That means two journeys.'

I would set off up the lane, slowly over Monty's Leap, past the farm buildings at the top, then on along the bumpy stretch to the main road. In a quarter of an hour I was at Penzance station being shepherded to one of the trucks of the flower train, and I would back the Volvo to the opening, and in five minutes it would be unloaded; and I would be off again to Minack.

After my second journey I would linger at the station. This was an opportunity for quiet enquiries casually made . . .

'What did the Scillies do today?' I would ask George Mills, the flower train foreman, or one of my other friends if he wasn't there.

'Three thousand boxes.'

'Might have been worse,' I might answer. Then put another question: 'What about Tomlin, and that Sennen man?'

'The Sennen man sent three hundred boxes in one load, and there are a couple of hundred still to come.'

'What chance has the rest of us? Three years ago good Cornish farming country. Now its beginning to look like part of Lincolnshire.'

'That's how it goes.'

The efforts of Jeannie and me and Geoffrey were so puny. We were each of us so full of enthusiasm for every extra box we were able to send each day, full of pride, too, for the quality of the blooms we sent; and yet the mite we sent compared with the gargantuan sendings of the others was laughable.

'What about Le Grice?' I asked, 'how's he getting on?'

'Funny that,' came the answer, 'he was only asking yesterday how *you* were getting on.'

'Tell him,' I said smiling, 'that I have already begun to send away untreated Actaea. That will worry him.'

Le Grice was a well-known grower, and a friend. It was amusing to have a joking rivalry with him.

'Tell him also,' I added, pretending again, 'that I will be sending our first box of White Lion away next week. That will worry him too.'

When I passed the farm buildings on the way to the station, everyone knew I was in a hurry and tried to keep out of the way. If I met my dear friend Walter Grose on a tractor, he slewed to the side as soon as he saw me coming, then

waved to me cheerily as I passed him. So too, Jack Cockram, his partner in the farm. Jack was a Londoner evacuated to a farm nearby at the beginning of the war; and became a naturalised Cornishman. Then often I met Bill Trevorrow and he was like the others. We were lucky in our neighbours. They were always ready to help whenever it was required.

But as I came back along the lane, my transport task completed, I had time to spare; and I would stop if I saw one of them and tell him all the news.

'Prices are up this week.'

'It's cooler. Holding them back, I expect.'

'Trouble is that prices are always better at the end of the week but we still have to send on Monday and Tuesday.'

'Glad I haven't got any.'

'We start the whites next week.'

'Hope you do well with them is all I can say.'

The whites could be our bonus. The yellows were the bread and butter of the harvest, but if the whites coincided with a good market we would show a profit for ourselves; and we would be able to relax for a while.

First Brunswick, then Early Bride, Barrett Browning, a pause, then Actaea and White Lion. They followed each other in succession, and they were all away by the end of March; and the beds they once filled had only their foliage left, dark green foliage spattered occasionally by the colour of a rogue daffodil.

The whites had flowered profusely. They had not disappointed us.

CHAPTER FOURTEEN

Daisy had haunted the field where we picked the whites. Jeannie found her once between two beds of Brunswick, and when Jeannie said, 'Hello Daisy,' there was a miaow in return. This was unexpected. She had never responded before. Jeannie immediately dropped the daffodil basket, went back to the cottage, filled one saucer with fish, another with milk; and returned. Daisy did not move as Jeannie put them down in front of her.

153

Next day Daisy was in the same place; and Jeannie again fetched two saucers. But this time she ran away when Jeannie returned.

'Showing her independence,' said Jeannie, 'she thought she had been too familiar yesterday.'

Nevertheless Daisy was causing us uneasiness. I found her, for instance, asleep in a patch of grass close to a ditch in the wood; and she didn't budge although I was within a yard of her. She always used to be on guard, so quick to jump away. I therefore felt uneasy because a routine was being disrupted. Daisy was not behaving according to form. I realised how I had taken her for granted over the years, as one takes people for granted . . . her slow walk over the stable meadow, the unexpected meeting in the cliff meadows, the grey, compact little figure was part of the scenery.

On April 8th, a week after the last of the whites had been sent away, I saw her moving slowly down the path towards the cliff. She seemed quite normal.

On April 10th, in the morning, visitors called and asked whether they might have a look round. A half an hour later on their way back, one of them told me they had seen a grey cat in the field, and it was crying. I went down to the field and saw Daisy. She was obviously distressed but, as usual, she ran away when I tried to get close to her.

That evening we found her in the grass near Monty's Leap. Her fur was wet and matted, and she would not touch the liver and fish we offered her.

The next morning she was still there; and Jeannie decided that we must catch her. All three of us, Jeannie, Geoffrey and myself, made a combined effort to do so; and we were about to succeed when a van came at speed down the lane. It stopped just in time . . . for Daisy was now lying in the lane.

We tried again. We had a box ready with a lid, and once she was in it we were going to carry her to the small greenhouse. Suddenly Jeannie succeeded in holding her. The first time in all the years that Jeannie had touched her.

We carried her to the greenhouse, and put the box on the floor and opened the lid. She jumped out, spitting fury and ran towards the earth beneath the lemon tree.

That evening she was still beneath the lemon tree; and again we tried to coax her to eat. Then I put down beside her

154

a small earthenware saucer with water in it . . . and a strange thing happened. She suddenly found the strength to bring her paw down so hard on the saucer that it broke into pieces.

A proud gesture. She had told us that she valued her independence more than her life.

SUN ON THE LINTEL
Derek Tangye

Derek Tangye's chronicles of Minack, the Cornish flower farm where he and his wife Jeannie live, are a major bestseller of our times.

In SUN ON THE LINTEL, he unfolds another enchanting tale of their remote and peaceful valley as he tells the story of his New Year resolutions and how the creatures who share his life – the ingratiating donkeys, Penny and Fred; the cats, Oliver and Ambrose; Broadbent the gull, and a determined young badger – conspire to help him break them all down.

JEANNIE
A LOVE STORY
Derek Tangye

When Jeannie and Derek Tangye withdrew to a cliff-top
flower farm in Cornwall, sophisticated London society
protested, but an even wider circle was enriched by the
enchanted life which they shared and which Derek
recorded in the MINACK CHRONICLES. Jeannie died
in 1986, and, in tribute to her extraordinary personality,
her husband has written this portrait of their marriage.
All the delight of the MINACK CHRONICLES is here –
the daffodils, the donkeys and the Cornish magic. And
all the fizzle and pop of champagne days at the savoy is
captured as Jeannie dazzles admirers from Danny Kaye
to Christian Dior.

THE CHERRY TREE
Derek Tangye

Many people have come to Minack and stood beside the cherry tree, both famous and unknown. They all have in common a desire to breathe the fresh, invigorating Cornish air and share a little in the peace and contentment of the Tangyes' life.

And their days are filled with enchantment and incident. In spring the daffodils must be picked. There are Fred and Merlin the donkeys to look after, especially when Merlin falls in love. What will be the fate of the first pair of buzzards ever to nest near the cottage? Then there's Cherry, the little black cat Jeannie found curled up at the foot of the cherry tree, starving. Will she be allowed to stay at Minack?

☐	A Gull on the Roof	Derek Tangye	£4.50
☐	Sun on the Lintel	Derek Tangye	£2.99
☐	Somewhere A Cat is Waiting	Derek Tangye	£5.99
☐	The World of Minack	Derek Tangye	£4.99
☐	The Cherry Tree	Derek Tangye	£4.99
☐	Jeannie	Derek Tangye	£4.99
☐	The Evening Gull	Derek Tangye	£4.99

Warner Books now offers an exciting range of quality titles by both established and new authors. All of the books in this series are available from:

Little, Brown and Company (UK),
P.O. Box 11,
Falmouth,
Cornwall TR10 9EN.

Alternatively you may fax your order to the above address. Fax No. 01326 317444.

Payments can be made as follows: cheque, postal order (payable to Little, Brown and Company) or by credit cards, Visa/Access. Do not send cash or currency. UK customers and B.F.P.O. please allow £1.00 for postage and packing for the first book, plus 50p for the second book, plus 30p for each additional book up to a maximum charge of £3.00 (7 books plus).

Overseas customers including Ireland, please allow £2.00 for the first book plus £1.00 for the second book, plus 50p for each additional book.

NAME (Block Letters) ....

....

ADDRESS ....

....

....

☐ I enclose my remittance for ....

☐ I wish to pay by Access/Visa Card

Number ⬚⬚⬚⬚⬚⬚⬚⬚⬚⬚⬚⬚⬚⬚⬚⬚

Card Expiry Date ⬚⬚⬚⬚